MW01234907

Chicago

December 2009

Edited by
Peter B Fitzgerald
Marc Heiden

Rev. 200911031000

CONTENTS

CONTENTS

CONTENTS

CONTENTS

Chicago *choosechicago.com* is the home of the blues and the truth of jazz, the heart of comedy and the idea of the skyscraper. Here, the age of railroads found its center, and airplanes followed suit. Butcher of hogs and believer in progress, it is one of the world's great cities, and yet the metropolitan luxuries of theater, shopping, and fine dining have barely put a dent in real Midwestern friendliness. It's a city with a swagger, but without the surliness or even the fake smiles found in other cities of its size.

As the hub of the Midwest, Chicago is easy to find — its picturesque skyline calls across the waters of Lake Michigan, a first impression that soon reveals world-class museums of art and science, miles of sandy beaches, huge parks and public art *p.115*, and perhaps the finest downtown collection of modern architecture in the world.

With a wealth of iconic sights and neighborhoods to explore, there's enough to fill a visit of days, weeks, or even months without ever seeing the end. Dress warm in the winter, and prepare to cover a lot of ground: the meaning of Chicago is only found in movement, through subways and archaic elevated tracks, in the pride of tired feet and eyes raised once more to the sky.

Districts

Many visitors never make it past the attractions downtown, but you haven't truly seen Chicago until you have ventured out into the neighborhoods. Chicagoans understand their city by splitting it into large "sides" to the

CHICAGO DISTRICTS

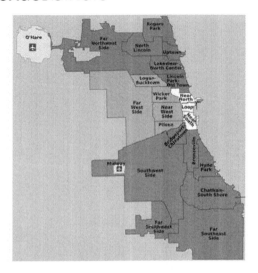

north, west, and south of the central business district (the Loop). Chicagoans also tend to identify strongly with their neighborhood, reflecting real differences in culture and place throughout the city. Rivalries between the North and South Sides run particularly deep, while people from the West Side are free agents in critical issues like baseball loyalty.

Downtown

The Loop *p.47* — the historic and business center of Chicago, the financial center of the Midwest, and the home of magnificent architecture, parks, and public art

Near North *p.71* — a ritzy shopping district, home to the Magnificent Mile, Navy Pier, and the Gold Coast, and many hotels

Near South *p.95* — a few big draws, including Printer's Row, the Museum Campus, McCormick Place, and Soldier Field

North Side

Lincoln Park-Old Town *p.123* — a wealthy neighborhood with museums, mansions, upscale boutiques, the Lincoln Park Zoo, and some of the city's top dining and theaters

Lakeview-North Center *p.139* — entertainment aplenty with the Chicago Cubs at Wrigley Field, storefront theaters, and **Boystown**, the center of Chicago's Gay-Lesbian-Bisexual-Transgender culture

Uptown *p.273* — a neighborhood with more than its fair share of Chicago history, Southeast Asian dining, Swedish and lesbian-friendly Andersonville, and a thriving entertainment district of edgy comedy and historic rock and jazz clubs

North Lincoln *p.313* — fun shopping at Lincoln Square, great Middle Eastern food on Kedzie and Korean food along Seoul Drive

Rogers Park *p.291* — thriving multi-ethnic communities, miles of laid-back beaches, Loyola University, and the totally Indian Devon Avenue

Far Northwest Side *p.363* — Polish Village, historic homes and theaters, and some undiscovered gems in the neighborhoods near O'Hare International Airport *p.397*

South Side

Hyde Park *p.157* — the University of Chicago's Gothic campus, brainy Hyde Park, old mansions aplenty, and great museums

Bronzeville *p.191* — the historic "Black Metropolis" is a mecca of African-American History, historic site of the Chicago Black Renaissance, and home to the nation's first museum of African-American History in the enormous Washington Park

Bridgeport-Chinatown *p.175* — home to Chicago's thriving Chinatown, the White Sox, and the city's South Side Irish power brokers

Chatham-South Shore *p.203* — one of the country's true centers of African-American culture, with great soul food, the best BBQ in the North, and unparalleled blues clubs on offer

Southwest Side *p.347* — Former home to the massive meatpacking district of the Union Stockyards, huge Polish and Mexican neighborhoods, and Midway Airport

Far Southeast Side *p.377* — a vast and weird section of the city home to most of the city's heavy industry and the historic planned Pullman community of labor history fame

Far Southwest Side *p.389* — Ireland in Chicago: authentic Irish pubs, brogues, galleries, and the odd haunted castle, all extremely far from the city center

West Side

Near West Side *p.215* — lots of attractions in one area: dining at Little Italy and Greektown, clubs and galleries in the West Loop, the Chicago Bulls, and what remains of Maxwell Street

Wicker Park *p.229* — Chicago's hippest bar and restaurant scene plus eccentric shopping right next to Ukrainian Village, a neighborhood of hipsters and the Orthodox

Logan-Bucktown *p.247* — a neighborhood riding on a wave of gentrification spillover from Wicker Park with some great dive bars and wide-ranging Latin-American dining

CHICAGO UNDERSTAND

Pilsen *p.259* — incredible Mexican food everywhere you look, Czech architecture, two thriving arts districts, the National Museum of Mexican Art, and a Little Italy not overrun by visitors

Far West Side *p.331* — so far off the beaten tourist track you might not find your way back, but that's OK given all the great food, a couple of top blues clubs, enormous parks, and the botanical gardens of the Garfield Park Conservatory

Understand

Chicago was known as a fine place to find a **wild onion** if you were a member of the Potawatomi tribe, who lived in this area of Illinois before European settlers arrived. It was mostly swamps, prairie and mud long past the establishment of Fort Dearborn in 1803 and incorporation as a town in 1833. It could be argued that nature never intended for there to be a city here; brutal winters aside, it took civil engineering projects of unprecedented scale to establish working sewers, reverse the flow of the river to keep it out of the city's drinking supply, and stop buildings from sinking back into the swamps — and that was just the first few decades.

By 1871, the reckless growth of the city was a sight to behold, full of noise, Gothic lunacy, and bustling commerce. But on October 8th, Mrs. O'Leary's cow reportedly knocked over a lantern in the crowded immigrant quarters

in the West Side, and the **Great Chicago Fire** began. It quickly spread through the dry prairie, killing 300 and destroying virtually the entire city. The stone Water Tower in the Near North *p.71* is the most famous surviving structure. But the city seized this destruction as an opportunity to rebuild bigger than before, giving canvas for several architects and urban planners who would go on to become legends of modern architecture.

At the pinnacle of its rebirth and the height of its newfound powers, Chicago was known as **The White City**. Cultures from around the world were summoned to the 1893 World's Colombian Exposition, to bear witness to the work of Louis Sullivan, Daniel Burnham, and the future itself. Cream of Wheat, soft drinks, street lights and safe electricity, the fax machine, and the Ferris Wheel bespoke the colossus now resident on the shores of Lake Michigan.

As every road had once led to Rome, every train led to Chicago. Carl Sandburg called Chicago the **Hog Butcher for the World** for its cattle stockyards and place on the nation's dinner plate. Sandburg also called it the **City of the Big Shoulders**, noting the tall buildings in the birthplace of the skyscraper — and the city's "lifted head singing so proud to be alive and coarse and strong and cunning." But Chicago is a city in no short supply of nicknames. Fred Fisher's 1922 song (best known in Frank Sinatra's rendition) calls it **That Toddlin' Town**, where "on State Street, that great street, they do things they don't do on Broadway." It's also referenced by countless blues standards like **Sweet Home Chicago**.

Chicago is also known as **The Second City**, which refers to its rebuilding after the fire — the current city is literally the second Chicago, after the one that disappeared in 1871. It can also refer to the city's long-held position as the United States' second largest city, after New York City, although it has since been surpassed in population by Los Angeles. And many know the nickname from Chicago's great comedy theater in Old Town *p.123*.

Chicago's history with corruption is legendary. During the Prohibition era, Chicago's criminal world, emblemized by names like Al Capone, Baby Face Nelson, and later Sam Giancana, practically ran the city. The local political world had scarcely more legitimacy in a town where voter turnout was highest among the dead and their pets, and precinct captains spread the word to "vote early, vote often." Even Sandburg acknowledged the relentless current of vice than ran under the surface of the optimistic city.

Today, Chicago is known as **The Windy City**. Walking around town, you might suspect that Chicago got this nickname from the winds off Lake Michigan, which shove through the downtown corridors with intense force. But the true origin of the saying comes from politics. Some say it may have been coined by rivals like Cincinnati and New

York as a derogatory reference to the Chicagoan habit of rabid boosterism and endless political conventions. Others say that the term originated from the fact that Chicago politicians change their minds as "often as the wind."

Finally, the city is known as the **The City That Works**, as promoted by current Mayor Richard M. Daley, which refers to Chicago's labor tradition and the long hours worked by its residents, its willingness to tackle grand civic projects and to make fortunes for a lucky few. Daley and his father, former Mayor Richard J. Daley, have ruled the city for decades in what can only be described as a benevolent dictatorship. The Daleys kept Chicago pre-eminent through decades when other Midwestern manufacturing cities went into decline, transforming it from a city of stockyards and factories to a financial giant at the forefront of modern urban design. It's not democracy, but it has worked pretty well for most (and not as well for a few others).

While the city has many great attractions downtown, most Chicagoans live and play outside of the central business district. To understand Chicago, travelers must venture away from the Loop and Michigan Avenue and out into the vibrant neighborhoods, to soak up the local nightlife, sample the wide range of fantastic dining, and see the sights Chicagoans care about most — thanks to the city's massive public transit system, every part of Chicago is only slightly off the most beaten path.

Climate

Weather is definitely not one of the attractions in Chicago. There's a good time to be had in any season, but it is a place where the climate has to be taken into consideration.

Obscured by Chicago's ferocious winters are the heat waves of summer. Many days in July and August are disgustingly hot and humid. Summer nights are more reasonable, though, and you'll get a few degrees' respite along the lakefront — in the local parlance, that's "cooler by the lake."

But then there are those winters. The months from December to March will see very cold temperatures, with even more bitter wind chill factors. Snow is usually limited to a handful of heavy storms per season, with a few light dustings in-between. (And a little more along the lakefront — again in the local parlance, that's "lake effect snow".) Ice storms are also a risk. It's a city that's well-accustomed to these winters, though, so city services and public transportation are highly unlikely to shut down.

That said, Chicago does have a few nice months of weather. May and September are pleasant and mild; April and June are mostly fine, although thunderstorms with heavy winds can also occur suddenly. Although there may be a chill in the air in October, it rarely calls for more than a light coat. The lake effect may prolong a pleasant autumn through October,

and sometimes into November.

Literature

Chicago literature found its roots in the city's tradition of lucid, direct journalism, lending to a strong tradition of social realism. Consequently, most notable Chicago fiction focuses on the city itself, with social criticism keeping exultation in check. Here is a selection of Chicago's most famous works about itself:

Karen Abbott's *Sin in the Second City* is a recent best-seller about Chicago's vice district, the Levee, and some of the personalities involved: gangsters, corrupt politicians, and two sisters who ran the most elite brothel in town.

Nelson Algren's *Chicago: City on the Make* is a prose poem about the alleys, the El tracks, the neon and the dive bars, the beauty and cruelty of Chicago. It's best saved for *after* a trip, when at least twenty lines will have you enraptured in recognition.

Saul Bellow's *Adventures of Augie March* charts the long drifting life of a Jewish Chicagoan and his myriad eccentric acquaintances throughout the early 20th century: growing up in the then Polish neighborhood of Humboldt Park *p.331*, cavorting with heiresses on the Gold Coast *p.71*, studying at the University of Chicago, fleeing union thugs in the Loop *p.47*, and taking the odd detour to hang out with Trotsky in Mexico while eagle-hunting giant iguanas on horseback. This book has legitimate claim to be *the* Chicago epic (for practical purposes, that means you won't finish it on the plane).

Gwendolyn Brooks' *A Street in Bronzeville* was the collection of poems that launched the career of the famous Chicago poetess, focused on the aspirations, disappointments, and daily life of those who lived in 1940s Bronzeville *p.191*. It is long out of print, so you'll likely need to read these poems in a broader collection, such as her *Selected Poems.*

Theodore Dreiser's *Sister Carrie* is a cornerstone of the turn of the 20th century Chicago Literary Renaissance, a tale of a country girl in the big immoral city, rags-to-riches and back again.

Stuart Dybeck's *The Coast of Chicago* is a collection of fourteen marvelous short stories about growing up in Chicago (largely in Pilsen *p.259* and Little Village *p.331*) in a style blending the gritty with the dreamlike.

Erik Larson's *Devil in the White City* is a best-selling pop history about the 1893 Colombian Exposition; it's also about the serial killer who was stalking the city at the same time. For a straight history of the Exposition and also the workers' paradise in Pullman, try James Gilbert's excellent *Perfect Cities: Chicago's Utopias of 1893.*

Audrey Niffenegger's *The Time-Traveler's Wife* is a recent love story set in Chicago nightclubs, museums, and libraries.

Mike Royko's *Boss* is the definitive biography of Mayor Richard J. Da-

ley and politics in Chicago, written by the beloved late Tribune columnist. *American Pharaoh* (Cohen and Taylor) is a good scholarly treatment of the same subject.

Carl Sandburg's *Chicago Poems* is without a doubt the most famous collection of poems about Chicago by its own "bard of the working class."

Upton Sinclair's *The Jungle* sits among the canon of both Chicago literature and US labor history for its muckraking-style depiction of the desolation experienced by Lithuanian immigrants working in the Union Stockyards on Chicago's Southwest Side *p.347*.

Richard Wright's *Native Son* is a classic Chicago neighborhood novel set in Bronzeville *p.191* and Hyde Park *p.157* about a young, doomed, black boy hopelessly warped by the racism and poverty that defined his surroundings.

Movies

Chicago is America's third most prolific movie industry and a host of very Chicago-centric movies have been produced here. These are just a few:

Ferris Bueller's Day Off (John Hughes, 1986). The dream of the northern suburbs: to be young, clever, and loose for a day in Chicago. Ferris and friends romp through the old Loop theater district, catch a game at Wrigley Field, and enjoy the sense of invincibility that Chicago shares with its favorite sons when all is well.

Adventures in Babysitting (Chris

7

Columbus, 1987). The flip side of Ferris Bueller — the dangers that await the suburbanite in the Loop at night, including memorable trips to lower Michigan Avenue and up close with the Chicago skyline.

The Blues Brothers (John Landis, 1980). Probably Chicago's favorite movie about itself: blues music, white men in black suits, a mission from God, the conscience that every Chicago hustler carries without question, and almost certainly the biggest car chase ever filmed.

The Untouchables (Brian De Palma, 1987). With a square-jawed screenplay by David Mamet, this is a retelling of Chicago's central fable of good vs. evil: Eliot Ness and the legendary takedown of Al Capone. No film (except perhaps *The Blues Brothers)* has made a better use of so many Chicago locations, especially Union Station (the baby carriage), the Chicago Cultural Center (the rooftop fight), and the LaSalle Street canyon.

High Fidelity (Stephen Frears, 2000). John Cusack reviews failed relationships from high school at Lane Tech to college in Lincoln Park and muses over them in trips through Uptown, River North, all over the city on the CTA, his record store in the rock snob environs of Wicker Park, and returning at last to his record-swamped apartment in Rogers Park.

Batman Begins (Christopher Nolan, 2005) and its sequel *The Dark Knight* (2008). Making spectacular use of the 'L', the Chicago

Board of Trade Building, Chicago skyscrapers, the Loop at night, and lower Wacker Drive, the revived action series finally sets the imposing power and intractable corruption of Gotham City where it belongs, in Chicago.

Others include Harrison Ford vs. the one-armed man in *The Fugitive,* the CTA vs. true love in *While You Were Sleeping,* and the greatest Patrick Swayze hillbilly ninja vs. Italian mob film of all time, *Next of Kin.*

Smoking

Smoking is prohibited by state law at all restaurants, bars, nightclubs, workplaces, and public buildings. It's also banned within fifteen feet of any entrance, window, or exit to a public place, and at CTA train stations. The fine for violating the ban can range from $100 to $250.

Tourist Information

Chicago's visitor information centers offer maps, brochures and other information for tourists.

Chicago Water Works Visitor Information Center, 163 E Pearson Ave, +1 877 244-2246, *egov.cityofchicago.org*, 7:30AM-7PM daily (closed Thanksgiving, Christmas Day, & New Year's Day). The city's main visitor information center is located on the Magnificent Mile in the historic Water Works. In addition to extensive free visitor materials, there is a popular gift shop inside.

Chicago Cultural Center Visitor Information Center, 77 E

Randolph St, +1 312 744-8000, *www.cityofchicago.org*, M-Th 10AM-7PM, F 10AM-6PM, Sa 10AM-5PM, Su 11AM-5PM. The Chicago Cultural Center is a good, centrally located place to pick up a host of useful, free materials relevant to virtually anyone visiting the city.

Get in

By plane

Chicago is served by two major airports: **O'Hare International Airport** *www.ohare.com* and **Midway Airport** *www.flychicago.com*. There are plenty of taxis from both to and from the city center, but they are quite expensive, especially during rush hours. Expect upwards of $40 for O'Hare and $30 for Midway. CTA trains provide direct service to both larger airports for $2.25 from anywhere in the city — faster than a taxi during rush hour and a lot less expensive.

Many large hotels offer complimentary shuttle vans to one or both airports, or can arrange one for a charge ($15-25) with advance notice.

O'Hare

O'Hare International Airport *p.397* (IATA: **ORD**) is 17 miles northwest of downtown and serves many international and domestic carriers. **United Airlines** *united.com* has the largest presence here (about 50%) followed by **American Airlines** *aa.com* with

about 40%. Most connecting flights for smaller cities in the Midwest run through O'Hare. It's one of the biggest airports in the world, and it has always been notorious for delays and cancellations. Unfortunately, it's too far northwest for most travelers who get stuck overnight to head into the city. As a result, there are *plenty* of hotels in the O'Hare area. See the O'Hare *p.397* article for listings.

The CTA Blue Line runs between the Loop and O'Hare in 45-60 sluggish minutes. On weekends, the Blue Line is usually getting some overdue repair work — this means you will have to take a (free) shuttle bus between stations, which can add even more time to the trip. If you've got a plane to catch, allow extra time.

Midway

Midway International Airport (IATA: **MDW**) is 10 miles southwest of downtown. **Southwest Airlines** *southwest.com* is the largest carrier here, followed by **AirTran** *airtran.com*. If it's an option for your trip, Midway is more compact, less crowded, has fewer delays, and usually cheaper.

The CTA Orange Line train runs between the Loop and Midway in around 25 minutes. There are a number of hotels clustered around Midway, too — see the Southwest Side article for listings.

CHICAGOGET IN

Others

Milwaukee's **General Mitchell International Airport** *www.mitchellairport.com* (IATA: **MKE**) is served by 7 Amtrak trains per day (6 on Sunday), and the Hiawatha Service was Amtrak's most on-time route in 2006. The trip from Chicago Union Station to Mitchell Airport Station is about one hour and 15 minutes.

By bus

Greyhound, 630 W Harrison St, +1 312 408-5800, *www.greyhound. com*, 24 hours. America's largest bus carrier offers service to destinations throughout the Midwest. The main terminal is near the southwestern corner of the Loop. There are secondary terminal at the CTA Red Line station at 95th/Dan Ryan and the CTA transit building (5800 N Cumberland). With advance purchase, the trip to Detroit costs about $27.

Megabus, 4400 S Racine Ave, +1 877 462-6342, *www.megabus.com/us*, M-Sa 6:30AM-10PM, Su 6:30AM-8PM. Popular in the United Kingdom, Megabus recently established a branch in Chicago. These buses stop in Chicago near **Union Station** (see below). At present, buses run express from Chicago to eleven other major Midwestern cities. With advance purchase, the trip to Detroit costs about $8.

By train

Chicago is historically the rail hub of the entire United States. Today, **Amtrak** *www.amtrak.com*, tel. +1 800 872-7245, uses the magisterial **Union Station** (Canal St and Jackson Blvd) as the hub of its Midwestern routes, making Chicago one of the most convenient U.S. cities to visit by train, serving the majority of the passenger rail company's long-distance routes, with options from virtually every major US city. With its massive main hall, venerable history, and cinematic steps, Union Station is worth a visit even if you're not coming in by train.

Most (but not all) Metra suburban trains run from Union Station and nearby **Ogilvie/Northwestern Station** (Canal St and Madison St), which are west of the Loop. Some southern lines run from stations on the east side of the Loop. The suburban trains run as far as Kenosha, Aurora, and Joliet, while the South Shore line runs through Indiana as far as South Bend. Several CTA buses converge upon the two stations, and the Loop *p.47* CTA trains are within walking distance.

By car

Chicagoans have a maddening habit of referring to some expressways by their names, not the numbers used to identify them on the signs you'll see posted on the U.S. interstate highway system, so you'll have to commit both name and number to memory. **I-55** (the **Stevenson Expressway**) will take you directly from St. Louis into downtown Chicago. **I-90/94** (**The Dan Ryan**) comes in from Indiana to the east (via the **Chicago Skyway** and **Bishop Ford Freeway**) and from central Illinois (via **I-57**). **I-90** (**The Kennedy**) comes in from Madison to the northwest. **I-94** (the **Edens Expressway**) comes in from Milwaukee to the north, but recent roadwork has slowed traffic considerably compared to I-90. **I-80** will get you to the city from Iowa which neighbors Illinois to the west.

If arriving downtown from Indiana, from the south on **I-94** or **I-90**, or from the north, Lake Shore Drive (**U.S. Highway 41**) provides a scenic introduction in both directions, day or night. If arriving on **I-55** from the southwest, or on **I-290** (the **Eisenhower Expressway**, formerly and sometimes still called **The Congress Expressway**) from the west, the skyline may also be visible from certain clear spots, but without the shore view. It should also be noted that I-55 from the southwest and I-90 through much of northwest Indiana are chock full of heavy industries with odors that'll knock your socks off, so plan your route downtown wisely.

Get around

Navigating Chicago is easy. Block numbers are consistent across the whole city. Standard blocks, of 100 addresses each, are roughly 1/8th of a mile long. (Hence, a mile is equivalent to a street number difference of 800.) Each street is assigned a number based on its distance from the zero point of the address system, the intersection of State Street and Madison Street. A street with a W (west) or E (east) number runs north-south, while a street with a N (north) or S (south) number runs east-west. A street's number is usually written on street signs at intersections, below the street name. Major thoroughfares are at each mile (multiples of 800) and secondary arteries at the half-mile marks. Thus, Western Ave at 2400 W is a north-south major thoroughfare, while Montrose Ave at 4400 N is an east-west secondary artery.

In general, "avenues" run north-south and "streets" run east-west, but there are numerous exceptions. (e.g., 48th Street may then be followed by 48th Place). In conversation, however, Chicagoans rarely distinguish between streets, avenues, boulevards, etc.

Several streets follow diagonal or meandering paths through the city such as Clark St, Lincoln Ave, Broadway, Milwaukee Ave, Ogden Ave, Archer Ave, Vincennes Ave, and South Chicago Ave.

By public transit

The best way to see Chicago is by public transit. It is cheap (basically), efficient (at times), and safe (for the most part). The **Regional Transportation Authority (RTA)** *www.rtachicago.com* oversees the various public transit agencies in the Chicagoland area. You can plan trips online with the RTA **trip planner** *tripsweb.rtachicago.com* or get assistance by calling 836-7000 in any local area code between 5AM-1AM. The RTA also has an official partnership with Google Maps, which can provide routes with public transit.

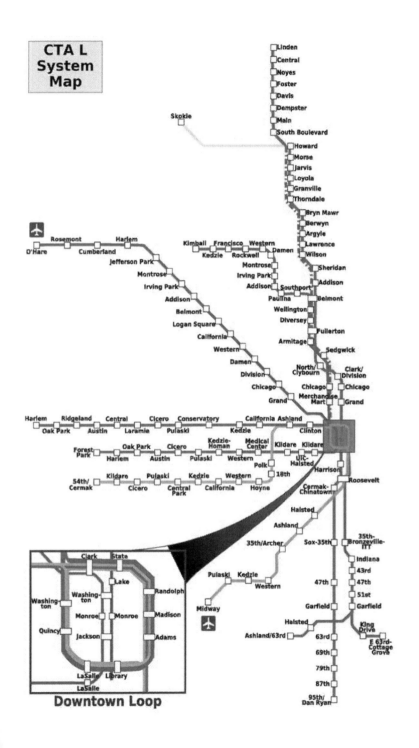

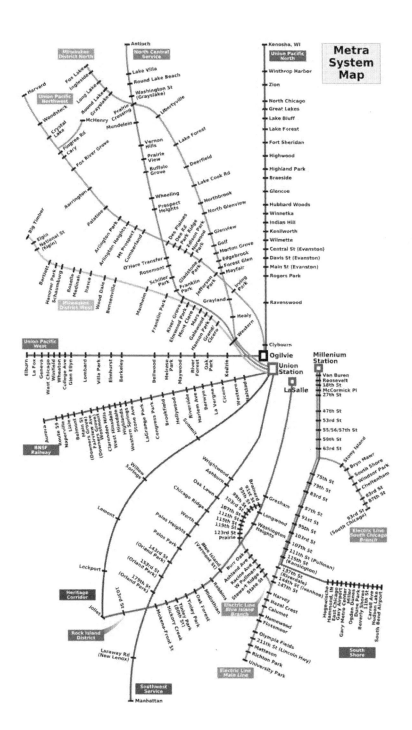

CTA

The **Chicago Transit Authority (CTA)** *www.transitchicago.com* operates trains and buses in the city of Chicago and some of the suburbs. Put simply, the CTA *is* Chicago. It is a marvel and a beast, convenient, frustrating, and irreplaceable. Even if you have the option of driving while you're in town, no experience of Chicago is complete without a trip on the CTA.

Fares are paid with **transit cards**, which can be purchased and refilled at kiosks in the lobby of every CTA station. All accept cash, and some accept credit cards. Many locals use the **Chicago Card**, which cannot be purchased at stations, but can be ordered online *www.chicago-card.com* and also purchased at grocery stores and currency exchanges. **Visitor passes** are sold for unlimited travel on the CTA and Pace: 1-Day (24 hours) for $5.75; 3-Days for $14; 7-Days for $23 and 30-Days for $86. These passes are on sale at certain train stations (notably, the O'Hare Blue Line station), currency exchanges and some convenience stores, and online *www. transitchicago.com*. Transit cards for single rides or larger increments can also be purchased online.

Train rides of any length, from one side of the city to another or just one stop, cost $2.25. At certain stations, you can transfer to other train lines at no extra cost. Once you have exited the turnstiles, entering another CTA station or boarding a CTA bus costs

$0.25 — and doing it a third time is free, provided it's still within two hours of when you started the trip.

Locals refer to Chicago's public train system as the "L". (Most lines run on **el**-evated tracks — get it?) All train lines radiate from the Loop *p.47* to every corner of the city. The "Loop" name originally referred to a surface-level streetcar loop, which predated the elevated tracks; that *any* form of transportation preceded the present one may come as a surprise, given how old some of the stations look. But they work.

CTA train lines are divided by colors: Red, Green, Brown, Blue, Purple, Yellow, Orange and Pink. All lines lead to the Loop except the Yellow Line, which is a non-stop shuttle between the suburb of Skokie and the northern border of Chicago. The Red and Blue lines run 24/7, making Chicago one of only two American cities with 24-hour rail service. Hours for the other lines vary somewhat by day, but as a general rule are from about 4:30AM-12:40AM, slightly later on weekends.

Before you travel, find out the name of the train stop closest to your destination, and the color of the train line on which it is located. Once you're on-board, you'll find route maps in each train car, above the door. The same map is also available online *www. transitchicago.com*. The name signs on platforms often have the station's location in the street grid, e.g. "5900 N, 1200 W" for Thorndale.

CHICAGO GET AROUND

There should be an attendant on duty at every train station. They can't provide change or deal with money, but they can help you figure out where you need to go and guide you through using the machines.

Buses run on nearly every major street in the city. Look for the blue and white sign, which should give a map of the route taken by the bus and major streets/stops along the way. Once inside, watch the front of the bus — a red LED display will list the names of the streets as they pass, making it easy to stop exactly where you'd like, even if it's a small side-street. To request a stop, pull the cord hanging above the window and make sure you hear an audible 'ding'. Hollering at the bus driver will raise tempers but works in a pinch.

Rides of any length cost $2 with a transit card or Chicago Card, and $2.25 in cash. Major bus routes run 7-15 minutes apart during daylight hours, depending on the route. Less-traveled routes or routes during off-peak hours may run less frequently. Check the sign to be sure the bus is still running. There are several bus routes that are on a 24 hour/7 day a week schedule — these are called OWL routes, and the signs usually have an owl to belabor that point. (See individual district articles for major bus routes through different parts of the city.)

If you have a web-enabled mobile device, the CTA runs a little godsend called the **CTA Bus Tracker** *ctabustracker.com*, which uses GPS to provide reliable, real-time tracking information for almost all bus routes.

CTA buses accept transit cards but do not sell them. They also accept cash, but do not provide change. If you overpay, the CTA keeps the extra cash, so carry exact change if possible.

In compliance with the Americans With Disabilities Act, all CTA buses and some train stations are accessible to wheelchairs. Wheelchair-accessible 'L' stations are indicated by the international wheelchair symbol and have elevators or are at ground level. If you are trying to get to a place with a non-accessible station, there will be alternate routes by bus — contact the CTA for more information.

Crime on the CTA is low, but as with any major urban area, travelers should be aware of their surroundings when traveling in the wee hours of the night, and sit close to the driver if you feel uncomfortable for any reason. Buses are being equipped with video cameras as the fleet is upgraded. Some train cars have a button and speaker for emergency communication with the driver, located in the center aisle of the car on the wall next to the door. Do not press this just to chat — the driver is required to halt the train until the situation has been confirmed as resolved, and your fellow passengers will be unamused.

Metra and South Shore

Metra *www.metrarail.com*, tel. +1 312 322-6777, runs commuter trains for the suburbs, providing service within Illinois, to Kenosha, Wisconsin, out west, and to the South Shore railroad, which provides service to South Bend, Indiana. Metra trains are fast, clean, and on-time, but unpleasantly crowded during rush hour. Generally, every car or every other car on the train has a bathroom.

Metra's **Electric Line** provides service to the convention center *p.95* (McCormick Place), Hyde Park *p.157* (Museum of Science and Industry, University of Chicago), and the Far Southeast Side *p.377*'s Pullman Historic District and Rainbow Beach. The Electric Line is *fast*, taking at most 15 minutes to reach Hyde Park from the Loop. Unfortunately, service outside of rush hours is infrequent (about once/hour), so be sure to check the schedules while planning your trip.

Although there are plans to change this in the future, none of the commuter trains currently accept CTA transit cards as payment. The fare to McCormick Place and Hyde Park, however, is only $2. Buy your tickets before boarding the train at a window or one of the automated vending machines. You can buy a ticket on the train, but that comes with an extra $2/ticket surcharge.

Ten-ride, weekly, and monthly passes are available. If you have a group of four or more people, it may be cheaper to purchase a ten-ride card and have all of your fares punched from that one card. If using Metra on Saturday and/or Sunday, you can purchase an unlimited ride weekend pass for just $5. Keep in mind that Metra only accepts cash at this time.

Pace

Pace *www.pacebus.com* runs buses in the suburbs, although some routes do cross into the city, particularly in Rogers Park *p.291* at the Howard (Red/Purple/Yellow Line) CTA station and the Far Northwest Side *p.363* at the Jefferson Park (Blue Line) CTA station. Pace provides paratransit services should you need to go somewhere inconvenient via CTA.

By car

Avoid driving in downtown Chicago if at all possible. Traffic is awful, pedestrians are constantly wandering into the street out of turn, and garages in the Loop can cost as much as $40 per day. And although downtown streets are laid out on the grid, many have multiple levels which confuse even the most hardened city driver. Even outside of the city center, street parking may not be readily available. If you do find a spot, check street signs to make sure that a) no residential permit is required to park here and b) parking is not disallowed during certain hours for "street cleaning", rush hour or something along those lines. Parking restrictions are swiftly and mercilessly enforced in the form of tickets and towing — be especially wary during snowy weather.

Parking meters are mixed between old coin-op meters and newer one-per-block kiosks, which will issue a slip for you to put in your front window.

Be advised: **talking on a handheld cell phone while driving is illegal** in Chicago, and the police are eager to write tickets for it. If you need to take a call, use a hands-free headset — or better yet, pull over.

The perpetual construction is bad enough, but drivers on the city expressways can be very aggressive. For those used to driving on expressways in the Northeast, this may be a welcome reminder of home. For everyone else, though, it can be intimidating.

By taxi

Chicago has some of the cheapest taxi fares in the US. Taxis are readily available throughout the major areas of interest for tourists and can be hailed from the street. All taxis are carefully regulated by the city. Taxi fares are standard and the initial charge ("flag pull") is $2.25 for the first 1/9 mile, then $0.20 for each additional mile or $0.20 for each elapsed 36 seconds. As of June 11, 2008, there is a $1.00 fuel surcharge added to the initial charge. There is also a flat $1.00 charge for the second passenger, and then a $0.50 charge for each additional passenger after that (for example, if four people take a taxi together, there will

be $2.00 in additional flat fees). There is no additional charge for baggage or credit card use. Taxi rides from O'Hare *p.397* and Midway to outer suburbs cost an additional one half the metered fee. Taxi drivers work best if you give them the nearest major intersection to which you are heading and then the specific address.

Outside of the downtown, North Side, Near West and Near South neighborhoods, you will likely have greater difficulty hailing a taxi directly from the street. In these situations, you can easily call for a taxi to come pick you up. Taxis typically take less than 10 minutes from the time you call to arrive. The principal Chicago taxi companies are:

American-United Taxi, tel. +1 773 248-7600

Checker Cab, tel. +1 312 243-2537

Flash Cab, tel. +1 773 561-1444 *www.flashcab.com*

Yellow Cab, tel. +1 312 829-4222 *www.yellowcabchicago.com*

The above applies only to City of Chicago taxis. Suburban-based taxi cabs have their own fares and rates, depending on the laws and regulations of the town in which they are based.

Your Name Here

Determined to shake off the burden of a world-class cultural heritage, Chicago has always found ways to undercut its own treasures in exchange for a quick buck. Of late, "naming rights" are all the rage; while official city tourism guides

CHICAGO SEE

rush to comply, using the new names will earn an eye roll or an oblivious look from most Chicagoans (and cab drivers). A few of the worst offenders:

Sears Tower — *26 years after it was built, North America's tallest building was redubbed the "Willis Tower" for a bunch of junk bond traders; even more surprising than the renaming was how little the owners got for it.*

Comiskey Park — *Winning the city's first World Series in nearly a century helped earn some acceptance for the "U.S. Cellular Field" ("The Cell") moniker, but it's still regarded as profanity by the old-timers in Bridgeport p.175, where the first Comiskey Park was built in 1910.*

Hollywood Beach — *The favorite beach of Chicago's GLBT community was renamed "Kathy Osterman Beach" for one of the mayor's Edgewater p.291 based political cronies, but more than a decade later, only city signage knows it by that name.*

By bicycle

Chicago has a bike path along the shores of Lake Michigan, making north-south travel very convenient if you're far enough east, as long as the weather is favorable by the lake. Most major city streets have bike lanes, and the biking culture is established enough that cars tend to accommodate and (grudgingly) yield to bicycles. Bike trips can also be combined with rides on the CTA. See the bicycling section below for more details.

See

Itineraries

Along the Magnificent Mile *p.109* — one day and night in Chicago, with skyscrapers, shopping, food, parks, and amazing views of the city from high and low.

Loop Art Tour *p.115* — a 2-4 hour walking tour of downtown Chicago's magnificent collection of modern sculpture.

Museums

Chicago's set of museums and cultural institutions are among the best in the world. Three of them are located within a short walk of each other in the Near South *p.95*, on what is known as the **Museum Campus**, in a beautiful spot along the lake: the **Adler Planetarium**, with all sorts of cool hands-on space exhibits and astronomy shows; the **Field Museum of Natural History**, which features "Sue," the giant Tyrannosaurus Rex skeleton, and a plethora of Egyptian treasures; and the **Shedd Aquarium**, with dolphins, whales, sharks, and the best collection of marine life east of California. A short distance away, in Hyde Park *p.157*, is the most fun of them all, the **Museum of Science and Industry** — or, as generations of Chicago-area grammar school students know it, the best field trip ever.

In the Loop *p.47*, the **Art Institute of Chicago** has a handful of iconic household names among an unrivaled collection of Impressionism, modern and classical art, and tons of historical artifacts. And in Lincoln Park *p.123*, a short trip from the Loop, the cheerful (and free) **Lincoln Park Zoo** welcomes visitors every day of the week, with highlights including the brand-new Great Ape House.

Those are the most famous ones, but Chicago has some knock-out small museums scattered throughout the city like the **National Museum of Mexican Art** in Pilsen, **The Polish Museum of America** (purportedly haunted by the once famous pianist Paderewski) in Wicker Park *p.229*, and the **Museum of Photography** in the Loop. The University of Chicago, in Hyde Park *p.157*, has several cool (and free) museums that are open to all visitors, including a spectacular collection of antiquities.

Discount packages like the **City-Pass** *citypass.com* and the **Go Chicago Card** *www.gochicagocard. com* can be purchased before you arrive in town. They cover admission to some museums and other tourist attractions, allowing you to cut to the front of lines, and may include discounts for restaurants and shopping.

Architecture

From the sternly classical to the space-age, from the Gothic to the coolly modern, Chicago is a place with an embarrassment of architectural riches, where the past meets the future. Modern architecture was born here. **Frank Lloyd Wright** fans will swoon to see his earliest buildings in Chicago, where he began his pro-

fessional career and established the Prairie School architectural style, with numerous homes in Hyde Park/Kenwood *p.157*, Oak Park, and Rogers Park *p.291* — over 100 buildings in the Chicago metropolitan area! He learned his craft at the foot of the *lieber meister*, **Louis Sullivan**, whose ornate, awe-inspiring designs were once the jewels of the Loop *p.47*, and whose few surviving buildings (Auditorium Theater, Carson Pirie Scott Building, one in the Ukrainian Village *p.229*) still stand apart.

The 1871 Chicago Fire forced the city to rebuild. The ingenuity and ambition of Sullivan, his teacher **William Le Baron Jenney** (Manhattan Building), and contemporaries like **Burnham & Root** (Monadnock, Rookery) and **Holabird & Roche/Root** (Chicago Board of Trade) made Chicago the definitive city of their era. The world's first skyscrapers were built in the Loop *p.47* as those architects received ever more demanding commissions. Later, **Mies van der Rohe** would adapt Sullivan's ethos with landmark buildings in Bronzeville *p.191* (Illinois Institute of Technology) and the Loop *p.47* (Chicago Federal Center). Unfortunately, Chicago's world-class architectural heritage is almost evenly matched by the world-class recklessness with which the city has treated it, and the list is long of masterpieces that have been needlessly demolished for bland new structures.

Architectural tours cover the landmarks on foot and by popular river boat tours, or by just standing awestruck on a downtown bridge over the Chicago River; see individual district articles for details. For a tour on the cheap, the short trip around the elevated Loop train circuit (Brown/Purple Lines) may be worth every penny of the $2 fare.

Chicago is also the birthplace of the **skyscraper**. It was here that steel-frame construction was invented, allowing buildings to rise above the limits of load-bearing walls. Naturally, competition with New York was fierce, but in the end, Chicago built them taller. Chicago boasts three out of America's tallest five buildings: the **Sears Tower** (1st), the Trump Tower (2nd), and the Aon Center (5th) (although the local favorite is actually #6: the John Hancock Center). For years, the Sears Tower was the tallest building in the world, but it's since lost the title by most measurements. Various developers insist they're bringing the title back. Until they do, though, the Sears Tower will have to settle for being the tallest building in North America, although the Hancock is not much shorter, is better located for tourists, has a better view, and is quite frankly better-looking.

African-American history

Chicago's African-American history begins with the city's African-American founder, **Jean Baptiste Pointe du Sable**. Born to a Haitian slave and a French pirate, he married a woman from the Potawatomi tribe, and built a house and trading post on the Chicago River on the spot of today's Pioneer Court (the square just south of the Tribune Tower in the Near North *p.71*). Du Sable lived on the Chicago River with his family from the 1770s to 1800, when he sold his house to John Kinzie, whose family and friends would later claim to have founded the city.

Relative to other northern cities, African-Americans constituted a fairly large part of Chicago's early population because of Illinois' more tolerant culture, which was inherited from fervent anti-slavery Mormon settlers. As a non-slave state generally lacking official segregation laws, Illinois was an attractive place to live for black freedmen and fugitive slaves.

By the 1920s, Chicago had a thriving middle class African-American community based in the Bronzeville *p.191* neighborhood, which at the time became known as "The Black Metropolis," home to a cultural renaissance comparable to the better-known Harlem Renaissance of New York. African-American literature of the time was represented by local poetess **Gwendolyn Brooks** and novelist **Richard Wright**, most famous for his *Native Son*, nearly all of which takes place in Chicago's Bronzeville *p.191* and Hyde Park/Kenwood *p.157*. The Chicago school of African-American literature distinguished itself from the East Coast by its focus on the new realities of urban African-American life. Chicago became a *major* center of African-American jazz, and *the* center for the blues. Jazz great **Louis Armstrong** got his start there; other famous black Chicagoans of the day included Bessie Coleman — the world's first licensed black pilot, the hugely influential African-American and women's civil rights activist **Ida B. Wells**, the great pitcher/manager/executive of Negro League Baseball **Andrew "Rube" Foster**, and many more.

Both fueling and threatening Chicago's black renaissance was the single most influential part of Chicago's African-American history: **the Great Migration**. African-Americans from the rural South moved to the industrial cities of the North due to the post-WWI shortage of immigrant industrial labor, and to escape the Jim Crow Laws and racial violence of the South. The massive wave of migrants, most from Mississippi, increased Chicago's black population by more than 500,000. With it came southern food, Mississippi blues, and the challenges of establishing adequate housing for so many recent arrivals — a challenge that they would have to meet themselves, without help from a racist and neglectful city government.

Black Chicago's renaissance was brought to its knees by the Great Depression; its fate was sealed ironically by the 1937 creation of the Chicago Housing Authority, which sought to build affordable public housing for the city. However well-intentioned the project may have sounded, the results were disastrous. The largest housing projects by far were the 1940 Ida B. Wells projects, which were designed to "warehouse" Chicago's population of poor African-Americans in a district far away from white population centers, the Cabrini Green projects, which developed a reputation as the most violent housing projects in the nation, and the massive 1962 Robert Taylor Homes in Bronzeville, which were forced to house an additional 16,000 people beyond their intended 11,000 capacity. The Black Metropolis proved unable to cope with this massive influx of new, impoverished residents, and the urban blight that came from concentrating such a great number of them in one place.

Further damaging to Chicago's black population was the phenomenon of "white flight" that accompanied the introduction of African-Americans to Chicago neighborhoods. Unwilling to live beside black neighbors, many Chicagoans fled desegregation to the suburbs. This trend was accelerated by the practice of "blockbusting," where unsavory real estate agents would fan racist fears in order to buy homes on the cheap. As a result, Chicago neighborhoods (with the notable exceptions of Hyde Park/Kenwood *p.157*, and Rogers Park *p.291*) never truly integrated, and the social, educational, and economic networks that incoming African-Americans hoped to join disintegrated in the wake of fleeing white communities. During this period, Chicago experienced a huge population loss and large sections of the city became covered with vacant lots, which in turn created the conditions for crime to flourish. A number of Chicago's major roads, most notably the Dan Ryan Expressway, were built in part to segregate these areas from more prosperous ones like the Loop *p.47*.

In 1966, **Dr. Martin Luther King, Jr.** decided to come north and chose Chicago as his first destination. However, from the moment of his arrival on the Southwest Side *p.347*, King was utterly confounded. The death threats that followed his march through Marquette Park were challenge enough, but nowhere in the South was there a more expert player of politics than Chicago's Mayor Richard J. Daley. King left town frustrated and exhausted, but **Rev. Jesse Jackson** continued civil rights efforts in Chicago through his Operation PUSH. The 1983 election of **Mayor Harold Washington**, the first black mayor of Chicago, was a watershed event for Chicago's African-American population, and although long battles with obstructionist white politicians lay ahead, it marked the moment when African-American elected officials became major, independent forces in Chicago.

Today, with a plurality of nearly 40%, Chicago's black population is the country's second largest, after New York. The broader South Side is the cultural center of Chicago's black community; it constitutes the largest single African-American neighborhood in the country and boasts

the nation's greatest concentration of black-owned businesses. Chicagoans ignorant of these areas may tell you that they are dangerous and crime-ridden, but the reality is much more complex. There are strong, middle and upper class black communities throughout the city, some of the more prominent of which include upper Bronzeville *p.191*, Hyde Park/Kenwood *p.157*, Chatham *p.203*, South Shore *p.203*, and Beverly *p.389*.

Bronzeville *p.191* is the obvious destination for those interested in African-American history, although Kenwood also boasts interesting recent history, as it has been (or is) home to championship boxer Muhammad Ali, Nation of Islam leaders Elijah Muhammad and Louis Farrakhan, and **President Barack Obama**. No one should miss the **DuSable Museum of African-American History** in Bronzeville *p.191*, the first museum of African-American history in the United States. And if your interest is more precisely in African-American culture than history, head down to Chatham and South Shore *p.203* to enter the heart of Chicago's black community.

Ethnic neighborhoods

Chicago is among the most diverse cities in America, and many neighborhoods reflect the character and culture of the immigrants who established them. Some, however, do more than just reflect: they *absorb* you in a place that, for several blocks at a time, may as well be a chunk of another country, picked up and dropped near the shores of Lake Michigan. The best of Chicago's ethnic neighborhoods are completely uncompromised, and that makes them a real highlight for visitors.

Chicago's Chinatown *p.175* is among the most active Chinatowns in the world. It even has its own stop on the CTA Red Line. It's on the South Side near Bridgeport *p.175*, birthplace of the Irish political power-brokers who have run Chicago government for most of the last century. More Irish communities exist on the Far Southwest Side *p.389*, where they even have an Irish castle to seal the deal. The Southwest Side *p.347* houses enormous populations of Polish Highlanders and Mexicans, as well as reduced Lithuanian and Bohemian communities.

No serious Chicago gourmand would eat Indian food that didn't come from a restaurant on **Devon Avenue** in Rogers Park *p.291*. It's paradise for spices, saris, and the latest Bollywood flicks. Lawrence Avenue in Albany Park *p.313* is sometimes called **Seoul Drive** for the Korean community there, and the Persian food on Kedzie Avenue nearby is simply astonishing. At the **Argyle** Red Line stop, by the intersection of Argyle and Broadway in Uptown *p.273*, you'd be forgiven for wondering if you were still in America; Vietnamese, Thais, and Laotians share space on a few blocks of restaurants, grocery stores, and even dentists. Neither the Swedish settlers who built Andersonville *p.273* or the Germans from Lincoln Square

p.313 are the dominant presence in those neighborhoods any more, but their identity is still present in restaurants, cultural centers, and other small discoveries to be made. Likewise, **Little Italy** and **Greektown** on the Near West Side *p.215* survive only as restaurant strips.

A more contemporary experience awaits in Pilsen *p.259* and Little Village *p.331*, two neighborhoods on the Lower West Side where the Spanish signage outnumbers the English; in fact, Chicago has the second largest Mexican and Puerto Rican populations outside of their respective home countries. Pilsen and its arts scene is an especially an exciting place to visit.

It's hard to imagine displacement being a concern for the Polish community on the city's Far Northwest *p.363* and Southwest *p.347* sides. The **Belmont-Central** business district is what you might consider the epicenter of Polish activity. Bars, restaurants, and dozens of other types of Polish businesses thrive on this strip, and on a smaller section of Milwaukee Avenue (between Addison and Diversey). **Taste of Polonia**, held over Labor Day weekend, draws an annual attendance of about 50,000 people.

Do

Beaches

Chicago is not well known as a beach destination, but Lake Michigan is the largest freshwater lake located entirely within the United States, and Chicagoans flock to it.

25

Anyone can show up and swim — virtually none of Chicago's lakefront is spoiled by "private" beaches. And despite the latitude, the water is quite warm in the late summer and early fall . The Chicago shore has been called the second cleanest urban waterfront *in the world*, although bacteria levels in the water do force occasional — but rare — beach closures (which are clearly posted at the beach, and online *www.chicagoparkdistrict.com*). Lifeguards keep a stern watch for safety, and if one's in a row boat, they're both keeping an eye out and setting a boundary for swimmers (usually waist-deep).

Oak Street Beach and North Avenue Beach (in the Near North *p.71* and Lincoln Park *p.123*) are the fashionable places to sun-tan and be seen, but Rogers Park *p.291* has mile after mile of less pretentious sand and surf. Hyde Park's *p.157* Promontory Point is beautiful, and offers skyline views from its submerged beach by the rocks (although a swim there is *technically* against city rules). Rainbow Beach in South Shore *p.203* is actually one of the city's nicest, although it is rarely visited by sun lovers from outside the neighborhood.

Parks

Where there are beaches, there are lakefront parks. During the summer months, the lakefront parks are a destination for organized and impromptu volleyball and soccer games, chess matches, and plenty more. There are also a couple of tennis courts in Lincoln Park *p.123*, Lakeview *p.139*, and Rogers Park *p.291*. There are also terrific parks further away from the lake. In the Loop *p.47*, **Grant Park** hosts music festivals throughout the year, and **Millennium Park** is a fun destination for all ages, especially during the summer. In Hyde Park *p.157*, **Midway Park** offers skating, and summer and winter gardens in the shadow of the academic giant, the University of Chicago, and **Jackson Park** has golf, more gardens and the legacy of the city's shining moment, the 1893 World's Colombian Exposition. In Bronzeville *p.191*, **Washington Park** is one of the city's best places for community sports. And that's just a brief overview. Almost every neighborhood in Chicago has a beloved park.

Events & Festivals

If you're *absolutely* determined and you plan carefully, you may be able to visit Chicago during a festival-less week. It's a challenge, though. Most neighborhoods, parishes, and service groups host their own annual festivals throughout the spring, summer, and fall *www.explorechicago.org*. There are a few can't-miss city-wide events, though. In the Loop *p.47*, Grant Park hosts **Taste of Chicago** in July, and four major music festivals: **Blues Fest** and **Gospel Fest** in June, **Lollapalooza** in August, and **Jazz Fest** over Labor Day Weekend. All but Lollapalooza are free. The Chicago-based music website **Pitchfork Media** also hosts their own annual three day festival of rock, rap, and more in the summer.

Sports

With entries in every major professional sports league and several universities in the area, Chicago sports fans have a lot to keep them occupied. The **Chicago Bears** play football at Soldier Field in the Near South *p.95* from warm September to frigid January. Since the baseball teams split the city in half, nothing seizes the Chicago sports consciousness like a playoff run from the Bears, who dominated the 2006 season before losing in the Super Bowl. Aspiring fans will be expected to be able to quote a minimum of two verses of the *Super Bowl Shuffle* from memory, tear up at the mention of Walter Payton, and provide arguments as to how Butkus, Singletary, and Urlacher represent the premier linebackers of their respective eras, with supporting evidence in the form of grunts, yells, and fists slammed on tables.

The **Chicago Bulls** play basketball at the United Center on the Near West Side *p.215*. After a few miserable years, the Bulls are in playoff form again, and while ticket prices may never reach Jordanera mania, they're still an exciting team to watch, even if the United Center doesn't hold in noise like the old Chicago Stadium did. The **Chicago Blackhawks** share a building with the Bulls. As one of the "Original Six" teams in professional hockey, they have a long history in their sport, and while they've been awful for

years, the team is experiencing a renaissance. Home games tend to sell out, but tickets can usually be found if you check in advance. Both the Bulls and the Blackhawks play from the end of October to the beginning of April.

It's baseball, though, in which the tribal fury of Chicago sports is best expressed. The **Chicago Cubs** play at Wrigley Field on the North Side, in Lakeview *p.139*, and the **Chicago White Sox** play at U.S. Cellular Field (Comiskey Park, underneath the corporate naming rights) on the South Side, in Bridgeport *p.175*. Both stadiums are open-air, and both franchises have more than a century's worth of history. Everything else is a matter of fiercely held opinion. Both teams play 81 home games from April to the beginning of October. The two three-game series when the teams play each other are the hottest sports tickets in Chicago during any given year. If someone offers you tickets to a game, pounce.

There are plenty of smaller leagues in the city as well, although some play their games in the suburbs. The **Chicago Fire** play soccer in the suburb of Bridgeview, the **Chicago Sky** play women's professional basketball at the UIC Pavilion on the Near West Side *p.215*, and the **Windy City Rollers** skate flat-track roller derby in neighboring Cicero. Minor league baseball teams dot the suburbs as well.

While college athletics are not one of the city's strong points, Northwestern football (in Evanston)

CHICAGO◌

and DePaul basketball (in Lincoln Park *p.123*) show occasional signs of life, and the University of Illinois at Champaign-Urbana is usually at least competitive. If you find yourself in Hyde Park *p.157*, ask someone how the University of Chicago football team is doing — it's a surefire conversation starter.

Theater

Modern American comedy — the good parts, at least — was born when a group of young actors from Hyde Park *p.157* formed The Compass Players, fusing intelligence and a commitment to character with an improvisational spark. One strand of their topical, hyper-literate comedy led, directly or indirectly, to Shelly Berman, Mike Nichols & Elaine May, Lenny Bruce, *M*A*S*H* and *The Mary Tyler Moore Show;* another strand, namely **The Second City**, led to *Saturday Night Live* and a pretty huge percentage of the funny movies and television of the last thirty years. Still in Chicago's Old Town *p.123* (and few other places as well), still smart and still funny, Second City does two-act sketch revues followed by one act of improv. As the saying goes, if you can only see one show while you're in Chicago, even if you have no particular interest in theater, Second City is one to see.

Improvisational comedy as a performance art form is a big part of the Chicago theater scene. At Lakeview *p.139* and Uptown *p.273* theaters like **The Annoyance The-**

ater, I.O., and **The Playground,** young actors take classes and perform shows that range from ragged to inspired throughout the week. Some are fueled by the dream of making the cast of *SNL* or Tina Fey's latest project, and some just enjoy doing good work on-stage, whether or not they're getting paid for it (and most aren't). There's no guarantee that you'll see something great on any given night, but improv tends to be cheaper than anything else in town, and it can definitely be worth the risk. Another popular theater experience is the comedy/drama hybrid **Too Much Light Makes The Baby Go Blind,** offering 30 plays in 60 minutes every weekend in Andersonville *p.273*.

Steppenwolf, in Lincoln Park *p.123*, is Chicago's other landmark theater. Founded in 1976, they have a history of taking risks onstage, and they have the ensemble to back it up, with heavyweights like Joan Allen, John Malkovich, and Gary Sinise. Steppenwolf isn't cheap any more, but they mix good, young actors with their veteran ensemble and still choose interesting, emotionally-charged scripts. It's the best place in town to see modern, cutting-edge theater with a bit of "I went to…" name-drop value for the folks back home.

Most of the prestige theaters, including the **Broadway in Chicago** outlets, are located in the Loop *p.47* or the Near North *p.71*. Tickets are expensive and can be tough to get, but shows destined for Broadway like *The Producers* often make their debut here. For the cost-conscious, the **League of Chicago Theatres** operates **Hot Tix** *www.hottix.org*, which offers short-notice half-price tickets to many Chicago shows.

One theater to see, regardless of the production, is **The Auditorium** in the Loop *p.47*. It's a masterpiece of architecture and of performance space. Designed by Dankmar Adler and Louis Sullivan, who were on a commission from syndicate of local business magnates to bring some culture to the heathen city, it was the tallest building in Chicago and one of the tallest in the world at the time of its opening in 1889, and it's still an impressive sight, inside and out.

Bicycles

Chicago has a strong, passionate bicycle culture, and riding opportunities abound. Pedaling your way around the city is one of the best ways to get to know Chicago. And the terrain is mostly flat — a boon for easy-going cyclists!

The scenic **Lakefront Trail** runs for 18 continuous miles along the city's beautiful shoreline. Even while riding at a moderate pace, traveling downtown along the lakefront can be faster than driving or taking the CTA! Further inland, many streets have bike lanes, and signs direct riders to major bike routes. The City of Chicago maintains helpful **bicycle resources online** *egov.cityofchicago.org*, including major civic bike events and (slow) interactive maps of major streets with bike lanes.

Bicyclists have to follow the same "rules of the road" as automobiles. Police officers will write citations for bicyclists in violation of traffic laws (especially disregarding stop signs and traffic lights). Bicycle riding is never allowed on sidewalks (except for children under age 12). This rule is strictly enforced in higher density neighborhoods, mostly areas near the lake, and is considered a criminal misdemeanor offense. You must walk your bike on the sidewalk.

Conveniently, CTA buses are all equipped with bike racks which carry up to two bicycles, and 'L' trains permit two bicycles per car *except* during rush hour (roughly 7-9:30AM and 3:30-6:30PM weekdays, excluding major holidays on which the CTA is running on a Sunday schedule). With the buses, inspect the rack closely for wear or damage and be absolutely certain that the bike is secured before you go, lest it fall off in traffic (and be immediately flattened by the bus). The CTA will fight tooth and nail to avoid reimbursing you for the loss, and the driver might not stop to let you retrieve it.

Bikes may be rented from the North Avenue Beach House (Lincoln Park *p.123*), Navy Pier, (Near North *p.71*), the Millennium Park bike station (Loop *p.47*), and from several bike shops in the city. Another option is to contact the terrific **Working Bikes Cooperative** *workingbikes.org*, an all-volunteer group of bike lovers that collects and refurbishes bikes, and then sells a few in Chicago to support their larger project of shipping bikes to Africa and South America. You could buy a cheap bike and donate it back when you're done, or even spend a day or two working as a volunteer.

For an opportunity to connect with the local bike community and take a memorable trip through the city, don't miss the **Critical Mass** *chicagocriticalmass.org* rides on the last Friday of every month, starting from Daley Plaza in the Loop *p.47* (5:30PM). With numbers on their side, the hundreds or even thousands of bike riders wind up taking over entire streets along the way, with themed routes that are voted upon at the outset of the trip. Anyone is free to join or fall away wherever they like. Police are generally cooperative — take cues from more experienced riders.

Learn

Several major and minor universities call Chicago home. The **University of Chicago** and **Northwestern University** are undoubtedly the most prestigious among them. The University of Chicago's Gothic campus is in Hyde Park *p.157*, which is, famously, "home to more Nobel Prizes per square kilometer than any other neighborhood on Earth." Further north, in the Bronzeville *p.191* area, is the **Illinois Institute of Technology**, which has notable programs in engineering and architecture. **Northwestern University** has its main campus in Evanston, just north of Chicago, but it also has campuses in the Near North *p.71* off Michigan Ave, including its med-

ical, law, and business schools.

On the North Side, there are two major Catholic universities with over a hundred years in Chicago: **DePaul University**, in Lincoln Park *p.123*, and **Loyola University**, in Rogers Park *p.291*. Both schools also have campuses in the Loop *p.47*. **Rush University Medical School**, on the Near West Side, traces its roots back even further, to 1837. Dating back to 1891, **North Park University** serves as another fine private liberal arts university in Albany Park *p.313* on the Northwest Side.

A handful of schools in the Loop *p.47* attract students in the creative arts. **Columbia College** has an enviable location on Michigan Avenue, and its programs in creative writing and photography are well-regarded. The **School of the Art Institute** is generally regarded as one of the top three art and design schools in the country and is one of the few art schools that does not require its students to declare majors. The **Illinois Institute of Art** specializes in different fields of art and design. The main campus of **Roosevelt University**, former home to Chicago heavyweights like Harold Washington and Ramsey Lewis, is in the Auditorium Building on the corner of Michigan Avenue and Congress Parkway. **Northwestern University** has its main campus in Evanston, just north of Chicago, but it also has campuses in the Loop including its medical, law, and business schools.

To the west of the Loop, built over the remains of Little Italy and

Maxwell Street neighborhoods is the brutalist Near West Side *p.215* campus of the **University of Illinois at Chicago (UIC)**, the second-largest member of the Illinois state university system.

The **City Colleges of Chicago** *www.ccc.edu* are scattered throughout the city. They include **Harold Washington College** (Loop *p.47*), **Harry S. Truman College** (Uptown *p.273*), **Malcolm X College** (Near West Side *p.215*), **Wright College** (Humboldt Park *p.331*), **Kennedy-King College** (Englewood *p.347*), **Daley College** (Southwest Side *p.347*), and **Olive-Harvey College** (Far Southeast Side *p.377*).

Work

Chicago still loves Carl Sandburg and his poems, but the city shucked off the hog butcher's apron a long time ago. In terms of industry, there's little that distinguishes Chicago from any other major city in America, save for size. The **Chicago Board of Trade** *www.cbot.com* and **Chicago Mercantile Exchange** *www.cme.com* are among the biggest employers, with stables of traders and stock wizards. **Boeing** *www.boeing.com* moved its headquarters to Chicago amid much fanfare a few years ago; **United Airlines** *www.united.com* is another international company with headquarters in town. **Abbott Labs** *www.abbott.com*, just outside city limits, is the biggest employer of foreign nationals in scientific fields. The Big Five consulting firms all have one or more offices in the Loop

p.47. And there's always construction work in Chicago, but with a strong union presence in the city, it's not easy for a newcomer to break into without an introduction.

For younger workers, the museums in the Loop *p.47* and the Near South *p.95* are always looking for low-paid, high-enthusiasm guides, and the retail outlets on the Magnificent Mile *p.71* also need seasonal help. And with so many colleges and universities in the city, study abroad opportunities abound.

In Chicago, business is politics, and there's one word in Chicago politics: **clout**. The principal measure of clout is how many jobs you can arrange for your friends. Hence, if you want to work in Chicago, start asking around — email someone from your country's embassy or consulate and see if they have any leads, or figure out if there is a cultural association that might be able to help you. It's no coincidence that the Mayor's Office *egov.cityofchicago.org* employs scores of Irish workers every summer. If you happen to contact somebody who met the right person at a fundraiser a few days ago, you might fall into a cushy job or a dream internship; it's worth a try.

Buy

Whatever you need, you can buy it in Chicago, on a budget or in luxury. The most famous shopping street in Chicago is a stretch of Michigan Avenue

known as **The Magnificent Mile**, in the Near North *p.71* area. It includes many designer boutiques, and several multi-story malls anchored by large department stores like 900 N Michigan and Water Tower Place. Additional brands are available from off-strip shops to the south and west of Michigan.

State Street used to be a great street for department stores in the Loop *p.47*, but it's now a shadow of its former self, with Carson Pirie Scott's landmark Louis Sullivan-designed building closed, and invading forces from New York holding the former Marshall Field's building hostage under the name Macy's. Discounts can still be found at places like Filene's Basement, though.

For a classic Chicago souvenir, pick up a box of **Frango Mints**, much-loved mint chocolates that were originally offered by Marshall Field's and are still available at Macy's stores. Although no longer made in the thirteenth-floor kitchen of the State Street store, the original recipe appears to still be in use, which pleases the loyal crowds fond of the flavor — and too bad for anyone looking to avoid trans-fats.

However, for a more unique shopping experience, check out the fun, eclectic stores in Lincoln Square *p.313*, or the cutting-edge shops in Bucktown *p.247* and Wicker Park *p.229*, which is also the place to go for **music fiends** — although there are also key vinyl drops in other parts of the city as well. **Southport** in Lakeview *p.139* and **Armitage** in Lin-

coln Park *p.123* also have browser-friendly fashion boutiques.

For **art** or **designer home goods**, River North is the place to go. Centered between the Merchandise Mart and the Chicago Avenue Brown Line "L" stop in the Near North *p.71*, River North's gallery district boasts the largest arts and design district in North America outside of Manhattan. The entire area is walkable and makes for fun window-shopping.

Goods from around the world are available at the **import stores** in Chicago's many ethnic neighborhoods; check See for descriptions and district articles for directions.

If you are the type that loves to browse through **independent bookstores**, Hyde Park has a stunning assortment of dusty used bookstores selling beat-up-paperbacks to rare 17th century originals, and the world's largest academic bookstore. **Printer's Row** in the Near South *p.95* is also a great stop for book lovers.

Eat

Chicago is one of the great restaurant towns in America. If you're looking for a specific kind of cuisine, check out the neighborhoods. Greektown *p.215*, the Devon Ave *p.291* Desi corridor, Chinatown *p.175*, and Chatham *p.203*'s soul food and barbecue are just the tip of the iceberg. Other areas are more eclectic: Lincoln Square *p.313* and Albany Park have unrivaled Middle Eastern, German, and Korean food, while Uptown *p.273* offers nearly the whole

Chicago's deep dish pizza is incredible

Southeast Asian continent with Ghanaian, Nigerian, contemporary American, stylish Japanese, and down-home Swedish a few blocks away.

If you're interested in celebrity chefs and unique creations, Lincoln Park *p.123* and Wicker Park *p.229* have plenty of award-winners. River North *p.71* has several good upscale restaurants, but don't waste your time on tourist traps like Rainforest Cafe, Cheesecake Factory or Hard Rock Cafe. In fact, you should never submit to standing in line—there are always equally good restaurants nearby. No matter what you enjoy, you'll have a chance to eat well in Chicago, and you won't need to spend a lot of money doing it—unless you want to, of course.

But while Chicago has a world class dining scene downtown, it is the low-end where it truly distinguishes itself. No other city on earth takes fast food so seriously; for those who don't concern themselves with calorie counting, Chicago is cheap, greasy heaven. A couple "culinary specialties" in particular deserve further description.

Chicago pizza

Chicago's most prominent contribution to world cuisine might be the **deep dish pizza**. Delivery chains as far away as Kyoto market "Chicago-style pizza," but the only place to be sure you're getting the real thing is in Chicago. To make a deep dish pizza, a thin layer of dough is laid into a deep round pan and pulled up the sides, and then meats and vegetables — Italian sausage, onions, bell peppers, mozzarella cheese, and more — are lined on the crust. At last, tomato sauce goes on top, and the pizza is baked. It's gooey, messy, not recommended by doctors, and delicious. When you dine on deep dish pizza, don't wear anything you were hoping to wear again soon. Some nationally-known deep dish pizza hubs are Pizzeria UNO and DUE, Gino's East, Giordano's, and Lou Malnati's, but plenty of local favorites exist. Ask around — people won't be shy about giving you their opinion.

But deep dish is not the end of the line in a city that takes its pizza so seriously. Chicago also prides itself on its distinctive thin-crust pizza and stuffed pizzas. The Chicago **thin crust** has a thin, cracker-like, crunchy crust, which somehow remains soft and doughy on the top side. Toppings and a lot of a thin, spiced Italian tomato sauce go under the mozzarella cheese, and the pizza is sliced into squares. If you are incredulous that Chicago's pizza preeminence extends into the realm of the thin crust, head south of Midway to Vito and Nick's, which is widely regarded among Chicago gourmands as the standard bearer for the city.

The **stuffed pizza** is a monster, enough to make an onlooker faint. Start with the idea of a deep dish, but then find a much deeper dish and stuff a *lot* more toppings under the cheese. Think deep-dish apple pie, but pizza. Allow 45 minutes to an hour for pizza places to make one of these and allow 3-4 extra notches on your belt for the ensuing weight gain. Arguably the best stuffed pizza in town is at Bella Bacino's in the Loop *p.47*, which somehow is not greasy, but other excellent vendors include Giordano's, Gino's, and Edwardo's.

The Chicago hot dog

This may come as a surprise to New Yorkers, but the Chicago hot dog is the king of all hot dogs — indeed, it is considered the **perfect hot dog**. Perhaps due to the city's history of Polish and German immigration, Chicago takes its dogs *way* more seriously than the rest of the country. A Chicago hot dog is always all-beef (usually Vienna beef), always served on a poppy-seed bun, and topped with what looks like a full salad of mustard, diced tomatoes, a dill pickle spear, sport (chili) peppers, a generous sprinkling of celery salt, diced onion, and a sweet-pickle relish endemic-to-Chicago that is dyed an odd, vibrant bright-green color. It's a full meal, folks.

Ketchup is regarded as an abomination on a proper Chicago-style hot dog. Self-respecting establishments will refuse orders to put the ketchup on the dog, and many have signs indicating that they don't serve it; truly serious hot dog joints don't even allow the condiment on the premises. The reason for Chicago's ketchup aversion is simple — ketchup contains sugar, which overwhelms the taste of the beef and prevents its proper enjoyment. Hence, ketchup's replacement with diced

A charred Chicago-style hot dog with all the trappings

tomatoes. Similarly, Chicagoans eschew fancy mustards that would overwhelm the flavor of the meat in favor of simple yellow mustard. And for the hungry visiting New Yorkers, the same goes for sugary sauerkraut — *just no.*

At most hot dog places, you will have the option to try a **Maxwell Street Polish** instead. Born on the eponymous street of the Near West Side *p.215*, the Polish is an all-beef sausage on a bun, with fewer condiments than the Chicago hot dog: usually just grilled onions, mustard, and a few chili peppers.

In a tragic, bizarre twist of fate, the areas of Chicago most visited by tourists (i.e., the Loop *p.47*) lack proper Chicago hot dog establishments. If you are down-town and want to experience a Chicago hot dog done right, the nearest safe bet is Portillo's. Although, if you're up for a little hot dog adventure, you can eat one right at the source, at the Vienna Beef Factory deli. Sadly, both baseball parks botch their dogs.

Italian Beef

The Italian Beef sandwich completes the Chicago triumvirate of tasty greasy treats. The main focus of the sandwich is the beef, and serious vendors will serve meat of a surprisingly good quality, which is slow-roasted, and thinly shaved before being loaded generously onto chewy, white, Italian-style bread. Two sets of options will come flying at you, so prepare yourself: sweet peppers or hot and dipped or not. The "sweet" peppers are sautéed bell peppers, while the hots are a mixed Chicago giardiniera. The dip, of course, is a sort of French dip of the sandwich back into the beef broth. (Warning: dipped Italian Beefs are sloppy!) If you are in the mood, you may be able to get an Italian Beef with cheese melted over the beef, although travelers looking for the "authentic Italian Beef" perhaps should not stray so far from tradition.

The Italian Beef probably was invented by Italian-American immigrants working in the Union Stockyards on the Southwest Side *p.347*, who could only afford to take home the tough, lowest-quality meat and therefore had a need to slow-roast it, shave it into thin slices, and dip it just to get it in chewable form. But today the sandwich has found a lucrative home downtown, where it clogs the arteries and delights the taste buds of the Chicago workforce during lunch break. Some of the city's favorite downtown vendors include Luke's Italian Beef in the Loop *p.47* and Mr. Beef in the Near North *p.71*, while the Portillo's chain is another solid option.

Four fried chickens and a coke...

With the Great Migration came much of what was best about the South: blues, jazz, barbecue — but following a legendary meal at which a young, hungry Harold Pierce saw the last piece of bird flee his grasp into the mouth of the local preacher, Harold made it his mission to add fried chicken to that prestigious list, and to ensure that no South Side Chicagoan ever run out.

Harold's Chicken Shack, a.k.a. the Fried Chicken King, is a South Side institution like no other. The Chicago-style fried chicken is considered by many connaisseurs to be some of the nation's best (certainly in the North), and it is fried in a home-style mix of beef tallow and vegetable oil, then covered with sauce (hot or mild). Crucially, it is always cooked to order — ensuring that essential layer of grease between the skin and the meat. A half chicken meal can come as cheap as $4 and includes coleslaw, white bread, and sauce-drenched fries — make like a local and wrap the fries in the bread.

Initially, the fried chicken chain spread throughout black neighborhoods, which were ignored by other fast food chains, but in later years the franchise has expanded its greasy fingers to the West and North Sides, as well as downtown. While chances are you will not find better fried chicken outside of Harold's walls, the quality, pricing, and character vary between individual locations. Your safest bets are on the South Side — if you are served through bullet-proof glass under signs bearing a chef chasing a chicken with a hatchet, rest assured you are getting the best.

Drink

Chicago is a drinking town, and you can find bars and pubs in every part of the city. It is believed that Chicago has the second highest bars-per-capita in the US (after San Francisco). Be prepared to be asked for identification to verify

your age, even at neighborhood dive bars. **Smoking** is banned in Chicago bars (and restaurants).

The best place to drink for drinking's sake is Wicker Park *p.229* and its neighbor Bucktown *p.247*, which have a world-class stock of quality dive bars. North Center *p.139* and Roscoe Village are also a great (and underrated) destination for the art of the cheap beer and the beer garden. Beware the bars in Lakeview *p.139* near Wrigley Field, though, which are packed on weekends, and jam-packed all day whenever the Cubs are playing. Just to the south, Lincoln Park *p.123* has bars and beer gardens to indulge those who miss college, and some trendy clubs for the neighborhood's notorious high-spending Trixies.

Ill-informed tourists converge upon the nightclubs of Rush and Division St *p.71*. The city's best DJs spin elsewhere, the best drinks are served elsewhere, and the cheapest beers are served elsewhere; the hottest of-the-moment clubs and in-the-know celebrities are usually elsewhere, too. For the last few years the West Loop's *p.215* warehouse bars were the place to be, but more recently the River North neighborhood has been making a comeback. Still, the Rush/Division bars do huge business. This area includes the "Viagra Triangle," where Chicago's wealthy older men hang out with women in their early 20s. Streeterville, immediately adjacent, exchanges the dance floors for high-priced hotel bars and piano lounges.

Although good dance music can be found in Wicker Park and the surrounding area, the best places to dance in the city are the expensive see and be seen clubs in River North and the open-to-all (except perhaps bachelorette parties) clubs in gay-friendly Boystown *p.139*, which are a lot of fun for people of any sexual orientation.

Jazz and Blues

The Lower Mississippi River Valley is known for its music; New Orleans has jazz, and Memphis has blues. Chicago, though located far away from the valley, has both. Former New Orleans and Memphis residents brought jazz and blues to Chicago as they came north for a variety of reasons: the World's Columbian Exposition of 1893 brought a lot of itinerant musicians to town, and the city's booming economy kept them coming through the Great Migration. Chicago was the undisputed capital of early jazz between 1917-1928, wih masters like Joe King Oliver, Louis Armstrong, Jimmie Noone, Johnny Dodds, Earl Hines, and Jelly Roll Morton. Most of Chicago's historic jazz clubs are on the South Side, particularly in Bronzeville *p.191*, but the North Side has the can't-miss **Green Mill** in Uptown *p.273*.

The blues were in Chicago long before the car chase and the mission from God, but *The Blues Brothers* sealed Chicago as the home of the blues in the popular consciousness. Fortunately, the city has the chops to back

CHICAGODRINK

that up. **Maxwell Street** *www. maxwellstreet.org* (Near West Side *p.215*) was the heart and soul of Chicago blues, but the wrecking ball, driven by the University of Illinois at Chicago, has taken a brutal toll. Residents have been fighting to save what remains. For blues history, it doesn't get much better than **Willie Dixon's Blues Heaven Foundation** (Near South *p.95*), and Bronzeville *p.191*, the former "Black Metropolis," is a key stop as well. Performance venues run the gamut from tiny, cheap blues bars all over the city to big, expensive places like **Buddy Guy's Legends** (Loop *p.47*) and the original **House of Blues** (Near North *p.71*).

But don't let yourself get *too* wrapped up in the past, because Chicago blues is anything but. No other city in the world can compete with Chicago's long list of blues-soaked neighborhood dives and lounges. The North Side's blues clubs favor tradition in their music, and are usually the most accessible to visitors, but offer a slightly watered down experience from the funkier, more authentic blues bars on the South and Far West Sides, where most of Chicago's blues musicians live and hang. If one club could claim to be the home of the real Chicago blues, **Lee's Unleaded Blues** in Chatham-South Shore *p.203* would probably win the title. But there are scores of worthy blues joints all around the city (many of which are a lot easier to visit via public transport). A visit to one of these off-the-beaten-path blues dives is considerably

more adventurous than a visit to the touristy House of Blues, but the experiences born of such adventures have been known to reward visitors with a life-long passion for the blues.

Although playing second fiddle to the blues in the city's collective consciousness, jazz thrives in Chicago, too, thanks in no small part to members of the Association for the Advancement of Creative Musicians (AACM) and their residencies at clubs like **The Velvet Lounge** and **The Jazz Showcase** (both of which see regular national acts) (Near South *p.95*), **The New Apartment Lounge** (Chatham-South Shore *p.203*) and **The Hideout** (Bucktown *p.247*), with more expensive national touring acts downtown at **The Chicago Theater** (Loop *p.47*). If you are staying downtown, the Velvet Lounge will be your best bet, as it is an easy cab ride, and its high-profile performances will rarely disappoint.

Fans should time their visits to coincide with **Blues Fest** in June, and **Jazz Fest** over Labor Day Weekend. Both take place in Grant Park (Loop *p.47*).

Concerts

Wicker Park *p.229* and Bucktown *p.247* are the main place to go for indie rock shows: the **Double Door** and the **Empty Bottle** are the best-known venues, but there are plenty of smaller ones as well. In Lakeview *p.139*, the **Metro** is a beloved concert hole, with **Schubas**, **The Vic Theatre**, and the **Abbey Pub** nearby (the latter

38

CHICAGO SLEEP

on the Far Northwest Side *p.363*). Other mid-sized rock, hip-hop and R&B shows take place at the **Riviera** and the awesome **Aragon Ballroom** in Uptown *p.273*. The Near South *p.95* has become an underrated destination for great shows as well.

The **Park West** in Lincoln Park *p.123* has light jazz, light rock, and other shows you'd sit down for; so does **Navy Pier** (Near North *p.71*), particularly in the summer. The venerable **Chicago Theater** in the Loop *p.47* is better-known for its sign than for anything else, but it has rock, jazz, gospel, and spoken-word performances by authors like David Sedaris. The **Chicago Symphony Orchestra (CSO)** is the main bulwark in the city for classical and classy jazz, with occasional curve-balls like Björk. You'll find musicians from the CSO doing outreach all over the city, along with their counterparts at the **Lyric Opera**. Both are in the Loop *p.47*.

A few big concerts are held at the **UIC Pavilion**, the **Congress Theater**, and the **United Center** on the Near West Side *p.215* every year, and some *huge* concerts have taken place at **Soldier Field** (Near South *p.95*). The **Petrillo Bandshell** in **Grant Park** and the **Pritzker Pavilion** in **Millennium Park**, both in the Loop *p.47*, tend to host big, eclectic shows and festivals in the summer, which are sometimes free.

Otherwise, most big shows are out in the suburbs, primarily at the **Allstate Arena** and the **Rosemont Theater** in Rosemont, the **Sears Centre** in Hoffman Estates, the **First Midwest Bank Amphitheatre** in Tinley Park, **Star Plaza** in Indiana, and the **Alpine Valley Music Theater** over the Wisconsin border. You'll also have to head out to the suburbs for **Ravinia**, which features upscale classical, jazz, and blues outdoors throughout the summer.

Sleep

Chicago hosts many major conventions each year and has plenty of places to stay. The majority are either at O'Hare Airport *p.397* or downtown in the Loop *p.47* and the Near North *p.71* (near the Magnificent Mile). If you want to explore the city, aim for downtown — a hotel near O'Hare is good for visiting one thing and one thing only, and that's O'Hare. However, if you have a specific interest in mind, there are hotels throughout the city, and getting away from downtown will give you more of a sense of other neighborhoods. You'll appreciate that if you're in town for more than a couple of days. Make sure that where you're staying is within your comfort level before committing to stay there, though. More far flung transient hotels will be suitable for those seeking to relive Jack Kerouac's seedy adventures around the country, but may alarm and disgust the average traveler.

Budget-priced places are usually pretty far from the Loop *p.47*, so when you're booking, remember that Chicago is vast. Travelers on a budget should consider accom-

39

modations away from the city center which can be easily reached via any of the several CTA train lines. There is a hostel in the Loop *p.47* and two others near the universities in Lincoln Park *p.123* and Rogers Park *p.291*, all of which are interesting neighborhoods in their own right, and close to the L for access to the rest of the city. For deals on mid-range hotels, there are good options far out from the center by Midway and in North Lincoln *p.313*.

Contact

Internet

The first Internet cafe in the United States was opened in Chicago, but they never really caught on here. There are still a few, though; check individual district articles. If you have a computer with you, free wireless Internet access is now standard-issue at coffee shops throughout the city — only the big chains like Starbucks charge for it. Most hotels above the transient level offer free wi-fi, too.

The good news is that all branches of the **Chicago Public Library** system offer **free internet access**, via public terminals and free, password-free, public wireless. If you do not have a Chicago library card, but you have a photo ID that shows you do not live in Chicago, you can get a temporary permit from the library information desk. (If you *are* from Chicago and don't have a library card, though, all you can get is a stern look and a brief lecture on how Chicagoans

need to support the library system.) The most centrally located branch is the giant **Harold Washington Library** in the Loop *p.47*, but there are branch libraries in every part of the city — again, see individual district articles.

Telephones

312 was the area code for all of Chicago for a long time; it's still the code of choice for the Loop *p.47*, and most of the Near North *p.71* and Near South *p.95*. **773** surrounds the center, covering everything else within city limits.

Suburban areas close to the city use **847** (north/northwest), **708** (south), **815** (southwest), and **630** (west).

Stay safe

As in almost the entire United States, dial **911** to get emergency help. Dial **311** for all non-emergency situations in Chicago.

Despite a big decline in the crime rate from the 1970's and '80's, Chicago is still a big city with big city problems. There are run-down areas within a few blocks of some well-traveled places such as near the United Center and US Cellular Field. The majority of the city's violent crimes occur within a relatively small number of neighborhoods well off the beaten path in the South and West Sides, but given the chance nature of crime, you should exercise the usual precautions wherever you go. And just because a neighborhood has a bad reputation, you might still have a perfectly good time there, as long as it falls within your comfort level.

Take caution in the Loop *p.47* at night — after working hours, the Loop gets quiet and dark in a hurry west of State Street, but you'll be fine near hotels, and close to Michigan Avenue and the lake. When disembarking a crowded CTA train, especially in the downtown-area subways, be wary of purse snatchers.

Beggars are common downtown *p.47*. They are very unlikely to pose any kind of problem, though. Some sell a local newspaper called *Streetwise* to make a living.

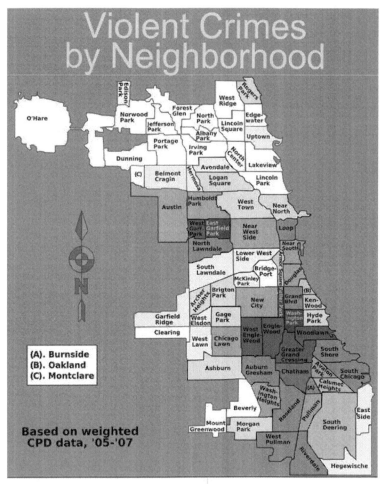

Violent Crimes by Neighborhood

O'Hare

Edison Park
Norwood Park
Forest Glen
West Ridge
Rogers Park
Jefferson Park
North Park
Edgewater
Lincoln Square
Albany Park
Uptown
Portage Park
Irving Park
North Center
Lakeview
Dunning
Avondale
(C)
Belmont Cragin
Logan Square
Lincoln Park
Austin
Humboldt Park
West Town
Near North
West Garf Park
East Garfield Park
Near West Side
Loop
North Lawndale
Lower West Side
Near South
South Lawndale
Bridgeport
McKinley Park
(B)
Grand Blvd
Ken-Wood
Archer Heights
Brighton Park
New City
Hyde Park
Garfield Ridge
West Elsdon
Gage Park
West Englewood
Englewood
Woodlawn
Clearing
Chicago Lawn
Greater Grand Crossing
South Shore
West Lawn
Ashburn
Auburn Gresham
Chatham
Avalon Park
South Chicago
Washington Heights
Calumet Heights
(A)
Beverly
Roseland
Pullman
East Side
Mount Greenwood
Morgan Park
South Deering
West Pullman
Riverdale
Hegewisch

(A). Burnside
(B). Oakland
(C). Montclare

Based on weighted CPD data, '05-'07

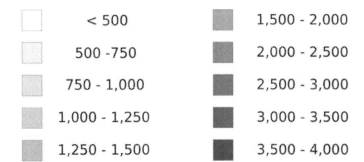

Per 100,000 Residents

< 500		1,500 - 2,000	
500 -750		2,000 - 2,500	
750 - 1,000		2,500 - 3,000	
1,000 - 1,250		3,000 - 3,500	
1,250 - 1,500		3,500 - 4,000	

In general, common sense will keep you safe in Chicago: avoid unfamiliar side streets at night, stay out of alleys at night, know where you're going when you set out, stick to crowded areas, and keep a $20 bill on hand for cab fare as a bail-out option.

Dress appropriately for the weather. Chicago's winter is famously windy and cold, so cover exposed skin and wear layers in the winter, but heat exhaustion is an equal risk in the summer months, especially July and August. Stay off the road during a snowstorm. Chicago's streets and sanitation department generally does a good job clearing the major roads in the center of the city, but the neighborhoods can take longer, and the construction-littered expressways are anyone's guess.

Cope

Publications

The Chicago Tribune (The Trib), *www.chicagotribune.com*. The Tribune is Chicago's oldest daily, recently converted into a tabloid format for newsstand purchases. New ownership has shed much of the Trib's former prestige with a debt-leveraged purchase and forced bankruptcy, widespread staff layoffs, and an ill-advised redesign.

The Chicago Sun-Times, *www. suntimes.com*. The Sun-Times is Chicago's other "major" newspaper. It has a long-standing reputation for aggressive (some might say "sensationalist") investigative

journalism. It has also been teetering on the verge of oblivion for some time, but at least it has Roger Ebert.

The Redeye, *www.redeyechicago. com*. Redeye is a free weekdays-only newspaper produced by the Tribune. Although its covers appear to report from some parallel universe where topics like sandwiches and being tired at work are the top stories of the day, it does have basic news coverage inside along with entertainment gossip.

The Chicago Defender, *www.chicagodefender.com*. The Defender is Chicago's biggest African-American daily, and it played a major role in the city's African-American history. Its distribution network today is comparatively small, though.

Hola Hoy, *www.hoyinternet.com*. Hola Hoy produces a free Spanish-language newspaper with wide distribution.

The Chicago Reader, *www.chicagoreader.com*. The Reader is a free weekly newspaper distributed throughout the city each Wednesday. It includes extensive listings of arts, music, and events. Nobody knows more about Chicago than the Reader, but it's definitely oriented toward locals.

Crain's Chicago Business, *www. chicagobusiness.com*. Crain's is a long-standing weekly newspaper covering the Chicago area business community, with a dash of politics and lifestyle — definitely worth a look if you're in town on business.

43

New City, *www.newcitychicago.com*. New City is a free weekly alternative arts and entertainment magazine, distributed every Wednesday. Event listings and local content are skimpy, but it is free.

Time Out Chicago, *www.timeoutchicago.com*. Time Out produces a weekly magazine available at most newsstands and bookstores. Its listings for events, bars, and restaurants are by far the most comprehensive and easiest to use for visitors to the city.

Religious services

There are places of worship all over the city; the front desk of your hotel will almost certainly be able to direct you to one nearby. If not, though, the following are centrally located in either the Loop *p.47* or the Near North *p.71*, unless otherwise noted.

For churches of specific Orthodoxies, check in neighborhoods that feature communities with ties to that region. There's a majestic Orthodox church in Ukrainian Village *p.229*, for example. Evangelical Christian ministries are mostly on the South Side, with some historic churches in Bronzeville *p.191*. For the Baha'i faith, visit the **Baha'i Temple** in Wilmette, easily accessible by the CTA Purple Line.

Anshe Sholom B'nai Israel, 540 W Melrose St (*Belmont Red Line*), +1 773 248-9200, *www.asbi.org*. Modern Orthodox Judaism. In a remarkably beautiful building by the lake. Shacharit Su 8:30AM,

M,Th 6:45AM, Tu,W,F 7AM; Mincha Su-Th 7:45PM.

Armitage Baptist Church, 2451 N Kedzie Blvd. (*Logan Square Blue Line*), +1 773 384-4673, *www.armitagechurch.org*. Sunday worship 9:30, 11AM, and 6PM.

BAPS Shri Swaminarayan Mandir, 4N739 IL Route 59, Bartlett, +1 630 213 2277, *chicago.baps.org*. Everyday worship 11:30 AM Aarti. Free.

Chicago's Central Synagogue, 15 W Delaware Place (*Chicago Red Line*), +1 312 787-0450 , *www.centralchicago.org*. Conservative Judaism. Shabbat services Sa 9:15AM.

Chicago Loop Synagogue, 16 S Clark St (*Madison/Wabash Brown/Purple/Green/Orange/Pink Line*), +1 312 346-7370, *www.chicagoloopsynagogue.org*. Traditional Judaism. Shachris Sa 9AM, Su 9:30AM; Mincha Sa 3:45PM, Su 4:15PM, M-F 1:05PM; Maariv 4:45PM.

Chicago Sinai Congregation, 15 W Delaware Pl (*Chicago Red Line*), +1 312 867-7000, *www.chicagosinai.org*. Liberal Reform Judaism. Torah study Sa 10:30AM; Shabbat Eve service F 6:15PM, Sunday service 11AM.

Downtown Islamic Center, 231 S State St (*Jackson Red Line*), +1 312 939-9095, *www.dic-chicago.org*. Open M-F 10:30AM-5:30PM. Friday prayers: Khutba 1:05PM / Aqama 1:30PM (1st Friday Jamaa), Khutba 2:05PM / Aqama 2:30PM (2nd Friday Jamaa).

Hindu Temple of Greater Chicago, 10915 Lemont Rd, Lemont, IL, +1 630 972-0300, *htgc.org*, M-F 10AM-8PM. 25 miles southwest of Chicago. Call temple to schedule priest services.

Holy Name Cathedral, 735 N State St (*Chicago Red Line*), *www.holynamecathedral.org*, Open for private prayer or reflection from 5:30AM-7PM. Flagship of the Catholic Archdiocese in Chicago. Sunday Masses at 7:00, 8:15, 9:30 (incl. sign language), 11:00 AM, and 12:30, 5:15 PM. See website for Saturday, weekdays, and Holy Days schedules, as well as other sacraments.

Saint James Cathedral, 65 E Huron St (*Chicago Red Line*), +1 312 787-7360, *www.saintjamescathedral.org*. Episcopalian services. Office hours M-F 9AM-4PM. Eucharist Su 8AM,10:30AM, W 5:30PM, Th,F 12:10PM

Get out

Illinois

There are forest preserves in the far north, northwest, and south-west sides, and into the nearby Chicagoland suburbs. They are excellent for biking, jogging, and picnics.

Evanston is over the northern border of Chicago, approximately 45 minutes from downtown on the CTA, or half an hour via car (during light traffic). It has shops, restaurants, bars and Northwestern University, as well as some historic homes and lovely lake-front. Just beyond that is Wilmette, with the fascinating **Baha'i Temple**.

Ravinia is the summer home of the Chicago Symphony Orchestra. Metra's UP-North line stops at the park gates, and the return train waits for late-ending concerts. The arts and crafts style architecture coupled with a dazzling array of acts make this a classic summer destination for Chicagoans and tourists. Bring food, a blanket, wine, and a citronella candle; buy anything you forgot on-site.

Brookfield is home to the Chicagoland area's other world-class zoo, the **Brookfield Zoo**.

Historic Galena, three hours west-northwest of Chicago via I-90 and US-20, is great for hiking, sightseeing, and antiquing.

Six Flags Great America, in Gurnee (40 miles north on I-94), has the biggest and wildest roller coasters in Illinois.

Peoria, in some ways a miniature Chicago, is a little over three hours away.

The Quad Cities — about 2.5–3 hours away via I-55 or I-80 or I-90 to I-74 — bridge the Mississippi River forming a unique metropolitan area on the border of Iowa and Illinois.

Indiana

The Indiana Dunes are a moderate drive away, and are also accessible via the South Shore commuter rail. If you've enjoyed the beaches in Chicago, you owe the Indiana

Dunes a stop — that's where all the sand came from.

Gary is just over the border on the Skyway, with a skyline that rivals Chicago's for strength of effect — industrial monstrosity, in this case — with casinos, urban ruins, and a few entries by Prairie School architects Frank Lloyd Wright and George Maher.

Also just over the Skyway (before you reach Gary) is East Chicago's bizarre 19th century planned community, **Marktown**, which looks like a small English village totally incongruous with the gigantic steel mills and the world's largest oil refinery which surround it.

Michigan

Further along the lake from the Indiana Dunes are Michigan's dunes and summer resorts in Harbor Country. Keep your eyes open: Mayor Daley, University of Chicago President Robert Zimmer, and other notables summer here.

Detroit has many of Chicago's most hated sports rivals, and although fallen on hard times, it also has a musical and architectural heritage to compare with the Windy City.

Wisconsin

Lake Geneva, across the Wisconsin border, is the other big summer getaway. Nearby are the Kettle Moraine state parks, with good mountain biking.

Milwaukee and its venerable breweries are less than two hours from Chicago on I-94, via Amtrak, and by intercity bus services.

Spring Green is an easy weekend trip from Chicago, about three and a half hours from town on I-90. It's the home of two unique architectural wonders: Frank Lloyd Wright's magnificent estate **Taliesin**, and Alex Jordan's mysterious museum **The House on the Rock**.

The Wisconsin Dells are another (wet) summer fun destination, just three hours north of the city by car (I-90/94), also accessible by Amtrak train.

Cedarburg is a popular festival town with a charming downtown featured on the National Register of Historic Places. It is located 20 miles north of downtown Milwaukee. Take 1-94 to Milwaukee and continue north on I-43.

LOOPUNDERSTAND

The Loop is the central business district of Chicago, bounded by the Chicago River to the north and west, Harrison Street to the south, and Lake Michigan to the east. It contains the tallest members of Chicago's skyline and much of the city's finest architecture, holding within them much of the city's working stiffs; for visitors, it also has the glitzy downtown theater district, and the biggest annual music festivals.

Understand

The Loop is the center of Chicago and without a doubt the most iconic section of the city. If you've never been to Chicago, begin here. Whether on an official architecture cruise along the Chicago River, or an unofficial one along the veritable river of elevated trains, only the most jaded could shake that feeling of awe at the canyons of LaSalle and the cliffs of Michigan Avenue. Moreover, the Loop contains a world-class collection of public art *p.115*, in the form of huge street-side statues by many of the 20th century's most famous sculptors.

The Loop initially got its name from the looping route of streetcars that served as the transit hub of early downtown Chicago, but the name has come to be defined by the modern era's looping route of elevated train tracks, serving seven CTA lines, which ensures the continued prominence of the area as the center of Chicago's working world. Despite the gradual northwards shift in the city's center of gravity and the centrifugal force of suburbanization, all tracks lead here and accordingly the Loop remains the most attractive location in the city for major businesses, and for most of the city's visitors.

On a work day, you won't have to walk around long to realize you are at the center of things. Busy-looking people in suits hurry in and out of tall buildings, major theaters hawk their big-name productions on neon marquees, and every block has a reminder of a scene from *Ferris Bueller's Day Off,* **The Dark Knight**, or another Chicago movie. The Loop is the United States' second largest central business district, owing largely to its historical position as the financial hub for the Midwest and the modern world's biggest futures market. Many of those suits walking by (as you stand and gape) work for one of four major financial exchanges, the largest of which is the recent merger between the Merc (the Chicago Mercantile Exchange) and the Chicago Board of Trade. The CBoT was the world's first modern futures exchange, set up principally to serve the needs of the Midwest agriculture market, and along with the other major exchanges in Chicago, pioneered the massive modern derivatives industry. Not too long ago the streets sagged under the enormous profits, as the Merc and CBoT traded over nine million contracts daily, worth over $4.2 trillion. Today's economic outlook has soured, though, and the ranks of those suits have been thinned by layoffs, golden parachuting, and other extreme sports.

Forget work, though – the fun of Millennium Park and the festivals of Grant Park are here, and the Art Institute is fantastic. A walk by the Sears Tower and the Chicago Board of Trade is a requisite Chicago experience, but the Loop is eclipsed by other parts of the city in terms of nightlife, shopping, and dining. Being as it is first and foremost a business district, things shut down when the commuters punch the clock and hop on the train, so even if you have a room at one of the Loop's classic old hotels, don't plan to spend all of your time here – even though your camera will likely receive no finer work-out anywhere else.

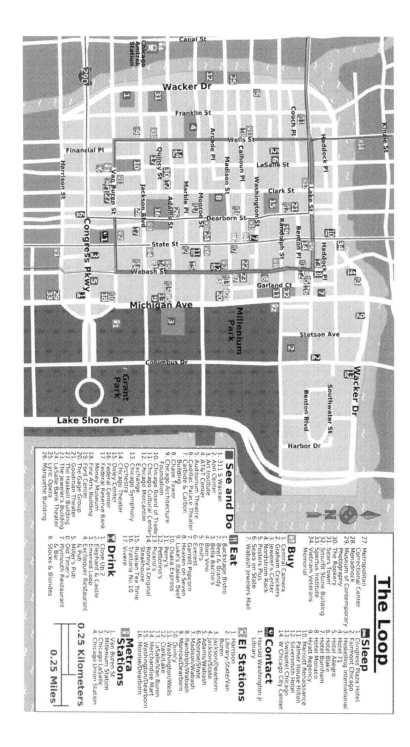

The Loop

Sleep
1. Congress Plaza Hotel
2. Fairmont Chicago
3. Hostelling International
4. Hotel Allegro
5. Hotel Blake
6. Hotel Burnham
7. Hotel Monaco
8. Hyatt Regency
9. Marriott Renaissance
10. Palmer Hilton
11. Silversmith Hotel
12. Swissotel Chicago
13. Wyndham
14. W Chicago City Center

Contact
1. Harold Washington Jr Library

El Stations
1. Harrison
2. Library-State/Van Buren
3. Jackson/Dearborn
4. Jackson/State
5. Adams/Wabash
6. Monroe/State
7. Randolph/Wabash
8. Randolph/Wabash
9. Monroe/Dearborn
10. Quincy
11. Washington/Wabash
12. Clark/Lake
13. LaSalle/Van Buren
14. State/Lake
15. Washington/Dearborn
16. Monroe/Dearborn

Metra Stations
1. Van Buren St
2. Millenium Station
3. Chicago LaSalle
4. Chicago Union Station

0.25 Kilometers
0.25 Miles

See and Do
1. 311 S Wacker
2. Aon Center
3. Art Institute
4. AT&T Center
5. Auditorium Theatre
6. Cadillac Palace Theater
7. Carbide & Carbon
8. Chase Tower
9. Chicago Architecture Foundation
10. Chicago Board of Trade
11. Chicago Cultural Center
12. Chicago Mercantile Exchange
13. Chicago Symphony Orchestra
14. Daley Center
15. Federal Center
16. Federal Reserve Bank
17. Monadnock
18. Fine Arts Building
19. Ford Center
20. The Gage Group
21. Goodman Theater
22. The Haskell Building
23. The Jeweler's Building
24. LaSalle Bank Theater
25. Lyric Opera
26. Marquette Building
27. Metropolitan Correctional Center
28. Monadnock
29. Museum of Contemporary
30. The Rookery
31. Sears Tower
32. Smurfit Stone Building
33. Spertus Institute
34. Vietnam Veterans Memorial

Buy
1. Central Camera
2. Graham's Crackers
3. Macy's Center
4. Nordstrom Rack
5. Posters Plus
6. Sears on State
7. Wabash Jewelers Mall

Eat
1. Backstage Bistro
2. Beef & Brandy
3. Bella Bacino's
4. Bon Vino
5. Deli's
6. Everest
7. Garrett Popcorn
8. Heaven on Seven
9. Luke's Italian Beef
10. Osaka Express
11. Perry's
12. Pettorino's
13. Prizano's
14. Roney's Original Steakhouse
15. Russian Tea Time
16. Trattoria No.10
17. Vivere

Drink
1. Close Up 2
2. Elephant & Castle
3. Emerald Loop
4. Exchequer Restaurant & Pub
5. Miller's Pub
6. Oasis Timer's
7. Plymouth Restaurant & Bar
8. Stocks & Blondes

Get in

By train

In Chicago, all tracks lead to the Loop. The astonishing, creaky elevated tracks of the CTA come in from virtually ever corner of the city, and through the smoother commuter rails of Metra and Amtrak, from the rest of the Chicagoland area and the country beyond.

The CTA **Red Line** spans from Rogers Park *p.291* at the city's northern border to the Far Southeast Side *p.377*. In the Loop, it runs under State Street, with key stops at Lake, Washington (closed til late 2008), Monroe, and Jackson.

The **Blue Line** from O'Hare International Airport *p.397*, the Far Northwest Side *p.363*, and the rest of the West Side also runs underground through the Loop along Dearborn, offering free connections with the Red Line at Washington (again, closed til late 2008) and Jackson.

Several other CTA lines ride the elevated tracks that travel through the Loop in, well, a loop. The **Brown Line** comes in from the Northwest *p.313* and North Center *p.139*, the **Purple Line** comes in from Evanston and Lakeview *p.139*, the **Pink Line** comes in from Pilsen *p.259* and further west, and the **Green Line** comes in from the Far West *p.331* and South *p.191*. If you are arriving at Midway Airport or stopping on the Southwest Side *p.347*, the swift, clean **Orange Line** goes straight from the airport terminal to the Loop. (The only CTA line that does not directly serve the Loop is the far north **Yellow Line**.)

From the suburbs, Metra commuter trains arrive at **Union Station** (Canal St and Jackson Blvd), **Ogilvie/Northwestern Station** (Canal St and Madison St), and **Millennium Station** (Michigan Ave between South Water St and Randolph St), all of which are within easy walking distance of the Loop and the CTA elevated lines. From beyond the suburbs, Amtrak connections arrive at Union Station.

By bus

Several dozen CTA bus lines travel through the Loop, but given the traffic, only a few will be useful for visitors traveling from the rest of the city. **20 Madison** heads west down Madison St, ideal for reaching the United Center on the Near West Side *p.215*.

147 Express runs through the Near North *p.71* before running express on Lake Shore Drive to Rogers Park *p.291*.

By car

Do not drive to the Loop if at all possible. It is not a very automobile-friendly place. You're unlikely to relish the memory of having driven through the Loop, but plenty of people do it every day. **Michigan Avenue** offers a scenic — if slow as mud — trawl through the east end of the Loop, marking the end of the commercial area and the beginning of the parkland along the lake. **Lake**

Shore Drive provides an equally lovely — and equally slow — route through the Loop. **I-90** lets out at Jackson Blvd, at the west end of the Loop.

If you do come by car, there are four underground parking garages near Grant Park and Millennium Park. *www.grantparkparking.com* Rates vary by garage and are more expensive for special events, but the East Monroe garage (near Millennium Park) is the cheapest ($13 up to 12 hours, $16 12-24 hours).

See

Itineraries

The Loop Art Tour *p.115* will take you down the Loop's main roads through Millennium Park and the downtown city plazas, all in the name of art.

Along the Magnificent Mile *p.109* is a one day and night itinerary that connects the Loop with the Near North *p.71* for shopping, food, skyscrapers, parks, and amazing views of Chicago from high and low.

Museums and galleries

Art Institute of Chicago, 111 S Michigan Ave (*Adams/Wabash Brown/Green/Orange/Purple/Pink Line*), +1 312 443-3600, *www.artic.edu*, M-W,F 10:30AM-5:00PM, Th 10:30AM-8PM, Sa-Su 10AM-5PM except Thanksgiving, Christmas, and New Year's Day. One of the premier museums in the US — and with the opening

of the sensational new **Modern Wing**, it's one of the largest, too. Set aside a whole day and arrive early! Iconic pieces on display include "American Gothic" by Grant Wood (the stoic farm couple), "Nighthawks" by Edward Hopper (the late-night diner), Georges Seurat's pointillist masterpiece "Sunday Afternoon on the Island of La Grande Jatte". The Art Institute also boasts the world's best collection of Impressionist painting outside of France. But there's a lot more to discover, including a great selection of early 20th-century painting, architecture, and photography, as well as archaeological finds covering 5,000 years of art and cultural history. Admission is $12 adults, $7 children and seniors; free Th 5-8PM.

Federal Reserve Bank Money Museum, 230 S LaSalle St (*LaSalle/Van Buren Brown/Orange/Pink/Purple Line*), +1 312 322-2400, *www.chicagofed.org*, M-F 9AM-4PM, except bank holidays. Currency wonks can study various denominations and practice counterfeit detections. Guided tours every day at 1PM. Free.

Museum of Contemporary Photography, 600 S Michigan Ave (*State/Van Buren Brown/Orange/Purple/Pink Line*), +1 312 663-5554, *mocp.org*, M-F 10AM-5PM, Th 10AM-8PM, Sa 12-5PM. A stimulating and innovative forum for the collection, creation, and examination of contemporary image-making in its camera tradition and in its expanded vocabulary of dig-

LOOPSEE

ital processes. Affiliated with Columbia College Chicago. Free.

Spertus Institute, 618 S Michigan Ave, +1 312 322-1700, *www.spertus.edu/museum*, Su,W 10AM-5PM; Th 10AM-6PM. A museum dedicated to Jewish culture and learning, in a dramatic, newly remodeled facility. There's a children's center, which promises hands-on exhibits, and a regular slate of exhibits and events on Jewish art, culture, and social issues, with points given for range that includes the Israeli-Palestinian Comedy Tour *and* lectures on Jewish-Catholic relations. The **Asher Library**, also on-site, keeps similar hours. $7 adults, $5 children and seniors; free W 10AM-noon, Th 2-6PM.

Parks and monuments

Grant Park, On the east side of Michigan Ave between Lake Shore Dr and Columbus Dr, +1 312 742-7648, *www.chicagoparkdistrict.com*, 6AM-11PM daily. Right at the center of Chicago, this has been a park space for almost the entire history of the city. Most citywide events and festivals (see below) are held in Grant Park and the **Petrillo Bandshell**. The centerpiece of the park is **Buckingham Fountain** (10AM-11PM), which is sometimes accompanied by music and colored lights (8-11PM, May-Sep). There are also tennis courts, softball fields, and a walking trail near the lake. Millennium Park is to the north and the Museum Campus is to the south, so there is a large area to wander. Entrance to the park and most events & festivals is generally free, although some concerts do have an admission charge; in that case, admission to other areas of the park is still free.

Millennium Park, On the east side of Michigan Ave between Randolph St and the Art Institute, +1 312 742-1168, *www.millenniumpark.org*, 6AM-11PM daily. Long before it opened, Millennium Park had become notorious for delays and cost-overruns, missing its titular date by a wide margin. However, when it was finished, the biggest shock of all came when it turned out to be quite nice. Aside from plenty of grass and open space, it has modern sculptures in steel and glass, including Chicago's newest must-photo for visitors, **The Bean** (properly known as **Cloud Gate**), and the Frank Gehry-designed **Pritzker Pavilion** for outdoor concerts. Kids will love getting wet in the **Crown Fountain** (mid-April to the end of summer) at Michigan and Monroe, in which the giant projected faces of Chicago residents spit water into a shallow reflecting pool where everyone is welcome to splash around. Look for tents offering guides to the park near the entrances at Randolph and/or Washington. Free.

Vietnam Veterans Memorial, 2 E Wacker Dr (*between Wabash Ave and State St*). Designed in coordination with the National Vietnam Veterans Art Museum in the Near South, this waterfront plaza features a timeline from the war, a list of Illinois veterans who were killed in action, and a nice vantage point toward a few iconic buildings down the river. After crossing over the river from the Near North, turn and take the stairs down to the lower level.

Visitor centers

Chicago Board of Trade Visitor Center, 141 W Jackson Blvd, 1st floor (*LaSalle/Van Buren Brown/Orange/Pink/Purple Line*), +1 312 435-3590, *www.cbot.com*, M-F 8AM-4PM. This monumental 1930 building is an Art Deco masterpiece and dominates its surrounding streets like no other in the Loop. The new Visitors Center features high-tech displays and historical artifacts on the history of financial trading. Sadly, the more exciting 5th floor observation deck, which lets you watch the frenzied action on the trading floor, is only open to group tours that have applied in advance. Admission to the Visitors Center is free.

Chicago Cultural Center, 78 E Washington St (*Washington Red Line*), +1 312 744-6630, *www.chicagoculturalcenter.org*, M-Th 8AM-7PM, F 8AM-6PM, Sa 9AM-5PM, Su 10AM-5PM, closed holidays. Built in 1897 as Chicago's first public library, the building now houses the city's Visitor Information Center, galleries, and exhibit halls. Worth a visit to see the beautiful interior — the ceiling of Preston Bradley Hall includes a 38-foot Tiffany glass dome, and the north wing includes the impressive Grand Army of the Republic Rotunda. Of late, amid various city-approved art and music events, some surprisingly good theater has been performed here. Free.

Chicago Mercantile Exchange Visitors Center, 20 S Wacker Dr (*Washington/Wells Brown/Purple/Orange Line*), +1 312 454-5326, *www.cme.com*, M-F 8AM-4:30PM. The 4th Floor Visitor Gallery is currently closed, but the lobby level Visitors Center has displays on the history and role of the exchange, and there's a gift shop. Free.

The Skydeck, 233 S Wacker Dr (*Quincy/Wells Brown/Purple/Orange/Pink*), +1 312 875-9447, *www.the-skydeck.com*, Apr-Sept 9AM-10PM, Oct-March 10AM-8PM; open every day of the year, including holidays. Once the tallest building in the world, the Sears Tower now has to settle for the title in North America alone, and even that's after a semantic battle with Near North) has a nicer view of the city, but the Sears Tower offers an incredible view of its own from "The Ledge", which lets visitors walk out in a transparent balcony suspended 1,353 feet above the street. To avoid the crowds, visit after 4PM. $14.95 adult, $10.50 children; there are express line tickets for $30.

Architecture

Most of these buildings are not fully open to the public, although some may be accessible through tours by the Chicago Architecture Foundation. Security procedures will, of course, vary. For some, you won't be able to make it past

53

the lobby; for others, a purposeful stride can take you anywhere you want to go.

Chicago Architecture Foundation, 224 S Michigan Ave, +1 312 922-3432, *www.architecture.org*, 9AM-6:30PM daily. Runs numerous river cruises and themed architecture walks covering the Loop and other parts of the city, with offerings suitable for general audiences and people with specific interests. There are some small, informative exhibits inside their 224 S Michigan headquarters and a gift shop. Walking tours are usually $15, $12 for students/seniors.

Buildings

Some of Chicago's greatest buildings, like the Chicago Board of Trade and the Auditorium Theatre, have major attractions inside to draw the appreciative eyes of visitors. Many other masterworks, though, don't have a specific attraction associated with them, so you'll have to seek them out.

Carbide and Carbon Building (Burnham Brothers, 1929), 230 N Michigan Ave. A beautiful Art Deco tower covered in dark green terra cotta and adorned with a gold terra cotta leaf at the pinnacle. It is rumored that the architects (the sons of city planner Daniel Burnham) intended the building to resemble a bottle of champagne. It's in great condition today, and can be visited through one of the bars in the lobby of the hotel inside.

Federal Center (van der Rohe, 1964/1975), 219/230 S Dearborn St. This plaza includes Mies' Dirksen Federal Building and Kluczynski Federal Building (built eleven years apart), with a low-rise post office enveloped in their sleek black lines. But the buildings are not quite as famous as the gigantic red constructivist flamingo statue by Alexander Calder in the plaza in front of the post office. An adventurous raccoon may have set a raccoon world climbing record by reaching the scaffolding on the 36th floor in 2006.

The Fine Arts Building (Beman, 1885), 412 S Michigan Ave. An old Michigan Avenue charmer whose worn stone walls looks even older than its 120+ years. Even though few artists could afford to keep studios on Michigan Avenue these days, it still has a creative air, thanks to the fanciful carvings on the walls, and an inviting snack shop on the first floor.

The Gage Group (Sullivan/Holabird & Roche, 1898-1902), 18-30 S Michigan Ave. Louis Sullivan designed the northernmost (18) of the three buildings here, and the team of Holabird & Roche added the next two (24 & 30). The roots of Mies-style modernism are easily apparent in the immaculate proportions here, although Sullivan's piers overflow like water-pipes with ornament at the top, and Holabird & Roche's two make an interesting contrast with the master.

The Haskell Building (Van Osdel, 1877), 18 S Wabash Ave. Originally designed by John Mills van Osdel, the city's first accredited architect after the Chicago Fire, this four-story building is one of the oldest in the Loop. The two bottom floors were remodeled by Louis Sullivan in 1896, adding some interesting cast-iron designs for its use as a department store.

The Jewelers' Building (Adler & Sullivan, 1882), 15-17 S Wabash Ave. Louis Sullivan was only a draftsman at the time this was built, but there are some interesting designs nestled into expressive facade and the classic, powerful masonry walls.

Marquette Building (Holabird & Roche, 1894), 140 S Dearborn. It's partially obscured by renovations, but this first-wave skyscraper still makes an immediate contrast with the modern Federal Center across the street. The lobby is decorated with Tiffany mosaics and bronze carvings of Pere Marquette, an early French explorer. There is plenty of first-floor retail to allow trips inside.

Monadnock Building (Burnham & Root, 1891), 53 W Jackson Blvd. Named appropriately for a mountain in New Hampshire, the Monadnock was the last tall building to be supported by its own walls (not a metal frame, although the 1893 addition by Holabird & Roche does use one). It's a masterpiece of simplicity and power in form. The block-long hallway that serves as a lobby has incredible ambiance: it's always kept at a level of brightness that sug-

gests gas lamps, and the small stores on the first floor (a coffee shop, a shoe-shine, a restaurant) are all turn-of-the-century tile-and-polish.

The Reliance Building (Root/Atwood, 1890/1895), 36 N State St. A then-unprecedented amount of glass was used in this early skyscraper, bewildering a public still used to masonry walls. Note the difference between the first two floors and the ones above: hold-outs among the previous building's tenants forced developers to build the foundation and the first two floors *under* the top three floors from the old building, and then knock off the top three when their leases had expired. It was restored when it became the Hotel Burnham (see below) in 1999, and can be explored with a stop at the Atwood Cafe (also below).

The Rookery (Burnham & Root, 1888), 209 S LaSalle St. The Rookery is gorgeous to be point of absurdity, with delight to be found in details in the rustic lower walls and the triumphant upper walls. (Note the helpful street names carved in the corners.) Named for pigeons' habit of roosting in the then-new skyscrapers, this was the first Loop building to be granted preservation status in 1972. The lobby was remodeled in 1907 by *enfant terrible* Frank Lloyd Wright, adding his own touch to the interior.

Skyline

Other buildings, however, you will not need to seek out — Chicago's tallest skyscrapers are attractions for anyone who happens to look up!

311 S Wacker Dr. 961 ft. This is perhaps the tallest building in the world without an official name, although locals know exactly what to call it: The White Castle Building. It is distinctive for its "crown," which is brightly illuminated at night. If you are nearby, head into its lobby to see its enormous indoor garden and fountain.

Aon Center, 200 E Randolph St. 1136 ft. Originally known as the Standard Oil Building, The Aon Center is America's fourth tallest building, after the Empire State Building in New York, and 15th tallest in the world. It was built in 1972 by architect Edward Stone and initially was faced with marble, but the windy city began to blow the marble off the sides of the building. The entire building had to be refaced with granite—a costly job at one-half of the entire building costs! A walk around the base can be particularly gratifying to admire the uninterrupted views straight up the shear walls and the "musical sculptures."

AT&T Corporate Center, 227 W Monroe St. 1007 ft. Built by Adrian Smith in 1989, the granite-clad AT&T Corporate Center is one of the city's more distinctive skyscrapers for its massive size, spiked roof pinnacles, and a style evocative of both Gothic and Japanese architectural styles. It's not well-known, but it is the eighth tallest building in the US.

Chase Tower, 21 S Clark St. 850 ft. Located at the exact epicenter of CTA's Loop transit system, this building is distinctive for its vertical curve. It has been re-named for each of the successive banks that have bought out its previous tenants — for example, it was the BankOne Tower until a couple years ago. The plaza outside is more interesting than the interior — it is home to an enormous mosaic by renowned Russian painter Marc Chagall.

Daley Center, 55 W Washington St. 648 ft. The 1965 Daley Center is Chicago's principal civic center and boasts a gigantic Picasso statue on the adjacent plaza. A true Chicago landmark, the Daley Center was featured in *The Blues Brothers*, who drive across Daley Plaza and crash through the glass walls of the building. The Mies-esque design was *intended* to age visibly: the color has faded in a rust-like direction from exposure to the elements.

Metropolitan Correctional Center, 71 W Van Buren St. 287 ft. While not very tall, this 1975 brutalist structure is one of the most distinctive and curious in the Chicago skyline. As its name suggests, it is a vertical prison skyscraper and its sharp triangular shape is designed to minimize the amount of time that it takes to patrol its corridors. Its prisoners have some of the prison world's best views as their exercise yard is located on top of the roof, although the narrow slits serving as windows do not allow such nice views from the cells. The prison houses male and female convicts of all security levels, waiting for transport to the courthouse nearby.

Smurfit-Stone Building (Diamond Building), 150 N Michigan Ave. 582 ft. Anyone who has seen *Adventures in Babysitting* should immediately recognize this 1984 building, as its slanted roof played a very important role in the film's climax. It's a hard building to miss, as it is just across the street from Millennium Park.

Trains

Although they're across the river and technically in the West Loop *p.215*, **Union Station** and **Ogilvie/Northwestern Station** are very much a part of the daily commute in the Loop. Union Station (1925) is a classical behemoth, lined with marble colonnades, and beautifully efficient on the inside. Ogilvie (1987), designed by Helmut Jahn, is tidy and efficient on the inside as well, with waterfalls of blue steel on the outside. If you'd like to compare a *third* era of Chicago transit, head over to the Near South *p.95* and check out **Dearborn Station** (1885), which no longer serves trains.

If you're taking the elevated train around the Loop, the **Quincy** stop may be worth a look, as it's done up like an old-timey station, complete with vintage advertisements. You can step off the train,

have a look around the platform, and get on the next train without paying again.

 Do

In the old days, the Loop was *the* theater district in Chicago. Few of the originals survived the demolition wave of the 1960s, but most of the ones that did are now part of the **Randolph Theater District**. The **Broadway in Chicago** consortium stages big-budget shows there, most of which are in previews before their Broadway debut (hence, the name). Tickets for hot shows are snapped up in droves, so inquire with your hotel concierge about dinner-and-a-show packages.

The **Chicago Cultural Center** is also a theater destination — see above.

The Auditorium Theatre, 50 E Congress Pkwy (*Library Brown/Purple/Orange/Green/Pink Line*), +1 312 431-2389, *auditoriumtheatre.org/wb.* Dankmar Adler and Louis Sullivan's masterpiece. Frank Lloyd Wright, who served as an apprentice on the project, called it "The greatest room for music and opera in the world — bar none." If the current production isn't worth seeing, take a tour of this gorgeous, acoustically-perfect theater instead. Tours are available Mondays at 10AM and 1PM by the theater itself, and at other times during the week from the Chicago Architecture Foundation. $8 per person.

Cadillac Palace Theater,

LOOP◯

151 W Randolph St, Box office +1 312 977-1700, *www.broadwayinchicago.com*, Hours vary. A Broadway in Chicago outlet, this opulent theater was built in 1926 for the vaudeville circuit and is now glossed up for high-profile productions with 2,300 seats per show. *The Producers* and the mighty Oprah's *The Color Purple* both enjoyed long runs here. $27.50-$77.50.

Chicago Symphony Orchestra, 220 S Michigan Ave (*Adams/Wabash Brown/Green/Orange/Purple/Pink Line*), +1 312 294-3333, *www.cso.org*, Box office M-F 10AM-6PM, Sa-Su 11AM-4PM. Home of Chicago's renowned orchestra; they spend a lot of time on the road, though, so visiting orchestras and stately jazz concerts can also be found here, as can the occasional curveball like a silent film. Student prices can run as low as $10; tickets for CSO events start from $25, but performances by traveling artists vary.

Chicago Theater, 175 N State St (*Lake CTA*), +1 312 462-6300, *www.thechicagotheatre.com*, Box office M-F 12-6PM. An old Balaban & Katz movie palace, refurbished as one of the city's premier performance venues. It hosts a wide range of events, from spoken word and stand-up comedy to jazz, gospel, and rock. Most people, however, know it for the iconic marquee out front. Tickets vary by event — generally $27.50 and up. Tours are available Apr-Sept Tu,Th 12PM and Oct-March Tu 12PM, also the third Saturday of every month at 11AM,12PM; $5 per person.

Ford Center for the Performing Arts (Oriental Theater), 24 W Randolph St, Box office +1 312 977-1700, *www.broadwayinchicago.com*, Hours vary. The Oriental Theater was once Chicago's most ornate movie palace, but this is now another Broadway in Chicago theater outlet. $29.50-$122.50.

Goodman Theater, 170 N Dearborn St (*Washington Red Line*), +1 312 443-3811, *www.goodman-theatre.org*, Box office M-F 10AM-5PM, Sa-Su 12-5PM. Non-profit theater company in an extremely expensive space; they pride themselves on new works, but are better known for revivals of plays from the American theater canon. Post-show discussions with the cast are held after Wednesday and Thursday night performances. Tickets vary by show, generally starting from $30 adults, $17 children.

Grant Park Music Festival (Grant Park Symphony Orchestra), *www.chicagofestivals.net*, 6:30-8PM. Chicago is spoiled for free music in the summer — the excellent Grant Park Symphony Orchestra plays in Millennium Park's Pritzker Pavilion about three times per week June-August, usually W,F-Sa. The symphony is hardly the only free show at the Pritzker Pavilion, though, and it's worth walking by on any night around 6:30PM to see if any other classical, dance, etc. performances are running.

LaSalle Bank Theater (Shubert Theater), 18 W Monroe St, Box office +1 312 977-1700, *www.broadwayinchicago.com*, Hours vary. Another Broadway in Chicago theater. Founded in 1906 to attract a classier vaudeville crowd, it saw performances from Harry Houdini, and was run by New York theater impresario Sam Shubert for more than forty-five years. *Monty Python's Spamalot* and *High School Musical* have been here more recently. $27.50-$82.50.

Lyric Opera, 20 N Wacker Dr   (*Washington/Wells Brown/Purple/Pink/Orange Line*), +1 312 332-2244, *www.lyricopera.org*. Extraordinary productions of major operas, in the impressive Civic Opera House, overlooking the river; local legend has it that the backstory behind business magnate Samuel Insull's decision to build it was the inspiration for the opera scenes in *Citizen Kane*. Although highly acclaimed today, there was a minor controversy among purists when they began to project English titles above the stage for non-English operas. Tickets start at $31 for weekdays and $42 for weekends.

Events & Festivals

The Loop is ground zero for Chicago festivals, and the festivals run long and large. Take note of these dates, as hotel reservations will become more difficult to find and prices will rise.

Saint Patrick's Day Parade, *www.chicagostpatsparade.com*. March 2010. Chicago has a large Irish-American population, and its one that punches above its weight — St Patrick's Day is a huge affair in the Windy City. The endless parade takes place on Columbus Drive along the Chicago River, which is dyed green for the occasion. The river dyeing is at 10:15AM, and the parade starts at noon.

Gospel Fest, *chicagogospelfestival. com*. Sa-Su, 6-7 June 2009. The world's biggest free outdoor gospel festival is in Grant Park! Like the Blues Fest, the performers are a combination of national and local acts. Chicago has a thriving gospel scene and this is one of the best ways to experience it for the uninitiated.

Blues Fest, +1 312 744-3315, *www. chicagobluesfestival.org*. F-Su, 12-14 June 2009. Top national and local blues musicians perform all day long throughout the festival just a couple miles from where modern blues was born. This is the world's premiere blues festival, and the list of greats who have performed here (like Albert King, B.B. King, Buddy Guy, Chuck Berry, Etta James, John Lee Hooker, Memphis Slim, Stevie Ray Vaughan, Willie Dixon) gets more impressive each successive year. Admission is free and the performances are spread out across six stages throughout Grant Park.

Taste of Chicago, +1 312 744-3315, *www.tasteofchicago.us*, 11AM-9PM. 26 June-5 July 2009. An outdoor showcase of Chicago restaurants, vendors, and performers, plus big name concerts. The specifics of the scheme vary from year to year, but generally, you buy a roll of tickets and then trade in those tickets for beer, drinks, food, and desserts. It's a great chance to sample the range of Chicago cuisine (at steeper prices). Also a great opportunity to watch Independence Day fireworks from the park and lakefront, but beware: it gets *crowded*.

Venetian Night, 6:30PM-10:30PM. Sa, 25 July 2009. A memorable night by the waterfront is ensured by the annual lighted boat parade on Lake Michigan, followed by a fireworks display, synchronized to music. The "best" viewing spots are at Shedd Aquarium in the Near South and Navy Pier in the Chicago/Near North, but rest assured that those spots will be crowded — you'll have fine views from the shoreline in Grant Park.

Lollapalooza, +1 888 512-7469, *www.lollapalooza.com*, F-Su 11AM-10PM. F-Su, 7-9 Aug 2009. Formerly a traveling tour, Lollapalooza has now found a permanent location in Chicago and grown quite a bit. It's a *massive* three day collection of popular and lesser-known national and local rock and hip hop bands. $80 one day, $165/$195 early/late three days.

Jazz Fest, *www.chicagojazzfestival. org*. 4-6, Sep 2009. The great Chicago Jazz Festival was inaugurated in 1974 just weeks after Duke Ellington's death to commemorate his life's work, and has since become one of the world's largest annual jazz festivals, pulling some of the biggest names in the jazz world each year.

And this one is free. If you have the means, you might want to come earlier in the week — there are usually a host of jazz-related events in the run up to the festival.

Buy

The Magnificent Mile *p.71* ends at the Chicago River, but there are still more than a few places to shop in the Loop, particularly on and east of State Street. The two landmark department stores that once anchored the area, **Marshall Field's** and **Carson Pirie Scott**, are both gone. The Carson's building, designed by Louis Sullivan, is being remodeled to serve as office space. Interior tours are still available through the Chicago Architecture Foundation (above), though.

The fate of Marshall Field's is a somewhat thornier one. Marshall Field himself was one of the original Chicago aristocracy, and his gorgeous store on State Street defined Chicago retail for several generations. In spite of its ties to Chicago culture and identity, when New York retailer Macy's bought the chain, they announced plans to rebrand all Field's stores as Macy's. Amid shock and uproar (among Chicagoans) and dire warnings (among industry analysts), Macy's executives assured reporters that focus group research had suggested people would, in fact, come to prefer the new brand. Today, sales have plunged, workers have been forced to take a sharp pay cut, and the interior is like a tomb. Ain't corporate hubris great?

Today, there are a few discount department stores, a few big stores for national chains like Old Navy and H&M, and a few amusingly shady joints on the streets under the elevated tracks.

Central Camera, 230 S Wabash Ave (*Monroe Red Line*), +1 312 427-5580, *www.centralcamera.com*, M-F 8:30AM-5:30PM, Sa 8:30AM-5PM. As the name suggests, this is a centrally-located place to deal with fussy cameras or upgrade to better ones. They've been in business since 1899, and have an awe-inspiring amount of spare and obsolete parts from over the years in storage, so don't be shy about asking for something you can't find anywhere else.

Graham Crackers, 77 E Madison St (*Washington Red Line*), +1 312 629-1810, *www.grahamcrackers. com*, M-F 10AM-6PM, Sa 11AM-5PM, Su 12-5PM. Comic book store right off Michigan Avenue, near the Art Institute.

Jeweler's Center, 5 S Wabash Ave (*Washington Red Line*), +1 312 236-2189, *www.jewelerscenter.com*, M-Sa 9AM-5PM, Su closed except four weeks prior to Christmas. An estimated 185 jewelers in one building by the elevated tracks give this a Wild West atmosphere — you could leave with a terrific deal, or...

Nordstrom Rack, 24 N State St (*Washington Red Line*), +1 312 377-5500, *shop.nordstrom.com*, M-Sa 9:30AM-9PM, Su 10AM-7PM. The outlet store for the Near North retailer. There's plenty of heavily-discounted merchandise, but shoes are where the serious mania lies.

Posters Plus, 200 S Michigan Ave (*Monroe Red Line*), +1 312 461-9277, *www.posterplus.com*, Su 10:30AM-6PM, M-W,F 10AM-6PM, Th 10AM-7PM, Sa 9:30AM-6PM. *The* place to buy Chicago images of all shapes and sizes. Posters Plus works with researchers on the side and single-handedly keeps a selection of memorable vintage Chicago posters in print. They also partner with the Art Institute across the street. It's worth a stop to have a look around their gallery even if you don't plan to buy anything.

Sears on State, 2 N State St (*Washington Red Line*), +1 312 373-6000, *www.sears.com*, M-F 10AM-8PM, Sa 10AM-8PM, Su 11AM-5PM. The *other* traditional Chicago retail giant opened this store in 2001. It has a few floors of moderately-priced, moderately-fashionable clothing and housewares.

Wabash Jewelers Mall, 21 N Wabash Ave (*Washington Red Line*), +1 312 263-1757, M-W,F 10AM-5:30PM, Th 10AM-6:30PM, Sa 10AM-5PM. The other bastion of Jeweler's Row, with several stores that specialize in loose diamonds.

Eat

It's easy to find cheap food during the day — this is where most of Chicago works, so this is where most of Chicago eats lunch. However, most of those places close when the work day ends, so it's more difficult to keep costs down

LOOPEAT

at night, when it's gourmet or bust. There's a sizable food court at Ogilvie/Northwestern Station (Canal and Madison) if you're on your way in or out of town.

In general, it's wise to avoid the restaurants right by major tourist attractions (e.g., the Art Institute, Millennium Park, etc.), as the quality of service and food tends to improve with distance from these one-time-visitor hot spots. There are some gems in the Loop, but you should also consider a quick cab ride west to one of downtown Chicago's premiere dining strips in Greektown *p.215*.

Budget

Artist's Cafe, 412 S Michigan Ave (*in the Fine Art building*), +1 312 939-7855, *www.artists-cafe.com*, Su-Th 6:30AM-11PM, F-Sa 6:30AM-12:30AM. In the beautiful old Fine Arts Building, this is easily the best outdoor seating in the Loop. It's sort of a diner with beer and wine also on the menu. The food and service are mediocre at best, but it's reasonably priced, brilliantly located, and more popular with the Columbia College students than it is touristy. $6-15.

Beef & Brandy (The B&B), 127 S State St, +1 312 372-3451, *www.beefbrandy.com*, M-Sa 7AM-9PM, Su 7AM-8PM. A nice spot to get good food at reasonable prices in the Loop — a good rib-eye steak here is just $15 (it's certainly the only place downtown to get a full diner breakfast for under $5). Best to be appraised that karaoke and DJs at the bar can make Wednesday-Friday nights a bit loud during dinner. $5-15.

Boni Vino, 111 W Van Buren St, +1 312 427-0231, M-F 10AM-midnight, Sa 10AM-5PM. Boni Vino, in addition to its pasta dishes, serves what is probably the best Chicago style thin crust pizza downtown — a good option if you want pizza, but fear the cholesterol-laden stuffed pizzas at Bella Bacino's. In addition to good pizza, this restaurant has lots of character and surprisingly low prices. $8-13.

Garrett Popcorn, 4 E Madison St, +1 888 4-POPCORN, *www.garrettpopcorn.com*, M-Sa 10AM-8PM, Su 11AM-7PM. Whether Garrett's shout-out-loud delicious popcorn is the cap to a good lunch or composes the entire meal is up to you and your conscience. "The Mix" is equal parts caramel- and cheese-coated popcorn; strange as it sounds, the combination is addictive. Sales went mad after an appearance on Oprah, so expect lines. There are a few other Loop stores, including 26 W Randolph and 2 W Jackson, but this is the most centrally located. Nice as it would be, signs warn that you can't bring Garrett's into the nearby theaters with you. S/M/L $3-5-7.

Heaven on Seven, 111 N Wabash Ave, +1 312 263-6443, *www.heavenonseven.com*, M-F 8:30AM-5PM, Sa 10AM-3PM, dinner: every third Friday of the month 5:30PM-9PM. If you are downtown when the craving hits for some down home comfort food, this is the place to go. While the South Side remains the

62

undisputed home of soul food in Chicago, this place holds its own. Heaven even boasts a floor length wall of hot sauces. $7-14.

Luke's Italian Beef, 215 W Jackson Blvd, +1 312 939-4204, M-F 10AM-4PM, Sa 10AM-5PM, Su 11AM-5PM. Luke's is where it's at for Italian Beef sandwiches in the Loop, and it's right next to the Sears Tower. The quality is a little unreliable at Luke's, but when they're on, they serve some of the best beef in the city. Hold the enormous portions of fries though, if you have any sympathy for your circulatory system. $3-6.

Osaka Express, 400 S Michigan Ave, +1 312 566-0118, M-Sa 11AM-8PM. A counter on a corner of Michigan Avenue with good, cheap seafood and vegetarian sushi. Be prepared for blank stares if you try ordering in Japanese, though. $5.

Perry's, 175 N Franklin St, +1 312 372-7557, *www.perrysdeli.com*, M-F 7:30AM-2:30PM. Absurdly huge sandwiches (including nine triple-deckers) and cheerful service. The lines at lunch are long, but you'll notice the way the regulars are content to wait for as long as it takes, knowing what's coming to them. (You'll also notice the prohibition against cell phones on the premises.) If in doubt, try "Perry's Favorite," a corned beef special named for the original owner's sandwich of choice. $6-8.

Mid-range

Miller's Pub and Exchequer in the Drink section serve food worth considering for a mid-range lunch.

Backstage Bistro, 180 N Wabash Ave, +1 312 475-6920, *www.artinstitutes.edu*, W-F 11:30AM-1PM 5:30PM-7PM (school months only). Somewhere between a restaurant and a classroom, the chefs and servers here are culinary arts students from the Illinois Institute of Art. The students are enthusiastic, and accordingly do a much better job than most "professionals" at the borderline tourist traps that proliferate around this section of town. Fine dining at very low prices, and you can even watch the chefs-in-training at work behind the kitchen's glass walls. It's small, so make reservations. $9-18.

Bella Bacino's, 75 E Wacker Dr, +1 312 263-2350, *www.bacinos.com*, M-Th 7AM-10PM, F 7AM-11PM, Sa 8AM-11PM, Su 8AM-10PM. Very good Italian food and simply incredible stuffed pizza. $12-$18.

Cellars Market, 141 W Jackson Blvd (*Chicago Board of Trade building, lower level*), +1 312 427-7440, M-F 7AM-2PM (approx.). A hidden gem serving breakfast and lunch only, this cafeteria closes soon after the trading floors upstairs do. Made-to-order deli sandwiches, homemade soups, a large salad bar, and daily specials prepared on-site. The turkey club sandwich is enormous, especially if you're polite and cheerful toward the person making it. $4-12.

Emil's, 101 N Wacker Dr, +1 312 332-4333, M-F 6AM-8PM. A strategically located, nice American/Italian restaurant just across the street from the Opera House. Emil's boasts a thoughtful menu, fine downtown dining, and a staff that will skillfully oblige patrons in a hurry to get to the show. $12-20.

Petterino's, 150 N Dearborn St, +1 312 422-0150, *www.leye.com*, M 11AM-9PM, T-Th 11AM-10:30PM, F 11:00AM-11PM, Sa 11:30AM-11PM, Su 3:30PM-7:30PM. Petterino's is a classic Chicago restaurant, serving high quality steaks, salads, and seafood dishes. The restaurant caters to the theater-going crowd, and reservations for dinner are wise. $12-40.

Pizano's, 61 E Madison St, +1 312 236-1777, *www.pizanoschicago.com*, Su-F 11AM-2AM, Sa 11AM-3AM. The closest deep dish pizza to Millennium Park and the Art Institute. Pizano's has roots in the family that produced UNO's and Lou Malnati's, but will serve a worthy thin-crust, too. $12-$20.

Ronny's Original Steakhouse, 340 S Wabash Ave, +1 312 939-6010, M-Sa 7AM-10PM. There are better steakhouses in downtown Chicago, but Ronny's earns points for being so drenched in the classic Chicago palette. Friendly Midwestern service, diner atmosphere, huge cuts of meat at low prices, and even a shadow-filled view out the window of the L. $9-15.

Splurge

Aria, 200 N Columbus Dr (*at the Fairmont Hotel*), +1 312 444-

9494, *www.ariachicago.com*, Su-Th 11:30AM-2:30PM 5PM-10PM, F-Sa 11:30AM-2:30PM 5PM-11PM. Fine dining in a romantic space attached to the Fairmont Hotel, offering what it describes as "culturally inspired, comfortably American" cuisine. $24-45.

Atwood Cafe, 1 W Washington St, +1 312 368-1900, *www.atwoodcafe.com*, Breakfast M-F 7-10AM, Sa 8AM-10AM, Su 8AM-3PM, Lunch M-Sa 11:30AM-3:45PM, Dinner Su-Th 5-10PM, F-Sa 5-11PM. Popular restaurant with a bar in the classic Hotel Burnham. Good location and atmosphere for dinner before a show. $17-$30.

Custom House, 500 S Dearborn St (*inside the Hotel Blake*), +1 312 523-0200, *www.customhouse.cc*, Su 5-9PM, M-F 11AM-2PM,5-10PM, Sa 5-10PM. Specializes in many varieties of red meat, with a menu created by award-winning Chef Shawn McClain. It's right on the border of Printer's Row in the Hotel Blake, with a name that slyly references the original vice district there. Three course dinner $46.

Everest, 440 S LaSalle St, 40th Floor, +1 312 663-8920, *www.everestrestaurant.com*, Tu-Th 5:30PM-9PM, F 5:30PM-9:30PM, Sa 5PM-10PM. Arguably the best restaurant in Chicago. The "Personal French Cuisine" of Executive Chef Jean Joho is world-renowned. The view from the top floor of the Chicago Stock Exchange is magnificent as well. Complimentary valet parking. $90-130/person.

ristorante we, 172 W Adams St, +1 312 917-5608, *www.ristorantewe.com*, M-Th 6:30AM-2:30PM 5PM-10PM, F 6:30AM-2:30PM 5PM-11PM, Sa 7AM-noon 5PM-11PM, Su 7AM-noon. Downtown Chicago steakhouse meets Tuscan fine dining in the very fashionable Hotel W. $26-48.

Russian Tea Time, 77 E Adams St, +1 312 360-0000, *www.russianteatime.com*, Su-Th 11AM-9PM, F-Sa 11AM-midnight. This is *the* place to try Russian cuisine in Chicago! Easily one of the best Russian restaurants in the world with an inventive menu and excellent management. Ask to be seated in the front section. Afternoon tea runs from 2:30-4:30PM. $22-$32.

Trattoria No.10, 10 N Dearborn St (*Washington Red Line*), +1 312 984-1718, *www.trattoriaten.com*, Lunch M-F 11:30AM-2PM; Dinner M-Th 5:30-9PM, F-Sa 5:30-10PM. A gourmet Italian restaurant; dinners are designed to include a *primi piatti* course of pasta and a *secondi piatti* of duck, veal, and other seasonal specialties, although they can be ordered separately. $40+.

Vivere, 71 W Monroe St, +1 312 332-4040, *vivere-chicago.com*, M-Th 11:30AM-2:30PM 5PM-10PM, F 11:30AM-2:30PM 5PM-11PM, Sa 5PM-11PM. One of Chicago's top Italian restaurants, with very creative decor and a romantic ambiance. $20-40.

Drink

The cost of real estate in the Loop means that most dives are priced out of the area, sending most of the after-work crowd to the places noted below. Friday nights after work can be a mob scene — if you're with a group, either make a reservation or be prepared to split up for a little while.

BIG Bar, 151 E Wacker Dr (*inside the Hyatt Regency*), +1 312 565-1234, *chicagoregency.hyatt.com*, M-Th 4PM-2PM, F-Sa 3PM-3AM, Su 11AM-2AM. Don't expect an intimate atmosphere or anything resembling a classic Chicago experience. Do expect all things comically out of proportion. The bar is 160 feet long and the margaritas can get so big that they actually mix them in a cement mixer. And the view is great.

Close Up 2, 416 S Clark St, +1 312 385-1111, *www.closeup2jazz.com*, T-F 4PM-2AM, Sa 9PM-3AM. A classy lounge that may be the best place in the city to relax and listen to smooth jazz. The clientèle is similarly classy, so come well dressed (business casual) and looking good. Cover: $5-10.

Elephant & Castle, 111 W Adams St, +1 312 236-6656, *www.elephantcastle.com*, 6:30AM-midnight. English-ish pub chain with the requisite fish & chips and other mid-range pub food, long hours, and a second location at 185 N Wabash. It's a good place for a long stay.

Emerald Loop, 216 N Wabash Ave, +1 312 263-0200, *www.vaughanhospitality.com*, M-F

7AM-2AM, Sa 11AM-3AM, Su 11AM-2AM. Irish-style pub in a elegant setting, with large tables to accommodate business lunches. The food's good, breakfast included.

Exchequer Restaurant & Pub, 226 S Wabash Ave, +1 312 939-5633, *www.exchequerpub.com*, M-Th 11AM-11PM, F-Sa 11AM-midnight, Su Noon-9PM. Family-friendly pub with pizza and ribs, under the L tracks and covered in Chicago memorabilia.

Miller's Pub, 134 S Wabash Ave, +1 312 263-4988, *www.millerspub.com*, Kitchen 11AM-2AM, Bar 10AM-4AM. Established in 1935 and bursting with faded celebrity photos, Miller's Pub serves ribs, steak, and sandwiches with its list of beer, wine, and martinis. It's a little too formal to sprawl out and relax, but perfect if getting a beer is a task of equal import to dinner.

Old Timer's Restaurant and Lounge, 75 E Lake St, +1 312 332-3561, M-F 6:30AM-2AM, Sa 7AM-1AM. The classic diner is worth a visit for breakfast, but the real gem is the divey bar that waits through the front door. You wouldn't expect a low-key, "regulars" atmosphere a block from Millennium Park, but here it is, with clientèle from *all* walks of life mingling over beer.

Plymouth Restaurant & Bar, 327 S Plymouth Ct, +1 312 362-1212, *plymouthgrill.com*, Su-Th 11AM-11PM, F-Sa 11AM-midnight. The Plymouth Restaurant is merely an adequate cafe serving diner-style

food, but come here instead for the rooftop bar. Sipping a cocktail while gazing off the balcony at the Harold Washington Library and various Louis Sullivan masterpieces is a fine way to cap off a day of sightseeing, provided that the blaring music doesn't drive you away.

Stocks & Blondes Bar & Grille, 40 N Wells St, +1 312 372-3725, *www.stocksandblondesbargrille.com*, M-Sa 11AM-1AM, Su 11AM-midnight. Stocks & Blondes, aside from the frightening pun, is a rarity in the Loop in that it is "just a bar." No fake Irish pub gimmickry, no failing attempts at trendiness, just a bare-bones bar atmosphere and good beer on tap.

Sleep

Although this is the most expensive real estate in Chicago, the hotels in the Loop are slightly cheaper than those in the Near North *p.71* simply because so much of the area shuts down at night. Still, these are some pretty nice digs, and being in the Loop makes transportation to any part of the city easy.

Budget

Congress Plaza Hotel, 520 S Michigan Ave (*Library Orange/Purple/Brown/Green/Pink Line, Jackson Blue Line*), +1 312 427-3800, *www.congressplazahotel.com*. The Congress Hotel has seen visits from most U.S. presidents since it was built in 1893. Today, other hotels have overtaken the Congress in the glamor class, leaving it behind as a great deal with a colorful past. Ask for a room with a view of the lake — if Buckingham Fountain is running, you will be treated to a magnificent view. Rooms from $100.

Hostelling International Chicago (J Ira & Nicki Harris Family Hostel), 24 E Congress Pkwy (*Library Orange/Purple/Brown/Green/Pink Line, Jackson Red Line, LaSalle Blue Line*), +1 312 360-0300, *www.hichicago.org*, Checkin: 3pm, Checkout: 11am. Quick and easy access to airports, bus terminal and train stations. Available 24 hours a day, 365 days a year. No curfew, no age restrictions (under 18 must be accompanied by adult). Ask for the coupon which gives $3 off the **Chicago Architecture Foundation** tours. Rates start at $27, plus $3 without HI membership.

Mid-range

Hard Rock Hotel, 230 N Michigan Ave (*inside the Carbide & Carbon Building*), +1 312 345-1000, *www.preferredhotels.com*. Near Millennium Park and the Magnificent Mile, with style points for being located in the beautiful Carbon & Carbide Building. Rooms come packed with audiovisual amenities apropos of the name. Rooms from $199.

Hotel 71, 71 E Wacker Dr, +1 312 346-7100, *www.hotel71.com*. Located on the Chicago River at Wacker Drive and Michigan Avenue with an impressive view, right on the border of the Near North. Rooms from $254.

Hotel Allegro, 171 W Randolph St (*Clark/Lake Blue Line*), +1 866-672-6143, *www.allegrochicago.com*. This lovely, Art Deco hotel calls itself a boutique, probably in reference to its friendly, full four-star service, designer decorated rooms and prices that are the same, or just a little bit more than you would pay for a blander three-star place just north of the river. Suites and some rooms have a double jacuzzi. Rooms from $209.

Hotel Blake, 500 S Dearborn St, +1 312 986-1234, *www.hotelblake. com*. Located across the street from Printer's Row, with an acclaimed restaurant in the lobby. Rooms from $169.

Hotel Burnham, 1 W Washington St, +1 312 782-1111, *burnhamhotel. com*. In the classic Reliance Building, near Millennium Park. A Kimpton Boutique hotel, like the Allegro. Rooms from $239.

Silversmith Hotel & Suites, 10 S Wabash Ave, +1 773 372-7696, *www.silversmithchicagohotel.com*. The Silversmith boasts an enviable location, good value, and perfectly adequate suites, but light sleepers should be sure to ask for a room away from the noisy L lines. Don't miss the dessert hour: free high quality cake, cookies, and coffee/tea in the lobby M-Th 9PM-10PM. Rooms from $180-315.

W Chicago City Center, 172 W Adams St, +1 312 332-1200, *www. starwoodhotels.com*. This outpost of the W Hotels chain is under the shadow of the Sears Tower, in the midst of the Loop, for a bit of stylish gloom at night. Rooms from $175.

Splurge

The Fairmont Chicago, 200 N Columbus Dr, +1 312 565-8000, *www.fairmont.com/chicago*. Upscale hotel that takes pride in its restaurants and offers a number of tour packages for Chicago attractions. Rooms from $269.

Hotel Monaco, 225 N Wabash Ave, +1 312 950-8500, *monaco-chicago.com*. The Monaco provides a bit better than four-star comfort at a bit less than four-star prices, though they are a little higher than at sister hotels like the Allegro or the Burnham. What you get for the extra money is a number of specialty services geared for business travelers, so if you are traveling for pleasure go for the Allegro. Rooms from $259.

Hyatt Regency Chicago, 151 E Wacker Dr, +1 312 565 1234, *chicagoregency.hyatt.com*. 2,000 guest rooms in two towers, a riverfront location, and what the management claims is the largest freestanding bar in the U.S. It's a favorite for convention groups, and is connected via covered walkways to the Illinois Center, which is a major business complex. Rooms from $259.

Marriott Renaissance Chicago Hotel, 1 W Wacker Dr, +1 312 372-7200, *www.marriott.com*. Elegant hotel with sweeping views and a Rejuvenation Center. Rooms from $259.

The Palmer House, 17 E Monroe St, +1 312 726-7500, *www1.hilton.com*. With over 1,600 rooms and no shortage of luxuries, the Palmer House is one of Chicago's most memorable hotels. It was originally built by business magnate Potter Palmer for his socialite wife Bertha. This is actually the third version of the Palmer House — the first opened two weeks before the Great Chicago Fire. (Can't beat that for timing.) The current version, overlooking State Street, enjoyed an extravagant renovation in 2008, with tasteful 1920s style guest rooms and a magnificent lobby bar (with magnificently overpriced drinks). Rooms from $259.

Swissotel Chicago, 323 E Wacker Dr, +1 312 565-0565, *www.swissotelchicago.com*. This sleek, new skyscraper offers great views over the Chicago River and the lake. Rooms from $217.

Contact

Harold Washington Library Center, 400 S State St (*Library Brown/Green/Orange/Purple/Pink*), +1 312 747-4999, *www.chipublib.org*, M-Th 9AM-9PM, F S 9AM-5PM, Su 1PM-5PM. Chicago's central library is in a gigantic, impressive, and stylistically bewildering building, named for Harold Washington, the city's first black Mayor. It holds exhibitions and author events, has an impressive permanent art collection, and is well-equipped with free computer and Internet services.

Get out

The Loop is rivaled only by the Near North *p.71* as Chicago's principal tourist destination. But the city has riches far beyond the tourist lure of downtown skyscrapers and big museums; to experience what makes Chicago "Chicago", venture into the neighborhoods where Chicagoans actually live.

The good news is that there is convenient public transportation from the Loop to virtually every corner of this massive city. Here are a few easy excursions if you are staying in the Loop that will really show you some of the city beyond the major tourist attractions:

Take the Metra Electric Line south from Millennium Park to spend half a day visiting the excellent museums or visiting the University of Chicago and the local independent bookstores in Hyde Park *p.157*.

Head south on the CTA Red Line to Chinatown *p.175* for a delicious Cantonese dinner.

Take the CTA Red Line north to Lawrence Avenue in Uptown *p.273* for a night of jazz at the historic Green Mill.

Hop on the CTA Blue Line to Damen Avenue in the epicenter of the ever-popular Wicker Park neighborhood, where you will find better dining options, way better bar options, and some eccentric shopping.

Take the CTA Brown/Purple lines north to Lincoln Park and Old Town *p.123* to visit Chicago's top comedy clubs and celebrity chefs, or to head into lovely Lincoln Park, home of the Lincoln Park Zoo and the famous North Avenue Beach.

The **Near North** is the shop-and-awe center of Chicago. It's bounded by North Avenue to the north, the Chicago River to the west and south, and Lake Michigan to the east.

With a whirlwind rush of department stores, restaurants, and luxurious hotels, there's no better place to abuse your budget than the Near North and its celebrated **Magnificent Mile**.

Understand

The Near North includes the neighborhoods of **River North**, full of art galleries, commercial lofts, and some tourist restaurants, nightclubs and bars; **Streeterville** and the Gold Coast, with expensive living for rich folks and many of the city's most impressive hotels; and the most prestigious shopping district in Chicago, the Magnificent Mile on Michigan Avenue, which includes one of Chicago's most beloved landmarks, the **Water Tower**.

This area has been a part of Chicago from the beginning, when Fort Dearborn was built on the other side of the river in 1803 (and burned to the ground nine years later, establishing an unfortunate civic trend). But ever since the early 1920s, when bridges were built to draw shoppers away from State Street in the Loop *p.47*, there has been too much to sell, too much awe to inspire, and not a minute to spare. That's why the Near North can be such a delight at a tourist's pace. The locals are in a hurry, but if you're not, the serene image of the old Water Tower or the resolutely quiet riverwalk can take on the feel of a private discovery, even with all of these people around.

That's not to say you can't have fun getting caught up in the hustle and bustle, of course. The sheer amount of shopping on Michigan Avenue cannot be overstated. The world's most elite fashion designers are all represented here, and the rest wish they were. River North has many of the city's busiest (if not best) clubs, with a dense row on Rush Street. In the Near North, you'll find a few significant members of the Chicago skyline, including the **John Hancock Center** and **Lake Point Tower**, which stands alone to the east at the end of a new, steel-and-glass future-scape in south Streeterville; it makes for an impressive view from Lake Shore Drive, and serves as an entryway to one of the city's most popular tourist spots, **Navy Pier**, a great place for entertaining children and catching the breeze from Lake Michigan with an evening stroll or a turn on the 150-foot tall **Ferris Wheel**.

Get in

What's that island?

That is Goose Island, an oddity of downtown Chicago, from which Chicago's biggest craft brewery takes its name. Named after an early Irish immigrant community that supposedly raised geese as livestock, the island was formed when landowner and Mayor William Ogden oversaw the building of a canal around its east side. Throughout its history, the island was an industrial center, although in recent times it seemed its riverfront location and splendid downtown views would ensure its conversion to condominiums. But that change was halted in 1990 when Mayor Daley backed its new status as a "Protected Manufacturing District."

By train

The CTA **Red Line** has stops near the entertainment in River North (Clark/Division) and the Magnificent Mile (Chicago, Grand).

The CTA **Brown Line** and **Purple Line** stop in the midst of the River North galleries (Chicago), and the Merchandise Mart has the next stop all to itself.

By bus

An intricate web of CTA bus lines serves the Near North, most converging upon the northern end of Michigan Avenue. Several express buses from other parts of the city serve Michigan Avenue, notably the **147 Outer Drive Express** from the north side and **3 King Drive Express** from the south side. Once you're here, though, you'll find it better to cover the Magnificent Mile on foot.

22 Clark is useful for travelers coming from the Loop *p.47* and the North Side to River North.

65 Grand travels down Grand Avenue, connecting with both the Red Line and the Blue Line further west.

66 Chicago travels down Chicago Ave from the lakefront to Michigan Avenue, through River North, and on to West Town *p.229*.

124 Navy Pier serves Navy Pier directly from train hub Union Station and Millennium Park in the Loop.

125 Water Tower Express brings you to the Water Tower from the other Loop train hub, Ogilvie/Northwestern Station, and the Merchandise Mart.

157 Streeterville runs close to Navy Pier and on to the Loop.

By trolley

Free trolleys run from Navy Pier through the area seven days a week, year round, during the pier's open hours.

By car

Don't drive to the Near North unless you have a very good reason for doing so. Streets are packed with taxis, confused tourists, desperate businessmen late for something or other, and even the occasional horse. Your knuckles don't need the strain.

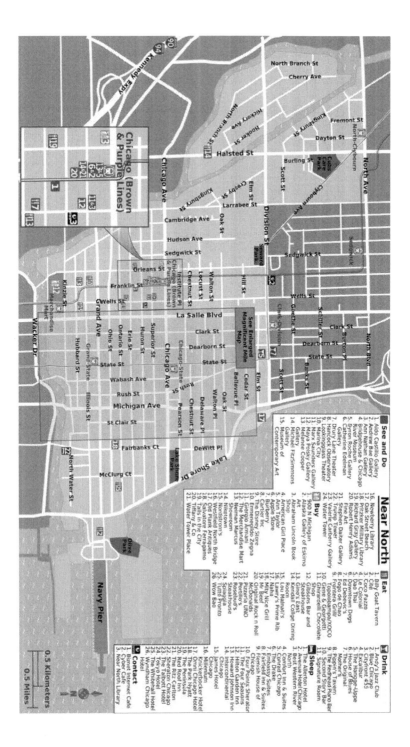

Chicago (Brown & Purple Lines)

See Enlarged Magnificent Mile Map

Chicago (Brown & Purple Lines)

Navy Pier

Olive Park

Kennedy Expy

North Branch St
Cherry Ave
North Branch St
Hickory Ave
Hooker St
North Cloburn
Fremont St
Dayton St
Halsted St
Burling St
Cubs Care Park
Scot St
North Ave
Clybourn Ave
Chicago Ave
Elm St
Crosby St
Kingsbury St
Larrabee St
Division St
Cambridge Ave
Oak St
Hudson Ave
Sedgwick St
Orleans St
Chicago (Brown & Purple Lines)
Walton St
Franklin St
Locust St
Chestnut St
Hill St
Wells St
Goethe St
Clark St
Sedgwick St
Schiller St
La Salle Blvd
Clark St
Clark-Division St
Dearborn St
Clark St
Dearborn St
State St
North Blvd
State St
Banks St
Scott St
Wabash Ave
Chicago Ave
Rush St
Chicago-State
Oak St
Cedar St
Elm St
Michigan Ave
Walton Pl
Bellevue Pl
St Clair St
Delaware Pl
Pearson St
Chestnut St
Illinois St
Grand-State
State St
Ontario St
Ohio St
Erie St
Huron St
Superior St
Hubbard St
Fairbanks Ct
DeWitt Pl
Lake Shore Park
McClurg Ct
North Water St
Wacker Dr
Kinzie St
Merchandise Mart
Grand Ave
Institute Pl

Lake Shore Dr

0.5 Kilometers
0.5 Miles

Near North

See and Do
1. Aldo Castillo Gallery
2. Andrew Bae Gallery
3. Ann Nathan Gallery
4. Bridgehouse & Chicago
5. Byron Roche Gallery
6. Catherine Edelman Gallery
7. Fine Art
8. Flatfile Gallery
9. Hancock Observatory
10. Lookingglass Theater
11. Marina City
12. Maya Polsky Gallery
13. Melanee Cooper Gallery
14. Stanley Fitzsimmons Gallery
15. Museum of Contemporary Art
16. Newberry Library
17. Oak Street Beach
18. Coco Pazzo
19. Printer Grate Library
20. Robert Henry Adams Fine Art
21. Stephen Daiter Gallery
22. Trap Door Theater
23. Tribune Tower
24. Water Tower

Buy
1. 900 N Michigan
2. Alaska Gallery of Eskimo Art
3. Abraham Lincoln Book Shop
4. American Girl Place
5. Apple Store
6. Burberry
7. Cartier Inc
8. Crate & Barrel
9. Disney Store
10. Ermenegildo Zegna
11. Giorgio Armani
12. The Merchandise Mart
13. Neiman Marcus Showroom
14. Niketown
15. Nordstrom's
16. Westfield North Bridge
17. Old Plank Antiques
18. Salvatore Ferragamo
19. Tails in the City
20. Tiffany & Co
21. Water Tower Place

Eat
1. Billy Goat Tavern
2. Clo
3. Coco Pazzo
4. Le Colonial
5. Excalibur
6. Gino's East
7. Downtown Dogs
8. Ed Debevic's
9. Frontera Grille
10. Gene & Georgetti
11. Ghirardelli Chocolate
12. Gibbons Bar and Steakhouse
13. Kendall College Dining Room
14. Lino's East
15. Lou Malnati's
16. Navy's Prime Rib
17. Mr. Beef Grill
18. Mitty Nice Grill
19. McDonald Rock n Roll Chicago
20. Pizzeria UNO
21. Portho's
22. RL Steakhouse
23. Saloon Steakhouse
24. Sisopia
25. Tutti Pronto
26. Wow Bao

Drink
1. Andy's Jazz Club
2. Blue Chicago
3. Cityfront 455
4. Excalibur
5. The Hangar-Uptop
6. House of Blues
7. The Original
8. Mother's
9. The Redhead Piano Bar
10. Second Story Bar
11. Signature Room

Sleep
1. Amalfi Hotel
2. Conrad Chicago
3. Best Western River North
4. Courtyard Inn & Suites
5. Sax Chicago
6. The Drake
7. Embassy Suites
8. Fairfield Inn & Suites
9. Intercontinental Chicago
10. Four Points Sheraton
11. Grand Chicago Inn
12. Hilton Garden Inn
13. Howard Johnson Inn
14. Intercontinental Chicago
15. James Hotel
16. Millennium Knickerbocker Hotel
17. Omni Chicago Hotel
18. The Park Hyatt
19. The Peninsula
20. Radisson Inn
21. The Ritz Carlton
22. Sheraton Chicago
23. The Talbott Hotel
24. The Westin Hotel
25. The Whitehall Hotel
26. Wyndham Chicago Hotel

Contact
1. Buznet Internet Cafe
2. Intelligentsia Coffee
3. Near North Library

Magnificent Mile

See

Along the Magnificent Mile *p.109* is a one day and night itinerary that connects the Near North with the Loop *p.47* for shopping, food, skyscrapers, parks, and amazing views of Chicago from high and low.

Bridgehouse & Chicago River Museum, 376 N Michigan Ave (*Lake CTA*), +1 312 977-0227, *bridgehousemuseum.org*, Th-M 10AM-5PM. Open late spring (mid-May), summer, and fall. A new, small museum spread over the five floors of the southwest tower of the Michigan Avenue Bridge. Visitors can see displays on the history of Chicago's famously abused river, and also check out the machinery used for raising the bridge. $3 adults, children under 5 are free.

Hancock Observatory, John Hancock Center, 875 N Michigan Ave (*Chicago Red Line*), 1-888 875-8439, *www.hancockobservatory.com*, 9AM-11PM. 360-degree view from the 94th floor. Not quite as high as the Sears Tower Skydeck, but with a better view. For drinks, see the Signature Room below. $15 adults, $9 children, $10 seniors; $3 for additional entry within 48 hours.

Marina City, 300 N State St, +1 312 222-1111, *www.marina-city. com*, M-F 9AM-5PM, Sa 10AM-2PM. No tours available, unless you're cheeky enough to fill out a fake rental application (24 hours in advance), but these iconic twin buildings are worth a photo. (You might recognize them from the cover of **Wilco**'s *Yankee Hotel Fox-* *trot*, among many others.) Designed to be "a city within a city," they include a wildly overpriced bowling alley and the **House of Blues** (see Drink below). If you like Marina City, be sure to visit the South Loop and architect **Bertrand Goldberg**'s other, lesser-known masterpiece, River City (800 S Wells St).

Museum of Contemporary Art, 220 E Chicago Ave (*Chicago Red Line*), +1 312 280-2660, *www.mcachicago.org*, Tu 10AM-8PM, W-Su 10AM-5PM. Contemporary art from around the world. The MCA has a great location and plenty of financial backing, but it's still fighting for recognition in the museum world; while not an upper-tier institution as yet, that has resulted in some interesting exhibitions. There isn't much of a permanent collection, so check what's on before you go. Also, Wolfgang Puck operates a lunch-only eatery in the MCA. $12 ($7 student, free Tuesdays).

Newberry Library, 60 W Walton St (*Chicago Red Line*), +1 312 943–9090, *www.newberry.org*, Reading rooms Tu-Th 10AM-6PM, F-Sa 9AM-5PM. The oldest public library in Chicago, although not part of the city library system. The collection focuses on the humanities, American and European history, and the age of exploration. Occasional author events are held. Free.

Pritzker Military Library, 610 N Fairbanks Ct (*Grand Red Line*), +1 312 587-0234, *www.pritzkermilitarylibrary.org*, M-F 8:30AM-4:30PM. A goldmine for people interested in military history, both scholarly and as told by the men and women who lived it, with a vast collection of books, prints, photos, and other military artifacts, and gallery exhibitions. Free evening events with major authors and Medal of Honor recipients are held throughout the year, mostly on Thursday nights; check the schedule on the website. Free.

Tribune Tower, 435 N Michigan Ave (*Grand Red Line*), +1 312 222-9100. Built in 1925, the walls of the Tribune Tower contain rocks from many famous world landmarks, including: the Taj Mahal, the Parthenon, the Great Pyramid, the Cathedral of Notre-Dame, the Great Wall of China, the Berlin Wall, and most recently from the demolished World Trade Center. The Tribune Tower even managed to get its hands on a moon rock, but so far NASA hasn't allowed it to add the rock to the wall.

The Trump Tower, 401 N Wabash Ave. 1362 ft. The Trump Hotel and luxury residential building is both the newest member of the Chicago skyline, completed at the beginning of 2009, and the tallest after the Sears Tower — indeed, it is the second tallest in the United States, ninth in the world. The Donald intended for it to be the tallest in the world, but decided to scale back to a mere "second tallest in North America" (after the Sears Tower) following the 9/11 terrorist attacks. The design features three prominent setbacks at the height of nearby buildings: the Wrigley Building, Marina City, and 330 N Wabash, which, combined with its

singularly reflective exterior, allow this supertall to blend into the skyline, almost to the point where you could overlook it. As intended, the building reflects and interacts with the Chicago skyline, rather than imposing itself upon it with its great height. Regardless, you will not likely miss this building, and it's plenty interesting to examine — its asymmetric form ensures that you will see something quite different from any different vantage point.

Water Tower, Chicago Ave & Michigan Ave (*Chicago Red Line*). In 1871, when Mrs. O'Leary's cow kicked over the lantern in her barn — or was framed for the act, depending on who you ask — the Gothic Revival spires of Water Tower were only two years old. Today, along with the Pumping Station on the other side of the street, the Water Tower is the last, dream-like symbol of the Old Chicago that disappeared in the Fire. Surrounded by hotels and colossal department stores, it's also *the* icon of the new city that arose. At night, the Water Tower is lit from within, and it's a memorable sight. Inside, the vintage machinery is long gone (along with the water), and the plain interior is occasionally used as a gallery space.

Galleries

Centered between the Merchandise Mart and the Chicago Brown Line station, with a few galleries that stray closer to Old Town *p.123* or Michigan Avenue, River North boasts the largest arts and design district in North America outside of Manhattan. Art galleries tend to be concentrated closer to Chicago Avenue, with more design galleries closer to the Merchandise Mart. The entire area is walkable and makes for fun browsing. Although everything on display is for sale, admission is almost always free, and visitors needn't fear gallery owners putting on the hard sell.

There is a free **art gallery tour** *www.chicagoartdealers.org* starting from the Starbucks under the Chicago Brown Line stop on Saturdays at 11AM. The tour usually visits four galleries and lasts about an hour and a half.

Aldo Castillo Gallery, 675 N Franklin (*Chicago Brown Line*), +1 312 337-2536, *www.artaldo.com*, Tu-Sa 11AM-6PM. Specializes in contemporary and classic Latin American art.

Andrew Bae Gallery, 300 W Superior (*Chicago Brown Line*), +1 312 335-8601, *www.andrewbaegallery.com*, Tu-Sa 10AM-6PM. Specializes in contemporary Asian art, particularly Korean and Japanese.

Ann Nathan Gallery, 212 W Superior (*Chicago Brown Line*), +1 312 664-6622, *www.annnathangallery.com*, Tu-F 10AM-5:30PM, Sa 11AM-5PM. Focuses on emerging artists, with an emphasis on contemporary realism, and some African tribal art.

Byron Roche Gallery, 750 N Franklin St (*Chicago Brown Line*), +1 312 654-0144, *www.byronroche.*

com, Tu-Sa 11AM-6PM. Contemporary art from an eclectic mix of media.

Catherine Edelman Gallery, 300 W Superior St (*Chicago Brown Line*), +1 312 266-2350, *www.edelmangallery.com*, Tu-Sa 10AM-5:30PM. Contemporary photography and mixed-media.

Marx-Saunders Gallery, 230 W Superior St (*Chicago Brown Line*), +1 312 573-1400, *www.marxsaunders.com*, Tu-F 10AM-5:30PM; Sa 11AM-5PM. Contemporary glass sculptures.

Maya Polsky Gallery, 215 W Superior St (*Chicago Brown Line*), +1 312 440-0055, *www.mayapolskygallery.com*, Tu-F 10AM-5PM, Sa 11AM-5PM. Consistently one of the most intriguing galleries in the area, with playful, well-displayed paintings and sculpture both local and from Russia.

Melanee Cooper Gallery, 740 N Franklin St (*Chicago Brown Line*), +1 312 202-9305, Tu-F 11AM-5PM, Sa 12-4PM. Fascinating contemporary art, mostly abstract and representational.

Michael FitzSimmons Gallery, 311 W Superior St (*Chicago Brown Line*), +1 312 787-0496, *www.fitzdecarts.com*, Tu-F 10AM-6PM, Sa 11AM-5PM. Textiles, ceramics, and antiques.

Richard Gray Gallery, 875 N Michigan Ave, Suite 2503 (Hancock Center) (*Chicago Red Line*), +1 312 642-8877, *www.richardgraygallery.com*, M-F 10AM-5:30PM. Big and very big names from modern and contemporary American and European art, including Millennium Park sculptor Jaume Plensa.

Robert Henry Adams Fine Art, 715 N Franklin St (*Chicago Brown Line*), +1 312 642-8700, *www.adamsfineart.com*, Tu-F 10AM-5PM; Sa 12-5PM. Big names from American art 1910-1970.

Stephen Daiter Gallery, 311 W Superior St (*Chicago Brown Line*), +1 312 787-3350, *stephendaitergallery.com*, W-Sa 11AM-6PM. Artistic and documentary photography from America and Europe.

Valerie Carberry Gallery, 875 N Michigan Ave, Suite 2510 (Hancock Center) (*Chicago Red Line*), +1 312 397-9990, *www.valeriecarberry.com*, M-F 10AM-5PM, Sa 11AM-5PM. Pre and post-war American art, particularly 1930-1949.

Navy Pier

600 E Grand Ave (*At the end of Illinois St*), +1 800 595-7437, *www.navypier.com*, Open 10AM daily; closes in summer Su-Th 10PM, F-Sa midnight, fall/spring Su-Th 8PM, F-Sa 10PM, winter M-Th 8PM, F-Sa 10PM, Su 7PM. Built in 1916, **Navy Pier** has had many different uses over the years; in 1994, it became a tourist attraction, with more than 50 acres of restaurants, shops, and activities by Lake Michigan. It's an easy place to entertain children. Unless otherwise noted, all of the attractions are open during Navy Pier operating hours. Several buses reach Navy Pier, including #29 State, #65 Grand, #66 Chicago, and #124 Navy Pier Express from the two Metra stations in the Loop. Parking available $19-23 per day.

AeroBalloon, +1 312 646 827-6287 for weather, +1 312 224-8827 to make reservations for rides between 8AM-10AM, In season, usually through October, and weather permitting: M-Th 8AM-10PM, F-Su 8AM-midnight. The hot air balloon stays tethered to the pier, but it heads 350 feet into the air for spectacular skyline views. $25 adults, $15 children; SpeedPass available for $5 more.

Amazing Chicago's Funhouse Maze, +1 888 893-7300, *amazingchicago.com*, Open 10AM daily. 4000 square feet of tunnels and mazes for adults & kids over 7 years old.

Bike Chicago, +1 888 245-3929, *www.bikechicago.com*, Summer 8AM-10PM, Spring/Fall 9AM-7PM. A wide variety of bikes, rollerblades, pedicabs and other wheeled vehicles are available for rent. Tours are also available. Rentals from $8/hr to $34/day.

Boat Cruises. Numerous boat cruises depart from the pedestrian-only "Dock Street," operated by several different companies. Some head inland on the Chicago River, and others stick to Lake Michigan. Double-decker tours also ply the boardwalk.

Chicago Children's Museum, 700 E Grand Avenue, #127, +1 312 527-1000, *www.chicagochildrensmuseum.org*, Su-W, F 10AM-5PM; Th, Sa

10AM-8PM. Hands-on exhibits for kids, including the popular Dinosaur Expedition. Admission $8, free Thursday after 5PM, free for children on the first Monday of every month.

Chicago Shakespeare Theater, 800 E Grand Ave (*Navy Pier*), +1 312 595-5600, *www.chicagoshakes.com*. The CST has offered high production values and somewhat bland production experiences since the company moved into their new, $24 million dollar theater in 1999; not *bad*, mind you, but not likely to leave you with much more than a pleasant, faintly-remembered evening. Still, if you're in the mood for Shakespeare, you'll find a professionally-mounted production of one of his major works here throughout the year. $54-$70.

Fireworks, Summer: W 9:30PM, Sa 10:15PM. You can watch the fireworks display from anywhere on the Pier. Booze and live music of varying quality are available at **The Beer Garden** (+1 312 595-5439, summer W-Sa to midnight, Su to 10PM).

IMAX Movie Theater, +1 312 595-5MAX, *www.imax.com/chicago*, Showtimes begin 10AM-8PM. Both Hollywood movies and IMAX films are shown on the six-story movie screen here. Tickets $9-$15.

Internet Access. Available at terminals next to the Haagen Dazs cafe about halfway down Dock Street, just past the Chicago Shakespeare Theater. $4/30min with ice cream purchase.

Pier Park, *www.navypier.com*, S-Th 10AM-8PM, F-Sa 10AM-10PM. Includes the signature **Ferris Wheel**, a mini-golf course, remote-controlled boats, and more. Each attraction $5, Ferris Wheel $6.

Skyline Stage, +1 312 902-1500, *www.navypier.com*, Box office 12-6PM, W-Sa. Shows of mild interest, ranging from jazz and blues to small touring circuses. Tickets $14.50-$29.50 for most shows.

Smith Museum of Stained Glass Windows, +1 312 595-5024, *www.navypier.com*. A mix of antique pieces, including several from Tiffany in New York, and also some contemporary work. Curator-led tours are available at 2PM on Thursdays. Free.

A few Chicago restaurants have branches here *www.navypier.com*. There's also a food court, and vendors along the dock during the summer. You're much better off making the short walk to one of the nearby restaurants off the pier, though — you'll save money and likely eat better. There's no cost for re-entry to Navy Pier, after all.

Among the restaurants, **The Billy Goat** and **Charlie's Ale House** serve beers that are brewed in-house. Try the dark beer from the Billy Goat or head down to the The Beer Garden to sample Chicago brewers Goose Island.

Shopping *www.navypier.com* is in plentiful supply, although it's pretty much limited to tourist-souvenir Chicago kitsch type stuff.

Do

Horse-drawn carriages ply routes along the Magnificent Mile and through Streeterville, usually beginning around the Water Tower. (You might see police officers on horses as well.) While there are too many cars to establish the kind of atmosphere you might expect in, say, Central Park, you'll probably know whether the night calls for a carriage ride, and choose accordingly. Expect to pay about $35 for a half-hour tour. College students also roam the area with small yellow cabs attached to the backs of bicycles for a low-cost, low-point alternative.

Drury Lane Theater, 175 E Chestnut St (Water Tower Place) (*Chicago Red Line*), +1 312 642-2000, *www.drurylanewatertower.com*, Box office opens 10AM, 11AM Sundays. Part of the Broadway in Chicago crew, although most of their offerings are locally-produced, amiable shtick. Tickets $59.50-$69.50. Dinner packages are offered with the Mity Nice Grill.

Lookingglass Theater, 821 N Michigan Ave (*Chicago Red Line*), +1 312 337-0665, *www.lookingglasstheatre.org*, Box office opens at 10AM on weekdays, 11AM weekends. Modern theater company, currently resident in the old Pumping Station across the street from the Water Tower, most famous for being co-founded by David Schwimmer. Tickets range from $20 on weekdays to $58 on weekends.

Oak Street Beach, between 500–1550 Lake Shore Dr, Open during the summer, from dawn to dusk. There is plenty of everybody doing everything at Oak Street Beach. Beyond swimming and sun-tanning, it's one of the city's most popular spots for beach volleyball, and there are concrete paths for cycling and skating. (Do not, however, plan to eat lunch at the restaurant on the beach.) To get here, cross under Lake Shore Drive through a pedestrian underpass.

Events & Festivals

Air & Water Show. Every August, the Blue Angels and the Thunderbirds headline a five-hour show over Lake Michigan. "Show Central" is at North Avenue Beach, but the action may be viewed anywhere from Northerly Island to Montrose Point, inland through Lincoln Park, and offshore by boat. (If you go by water, take a big boat, as the heavy traffic makes for choppy, seasickness-inducing waves.) A dress rehearsal takes place on Friday, often with multiple run-throughs by the headlining act. You won't see 100% of the weekend show, but it's a great way to avoid the crowds.

Magnificent Mile

One of the most prestigious shopping streets in the world, this stretch of Michigan Avenue is home to massive department stores, wildly expensive boutiques, and larger-than-usual stores for national chains like **The Gap**, **Banana Republic**, and **Crate & Barrel**. Some retailers even have two or more branches here: one standing alone, and another in one of the department stores. This isn't the place to look for discounts, though. Remember, you're not shopping here because it's cheap — you're shopping here because it's the Magnificent Mile.

900 N Michigan Ave (*Chicago Red Line*), +1 312 915-3916, *www.shop900.com*, M-Sa 10AM-7PM, Su noon-6PM. 70 specialty shops in the most stunning of the Michigan Avenue department stores. Includes **MaxMara**, among the most expensive stores for women's apparel on a street that's known for expense.

American Girl Place, 111 E Chicago Ave (*Chicago Red Line*), +1 877-247-5223, *www.americangirl.com*, Su-W 9AM-7PM, Th-Sa 9AM-9PM. Dolls. Doll houses. Doll hair salon. A doll hospital. Doll photo studio. Tea with dolls. Brunch, lunch, and dinner with dolls. Stories about dolls. Theater with dolls. Dolls starting controversies by calling Pilsen an unsafe place to grow up. Other than that,

pretty much your average store.

Ann Taylor, 600 N Michigan Ave (*Grand Red Line*), +1 312 587-8301, *www.anntaylor.com*, M-Sa 10AM-8PM, Su 11AM-6PM. Money rushes out of wallets at this fashionable women's store, anchor of the 600 N Michigan shopping complex. If you like what you see, also check out the **Ann Taylor Loft** *www.anntaylorloft.com* at 520 N Michigan, and another at Water Tower Place (see below).

Apple Store, 679 N Michigan Ave (*Chicago Red Line*), +1 312 981-4104, *www.apple.com*, M-Sa 10AM-9PM, Su 11AM-6PM. For some, a welcome respite from all of the clothes; for others, just more expensive fashion. This Apple-sleek showroom carries the full line of the company's products and accessories, and is usually packed with on-lookers pawing at all of the pretty designs. Several workshops are held each day for the true believers.

Burberry, 633 N Michigan Ave (*Grand Red Line*), +1 312 266-7440, *www.burberry.com*, M-Sa 9:30AM-6PM, Su 12-5PM. Fashion for men, women, and children from the English retail legend, famous for their made-to-order trench coats.

Cartier Inc., 630 N Michigan Ave (*Grand Red Line*), +1 312 787-2500, *www.cartier.com*, M-Sa 10AM-6PM. Boutique for the French jeweler and watchmaker.

The Disney Store, 717 N Michigan Ave (*Chicago Red Line*), +1 312 654-9208, M-F 10AM-8PM, Sa 10AM-7PM, Su 11AM-6PM. You know what you're getting into when you walk through these doors. It's the perfect place to reward a Disney fan who's been well-behaved during your family trip, but if you're on a budget, don't risk coming within two blocks.

Ermenegildo Zegna, 645 N Michigan Ave (*Grand Red Line*), +1 312 587-9660, *www.zegna.com*, M-Sa 10AM-6PM, Su 12-5PM. All of the elements for an excessively fashionable man, from shoes to shirts to suits.

Giorgio Armani, 800 N Michigan Ave (*Chicago Red Line*), +1 312 751-2244, *www.giorgioarmani.com*, M-Sa 10AM-6PM, Su 12-5PM. Boutique for the star Italian designer of men and women's fashion.

Neiman Marcus Showroom, 737 N Michigan Ave (*Chicago Red Line*), +1 312 642-5900, *www.neimanmarcus.com*, M-Sa 10AM-7PM, Su 12-5PM. Prada, Chanel, and other designer accessories in this distinctive Michigan Avenue store.

Niketown, 669 N Michigan Ave (*Grand Red Line*), +1 312 642-6363, *www.niketown.com*, M-Sa 10AM-8PM, Su 10AM-6PM. Not quite the hot-spot it was after it opened in 1993, when lines wrapped around the block to get in, but Niketown still exists somewhere between a store and a shrine to Nike products. Athletes from visiting sports teams can often be seen here paying homage (and cash).

Nordstrom's, 55 E Grand Ave (*Grand Red Line*), +1 312 464-1515, *www.nordstom.com*, M-Sa 10AM-8PM, Su 11AM-6PM. Clothes and accessories for men, women, and children, including a wide selection of shoes.

Old Plank Antiques, 3 E Huron St (*Grand Red Line*), +1 312 981-7000, *www.oldplankonhuron.com*, M-Sa 11AM-5PM. Antiques from around the world, intended to be accessible to budgets large and small.

Salvatore Ferragamo, 645 N Michigan Ave (*Grand Red Line*), +1 312 397-0464, *www.ferragamo.com*, M-Sa 10AM-6PM, Su 12-5PM. Fashionable boutique for women's apparel and accessories. The store is far from cluttered; what they have will sell, and they know it.

The Shops at North Bridge, 520 N Michigan Ave (*Grand Red Line*), +1 312 327-2300, *www.theshopsatnorthbridge.com*, M-Sa 10AM-8PM, Su 11AM-6PM. Includes another Nordstom, a Spa Nordstom, a LEGO store, fifty more specialty shops, and physically connected to the Conrad Chicago hotel.

Tails in the City, 1 E Delaware Pl (*Chicago Red Line*), +1 312 649-0347, *www.tailsinthecity.com*, M-Sa 10AM-6PM, Su 12-5PM. Designer treats and accessories for the fashion-conscious cat and the trend-minded dog.

Tiffany & Co., 730 N Michigan Ave (*Chicago Red Line*), +1 312 944-7500, *www.tiffany.com*, M-Sa 10AM-6PM, Su 12-5PM. Internationally renowned retailer of jewelry, sterling silverware, china, crystal, and more.

NEAR NORTHEAT

Water Tower Place, 835 N Michigan Ave (*Chicago Red Line*), +1 312 440-3166, *www.shopwatertower.com*, M-Sa 10AM-9PM, Su 11AM-6PM. Features an eight-level atrium and over a hundred stores, from fashionable clothes to the Chicago Cubs Clubhouse.

Other shops

Abraham Lincoln Book Shop, 357 W Chicago Ave (*Chicago Brown Line*), +1 312 944-3085, M-W,F 9AM-5PM, Th 9AM-7PM, Sa 10AM-4PM. Offers "Historical Americana," namely Lincoln and Civil War items, rare and autographed books, an amazing collection of Civil War photographs and salt prints, and all sorts of fascinating miscellany. Check out their "Essential" shelves for aspiring collectors and see how your own stacks up. Appraisal services are also available.

Alaska Gallery of Eskimo Art, 104 E Oak St, +1 312 943-3393, *www.alaskainuitart.net*, M-F 11AM-3PM, Sa 12:30PM-5PM. Probably one of the better places to buy Inuit Art in the world, with an expert, honest staff and high-quality Inuit carvings for sale.

The Merchandise Mart, 222 Merchandise Mart Plaza (*Merchandise Mart Brown Line*), +1 312 527-7990, *www.merchandisemart.com*, Hours vary by store. The Mart strides the barrier between River North and the Loop, with a train station and a zip code all to itself, not to mention a Holiday Inn, several offices, a school, two radio stations, restaurants, and, of course, shopping. It also includes the Chicago Apparel Center *www.merchandisemart.com*. None of the stores are considered major destinations by themselves, but there are frequent trade shows, and many other reasons for business travelers to find themselves at the Mart.

Eat

Budget

This is expensive territory — if you're on a tight budget, you're likely to be stuck with fast food. Most of the department stores on Michigan Ave have food courts.

The Billy Goat, 430 N Michigan Ave, Lower Level (*Grand Red Line*), +1 312 222-1525, *www.billygoattavern.com*, M-F 6AM-2AM, Sa 10AM-2AM, Su 11AM-2AM. The original location of the famous cheezborger joint. Due to its location under the Tribune Tower, this one has been a haunt for Chicago newspapermen for decades. The burgers are dry and little more than patty and cheese, but delicious nonetheless. $4-7.

Dao Thai, 230 E Ohio St (*Grand Red Line*), +1 312 337-0000, *www.daothai.com*, Su-Th 11AM-10PM, F-Sa 11AM-11PM. Thai food in a spacious, beautiful dining room with plenty of flavor and filling portions. The service can get a bit distracted, but the cooks are always focused. $7-9.

Downtown Dogs, 804 N Rush St (*Chicago Red Line*), +1 312

951-5141, M-Th 11AM-8PM, F-
Sa 11AM-9PM, Su 11AM-7PM.
Chicago-style hot dogs, all the
way down to the traditional prohibition on ketchup. And dog lovers
(of the furry kind) will likely be
tickled pink by the wild, mixed-
media canine propaganda.

Mr. Beef, 666 N Orleans St
(*Chicago Brown Line*), +1 312
337-8500, 8AM-5PM M-Th,
10:30AM-4AM F-Sa. Should Mr.
Beef ever decide to raise an army,
city hall ought to be concerned;
his Italian beef sandwiches have
a fiercely loyal following among
the River North lunch crowd,
some of whom won't bother with
anywhere else. It's closed for
dinner, but open for the late-night
weekend club scene.

**Original Rock 'n Roll McDon-
ald's**, 600 N Clark St (*Grand Red
Line*), +1 312 664-7940, Open 24
hours. It's still McDonald's, with
all that entails, and reportedly the
third-busiest one in the United
States; but there's vintage rock
and roll memorabilia to excuse the
visit to your conscience, if that's
possible.

Portillo's, 100 W Ontario Ave
(*Grand Red Line*), +1 312 587-8910,
www.portillos.com, 10AM-11PM.
Polishes, Italian Beef, Burgers,
and everything else you would
expect at a hot dog place, plus
one surprise—the chocolate cake
milkshake (it's not on the menu,
but order a "cake shake," and
sweet tooths will have their day).
This location, which includes
a drive-thru, is decked out in
a "Gangster" theme, which is
known to produce delight in

tourists and queasiness in locals.

Wow Bao, 835 N Michigan Ave,
+1 312 642-5888, M-F 10AM-8PM,
Sa 10AM-9PM, Su 10:30AM-6PM.
A good way to fill up on cheap
delicious food on the Magnificent
Mile, Wow Bao offers carryout
steamed Chinese buns filled with
all sorts of wonderful meaty good-
ness. $1-3.

Mid-range

Café Iberico, 739 N LaSalle St, +1
312 573-1510, *www.cafeiberico.com*,
M-Th 11AM-11:30PM, F 11AM-
1:30AM, Sa Noon-1:30AM, Su
Noon-11PM price=$18-30. Span-
ish tapas place, usually crowded.
Quite good food.

Le Colonial, 937 N Rush St, +1 312
255-0088, Lunch: noon-2:30PM
daily, Dinner: M-F 5PM-11PM,
Sa 5PM-midnight, Su 5-10PM.
Excellent upmarket Vietnamese
cuisine with a French Indochina
theme. Reservations would be a
good idea. $18-30.

Ed Debevic's, 640 N Wells St
(*Chicago Brown Line*), +1 312
664-1707, *www.eddebevics.com*,
Su-Th 11AM-10PM, F-Sa 11AM-
11:30PM. Affable tourist trap
with burgers, mock-rude service
and occasional *Grease* style song-
and-dance performances by the
wait-staff.

Frontera Grill, 445 N Clark St
(*Merchandise Mart Brown Line*), +1
312 661-1434, *www.rickbayless.com*,
Lunch Tu-F 11:30AM-2:30PM, Sa
10:30AM-2:30PM; Dinner Tu 5:20-
10PM, W-Th 5-10PM, F-Sa 5-
11PM. Renowned chef **Rick Bay-**

NEAR NORTH EAT

less presents authentic Mexican cuisine as most have never experienced it (outside of Mexico), with a particular emphasis on seafood. Frontera won the 2007 James Beard Award for Outstanding U.S. Restaurant.

Topolobampo, 445 N Clark St, +1 312 661-1434, *www.rickbayless.com*, Tu 11:45AM-2PM, W-F 11:30AM-2PM; Dinner Tu-Th 5:30-9:30PM, 5:30-10:30PM F-Sa. The high-class, dressier side of the house. Frontera is more casual, though still top-notch. Reservations are necessary at Topolobampo, while Frontera is first-come, first-serve.

XOCO, 449 N Clark St, +1 312 334-3688, *www.rickbayless.com*, Tu-Th 7AM-9PM, F 7AM-10PM, Sa 8AM-10PM. The newest outlet in the Bayless empire focuses on "street food" of Mexico, with highlights including the red chile chicken and the Xoco salad (pork carnitas, mixed greens, and avocado-lime dressing). Good soups are on later in the day. No reservations are taken — just line up and watch the chefs at work, as the kitchen is in full view. $10-14.

Ghirardelli Chocolate Shop, 830 N Michigan Ave (*Chicago Red Line*), +1 312 337-9330, *www.ghirardelli.com*, Su-Th 10AM-10:30PM, F-Sa 10AM-midnight. Right behind the Water Tower; stop in for the soda fountain, the hot fudge sundae, and other chocolate treats.

Gino's East, 633 N Wells St (*Grand Red Line, Chicago Brown Line*), +1 312 943-1124, *www.ginoseast.com*, M-Th 11AM-10PM, F-Sa 11AM-11PM, Su noon-9PM. Deep-dish and thin-crust pizza.

Kendall College Dining Room, 900 N North Branch St (*3rd floor*), +1 312 752-2328, *culinary.kendall.edu*, Lunch: M-F noon-1:30PM, Dinner: T-F 6PM-8PM, Sa 6PM-8:30PM. Fine dining, *fantastic* skyline views, very reasonable prices, all prepared by student chefs. Goose Island is out of the way, but there is a free parking lot. Some of Chicago's top chefs learned their trade at Kendall College, so expect to be in for a treat. Open only seasonally, so check the website in advance of your visit. $20-30.

Lou Malnati's, 439 N Wells St (*Merchandise Mart Brown Line*), +1 312 828-9800, *www.loumalnatis.com*, M-Th 11AM-11PM, F-Sa 11AM-midnight, Su noon-10PM. One of the deep dish pizza giants; pleasant hole-in-the-wall atmosphere a short walk from the Merchandise Mart.

Mity Nice Grill, 835 N Michigan Ave, Water Tower Place Mall, 2nd floor, +1 312 335-4745, M-F 11AM-9PM, F-Sa 11AM-10PM, Su 11AM-8PM. Billed as a "1940s Style Bar and Grill." Even on busy nights, you won't wait long for a table, but reservations are accepted. Fare includes steaks, seafood selections, pasta, and excellent recurring daily specials like meatloaf and a turkey dinner.

Pizzeria UNO, 29 E Ohio St (*Grand Red Line*), +1 312 321-1000, *www.unos.com*, Su 11AM-11:30PM, M-F 11AM-1AM, Sa 11AM-2AM. By some reckonings, the original deep dish pizza joint. The name has been diminished over the last few years by over-expansion, but this is the original location — they do it better here. Their Italian beef is excellent as well. See also DUE, around the corner at 619 N Wabash.

Tutto Pronto, 401 E Ontario St, +1 312 587-7700, *www.tuttoprontoitaliano.com*, M-Th,Su 7AM-10PM, F-Sa 7AM-111PM. It's not right for a place that's this good to be this little known. Tutto Pronto is a gourmet Italian deli with an import store for wine and other niceties, and an ideal lunch spot. They serve panini sandwiches unlike anywhere else that are eyes-watering good every time. $10-18.

Weber Grill, 539 N State St (*inside the Hilton Garden Inn*), +1 312 467-9696, *www.webergrillrestaurant.com*, M-Th 11AM-11PM, F 11AM-midnight, Sa 11:30AM-midnight, Su 11:30AM-11PM. A local grill & BBQ chain from the suburbs serving up the best BBQ in downtown Chicago. But keep in mind that the steaks are of low quality and overpriced and that the best of Chicago barbecue is off in the neighborhoods — look for Smoque on the Far Northwest Side or any of the great South Side Memphis-style BBQ joints. $12-36.

Splurge

Cité, 505 N Lake Shore Dr, +1 312 644-4050, *www.citechicago.com*, Su-Th 5:30PM-10PM, F-Sa 5:30PM-11PM. An upscale French/American restaurant

most notable for its 360 degree views from the 70th floor of the Lake Point Tower. The food, while very good, does not quite live up to its price, but the view is really what you come here for anyway. Jacket required. $51+.

Coco Pazzo, 300 W Hubbard St, +1 312 836-0900, *www.cocopazzochicago.com*, Lunch M-F 11:30AM-2:30PM, Dinner M-Th 5:30-10:30PM, F-Sa 5:30-10:30PM, Su 5-10PM. Very tasty Italian cafe. Try the gnocchi, and save some room for the fruit desserts. $30+.

Fogo de Chao, 661 N LaSalle St, +1 312 932-9330, *www.fogodechao.com*, Lunch M-F 11AM-2PM, Dinner M-Th 5-10PM, F 5-10:30PM, Sa 4:30-10:30PM, Su 4-9:30PM. Brazilian steakhouse with a twist: diners receive a disc to put in front of their plate, and if it's green, waiters will surround you with skewers of hot meats, unrelenting until you flip the disc over to red. prix fixe, lunch: $24.50, dinner: $38.50.

Gene & Georgetti, 500 N Franklin St, +1 312 527-3718, *www.geneandgeorgetti.com*, 11AM-midnight. This venerable Chicago steakhouse (over 60 years old) has played host to venerable Chicago steak eaters like Frank Sinatra and Lucille Ball as well as contemporary big shots. It is a traditional Italian-American steakhouse and serves some of the best steak in a city that takes these things seriously.

Gibsons Bar and Steakhouse, 1028 N Rush St (*Clark/Division*

Red Line), +1 312 266-8999, www.gibsonssteakhouse.com, 11AM-midnight; bar 11AM-2AM. Look on the wall at the pictures of countless celebrities who have dined at Gibsons and you'll see why it's a must for those who want to stretch their wallets during a visit to Chicago. You may run into a celebrity yourself.

Lawry's Prime Rib, 100 E Ontario St, +1 312 787-5000, www.lawrysonline.com, Lunch M-Sa 11:30AM-2PM, Dinner M-Th 5-10:30PM, F-Sa 5-10PM, Su 3-10PM. As elegant an interior as any Chicago restaurant can offer. Mind the dress code, and come carnivorous or don't come at all.

Naha, 500 N Clark St, +1 312 321-6242, www.naha-chicago.com, Lunch: M-F 11:30AM-2PM, Dinner: M-Th 5:30PM-9:30PM, F-Sa 5:30PM-10PM. An exceptional fusion restaurant headed by a star Armenian-American chef and specializing in Californian and Mediterranean-inspired dishes. $40-80.

Rosebud's Steakhouse, 192 E Walton Pl (Chicago Red Line), +1 312 397-1000, www.rosebudrestaurants.com, M-Th 11:30AM-11PM, F 11:30AM-midnight, Sa 3PM-midnight, Su 3-10PM. A strong contender in the Best Burger in Chicago stakes, and not bad for steaks either. There's also **Rosebud's on Rush** www.rosebudrestaurants.com, an older branch with more celebrity photos on the wall, but the Walton location is more of a favorite with the neighborhood.

Spiaggia, 980 N Michigan Ave (Chicago Red Line), +1 312 280-2750, www.levyrestaurants.com, M-Th 6-9:30PM, F-Sa 5:30-10:30PM, Su 6-9PM; Lounge 5:30-11PM. World-class contemporary regional Italian fair with classic touches in a remarkable dining room overlooking the Magnificent Mile. Jackets required for men, though ties are optional. $30-90.

Drink

Rush Street is probably the single best-known street for drinking and clubbing in Chicago. It's lined with late-night bars, both fashion-of-the-moment designer clubs and generic fake-Irish pubs. Rush Street branches off from State south of Elm and runs parallel to State from there, although the action is north of Chicago Avenue. There's also a similar densely-populated strip of late-night clubs on **Division**, between Clark and State.

Andy's Jazz Club, 11 E Hubbard St, +1 312 642-6805, M-F 11:30AM-1:30AM, Sa 5PM-2AM, Su 5PM-1AM. A nice and slightly less pretentious jazz club featuring straight-ahead performances nightly. Admission: Su-Th $5, F-Sa $10, Dinner: $15-25.

Blue Chicago, 736 N Clark St (Chicago Brown Line), +1 312 642-6261, www.bluechicago.com, Su-F 8PM-2AM, Sa 8PM-3AM. Live blues most nights of the week, except for Sundays. Has a sister club by the same name just a couple blocks away at 536 N Clark (312 661-0100, no music on Mondays).

Cover Su-Th $8, F-Sa $10.

Cityfront 455, 455 N Cityfront Plaza (*in the NBC Tower*), +1 312 494-1452, M-Th 4PM-10PM, F-Sa 4PM-midnight. A very nice wine bar in the NBC Tower lobby with helpful staff. Also serves high quality vodkas and martinis.

Excalibur, 632 N Dearborn St, +1 312 266-1944, *www.excaliburchicago.com*, Open 5PM-4AM most nights, until 5AM on Saturdays. Listed more for the spectacle than the actual experience of drinking and dancing here, this dance club has been attracting minor celebrities and hordes of hook-up seeking citydwellers and suburbanites for years. Just watching partygoers totter in from the outdoor seating at Pizzeria UNO (see above) can be hysterical.

The Hangge-Uppe, 14 W Elm St, +1 312 337-0561, *www.rushanddivision.com*, Su-F to 4AM, Sa to 5AM. The best bar in the Rush/Division nexus. Drinks aren't over-priced, the decor is cool, and there are two floors for dancing, depending on whether you prefer retro or modern beats.

House of Blues, 329 N Dearborn St, +1 312 923-2000, *www.hob. com*, Hours vary by event; Sunday morning gospel brunch starts at 10AM. Food, drinks, and music. Blues fans may find something good, but the roster of bands can stray from the classic old bluesman with a guitar to the worst of twentieth-century music (no genre excepted), so don't show

up without checking the schedule first. Tickets can run as low as $10 and upwards of $55 for some national touring acts.

The Original Mother's, 26 W Division St, +1 312 642-7251, *www.rushanddivision.com*, Su-F 8PM-4AM, Sa to 5AM. Hugely popular bar that trades on old rock-and-roll cred — Cream, The Velvet Underground played here long ago — to adorn a modern dance floor and pool tables.

Pippin's Tavern, 806 N Rush St (*Chicago Red Line*), +1 312 787-5435, *www.rushanddivision.com*, Su-F to 4AM, Sa to 5AM. Fake Irish pub, notable mainly for being tucked away behind the Water Tower, right off the Magnificent Mile. The after-work crowd is generally laid back, and the lack of (excessively) loud music and sports TV makes this a decent choice for exhausted shoppers in need of a beer.

The Redhead Piano Bar, 16 W Ontario St, +1 312 640-1000, *www. theredheadpianobar.com*, Sat 7PM-5AM, Sun-Fri 7PM-4AM. Cocktails, live music, and a schmaltzy sort of elegance.

Second Story Bar, 157 E Ohio St, Apt 2 (*Grand Red Line*), +1 312 923-9536, Su-F noon-2AM, Sa noon-3AM. It's no small feat to find this place — look for the pink-lettered sign up on, well, the second story. Inside, you'll find a gay bar that falls on the fun side of sleazy (or the sleazy side of fun), far more of a dive than you would expect in these surroundings and the perfect antidote to hotel bars.

Signature Room, John Hancock Center, 875 N Michigan Ave (*Chicago Red Line*), +1 312 787-9596, *www.signatureroom.com*, Su-Th 5-10PM, F-Sa 5-11PM. Just above the Hancock Observatory (above). Expensive drinks on the 95th floor, with live jazz on the weekends. Skip the over-priced food, but the view makes this a great place for evening cocktails, and a more civilized alternative to the sometimes over-crowded observatory one floor below.

Sleep

Again, this is expensive territory — nearly every tourist stays here, and the rates reflect that. If price is a concern, remember that this area is well-served by public transportation from every direction, including places where you can sleep a bit cheaper. On the other hand, if part of the vision for your vacation is a memorable hotel, this is definitely the place to be.

Budget

The Allerton Hotel Chicago, 701 N Michigan Ave (*Chicago Red Line*), +1 312 440-1500, *www.theallertonhotel.com*. Classic Chicago building with modern interiors; generations have known it for the neon TIP TOP TAP at the top of the building, referring to the swanky club that operated up there in the 1950's (but not any more). Rooms from $189 a night.

Best Western River North, 125 W Ohio St (*Chicago Brown Line*), +1 800 704-6941, *www.rivernorthhotel. com*. A little bit out of the way, but close to I-90/94 for easy travels by car; amenities include free parking and an indoor pool. Rooms from $159 per night.

Comfort Inn & Suites Downtown Chicago Hotel, 15 E Ohio St (*Grand Red Line*), +1 312 894-0900, *www.chicagocomfortinn.com*. Rooms from $179 a night.

Fairfield Inn & Suites by Marriott, 216 E Ontario St (*Grand Red Line*), +1 312 787-3777, *www.fairfieldsuiteschicago.com*. 185 rooms and suites just one block east of Michigan Avenue on the corner of Ontario St and N St Clair St. Rooms from $129.

Flemish House of Chicago, 68 E Cedar St, +1 312 664-9981, *www. innchicago.com*. Furnished studio and one bedroom apartments in a historic 19th century greystone on a quiet Gold Coast street. Rooms from $150.

Howard Johnson Inn Downtown Chicago, 720 N LaSalle St (*Chicago Brown Line*), +1 312 664-8100, *www.hojo.com*. Slightly inconspicuous, but in a great location for sights throughout the Near North and the Loop. Parking available. Rooms from $139 per night.

Red Roof Inn, 162 E Ontario St (*Grand Red Line*), +1 312 787-1299, *www.redroof-chicago-downtown. com*. A bit incongruous, but right in the middle of things. Rooms from $139.

Tokyo Hotel, 19 E Ohio St (*Grand Red Line*), +1 312 787-4900. Seedy to the hilt, but it's in a safe neighborhood, and a historic building. Popular with international backpackers. The hotel has two budget restaurants by its street entrance: **Ginza** (Japanese, +1 312 222-0600) and **Yu Shan** (Chinese, +1 312 527-4400). Rooms from $45.

The Whitehall Hotel, 105 E Delaware Pl (*Chicago Red Line*), +1 312 944-6300, *www.thewhitehallhotel.com*. An independent, high-rise hotel in a quiet pocket just down the street from the Hancock and Water Tower Place. Rooms from $169 a night.

Mid-range

Avenue Hotel Chicago, 160 E Huron St (*Grand Red Line*), +1 877 283-5110, *www.avenuehotelchicago.com*. Located in the heart of Magnificent Mile, formerly the Radisson. Rooms from $209 a night.

Conrad Chicago, 521 N Rush St (*Grand Red Line*), +1 312 645-1500, *conradhotels1.hilton.com*. Adjoins The Shops at North Bridge. Rooms from $215.

The Drake, 140 E Walton Pl (*Chicago Red Line*), +1 312 787-2200, *www.thedrakehotel.com*. It was swallowed into the Hilton chain some years ago, but the Drake is still the definition of old Chicago elegance. Founded in 1920, it's on the National Register of Historic Places, and probably has a longer list of celebrity guests than any hotel in the city, save possibly the Palmer House in the Loop. It's right off Michigan Avenue and the prime shopping district. Rooms from $255 a night.

Embassy Suites Chicago-Downtown Magnificent Mile (Grand Red Line), 600 N State St, +1 312 943-3800, *www.embassysuiteschicago.com*. Not right on Michigan Avenue, despite the name, but an easy walk. Rooms from $249 a night.

Four Points by Sheraton Chicago, 630 N Rush St, +1 312 981-6600, *www.fourpointschicago.com*. New hotel with 226 rooms and suites that include in-room refrigerators and microwaves; many rooms also feature balconies and whirlpool tubs. Service is excellent, and this is a good place to find cheap rates during slow periods. Rooms from $275.

Hilton Garden Inn Chicago Downtown Magnificent Mile, 10 E Grand Ave, +1 877 782-9444, *hiltongardenchicago.com*. Located just off the Magnificent Mile, and adjacent to the River North dining & entertainment area. Rooms from $229 a night.

James Hotel Chicago, 55 E Ontario St (*Grand Red Line*), +1 877 526-3755, *www.jameshotels.com*. A boutique hotel with a gym, restaurant, and modern touches such as large LCD TV's, iPod docks, wireless internet, and martini glasses in the mini-bar. Rooms from $279 a night.

Omni Chicago Hotel, 676 N Michigan Ave (*Chicago Red Line*), +1 312 944-6664, *www.omnihotels.com*. Among the amenities are an indoor swimming pool and two rooftop sundecks. Rooms from $229.

NEAR NORTH SLEEP

Sheraton Chicago Hotel and Towers, 301 E North Water St (*Grand Red Line*), +1 877-242-2558, *www.sheratonchicago.com*. The Sheraton does enormous business for business meetings and conventions. Most rooms offer views over the Chicago River. The hotel has a steak house (Shula's) and a burger joint, as well as an indoor swimming pool. Rooms from $199 a night.

The Talbott Hotel, 20 E Delaware Pl (*Chicago Red Line*), +1 312 944-4970, *www.talbotthotel.com*. 16-story boutique hotel down the block from the Hancock. Though built in 1927, they tout their eco-friendly updates. *Crain's* ranked it the city's best hotel for business travelers. Rooms from $209 a night.

Wyndham Chicago Hotel, 633 N St Clair St, +1 312 573-0300, *www.wyndham.com*. Friendly staff, decent rooms with plenty of business amenities. If you register for the Wyndham ByRequest "frequent traveler" program, when you arrive, your favorite music will be playing in your room and a plate of fruit and iced tea (or whatever you choose) will be waiting for you. Rooms from $233.

Splurge

The Four Seasons, 120 E Delaware Pl (*Chicago Red Line*), +1 312 280-8800, *www.fourseasons.com*. Right across from the Hancock. Rooms from $470 a night.

InterContinental Chicago, 505 N Michigan Ave (*Grand Red Line*), +1 312 944-4100, *www.icchicagohotel.com*. Originally built as an athletic club, the InterContinental is flush with gorgeous 1920's design flourishes. The grand swimming pool on the 14th floor is simply astonishing — worth a look whether you've brought your trunks or not. (If you're not staying here, $15 can usually get you access to the sauna and pool.) Rooms from $349 a night.

Millennium Knickerbocker Hotel, 163 E Walton Pl (*Chicago Red Line*), +1 312 751-8100, *www.millenniumhotels.com*. Across from the Drake and right around the corner from Michigan Avenue, with **Nix**, a quiet, knockout-delicious cafe/restaurant on the first floor (at knockout-expensive prices). Rooms from $329.

The Park Hyatt, 800 N Michigan Ave (*Chicago Red Line*), +1 312 335-1234, *parkchicago.hyatt.com*. A bona-fide member of the Chicago skyline, towering over the Water Tower and the Magnificent Mile. Guest rooms are sleek, stylish, and comfortable, and the hotel's NoMi restaurant is quite good. Rooms from $495 a night.

The Peninsula, 108 E Superior St (*Grand Red Line*), +1 866 288-8889, *chicago.peninsula.com*. The Peninsula has been recognized by AAA with a Five-Diamond award. That combined with its high prices and the Mag Mile address mean top-notch service, bells & whistles, and impressive views. Those not sleeping here may want to stop by on a Friday or Saturday night for the Lobby's all-you-can-eat high-end chocolate buffet

(8PM-11:30PM, $26). Rooms from $525 a night.

The Ritz Carlton, 160 E Pearson St (*Chicago Red Line*), +1 312 266-1000, *www.fourseasons.com*. Atop the Water Tower Place shopping center. Rooms from $470 a night.

Contact

Biznet Internet Cafe, 205 E Ohio St (*Grand Red Line*), +1 312 645-0065, M-F 9AM-9PM, Sa-Su 12-7PM. Tucked away on a side street, but only a short distance from Michigan Avenue. $5/hour.

Chicago Public Library, Near North Branch, 310 W Division St (*Clark/Division Red Line to 70 Division bus*), +1 312 744-0991, *www. chipublib.org*, M-Th 9AM-9PM, F-Sa 9AM-5PM. Public internet access. It's between the Sedgwick and Chicago Brown Line stations, but a long walk from either. The area is safe during the day, but don't walk far by night.

Cyber Cafe, 25 E Pearson St, +1 312 915-8595, M-Th 7AM-9:30PM, F-Sa 7AM-5PM. A Jesuit run internet cafe with coffee, snacks, antiques, and a quiet atmosphere.

The **Apple Store** (see Buy) is a de facto free internet cafe, with all of the floor models hooked up to wi-fi, and the salesmen-to-customer ratio virtually ensures nobody will bother you if you want to dash off a few emails home.

Get out

Old Town *p.123* is just north, and segues neatly into the Near North with smaller boutiques, smaller palatial mansions, and the city's landmark theaters Steppenwolf and Second City.

Wicker Park *p.229* offers a parallel Magnificent Mile of hip, independent stores, bars and clubs. Lincoln Square *p.313* is another exceptional shopping destination.

NEAR SOUTH UNDERSTAND

The **Near South** area of Chicago is bounded by Harrison St to the north, the Chicago River and Clark St/Federal St to the west, 26th St to the south, and Lake Michigan to the east. It includes the eclectic neighborhoods of **Printer's Row** and the **South Loop**.

Grant Park overflows from the Loop *p.47* into the Near South, leading right up to the main attractions on the lakefront: the splendid **Museum Campus**, with three world-class (and fun!) natural science museums; **Soldier Field**, home of the NFL's Chicago Bears; and **McCormick Place**, the city's massive convention center.

There's more to be found at the street level, though. The fascinating and eerie **Prairie Avenue** neighborhood was the first "prestige address" in Chicago. Forgotten for many years, it's now a portal into the Gilded Age. Also, there

are a couple of major **jazz** and **blues** landmarks.

Understand

The neighborhoods of the Near South are among the oldest settlements in Chicago. They were once the most prestigious — and notorious — in the entire city. After being forgotten for several decades, they have recently been re-discovered and are buzzing with new activity.

Prairie Avenue, in particular, was the heart of Gilded Age Chicago, when the city was building fortunes at a rate unlike any the world had ever seen. At the time of the World's Columbian Exposition in 1893, held a few miles to the south *p.157*, 75 of the world's richest men lived on "Millionaire's Row," in mansions with gaslit grand ballrooms, golden chandeliers, and no pretense of modesty. Eventually, the city's elite

95

moved to the Gold Coast *p.71*, and the area fell into rapid decline; soon, it was all but abandoned. Today, of the eleven surviving residences on Prairie Avenue, nine are protected as Chicago landmarks. This is the Gilded Age as if the millionaires simply got up and left, leaving their mansions to weather the elements for over a hundred years.

The **Museum Campus** was born shortly before the 1933 World's Fair, as Chicago's business community set about to recapture the energy of the landmark 1893 Exposition. The Field Museum was already there; it had opened in the building that now houses the Museum of Science and Industry, and moved to this choice location by the lake in 1921. All three institutions received generous financial support put it support to good use in its early years, building world-class collections within their respective fields. They are housed in beautiful, historic buildings along the lakefront and rolling green-space, making a stroll through the area worth your time even if your budget won't let you past the front gates.

Printer's Row is a small and surprisingly tight-knit neighborhood just south of the Loop, centered around Harrison and Dearborn. In its early days, as an off-shoot of the infamous Levee District a few blocks south, it was the yin to Prairie Avenue's yang. In time, crusaders managed to force the closure of the bordellos and gambling houses, and Printer's Row earned its current, more respectable name, from its role as

the center of Chicago's publishing industry. The area fell into disuse, but then fortunes changed again; those warehouses and publishing houses became perfect stock for conversion to trendy loft residences. It has a reputation as an eclectic home to artists and writers, who moved in to enjoy the cheap downtown real estate along Dearborn Street. To be sure, the outrageous boom in downtown Chicago property values is bringing in a more white-collar crowd of lawyers and traders, but the neighborhood retains its eclectic, book-loving feel and is a pleasant evening alternative to the Near North *p.71* when you are looking for a helping of Chicago blues or an interesting restaurant.

Similarly, the **South Loop** was once as busy as the rest of the Loop *p.47*, and then, as development shifted northward, it became known as the place where the hustle and bustle of the Loop trailed off, a quiet zone between Bronzeville *p.191* and the central business district. Today, however, it's something else entirely — a mad rush of new construction has overtaken the place, with historic stone edifices interspersed among new steel-and-glass towers in varying stages of readiness, and trendy restaurants to exercise the wallets of the people who can afford to live there.

Get in

By train

The CTA Red Line stops near Printer's Row (Harrison) and in

the South Loop (Roosevelt/State, Cermak-Chinatown). Printer's Row is within reach of the Blue Line (LaSalle/Congress), too. The Orange and Green Lines also stop in the South Loop (Roosevelt/Wabash).

Both stations on Roosevelt are within walking distance of the Museum Campus, although buses and free trolleys also run the route.

By bus

The CTA runs a few convenient buses through the area:

4 Cottage Grove is a convenient north/south route along Michigan Ave, which leads to and from the South Side along Dr Martin Luther King Jr Dr, and Cottage Grove Ave.

6 Jeffrey Express comes from the South Side along Lake Shore Dr and stops at Roosevelt and Congress, which is close enough to reach the major attractions.

12 Roosevelt meets the CTA train stations and runs down Roosevelt to the edge of the Campus.

130 Grant Park runs directly from Union Station in the Loop *p.47* during the summer.

146 Michigan is a tourist favorite, running southbound from Michigan Avenue in the Near North *p.71*, though the Loop and past Grant Park, and arrives at Soldier Field and the Museum Campus.

Near South

■See and Do
1. Adler Planetarium
2. Arie Crown Theatre
3. Charter One Pavilion
4. Dearborn Station
5. Field Museum
6. Hilliard Homes
7. John G Shedd Aquarium
8. Clarke House Museum
9. Glessner House Museum
10. Marshall Field Jr Mansion
11. McCormick Place
12. National Vietnam Veterans Art Museum
13. Second Presbyterian Church
14. Soldier Field
15. Willie Dixon's Blues Heaven

▣Buy
1. Canady le Chocolatier
2. Loopy Yarns
3. Printer's Row Fine & Rare Books
4. Sandmeyer's Bookstore

▥Eat
1. Bongo Room
2. Cafe Mediterra
3. Chicago Firehouse Restaurant
4. Eleven City Diner
5. Gioco
6. Hackney's
7. Harold's Chicken Shack
8. Kroll's Chicago
9. La Cantina Grill
10. Opera
11. Oysy Japanese Sushi
12. Panozzo's Italian Market
13. Pat's Pizzeria
14. South Coast
15. Standing Room Only
16. Tamarind
17. Trattoria Caterina
18. Yolk
19. Zapatista

▣Drink
1. Buddy Guy's Legends
2. Kasey's Tavern
3. M Lounge
4. Reggie's
5. The Velvet Lounge

▤Sleep
1. Best Western Grant Park
2. Chicago Hilton & Towers
3. Essex Inn
4. Hyatt Regency McCormick Place
5. The Wheeler Mansion

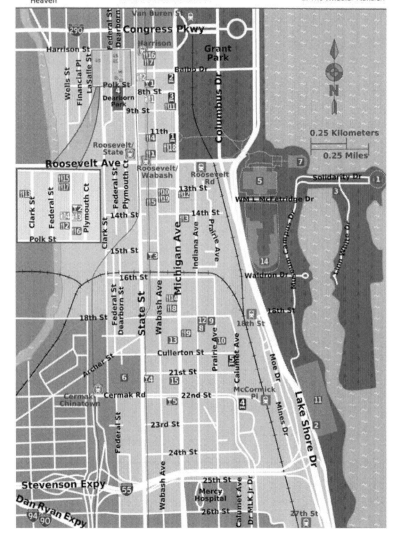

By car

Don't drive to the Near South without a good reason; parking is scarce and often expensive, especially around Soldier Field, the Museum Campus, and Mc-Cormick Center.

If you choose to drive, **Lake Shore Drive** is the key artery from the north or south, passing Soldier Field, McCormick Place, and the Museum Campus. Exits are clearly marked with lists of attractions. For the Museum Campus and Soldier Field, exit at 18th Street/McFetridge Drive. Coming from the Loop *p.47* to the north and Bronzeville *p.191* to the south, **Michigan Avenue** runs through the commercial and residential center of the area. Coming along the Stevenson Expressway, there are exits on to State Street, King Drive, and Lake Shore Drive.

In Printer's Row and the South Loop, parking is more or less what you would expect in the Loop *p.47* — look for a multi-story garage and expect to pay over $10 for a couple of hours. For the museums and McCormick Place, parking is available at public lots for $15 on days without special events, and totally unavailable on Sunday home games for the Bears; in that case, you'd be much better advised to come back another day.

Museum Campus

All three museums are within a short, pleasant walk from each other, even with toddlers and strollers in tow, so it's worth setting aside an entire day for your visit. Try to get your tickets in advance, though, as lines can be *hellacious*. Both the Field Museum and Shedd Aquarium sell tickets by phone and on-line, eliminating the wait; sadly, the Adler Planetarium is still walk-up only. The two major discount packages, **City-Pass** *citypass.com* and **Go Chicago Card** *www.gochicagocard.com*, may come in handy if you're planning to visit all three, but they do not necessarily cover admission to special exhibits. If you're staying with family and you can pass for Aunt Millie or Uncle Chuck, borrow their ID; Chicago residents receive a discount with proof of residency. Mondays and Tuesday are sometimes discounted, depending on the season.

Adler Planetarium, 1300 S Lake Shore Dr, +1 312 922-7827, *www.adlerplanetarium.org*, Daily 9:30AM-4:30PM, to 6PM in the summer, to 10PM on the first Friday of the month. It's the smallest and probably the least impressive of the three museums, but the oldest planetarium in the Western Hemisphere still packs a lot of fun. There are some interactive exhibits on the second floor, a scale model of the solar system, a few space rocks, and two high-tech dome theaters with nifty "star shows" throughout the day. Admission $10 adult, $6 children, $8 seniors, and shows $9/$15 for one/both. Chicago residents save $1-2.

Field Museum of Natural History, 1400 S Lake Shore Dr, +1 312 922-9410, *www.fieldmuseum.*

NEAR SOUTHSEE

org, Daily 9AM-5PM, last admission 4PM. The largest museum on the campus; highlights include Sue, the largest *Tyrannosaurus Rex* skeleton in the world, and the man-eating Tsavo lions; it might be the biggest collection of taxidermy in the world, in fact. Part of the collection came directly from the 1893 World's Columbian Exposition, adding a layer of intrigue to all of those dusty old animals. Another highlight is the great, kid-friendly Egyptian exhibit, and the Hall of Gems will impress, too. Traveling exhibitions tend to be excellent, so this is one place where it's worth shelling out for the extra shows. Regular admission $15 adults, $10 children, $12 seniors and students; Admission for 1/2/3 special exhibits is $23/29/34 adults, $13/16/18 children, $20/26/31 seniors and students. Chicago residents save $1-2.

John G. Shedd Aquarium, 1200 S Lake Shore Dr, +1 312 939-2438, *www.sheddaquarium.org*, M-F 9AM-5PM, Sa-Su 9AM-6PM; summer F-W 9AM-6PM, Th 9AM-10PM. Home to a massive collection of marine life from throughout the world, among the very best you'll ever see. The Pacific Northwest-themed Oceanarium features otters, beluga whales, and a panoramic view of Lake Michigan, although you'll need to arrive extremely early for the (free) dolphin show. The terrific new Wild Reef exhibit offers floor-to-ceiling windows for an extraordinary view of a Philippine coral reef environment, complete with dozens of sharks.

Admission is $24.95 adults, $17.95 children and $21.95 seniors, plus $2 for special exhibits. Chicago residents save 25%.

Prairie Avenue

The Prairie Avenue Historic District includes the 1800 and 1900 blocks of South Prairie, the 1800 block of South Indiana and 211 through 217 East Cullerton. Neighborhood tours are led by the Glessner House Museum a few times each year. If you happen to be in the area on Halloween, move heaven and earth to join the evening ghost tour, which roams through the Glessner House, meeting a magician a few times along the way, and then heads out to the wonderfully spooky street for a walking tour.

The Clarke House Museum, 1827 S Indiana Ave, +1 312 745-0041 (312 326-1480 for tours), *www.cityofchicago.org*, W-Su 12&2PM. Built in 1836, this unassuming little white house is the oldest surviving structure in Chicago. Tours are available through the Glessner House, but it's free to walk around the lovely Women's Park & Gardens that surround it. $10 adults, $9 students/senior, $5 children; add $5 to visit the Glessner House as well. Wednesdays free.

The Glessner House Museum, 1800 S Prairie Ave, +1 312 326-1480, *www.glessnerhouse.org*, Tours W-Su 1&3PM. A stately Arts & Crafts mansion from 1887, now fully restored and refurnished to its original Gilded Age atmosphere. The staff are hardworking, knowledgeable, and enthusiastic, and they take pride in the House and its history. $10 adults, $9 students/senior, $5 children; add $5 to visit the Clarke House as well. Wednesdays free.

Marshall Field Jr. Mansion, 1919 S Prairie Ave, +1 312 915-4713, *www.marshallfieldjrmansion.com*. No tours are offered, as this long-derelict property is being rehabbed for future residential use. This was the site of one of the great scandals of the Gilded Age. It was built by Marshall Field, the richest and most powerful man in Chicago, for his son. In 1905, the younger Field was found dead in his home under mysterious circumstances from a bullet wound. After two days, the family made the announcement that the bullet had been fired by accident during preparation for a hunting trip. According to rumors, though, he had been shot in a brothel in the notorious Levee. The elder Field died the next year, and the end of the Prairie Avenue era had begun.

National Vietnam Veterans Art Museum, 1801 S Indiana Ave, +1 312 326-0270, *www.nvvam.org*, Tu-F 11AM-6PM, Sa 10AM-5PM. A collection of over 500 evocative pieces of art, created by artists who served in Vietnam. Recently, the museum has also begun to hold exhibitions on the Iraq war. $10 adults, $7 children.

Second Presbyterian Church, 1936 S Michigan Ave, +1 312 225-4951, *www.2ndpresbyterian.org*, Worship Su 11AM (10AM July-August); open W-F 8AM-4PM, Sa 8AM-12PM, Su 8AM-2PM. Tours by appointment. Windows

designed by Louis Tiffany and other stained-glass masters for a proudly diverse congregation.

Willie Dixon's Blues Heaven Foundation (Chess Records Studio), 2120 S Michigan Ave., +1 312 808-1286, *www.bluesheaven.com*, M-F 12-3PM, Sa 12-2PM. A major blues hotspot where Muddy Waters, Ahmad Jamal, Chuck Berry, Aretha Franklin, Bo Diddley, Etta James, Buddy Guy, John Lee Hooker, Ramsey Lewis, and many other greats recorded during Chicago's bluesiest period. The Rolling Stones also recorded here, paying tribute in their instrumental "2120 S Michigan Avenue." Public tours.

Printer's Row

As the Loop *p.47* trails off into Printer's Row, there are still a few impressive buildings to be seen, especially on Dearborn and Plymouth. The Pontiac Building at **542 S Dearborn** is one of Chicago's oldest skyscrapers (Holabird & Roche, 1891), and the buildings at **731 S Plymouth** and **718 S Dearborn** have intriguing details that call back to their publishing past.

Today, the major draws of Printer's Row are the bookstores — see below.

Dearborn Station, 47 W Polk St, +1 312 554-4408, *www.dearbornstation.com*. Built in 1885, this was one of the great stations of the railroad era, the first glimpse of Chicago for countless visitors from across the country. (It also became a focal point for the anti-vice crusaders, with pamphlets describing lurid tales in which innocent farm girls fresh off the train were seized and sold into prostitution.) The rail yard is gone, with traffic having ceased in 1971, but the station house has been renovated into mixed-use commercial space, with a bar and restaurant on the ground floor.

Printer's Row Book Fair, Dearborn St & Polk St (*In Dearborn Park*), +1 312 222-3986, *www. printersrowbookfair.org*. Every June, readers converge upon Printer's Row for a celebration of books. Events with authors famous and obscure are held throughout the weekend, and almost 200 booksellers set up shop.

Hilliard Homes

In the architecture of these massive public housing projects lies the South Side's tongue-in-cheek answer to the North Side's Marina City—in fact, they were built by the same architect, Bertrand Goldberg. With its enormous corncob towers and northern semicircular wall, the Hilliard Homes are impossible to miss when traveling between Downtown and Chinatown *p.175*. Despite the architectural distinction of being the only public housing projects to get on the National Register of Historic Places, the towers have not always been a great place to live, suffering from urban blight similar to that found in public housing throughout the country. The complex is currently undergoing a major renovation that will lead to the cre-

ation of a mixed-income residential development. Located at State St and Cermak Ave.

Do

Arie Crown Theater, 2301 S Lake Shore Dr, +1 312 791-6190, *www.ariecrown.com*, Box Office: M-Sa 10AM-6PM. Comfortable sit-down music venue in the midst of McCormick Place. It hosts big pop, rock, gospel, and R&B concerts as well as occasional musical.

Charter One Pavilion at Northerly Island, 1300 S Lynn White Dr, +1 312 540-2668, *www.charteronepavilion.com*, Box office 12-9PM. This small peninsula, jutting out into Lake Michigan, was the site of Meigs Airport until Mayor Daley's midnight demolition raid a few years ago; now it's a 7500-seat concert venue for touring rock and hip-hop acts. Tickets vary by event, although if you don't mind not being able to see the stage, you'll hear the show just fine anywhere on the lakefront near the Museum Campus.

McCormick Place, 2301 S Lake Shore Dr, +1 312 791-7000, *www.mccormickplace.com*, Prices and hours vary by event. Mayor Richard J. Daley believed firmly — as his son, Mayor Richard M., does after him — in total, ruthless domination of the convention circuit. Hence, the massive complex of McCormick Place, which gets a makeover every few years for no reason other than to stay far ahead of the competition.

There's little reason to seek out McCormick Place if your business isn't already sending you there, but the auto shows are a draw for some visitors. Parking $16, regardless of time spent.

Soldier Field, 1410 S Museum Campus Dr, +1 312 235-7000, *www.soldierfield.net*. Home of the **Chicago Bears**. *www.chicagobears.com* If you'd like to see a Bears game, then you have something in common with many Chicagoans; there's no point in listing ticket prices, because they sell out long before the season starts. The original Soldier Field was built in 1924 to honor veterans of the First World War, and was added to the National Register of Historic Places in 1984. By 2002, the stadium was in dire need of renovations, and the Bears promised to preserve the majestic colonnades of the old stadium. However, when the renovations were complete, what appeared to be a giant spaceship had landed at mid-field. The amenities have improved, and it really is a nice facility…on the inside. On the outside, it's hard to say *what* it is, other than probably the strangest-looking sports arena in America. (It's not a Historic Place any more, having been stripped of that designation in 2006.) Tours are available during the week, M-F 9AM-5PM, by phone appointment; $15 adults, $10 students, $7 seniors, $4 children.

Buy

The Near South is not a shopping destination; there is no need

really, given that some of the world's most intense shopping experiences may be had in the two miles to the north. But a trip to **Printer's Row** can be a refreshing change of pace for downtown visitors who would prefer to browse independent bookstores.

Canady le Chocolatier, 824 S Wabash Ave, +1 312 212-1270, *www.canadylechocolatierchicago. com*, M-F 10:30AM-9PM, Sa-Su 11AM-9:30PM. Premium chocolate served in every form you might want it in. Some seating available. Great ice cream in summer.

Loopy Yarns, 719 S State St, +1 312 583-9276, *www.loopyyarns.com*, M-Th 11:30AM-7PM, F 11:30AM-9PM, Sa 10AM-6PM, Su 1-5PM. Yarn powerhouse. Classes are available, and Friday nights are an open-knitting party.

Printer's Row Fine and Rare Books, 715 S Dearborn St (*Harrison Red Line*), +1 312 583-1800, *www.printersrowbooks.com*, Tu-F 10AM-7PM, Sa-Su 11AM-5PM. Specializes in old and autographed books, although that doesn't mean visitors aren't welcome to relax and browse; actually, the decor insists upon it.

Sandmeyer's Bookstore, 714 S Dearborn St (*Harrison Red Line*), +1 312 922-2104, *www.sandmeyersbookstore.com*, M-W,F 11AM-6:30PM, Th 11AM-8PM, Sa 11AM-5PM, Su 11AM-4PM. A classic creaky-floors-and-cluttered-shelves kind of place.

NEAR SOUTHEAT

Eat

There are restaurants in each of the museums on the Museum Campus; the prices will replace the wonder of science with the wince of cold, hard economics. (It's odd enough that the Shedd Aquarium has a seafood restaurant, but no, you are not allowed to make selections from the aquarium floor.) If the weather's nice, take advantage of the beautiful scenery and bring a picnic lunch.

Budget

Cafe Mediterra, 728 S Dearborn St, +1 312 427-2610, M 7AM-9PM, Tu-F 7AM-10PM, Sa 8AM-9PM, Su 8AM-8PM. Greek and Mediterranean food, with plenty of space for lounging with drinks after your meal. A nice place, but it is a real shame that it replaced the quintessential Printer's Row coffee shop, Gourmand. $7-12.

Eleven City Diner, 1112 S Wabash Ave, +1 312 212-1112, *www.elevencitydiner.com*, M-Th 7:30AM-10PM, F 7:30AM-12AM, Sa 9AM-12AM, Su 9AM-9PM. New York-style Jewish diner. $7-14.

Hackney's, 733 S Dearborn St, +1 312 461-1116, *www.hackneysprintersrow.net*, M-F 10:30AM-11PM, Sa-Su 8:30AM-11:30PM. Printer's Row branch of the Chicagoland area beer 'n burgers chainlet. $8-10.

Harold's Chicken Shack No 62, 636 S Wabash Ave, +1 312 362-0442, 9AM-9PM. The prices are higher and the quality lower at

this central location of the great South Side chain, but it's still a great cheap eat. $4-7.

Panozzo's Italian Market, 1303 S Michigan Ave, +1 312 356-9966, *www.panozzositalianmarket.com*, Tu-F 10:30AM-7PM, Sa 10AM-5PM, Su 10AM-4PM. A neighborhood deli with sandwiches and such. Perfect place to prepare a picnic lunch for a day at the Museum Campus. $5-8.

Pat's Pizzeria, 638 S Clark St, +1 312 427-2320, 11AM-10PM. Cheap thin-crust pizza with a devoted following. Lunch during the work-week is crowded. $8-14.

Standing Room Only, 610 S Dearborn St, +1 312 360-1776, *www.srochicago.com*, M-Sa 4-11PM, Su 4-10PM. Burgers of the standard, turkey, and veggie variety. Standing room only. $8 delivers a whole sandwich meal.

Yolk, 1120 S Michigan Ave, +1 312 789-9655, *www.yolk-online.com*, M-F 6AM-3PM, Sa-Su 7AM-3PM. Breakfast place with egg-based dishes (obviously) and bright yellow walls (you've been warned). $8-10.

Mid-range

Bongo Room, 1152 S Wabash Ave, +1 312 291-0100, M-F 8AM-2:30PM, Sa-Su 9AM-2PM. Great breakfast/brunch location with no signage, a spin-off of the original Wicker Park restaurant. $9-14.

Kroll's Chicago, 1736 S Michigan Ave, +1 312 235-1400, *www.krolls-chicago.com*, Su-Th 11AM-10PM, F-Sa 11AM-11PM, lounge with limited menu open F-Sa until 2AM. Sister branch of a Green Bay fixture, which is a controversial move in the heart of Bears territory. They offer a big menu of seafood and sandwiches from a charcoal grill. Plenty of beer is available, but kids are welcome. $8-15.

La Cantina Grill, 1911 S Michigan Ave, +1 312 842-1911, *www.lacantinagrill.com*, M-Th 11AM-10PM, F 11PM-1AM, Sa 4PM-1AM, Su 4-10PM. Unpretentious, good Mexican cuisine. $10-$15.

Oysy Japanese Sushi, 888 S Michigan Ave, +1 312 922-1127, *www.oysysushi.com*, M-F 11:30-2:30,5-9:30PM; Sa 5-11PM, Su 5-9PM. Models itself upon a Japanese izakaya, and offers reasonably priced Japanese dishes like tempura and sushi rolls near Grant Park. $10-15.

South Coast, 1700 S Michigan Ave, +1 312 662-1700, *www.southcoastsushi.com*, M-Sa 4-11PM, Su 4-10PM. BYOB sushi bar. $15-$25.

Tamarind, 614 S Wabash Ave, +1 312 379-0970, *www.tamarindsushi.com*, 11AM-11PM. Japanese, Vietnamese, Thai and Chinese food. $8-25.

Trattoria Caterina, 616 S Dearborn St, +1 312 939-7606, M-Th 11AM-9PM, F 11AM-10PM, Sa 5-9PM. Hole-in-the-wall Italian restaurant. You can select from their wines or BYOB as you prefer. $9-15.

Zapatista, 1307 S Wabash Ave, +1 312 435-1307, *www.zapatistamexicangrill.com*, M-Th 11:30AM-10PM, F-Sa 11:30AM-11PM, Su 12-9PM. Stylish Mexican restaurant named for the revolutionary Emiliano Zapata; it's a little pricey during the week, but check out the Saturday and Sunday $5 brunch specials. $14-30, $5 for weekend brunch.

Splurge

Chicago Firehouse Restaurant, 1401 S Michigan Ave, +1 312 786-1401, *www.mainstayhospitality.com*, M-Th 11:30AM-10PM, F 11:30AM-10:30PM, Sa 5-10:30PM, Su 4:30-9PM. Fine American dining. $20-60.

Gioco, 1312 S Wabash Ave, +1 312 939-3870, *www.gioco-chicago.com*, Lunch: M-F 11:30AM-2:30PM, Dinner: Su-Th 5-10PM, F-Sa 5PM-midnight. Offers "rustic Italian" dishes. $15-$40.

Opera, 1301 S Wabash Ave., +1 312 461-0161, *www.opera-chicago.com*, Su-Th 5PM-10PM, F-Sa 5PM-12AM. Executive Chef Paul Wildermuth offers Chinese cuisine with "modern presentations," in a renovated Paramount film warehouse. $16-26.

Drink

Blues and jazz fans staying downtown have a real reason to come to the Near South at night in the form of two legendary clubs: Buddy Guy's Legends for the blues and the Velvet Lounge for jazz.

Buddy Guy's Legends, 754 S Wabash Ave (*corner of E 8th St*), +1 312 427-0333, *www.buddyguys. com*, M-F 11AM-2AM, Sa 5PM-3AM, Su 6PM-2AM. A famous, fairly large blues club with a cajun/soul food menu and frequent big-name acts.

Kasey's Tavern, 701 S Dearborn St (*Harrison Red Line*), +1 312 427-7992, *www.kaseystavern.com*, Su-F 11AM-2AM, Sa 12PM-3AM. Excellent dive bar in historic Printer's Row. Extensive beer selection, disgusting bathrooms and "Absolutely No Dancing." Kasey's is good for a drink before or after a Sox game.

Kitty O'Shea's, 720 S Michigan Ave (*inside the Chicago Hilton*), 312-294-6860, *www1.hilton.com*, Su-Th 11AM-1AM, F-Sa 11AM-2AM. Better than your average hotel bar, with a stately ambiance that's nevertheless hospitable to Bears fans on their way back from Soldier Field or Grant Park festival-goers.

Jazz Showcase, 806 S Plymouth Ct (*Harrison Red Line*), Box office +1 312 360-0234, *www.jazzshowcase. com*, Sets at 8 and 10 Mon-Sat, and at 4 PM and 8 and 10 on Sundays. Started in 1948 by Joe Segal, this historic jazz club is home to both national touring acts and the finest local jazz musicians Chicago has to offer. Currently located in the historic Dearborn Station building in the South Loop, Segal continues to maintain the high standard for acoustic jazz that over the years has featured luminaries from Dizzy Gillespie to Chick Corea.

M Lounge, 1520 S Wabash Ave, +1 312 447-0201, *www.mloungechicago.com*, Tu-Th 6PM-1AM, F-Sa 6PM-2AM. Martinis and jazz; live performances Tu-W, 7PM-10PM. Nights with music supposedly have a two drink minimum, but for cheapskates, it is unclear how this policy would be enforced. $12 martinis. $4+ beer, no cover.

Reggie's, 2105 & 2109 S State St, Joint: +1 312 949-0120, Club: +1 312 949-0121, *www.reggieslive.com*, Joint: Su-F 11AM-2AM, Sa 11AM-3AM; Club: hours vary by show. Reggie's Music Joint is a nice bar and grill that offers nightly live music, mostly by local rock bands, as well as a professional blues jam session every Wednesday night. The newly opened Reggie's Rock Club features bigger-name touring rock acts. If you want to take some music home, head upstairs over the Rock Club to Record Breakers, which sells new and used cds, lps, and other rock paraphernalia. Joint: no cover, Club: $7-15.

The Velvet Lounge, 67 E Cermak Rd, +1 312 791-9050, *www. velvetlounge.net*. Another essential stop on The Jazz Track, best reached by taxi. If you want to go to a bar that represents the real Chicago jazz tradition from Louis Armstrong right up to Pharaoh Sanders, then you must go to the Velvet Lounge.

Sleep

Since there are so many hotels in the Loop *p.47* and the Near North *p.71*, there has never been much demand for them here. Any Loop hotels that are close to Grant Park will also be within pretty reasonable distance of the Museum Campus and McCormick Place.

Best Western Grant Park, 1100 S Michigan Ave, +1 312 922-2900, *www.bestwesternillinois.com*. Includes wi-fi and an outdoor pool, weather permitting. Rooms from $153.

The Chicago Hilton and Towers, 720 S Michigan Ave, +1 312 922-4400, *www.hiltonchicagohotel.com*. One of the finest Hilton hotels in the chain, with many luxury suites and rooms, including ambassador and presidential suites. It has a wonderful view of Grant Park. The Chicago Hilton and Towers is located right on the border of the business Loop. Rooms from $199.

Essex Inn, 800 S Michigan Ave, +1 800 621-6909, *www.essexinn.com*. Offers clean, fully equipped, and recently renovated rooms, a fantastic pool and fitness center and free wi-fi. Rooms from $120.

Hyatt Regency McCormick Place, 2233 S Dr Martin Luther King Jr Dr, +1 312 567 1234, *mccormickplace.hyatt.com*. Nothing exceptional, except some of the views — if you are staying here, spend whatever extra money is required for the spectacular cityscape views. $180-$300.

The Wheeler Mansion, 2020 S Calumet Ave, +1 312 922-2900 , *www.wheelermansion.com*. One of the few mansions to survive the fire of 1871 is now a very charming four star bed and breakfast with spacious rooms adorned with antiques. $230-$280.

Contact

For internet access, the closest public libraries are the Chinatown *p.175* Branch, just west of the Velvet Lounge, and the Harold Washington Center just north of Printer's Row in the Loop *p.47*.

Get out

If you came here looking for blues and jazz, you may want to head further to the South Side home of the blues in Chatham-South Shore *p.203*.

And if you had fun at the Museum Campus, even more awaits you at the **Museum of Science and Industry** in Hyde Park *p.157*.

Hurting for good Chinese food? Find *great* Chinese food in nearby Chinatown *p.175*. Take bus #18 from Prairie Avenue or #21 from McCormick Place.

A long the Magnificent Mile is a one day and night sightseeing tour of Chicago.

Understand

Most of Chicago lives in apartments, bungalows, condos, and houses on the North Side or the South Side, but this is where they all come together: to work amid the skyscrapers of the Loop *p.47*, to relax in the parks and beaches along the lake, and to blow their hard-earned cash in the department stores on the Magnificent Mile. In this itinerary, you'll follow **Michigan Avenue** as it evolves from shopping district to recreation space, and then you'll take a turn into the canyons of the commerce-oriented Loop before heading off for a terrific dinner.

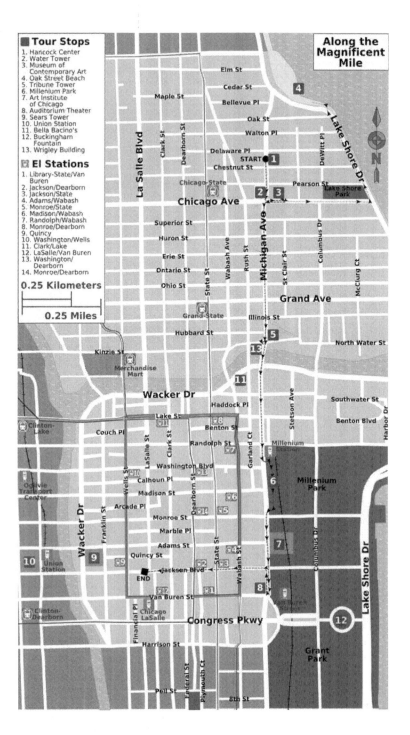

Along the Magnificent Mile

Tour Stops
1. Hancock Center
2. Water Tower
3. Museum of Contemporary Art
4. Oak Street Beach
5. Tribune Tower
6. Millenium Park
7. Art Institute of Chicago
8. Auditorium Theater
9. Sears Tower
10. Union Station
11. Bella Bacino's
12. Buckingham Fountain
13. Wrigley Building

El Stations
1. Library-State/Van Buren
2. Jackson/Dearborn
3. Jackson/State
4. Adams/Wabash
5. Monroe/State
6. Madison/Wabash
7. Randolph/Wabash
8. Monroe/Dearborn
9. Quincy
10. Washington/Wells
11. Clark/Lake
12. LaSalle/Van Buren
13. Washington/Dearborn
14. Monroe/Dearborn

0.25 Kilometers

0.25 Miles

Prepare

You're walking for most of this itinerary, so wear comfortable shoes, and dress for the climate. If it's a warm day in the spring, summer, or early fall, bring a small towel for splashing in the fountains at Millennium Park. This route starts in the Near North *p.71*, proceeds to the Loop *p.47*, veers off to the Near West Side *p.215*, and returns to the Near North *p.71*. Although the route is very straightforward and easy to follow, you may wish to print out the articles for those districts, if only for a few alternate recommendations and further illustration of what you'll see along the way.

If you skip the shopping and stick with your feet, the day won't cost very much. Only dinner, the Art Institute, and the Hancock/Sears Tower will put any kind of crimp in your wallet. To cut out the taxi fares, get the exact addresses from the Near North *p.71*, Loop *p.47*, and Near West Side *p.215* guides, and plot public transit routes using the **CTA Trip Planner** *tripsweb. rtachicago.com*.

Morning

Start early! On your way out of the hotel, ask the concierge whether the water is flowing at Buckingham Fountain yet; this will be important later. Grab a quick pastry and cup of coffee or juice to tide you over for the next couple of hours.

If you're starting on the CTA, take the Red Line subway to the Chicago stop, and walk three blocks east, toward the lake. Skip a couple paragraphs ahead and begin there, as you'll be walking right by the Water Tower.

Otherwise, take a taxi from your hotel to the **Hancock Center**. This is only the third-tallest building in Chicago (fifth-tallest in the United States), but it's better-liked and better-looking than the other two, and it definitely has the best view. Take an elevator up to the **Observatory** on the 94th floor. Admission is $9.75 adult, $6 child. Survey the city and the lake, and be sure to look south, for there lies the day's conquest. There's a bar with expensive drinks one floor up. Don't booze it up now, but you might come back for drinks later on.

One block south, at Michigan and Chicago, have a look at the old **Water Tower**. This is a Chicago icon, and the most famous survivor of the 1871 Chicago Fire, along with the less-celebrated **Pumping Station** on the other side of Michigan Avenue. Street performers may be in the small square behind the Water Tower. (Don't bother tours of the interior, though — it's been scrubbed of any historical traces, and is occasionally used as a gallery space now.) Behind the pumping station on Chicago Ave is a turn-of-the-century **firehouse**; not quite as old as the other two, but it's still in use, and you'll see members of the Chicago Fire Department (human and canine) relaxing out front if they're not away on a call.

Now, you have two options. If you're in the mood for sand, head east down Chicago Avenue. You might check to see if the **Museum of Contemporary Art** has any interesting public art outside its building at Mies van der Rohe Way. When you've reach the end of Chicago Avenue, turn left and walk a few blocks north. Use the pedestrian tunnel to cross under **Lake Shore Drive**. You are at **Oak Street Beach**. You should have a nice view of Lincoln Park *p.123* and the North Side. When you're done, walk back the way you came, or take a taxi directly to the Tribune Tower — back-tracking will make it kind of a long walk.

Alternatively, skip the beach and stroll down Michigan Avenue. This is the heart of the **Magnificent Mile**, with block after block of fashionable department stores. Pop into as many as you like, but this is expensive territory — and remember, you'll be carrying whatever you buy for the rest of the day. (That said, if cost is not a concern, stores will be more than happy to have packages wrapped and sent to your hotel while you carry on.) You'll want to backtrack to **900 N Michigan** and **Water Tower Place**, and then keep heading south on Michigan.

When you've almost reached the river, stop. On your left is the **Tribune Tower**. Walk along its north and south walls; embedded in them are stones from famous sites across the country and across the world. Bore your family with your knowledge of history.

Now, cross over to the west side of the street and look for a curious opening in the sidewalk. There

might even be a placard advertising a restaurant down there. Descend to **lower Michigan Ave**. At this point, your heart will be racing and you will fear for family's safety. Perhaps a scene from *Adventures in Babysitting* will play in your mind. Fight these feelings; there is nothing to fear.

Walk to the corner, towards the river, and you will see the **Billy Goat Tavern**. This legendary haunt for Chicago newspapermen was made famous by John Belushi's "cheeseburger-cheeseburger-not-Coke-Pepsi" sketch on Saturday Night Live. Go in and have a quick, cheap lunch.

Afternoon

When you are finished eating, head back upstairs and cross the river. If you are lucky, the bridge will be temporarily raised for some water traffic. Regardless, take in the views both east to the lake and west inland.

Millennium Park begins at Michigan and Randolph, although most of the action is a little further south, closer to Madison. If it's warm, this place will be hopping. Don't miss **The Bean** (you'll know it when you see it) or the giant **projection fountains**. Get your feet wet — you've done plenty of walking already, and there's plenty more ahead of you. (If you were hoping to have your kids burn off any excess energy, let them go buckwild in the fountain.)

Then continue down Michigan to

MAG MILE TOUREVENING

Adams, where two lions guard the entrance of the world-renowned **Art Institute of Chicago**. (Admission is $12 for adults, $7 for children and seniors. If this is a Thursday afternoon and you're running late, you're in luck: admission is free after 5:30PM.) Choose a couple areas of interest and check those out; perusing the whole collection would take you the better part of the day. There are some iconic American paintings (Wood's "American Gothic" and Hopper's "Nighthawks") and a number of seminal European paintings (most notably Seurat's "A Sunday Afternoon at La Grande Jatte").

Once you're finished browsing, continue south on Michigan to Congress Parkway. At the corner are the colossal stone walls of **The Auditorium Theatre**, designed by the great Louis Sullivan (with Frank Lloyd Wright toiling as his apprentice), once the tallest building in Chicago. A tour or a show here is well worth the cost, if you can arrange it. Have a look inside the grand lobby and the staircase if it's open, and leave before someone kicks you out.

Turn around and head back north for two blocks to Jackson, and then turn left. In the sky are the looming black metal blocks of the **Sears Tower**. Until recently the tallest building in the world, it now carries that title only for North America. If you didn't go to the Hancock Observatory earlier, you can have a look from the SkyDeck at the Sears Tower instead ($9.95 adult, $6.95 child). It's probably late in the afternoon by

now, and most Chicagoans are beginning their commute home. The streets of the Loop will be full of the rumble of elevated trains and the air of people who are tired from a full day's work.

This is Chicago.

Evening

If you're a train geek and you have some time left before dinner, it might be worth your while to continue west on Jackson, cross the river, and then turn left on Canal St. to check out **Union Station**. Once, all the railroads in America ran through Chicago, and you can still catch traces of that in this monumental neoclassical building. It will also be full of people on their way home from work, catching Metra trains for the suburbs. Join the march between the giant marble columns and down the grand steps, and where the falling baby-carriage climax of *The Untouchables* was filmed. (Please remove actual babies from carriages before attempting to re-enact the scene, though). Check out the enormous atrium and its long, stately wooden benches. Hang out for a few minutes if you're not in a hurry — this is a great spot for people-watching — or head back out to the street.

Time to decide: what do you want for dinner? Armed with your guide for the Near West Side *p.215*, catch a cab and tell the driver to take you to **Little Italy** or **Greektown**, just west of the Loop. (If the weather's favorable, you can walk to Greektown

113

in a few minutes). Have a nice, long, leisurely dinner at a family-run restaurant. You'll be spoiled for choice. If you'd prefer to stay closer to the Loop *p.47*, try **Bella Bacino's** for the best stuffed pizza in Chicago — and, by definition, anywhere.

If the concierge told you that **Buckingham Fountain** is on, and if it's near 8PM, catch a cab to **Grant Park**, and head to the fountain. When night falls, the water dances and soars and is illuminated by lights. Celebrate a successful day in Chicago with an ice cream cone from the **Bobtail stand** near the fountain.

Otherwise, have the cabbie take you to Michigan and Randolph, and walk north on Michigan, back towards the river. On the bridge, have another look east and west. Cross the river; the building on your left is the **Wrigley Building**. (It will be impossible to miss.) Look down Michigan at the lights and the people for a memorable view. If you're a fan of coming full circle, you might take a taxi back to the **Hancock Center** for drinks on the 95th floor, and see how the night view compares to the one you saw at the start of the day.

Stay safe

Once again, Chicago's climate is not to be underestimated. Bundle up in winter and keep hydrated in the height of the summer. You're unlikely to encounter any safety concerns during the day, save for the remote possibility of pick-pockets in crowded areas.

After dark, don't stray more than a couple of blocks from Union Station and Little Italy/Greektown. Both are safe for tourists, but there are some rough areas within walking distance.

LOOP ART TOUR

The **Loop Art Tour** is a guided walking tour of Chicago's impressive collection of public art in the Loop *p.47*, taking 2-4 hours depending on how long you linger at each sight.

Understand

Most visitors to Chicago make a point of visiting the endless collections at the Art Institute, but many overlook the world-class collection of public art on display throughout Chicago's commercial center. The Loop is a veritable open air museum of sculptures by the world's most famous modern artists (Picasso, Calder, Miro, Lewitt, etc.), and it's all, of course, free. These monumental sculptures are a both part of Chicago's distinctive character and a major source of civic pride. This itinerary will guide you along an efficient route to visit all the most famous of Chicago's downtown public art installations, as well as more than a few lesser-known gems.

Chicago's wealth of public art is also a great excuse to get out and enjoy the city in all its aesthetic glory. A major side benefit of this walking tour is that you'll quickly get to know the Loop and its main streets. The tour takes you past many of the Loop's most prominent landmarks, like Millennium Park, the Chicago Theater, the Chicago Board of Trade, the various central plazas, and the Sears Tower.

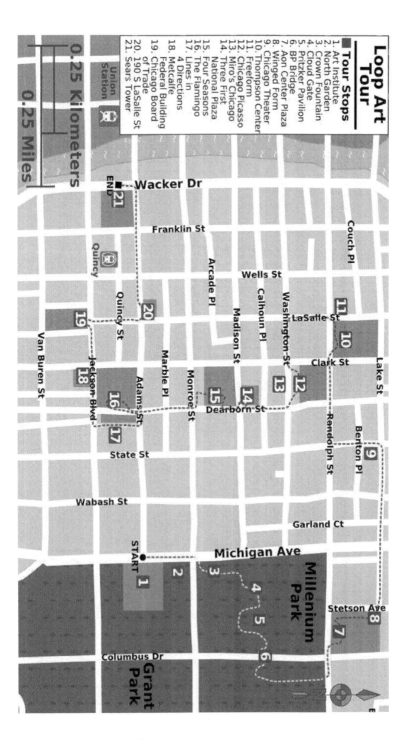

Prepare

You won't need to bring much else besides this guide. If you are planning on doing the full itinerary, be sure to wear comfortable shoes. In total it's a 2.7 mile walk, and that doesn't include time spent indoors. Inclement weather will make the walk less enjoyable, but only a real storm or the most frigid weather would really stop you from making the journey. Check the weather before you head out and bring rain/snow gear as appropriate. Don't forget your camera and consider bringing along the map of the Loop *p.47*, in case you want to stop in a cafe or finish with a beer.

One of the best things about public art is that you get to enjoy it without paying any money. The only costs you'll encounter are from the many temptations along the way. If you want to visit the Art Institute at the beginning, that will be $12 for adults and $7 for children/seniors; the Sears Tower Skydeck at the end will set you back $12.95/adult, $9.50/child. Set out in the morning or the afternoon, just so long as you'll finish the trip before dinner time, when many of the buildings close, denying you access to any indoor sculptures.

Art Institute

The walk begins at the world famous Art Institute of Chicago, and the more ambitious might want to plan an extra several hours at the beginning of the day to see some highlights from its collections (for information on how to get here, check the guide to the Loop *p.47*). Don't wear yourself out before you begin the walk, though! There are several interesting public statues on the grounds of the Institute that don't require admission fees. You are walking north anyway, so take a look at the three rather famous statues in the North Garden. Hold Calder's whimsical **Flying Dragon** and Sir Henry Moore's pondering **Large Interior Form** in your mind — you'll see two monumental echoes of these two statues farther on. The other statue on hand is David Smith's **Cubi VII**, the seventh such statue in a series displayed around the world. At first glance David Smith's work looks like a boxy, metal tree, but there's more to it than that. Smith's metal sculptures are oddly textured, causing the steel faces to catch light in a different way for every new day.

Millennium Park

Across Monroe Street, Millennium Park's **Crown Fountain** (Jaume Plensa) comes into view, and makes an impression! These two mini-skyscrapers project faces of Chicagoans, who occasionally spew water through their "mouths" into the large black granite fountain between them. If you've brought kids along, now is a good time to collect their shoes and let them splash around a bit.

Continuing northwards, you'll see the hard-to-miss **Cloud Gate** (Anish Kapoor). Better known as *the Bean*, it's a kidney-shaped structure of smooth stainless steel weighing 110 tons. It's the favorite sculpture of Millennium Park's throngs of visitors, as it reflects the surrounding skyscrapers (and tourists) like a funhouse mirror. That and it is rather graceful, isn't it?

After taking either artistic or goofy photos with the Bean, head east through the park, around the edge of the huge **Pritzker Pavilion** (Frank Gehry). Its giant steel trellis performs an important function besides aesthetic appeal; it supports much of the stage's sound and lighting systems. At the eastern edge of the pavilion (and of Millennium Park), take the long, winding **BP Bridge** over Columbus Drive and be sure to stop along the way to enjoy the views of the skyline and Lake Michigan.

Aon Center Plaza

After crossing the bridge, you are in Grant Park. Turn left, head up to Randolph Street and cross it to Aon Center. There is not a single setback on Aon Center, and you can walk right up to the base and look straight up 83 stories to the 1136 foot pinnacle. The plaza is pleasant enough and there are two **Sounding Sculptures** (Henry Bertoia) at the southeast and southwest corners. These "musical sculptures" are inspired by the image of Midwestern wheat fields swaying in the breeze. These wheat stalks are hollow and made of thin copper, so when the wind blows (and it always blows in the Windy City), the rods produce a strange metallic music. Follow the plaza around to the west of the

tower past some smaller statues and Richard Hunt's **Winged Form** (his more spectacular *Freeform* is yet to come), then head down the steps onto Lake Street.

Thompson Center

Continue a couple blocks to State Street and turn left. The giant Chicago sign on the left is one of Chicago's most famous landmarks, at the Chicago Theater. Walk past the theater and then turn right on to Randolph Street. Two blocks more and you will be before one of Chicago's most distinctive buildings, the Thompson Center (named for an Illinois governor). In the plaza on Randolph stands one of Chicago's most famous statues, Jean Dubuffet's **Monument with Standing Beast**. It's a strange sculpture of white, organic shapes, with thick black outlines, and usually a host of kids running in and out of it.

Make a point of wandering past the curved glass walls of the Thompson Center into its enormous atrium. The building is often compared to a spaceship, but few spaceships can claim the collection of public art that the Thompson Center has. Once you've finished inside, head back out to Randolph, turn right and head to the corner at LaSalle Street. Look across LaSalle and look up. Up on the State of Illinois Building is Richard Hunt's three ton, 2.5 story-tall, flame-like **Freeform** sculpture. If your neck starts to ache from looking up so much, look back down LaSalle and head south a block before turning left on to Washington Street.

Daley Center

Two blocks down Washington and you are at the Daley Center and Chicago's most famous work of art, **the Chicago Picasso**. Resembling an elephant, a sphinx, or whatever your mind comes up with, the Chicago Picasso was the first monumental public art downtown (donated by the artist) and sparked the spate of public art acquisitions that you are now enjoying. It was "controversial," however, when it first arrived for its "abstract" "non-traditional" design. But the reactionary grumps have bit their tongues (after having removed their foots from their mouths) and the statue is celebrated today by a city that loves art. Kids, in particular, enjoy sliding down the statue's base.

Turn around and look across Washington Street for **Joan Miro's Chicago**, a strange surrealist, anthropomorphic figure. The fork on its head is said to represent a star.

Go down Dearborn Street one block and take a left onto Madison Avenue to make a quick venture into Three First National Plaza (70 W Madison St). The atrium is attractive and full of plants, complemented by one very large Sir Henry Moore statue, **Large Upright Internal/External Form**. Henry Moore's titles are purposefully devoid of descriptive content. He argued:

All art should have a certain mys-

tery and should make demands on the spectator. Giving a sculpture or a drawing too explicit a title takes away part of that mystery so that the spectator moves on to the next object, making no effort to ponder the meaning of what he has just seen.

If the two Henry Moore statues you've seen today made an impression, you may want to plan a visit to his *Nuclear Energy* statue in Hyde Park *p.157.*

Chase Plaza

Head back to Dearborn and continue south. Dominating the next block is the curved Chase Tower and the large plaza at its feet. Courtesy of the Russian-Jewish painter Marc Chagall, this plaza has become a must-see attraction for art lovers in Chicago. **The Four Seasons** is a 70 foot long mosaic/mural featuring light-hearted surrealist depictions of Chicago. After you have finished here continue south on Dearborn Street.

Federal Plaza

Two blocks down Dearborn from Chase Plaza is Federal Plaza, a full city block planned by renowned modernist architect Mies Van der Rohe. In the center of the plaza is the second Alexander Calder statue of the day, **The Flamingo**. Whimsical and constructivist (meaning: constructed of big industrial materials bolted together) are not words that usually belong side by side, but both Calder statues of the day nonetheless fit this description. The giant

"Calder-red" flamingo poses a graceful, curving counterpoint to the hard edges and straight lines of the surrounding skyscrapers that reflect the statue in their windows.

The next sculpture is a eight stories tall, but easy to miss! Head south across Adams Street and then head around to the backside of the building on the left. Behind this building and on the side of another is Sol Lewitt's monumental, yet very understated **Lines in Four Directions**. The sculpture consists of four giant panels covered in long strips of aluminum painted white, facing in four directions (hence the title). Similar to David Smith's *Cubi VII* back at the Art Institute, the emphasis here is on how one work of art can change depending on its environment and the position of the viewer. Depending on where you are standing, and the day's lighting, different patterns will emerge as the light hits the differently aligned aluminum strips.

If you are feeling tired, now is a good time to call an early day — you've already seen the most famous of Chicago's downtown sculptures. Otherwise, head south on to Jackson Boulevard and make a right.

CBoT

The Metcalfe Federal Building's lobby on the left at the intersection of Jackson and Clark contains another larger than life statue. Frank Stella has created a whole series of Moby Dick related abstract sculp-

tures; this one is named after a specific chapter, **The Town-Ho's Story**. It's a terrific mess of 13,000 lbs. of steel and aluminum. The link to Melville's novel is not very clear, but the sculpture is impressive and purposefully abrasive.

The next block of Jackson Boulevard is the gigantic Art Deco Chicago Board of Trade Building (CBoT). The main lobby itself is a work of art, and a good quick stop along the way. From here turn up LaSalle Street. Turn left at Adams Street and cross the intersection to stop in the building at 190 South LaSalle Street to admire its beautiful lobby. The high vaulted ceiling is covered with $1 million of gold leaf, but lest you strain your neck, focus your attentions on the large bronze statue at the end of the room, **Chicago Fugue** (Sir Anthony Caro). The statue is a cubist jumble of musical instrument-like shapes: a keyboard, organ pedals, cymbals, and any others you may "find" in it. The lobby's leather couches are another good reason to come in here, by the way.

Sears Tower

The final stretch of the tour takes you another three blocks west on Adams Street. When you reach Wacker Drive, turn left around the Sears Tower and head into the main lobby. The Sears Tower likely needs no introduction, but the massive art installation inside is less well known. **Universe** is the last of the day's sculptures by Alexander Calder, and unlike the other "stabiles," this sculpture is fully "mobile." Held to represent the effect of the Big Bang at the origin of the universe, the work is comprised of rotating shapes meant to resemble heavenly bodies.

Your tour ends here in the Sears Tower, and you might want to take this opportunity to ride the 20 miles per hour elevator to the Sears Tower Skydeck for some grand views of the journey you've just taken.

If you are thinking of dinner at this point, you are just a block away from the Quincy L station — you have your choice of neighborhoods to visit for dinner. Some especially good "ethnic" dining options not too far from the Loop are in Greektown *p.215* a short walk across the river, Chinatown *p.175* to the south (Red Line), and authentic Mexican cuisine in Pilsen *p.259* (Pink Line).

I n **Lincoln Park**, collegians mix with freshly-minted lawyers and barrel-chested brokers, all come to sing their good fortune in beer gardens on the north side of Chicago, a short walk from miles of beautiful parks and the fabulous **Lincoln Park Zoo**. Just south is **Old Town**, a striking collision of rich and poor, and home of Chicago's two most celebrated theaters, **Steppenwolf** and **Second City**.

Understand

The flames of the Great Chicago Fire of 1871 lapped at the borders of Lincoln Park, and burned no further than Fullerton Avenue. It was, then, a small community of Polish and German settlers near the northern boundaries of the city, named Lake Park for the swamplands (and cemeteries) that were drained by the lake, and re-

named Lincoln Park for the slain president in 1865.

Back to that fire, though: refugees poured into the neighborhood for safety, and with their former homes in ashes, plenty of them decided to stay. Lots were sold to "worthy families," and it suddenly became a very fashionable place to live. With the arrival of the elevated train, a construction frenzy began. In fact, an estimated 60% of the buildings that currently stand in Lincoln Park date from the three decades after the fire. Cultural institutions emerged to match: for example, with the $10 purchase of a bear cub, the **Lincoln Park Zoo** opened to visitors in 1874, and **DePaul University** evolved from a small religious college to the center of life for the neighborhood, with strong academic and sports programs throughout much of the

twentieth century. (Long-time basketball coach Ray Meyer intro-
duced the concept of the skilled
seven-footer to the sport when
he recruited George Mikan in the
1940s.)

The area now known as Old Town
was not so lucky in the Fire, but
was spared the extensive damage
of the city center. Today, its pre-fire
history can be seen in the winding layout of the streets in the Old
Town Triangle Historic District,
and can be heard in the bells of
St. Michael's Church, one of the
few structures to stand in the path
of the fire and survive. The neighborhood was hit hard by the urban
flight of the 1950s, and many of
those classic structures were converted into boarding houses that
became affordable for beatniks:
artists, folk musicians, actors, and
others moved in and made Old
Town into the counterculture capital of Chicago for the next two
decades. Miles, Janis, Dylan, and
Seeger played in and outside of
the clubs in Old Town. It was
where teens from staid neighborhoods (like Lincoln Park) came to
feel the edge. Guitars! Long hair!
Loitering! Old Town had it all.

Into this environment came the
city's greatest comedic force, a
group of ex-pats from Hyde Park
p.157 who named their new theater **The Second City**, and reinvented American comedy. Years
later, a similarly talented band of
college actors arrived to establish
Steppenwolf, who set the tone for
the next two decades of dramatic
theater.

The shocking violence of the 1968

Democratic Convention spelled
the end of the hippie era in Old
Town. Soon, property values were
on the rise, and only the more
financially successful countercul-
tural outlets could stay in business. Today, you'll find a historic district and the new **Chicago
History Museum** to guide you
around, and you can split an
amazing night at the theater with
one of the trendy restaurants
nearby. Old Town is divided,
though: crumbling buildings sit
on one side of North Avenue without ever much affecting a trip to
Steppenwolf on the other side.
Old Town is a neighborhood that
knows the contradictions within
its boundaries, and lives with
them.

Lincoln Park, on the other hand, is
oblivious. Most of the North Side
wouldn't live in Lincoln Park if
you paid them to do it, and most
of Lincoln Park would refuse to
live anywhere else, understanding other neighborhoods only as
wastelands with poorly groomed
people and an unacceptable shortage of Starbucks. Thanks to the
presence of DePaul, Lincoln Park
has a distinctly collegiate atmosphere, created not only by students but also by young professionals with fond memories of
having been students within the
last two decades. The weekend
club scene in Lincoln Park will either offer an exhilarating trip back
to your college years or a vision of
hell on earth. That aside, Lincoln
Park also has a row of shopping
boutiques that is the envy of much
of the rest of the city, and the taxes
that churn through the local econ-

omy go to the well-maintained expanses of the eponymous park,
the lakefront bike and jogging
trails, and **North Avenue Beach**.

Also, to its credit, the Lincoln Park
Zoo didn't rest on its laurels after
it got that bear.

Get in

By train

The CTA **Red Line** runs along
Sheffield Avenue and stops at
Fullerton in Lincoln Park and
North/Clybourn at the edge of
Old Town. The **Brown Line**, fur-
ther west, connects with the Red
Line at Fullerton, but also makes
stops in Lincoln Park at Armitage
and Diversey, and in Old Town at
Sedgwick.

The Metra **Union Pacific District
Northwest Line** and **Union Pa-
cific North Line** both stop at the
Clybourn station just across the
Chicago River in Logan *p.247*,
from which you can catch the 73
Armitage bus into Lincoln Park.

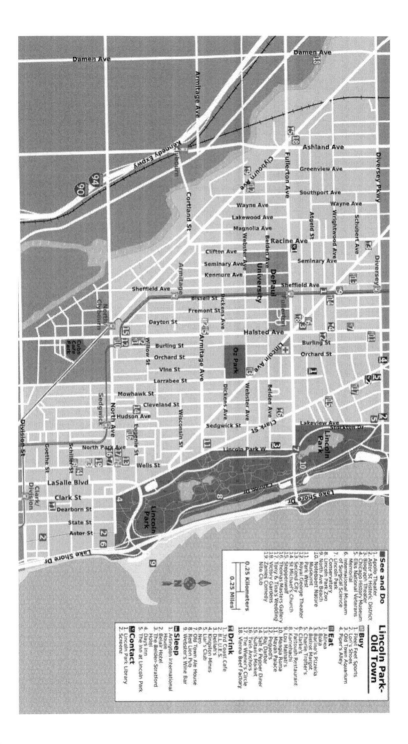

Lincoln Park-Old Town

See and Do
1. Apollo Theater
2. Astor St Historic District
3. Biograph Theater
4. Chicago History Museum
5. Elks National Veterans Memorial
6. International Museum of Surgical Science
7. Lincoln Park
8. Lincoln Park Zoo
9. North Ave Beach
10. Notebaert Nature Museum
11. Park West
12. Peggy Notebaert Nature Museum
13. Royal George Theatre
14. St. Clement Church
15. St. Michael's Church
16. Steppenwolf
17. Thomas Masters Gallery
18. Tony & Tina's Wedding
19. Victory Gardens
19. Zanies Comedy Nite Club

Buy
1. Fleet Feet Sports
2. Lori's Shoes
3. Shane Campbell
4. Paper Source

Eat
1. Salt & Pepper Diner
2. Aloha Eats
3. Bacino's Pizzeria
4. Nookies
5. Charlie Trotter's
6. Charlie's
7. Pattouch Restaurant
8. Clarke's
9. Lou Malnati's
10. Mama Roma
11. Pequod's
12. Peggy's Palace
13. Big Dan Bar
14. Salt & Pepper Diner
15. Stars & Mouse
16. Twin Anchors
17. The Wiener's Circle
18. Vienna Beef Factory

Drink
1. 3rd Coast Cafe
2. LUJ LSL
3. Delilah's
4. Kingston Mines
5. Nari's Club
6. Neo's
7. Old Town Ale House
8. Red Lion Pub
9. Webster's Wine Bar

Sleep
1. Arlington International House
2. Belair Hotel
3. Hotel Lincoln-Stratford
4. Days Inn
5. The Inn at Lincoln Park

Contact
1. Lincoln Park Library
2. Screens

0.25 Kilometres
0.25 Miles

By bus

8 Halsted runs past Steppenwolf's front door in Old Town.

11 Lincoln is a *slow* bus, but it does run down Lincoln Park's key artery.

22 Clark runs all night north/south down Clark Street, from the Near North *p.71* and through both Old Town and Lincoln Park, before heading on to Lakeview *p.139*.

72 North runs on North Avenue, into the heart of Old Town, and on to Bucktown *p.247*.

73 Armitage serves the Armitage shopping corridor.

74 Fullerton runs east/west on Fullerton, the major artery in Lincoln Park.

76 Diversey runs east/west on Diversey, the border between Lincoln Park and Lakeview, and continues to Logan Square *p.247*.

151 Sheridan and **156 LaSalle** both reach the **Lincoln Park Zoo** and the lakefront from the Near North *p.71*. The 151 runs all night.

By car

Lake Shore Drive has exits at Fullerton for Lincoln Park and North Avenue for Old Town. From the **Kennedy Expressway**, take any of the eastbound exits at Division, North, Fullerton, and Diversey.

Traffic is not swift on the streets of Lincoln Park and Old Town, but it's generally manageable. Be-

ware of parking on side streets that require residential permits. (If you're not parking at a meter, take a quick walk up and down the block to make sure that a permit isn't required to park there.)

There are parking garages in close proximity to the theaters (notably Piper's Alley in Old Town) and on the grounds of the Lincoln Park Zoo ($14, 1-3 hours).

See

The **Lincoln Park Zoo** and the lakefront are the biggest highlights for a day here, especially with kids, but a few sights, particularly the **Biograph Theater** and the **historic districts**, are at their most powerful by night.

Biograph Theater, 2433 N Lincoln Ave (*Fullerton Red/Brown/Purple Line*). Plays are shown here (see Victory Gardens below), but the theater itself is still best known as the place where John Dillinger went down in 1934. America's most famous bank robber was leaving after a movie with the Lady in Red when FBI agents opened fire. The owners of the theater have never been keen to play up the connection, but the classic marquee is still there. Reportedly, Dillinger fans hold gatherings outside on July 22, the anniversary of his death.

Chicago History Museum (Chicago Historical Society), 1601 N Clark St (*Clark/Division Red Line, Sedgwick Brown Line*), +1 312 642-4600, *www.chicagohistory.org*, M-W noon-8PM, Th-Sa 9:30AM-4:30PM, Su noon-5PM. A creative urban history museum. Exhibits include *The Pioneer,* the first railroad locomotive to operate in Chicago, and the bed upon which Abraham Lincoln died; more fun for kids is the Chicago-style Hot Dog showcase, which supplies all the giant plastic ingredients you'll need to turn yourself (or your little brother) into a life-sized hot dog (no ketchup, of course). They also host regular tours of different CTA lines and walking tours of Lincoln Park and Old Town. Suggested admission $5 adult, $1 child, free on Mondays.

Elks National Veterans Memorial, 2750 N Lakeview Ave, +1 773 755-4876, *www.elks.org/memorial,* M-F 9AM-5PM; also Sa-Su 10AM-5PM from 15 April-15 November. This neoclassical veterans memorial is truly grand. Its interior is an extravagant ensemble of marble, bronze sculptures, stained glass, and huge murals. Free admission and tours.

International Museum of Surgical Science, 1524 N Lake Shore Dr, +1 312 642-6502, *www.imss. org/index.htm,* Tu-Su 10AM-4PM. Four floors of artifacts and artwork, both scientific and whatever an embroidered x-ray can be classified as. $8 adults, $4 students/seniors.

Lincoln Park. The 1.5 mile-long park from which the neighborhood draws its name is dotted with statues of people with ties to Chicago or Germany (like Goethe), and features plenty of paths for running wide-open green space for sports, and even a rowing lagoon to the west.

Lincoln Park Conservatory, 2400 N Stockton Dr, +1 312 742-7736, *www.chicagoparkdistrict.com,* 9AM-5PM. Built more than a century ago, the conservatory is right next to the zoo. Even though they're overshadowed by the animals next door, the plants receive an equal amount of care, and there are usually some eye-popping floral displays in the spring. Volunteer-led tours are sometimes available at no cost. Free.

Lincoln Park Zoo, 2200 N Cannon Dr (*Fullerton Red/Brown/Purple Line, or see bus routes*), +1 312 742-2000, *www.lpzoo.com,* Daily 9AM-6PM, winter 9AM-5PM, summer weekends 9AM-7PM. Few things in Chicago are finer than the Lincoln Park Zoo. It's world-class, yet admission is free; its winding, expansive grounds have the charm of age, yet its facilities are modern and the animals are healthy, happy, and personable. The brand new Great Ape House is one to see, and the Farm In The Zoo features plenty for kids to do, but everyone has their own favorites (penguins). Free.

Notebaert Nature Museum, 2430 N Cannon Dr, +1 773 755-5100, *www.naturemuseum.org,* M-F 9AM-4:30PM, Sa-Su 10AM-5PM. Carefully positioned within walking distance of the Lincoln Park Zoo in hopes of being parents' second stop while they're in the area, the Notebaert Nature Museum is...okay. Exhibits are geared toward kids and are sometimes hands-on. The only consistent must-see is the butterfly haven.

Adults $9, children 3-12 $6, Th free.

Oz Park, 2021 N Burling St, +1 312 742-7898, *www.chicagoparkdistrict. com*. Young children might enjoy this Wizard of Oz-themed park with statues and playlots. Free.

Thomas Masters Gallery, 245 W North Ave (*Sedgwick Brown/Purple Line*), +1 312 440-2322, *www.thomasmastersgallery.com*, W-F 12-6PM, Sa 11AM-6PM, Su 12-5PM. A member of the River North gallery scene, with contemporary art, including paint, drawings and sculpture.

Historic districts

These areas have some of the most impressive homes in Chicago, and can be covered easily on foot. For guided walking tours, check with the Chicago History Museum (above).

Astor Street Historic District, Astor St, between Division and North, *www.cityofchicago.org*. Near Old Town, on what's often referred to as the Gold Coast, Astor Street was named for the fur tycoon John Jacob Astor, and does him tribute on his favored terms — these are the most expensive houses in Chicago. The atmosphere is the main attraction, but the 1892 **Charnley House** (1365 N Astor St) is particularly interesting, marking a halfway point between the distinctive styles of master architect Louis Sullivan and his apprentice Frank Lloyd Wright. There are also some interesting Art Deco homes like Holabird & Root's design at 1444 N

Astor St.

Mid-North Historic District, Between Fullerton Ave, Clark St, Armitage Ave, Lincoln Ave, and Orchard St, *www.cityofchicago.org*. There are several nice blocks of Lincoln Park near the lake, but the Italianate, Queen Anne, and Romanesque homes of the Mid-North District are especially lovely. Three survived the Chicago Fire (2121 N Hudson, 2339 N Cleveland, 2343 N Cleveland), and two were early designs of Louis Sullivan (440 W Belden Ave, 2147 N Cleveland St). The 1882-89 row houses between Belden and Fullerton are worth a look, too. As you walk, you'll see the faded white-and-blue signs of the Church of Our Savior (530 W Fullerton Ave), founded in 1867 (although the present structure dates from 1889).

Old Town Triangle District, Between North Ave, Lincoln Ave, and Wells St, *www.cityofchicago. org*. Several blocks of beautiful cottages and row houses, notably the five at 1826-34 N Lincoln Park West, which were designed by Louis Sullivan in 1885. The anchor of the district is St. Mike's (below).

St. Michael's Church, 1633 N Cleveland Ave, +1 312 642-2498, *www.st-mikes.org*, Services Su 9AM,11AM,7PM, M-Sa 8AM, Tu 6PM. Unveiled in 1869, the walls of St Mike's were all that remained after the Chicago Fire swept through Old Town, making it one of only six structures to survive — and the tallest in the city until 1885. A tower was added in 1887, and the current stained glass windows date from 1902. It serves the Redemptorist faith, a branch of Catholicism, with seating for more than 1000 people.

Do

North Avenue Beach, 1603 N Lake Shore Dr, +1 312 742-7529, *www.chicagoparkdistrict.com*. Quite possibly the beach volleyball capital of the Midwest. There are semi-pro leagues here, and plenty of nets for amateurs to show up and play. There's also an enclosed roller-hockey rink and plenty of people whizzing past on the wide bike lanes. The North Avenue Beach House is a big boat-shaped structure at the center (look for the red smokestacks) where there are a few food and drink options, occasional live music, and Park District offices. A couple blocks south, toward Oak Street Beach, there are chess tables.

Events & Festivals

Summers in Lincoln Park are full of festivals, with one for every major street and parish. Expect beer, non-descript food and a few jam bands. Old Town has one that's definitely worth singling out, though.

Old Town Art Fair, Just north of North Ave at Lincoln Ave and Wisconsin St, +1 312 337-1938, *www.oldtownartfair.org*, One weekend in early-to-mid June, 10AM-6PM. One of the premiere neighborhood festivals in Chicago, for almost 60 years. There's plenty of pretty stuff to buy, of course, with roughly 250 artists selected by a

jury to participate and again at the fair for award purposes. But there's also food and good live music (local high school and national performers), garden walks through the historic district and the neighborhood at its early summer best. Requested donation $5. Expect surly volunteers if the 'request' is not met, though..

Theaters

Apollo Theater, 2540 N Lincoln Ave (*Fullerton Red/Brown/Purple Line*), +1 773 935-6100, *www.apollochicago.com*, Box office M-Tu 10AM-6PM, W-Sa 10AM-8PM, Su 11AM-4PM. An eclectic mix on two stages includes solo shows, major contemporary plays like "Ragtime" and "The Vagina Monologues," and the popular improvised musicals of **Baby Wants Candy** *www.babywantscandy.com* (Sa 10:30PM, $15). Studio shows around $20, mainstage $35-$50.

Park West, 322 W Armitage Ave (*between Clark St and Lincoln Ave*), +1 773 929-5959, *www.parkwestchicago.com*. This converted movie theater (and former burlesque hall) has some of the best acoustics in the U.S., and it's surprisingly intimate considering it can seat up to a thousand. None other than Ringo Starr has said that Park West is second only to London's Royal Albert Hall. Fans will crowd the stage, but the best seats are toward the back, near the main bar and in the balconies... or call in advance to reserve a booth. Tickets usually $25-45.

Royal George Theater, 1641 N Halsted St (*North/Clybourn Red Line*), +1 312 988-9000, *www.theroyalgeorgetheatre.com*, Box office M 10AM-6PM, Tu-Sa 10AM-8PM, Su 12-5PM. Home to the *long*-running *Late Night Catechism* and its variations, the Royal George has a couple of stages for "cheeky" parodies and satires that go down nice with moderately wealthy white folks. $30-$50.

Second City, 1616 N Wells St (*Sedgwick Brown Line*), +1 312 337-3992, *www.secondcity.com*, 8PM (Su 7PM), F-Sa also 11PM. The list of Second City alumni in show business has become something of a cliche — Alan Alda, John Belushi, Bill Murray, on and on — and it's still going strong today, with recent graduates like Stephen Colbert, Steve Carell, and Tina Fey. The separate revues on the **Mainstage** and the **e.t.c.** theaters are consistently smart, timely, and funny. (The third stage, Donny's Skybox, is rented out to local sketch troupes outside the artistic direction of Second City, and is hit-or-miss.) The third act of the night is fully improvised, and if there's space left among the paying customers from the first two acts, admission is free. Tickets M $14, Su,Tu-Th $19, F-Sa $24.

Steppenwolf, 1650 N Halsted St (*North/Clybourn Red Line*), +1 312 335-1650, *www.steppenwolf.org*, Box office M-Sa 11AM-5PM, Su 1-5PM. The creation of John Malkovich, Gary Sinise, and many others, Steppenwolf features cutting-edge theater and doesn't trade on the famous name, offering both original material and incisive re-stagings of classic plays (like a terrific recent production of *The Crucible*). Unlike Second City, the famous alumni of Steppenwolf make occasional returns to the stage as their schedules allow. Tickets from $40.

Tony & Tina's Wedding, 230 W North Ave (*Sedgwick Brown Line*), +1 312 664-8844, *www.tonyntina. com*, Su 5PM, W-Th 7:30PM, F 8PM, Sa 7PM. Dinner theater is definitely an acquired taste, but if you're a fan, this is about as good as it comes. Tony, Tina, and their cartoon Italian families have been getting married for more than a decade, interacting with their "guests" at the bar, during the dinner (pasta, naturally), and an after-party. $55-65.

Victory Gardens, 2433 N Lincoln Ave (*Fullerton Red/Brown/Purple Line*), +1 773 871-3000, *www.victorygardens.org*, Box office Tu-Sa 12-8PM, Su 12-4PM. One of the premier Off-Loop theaters in Chicago, Victory Gardens hosts a noteworthy slate of original plays and adaptations both fun and dramatic. Among their several stages is the Biograph Theater, and they're kind enough to screen classic movies there ($5) from time to time so people can relive old Hollywood and ill-fated dates of John Dillinger. Tickets $15-45.

Zanies Comedy Nite Club, 1548 N Wells St (*Sedgwick Brown Line*), +1 312 337-4027, *www.chicago.zanies.com*, Su-Th 8:30, F 8:30 & 10:30, Sa 7PM, 9PM, & 11:15PM. This is Chicago's flagship stand-up comedy club and hosts all the big international stand-up touring acts. $20 cover & 2-item order minimum, cover may vary.

Buy

Trendy boutique shopping can be found at the shops on Armitage between Halsted and Sheffield in Lincoln Park.

Fleet Feet Sports, 210 W North Ave, Piper's Alley (*Sedgwick Brown/Purple Line*), +1 312 587-3338, *www.fleetfeetchicago.com*, M-F 10AM-8PM, Sa 10AM-6PM, Su 11AM-5PM. Reinforce tired feet and outdoor gear here. Fun runs on M-W at 6:30PM (Tu women only).

Lori's Shoes, 824 W Armitage Ave (*Armitage Brown/Purple Line*), +1 773 281-5655, *www.lorisshoes.com*, M-Th 11AM-7PM, F 11AM-6PM, Sa 10AM-6PM, Su 12-5PM. Reinforce unfashionable feet and unremarkable soles here. Handbags and jewelry available as well.

Old Town Aquarium, 1538 N Wells St, +1 312 642-8763, *www.oldtownaquarium.com*, M,W,F 12-7PM, Tu-Th 12-8PM, Sa 11AM-6PM, Su 12-6PM. If you can't make it to Shedd, at least you can go to one of their sources, and without the price of admission. Old Town Aquarium stocks freshwater and saltwater fish from around the world, and they have an extensive portfolio of custom aquarium designs to their credit.

Piper's Alley, 210 W North Ave (*Sedgwick Brown Line*), Hours vary by store. A good indoor mall with several floors of stores and restaurants. Piper's Alley houses a lot of the entertainment in Old Town, including an art-movie multiplex, Tony & Tina's Wedding, and the entrances to Second City's e.t.c and Skybox stages. If you've been to a show here and parked in the garage, you might as well go fishing to see if a small purchase anywhere might get your parking validated.

Eat

The Lincoln Park Zoo may be free, but the food court and the concessions are a bit steep. If you need to eat at the zoo, take some solace in remembering how much you paid to get in!

Budget

The DePaul area has a lot of fast food targeted at students, mostly sandwich and noodle shops.

Clarke's, 2441 N Lincoln Ave (*Fullerton Red/Brown/Purple Line*), +1 773 472-3505, *clarkesdiner.com*, 24 hours. Breakfast all day and night, although burgers are available, too. The food is decent at best, but the hours make it a must-know for anyone on the Lincoln Park bar scene. $3-8.

Salt n' Pepper Diner, 2575 N Lincoln Ave (*Fullerton Red/Brown/Purple Line*), +1 773 525-8788, 7AM-4PM daily. If you need an early breakfast or a cheap lunch, Salt & Pepper sticks to the basics and does them well, with an acclaimed rockabilly jukebox.

$4-9.

Sultan's Market, 2521 N Clark St, +1 312 638-9151, *chicagofalafel.com*, M-Th 10AM-10PM, F-Sa 10AM-midnight, Su 10AM-9PM. Take note if you're in the park by the lakefront, or if you're carrying a lighter wallet after a trip to the Century Shopping Centre in Lakeview a couple blocks north. The prices are absurdly low for the amount of satisfaction you'll get from the Mediterranean salad bar or falafel sandwiches here. They also do a fine shawerma. $3.50-8.

Vienna Beef Factory, 2501 N Damen St, +1 773 235-6652, *www.viennabeef.com*, Deli: M-F 6:30AM-2PM, Sa 10AM-2:30PM. Hoo boy, it's the motherlode. This is where all Chicago's hot dogs are born (not to mention Polish sausages, Italian Beef, and other assorted deli meats). You cannot eat a truer Chicago hot dog than in the factory itself, and the prices are among the best in the city. Parking is easy in the outside lot. $1.50-5.

The Wiener's Circle, 2622 N Clark St (*Fullerton Red/Brown/Purple Line*), Su-Th 11AM-4AM, F-Sa 11AM-5AM. The food is only so-so, the prices fair, but what makes this walk-up joint famous is the staff, who have zero patience for customers and the colorful language skills of a bartender at the seediest dockside bar imaginable. A favorite of the late-night crowd, who after a long night of drinking seem to find major entertainment value in being served a massive dose of profane invective with their greasy chili fries and Chicago-style hot dogs.

$3-7.

Mid-range

Lincoln Park is crammed with mid-range Italian restaurants. Sushi places aren't rare, either.

Bacino's Pizzeria, 2204 N Lincoln Ave, +1 773 472-7400, *www.bacinos.com*. A Lincoln Park branch of the Loop favorite that serves what many call the city's best stuffed pizza. $12-20.

Bistrot Margot, 1437 N Wells St (*Sedgwick Brown Line*), +1 312 587-3660, *www.bistrotmargot.com*, M 11:30AM-9PM, Tu-Th 11:30AM-10PM, F 11:30AM-11PM, Sa 10:30AM-11PM, Su 10:30AM-9PM. Casual French bistro at reasonable prices, with an enthusiastic chef and charming decor. There's a bar on the second floor. $18-26.

Fattoush Restaurant, 2652 N Halsted St (*Diversey Brown Line*), +1 773 327-2652, *www.fattoushrestaurant.com*, M-Tu 11AM-10PM, F-Sa 11AM-11PM, Su 11AM-9PM. Lebanese cuisine on Halsted, good for a quick bite before the B.L.U.E.S. or the Kingston Mines. $7-15.

Kamehachi, 1400 N Wells St (*Sedgwick Brown Line*), +1 312 664-3663, *www.kamehachi.com*, M-Sa 11:30AM-2AM, Su 4:30PM-midnight. Reliable and sometimes exceptional sushi at this Old Town outlet of the Chicago sushi chainlet. There's relief for vegetarians as well: try the agedashi tofu. $16-22.

Lou Malnati's, 958 W Wrightwood Ave (*Fullerton

LINCOLN PARK EAT

Red/Brown/Purple Line), +1 773 832-4030, *www.loumalnatis.com*, M-Th 4-10PM, F-Sa 11AM-11PM, Su 11AM-10PM. Lincoln Park branch of the deep-dish pizza giant. This location has outdoor seating and a nice park across the street. $7-12.

Mangia Roma, 1623 N Halsted St (*North/Clybourn Red Line*), +1 312 475-9801, *www.mangiaromaitalian.com*, Tu-Th 11AM-10PM, F-Sa 11AM-10:30PM, Su noon-10PM. Near Steppenwolf and the Royal George — the casual pizza dinners get cheaper if you're also going to a show. $9-16.

Mayan Palace, 2703 N Halsted St (*Diversey Brown Line*), +1 773 935-4200, *www.themayanpalace.com*. Good Mexican food in a relaxed atmosphere, indoor and outdoor seating. Don't put much stock in their claim regarding the best margaritas in the world (1/2 price Tu&Th), but their *mole* sauce and their fried ice cream *are* worth bragging about. $8-13.

Pequod's, 2207 N Clybourn Ave, +1 773 327-1512, *www.pequodspizza.com*, M-Sa 11AM-2AM, Su 11AM-midnight. Great place to get caramelized/burnt crust Chicago style deep dish pizza, considered a secret favorite. $6-12.

Raj Darbar, 2660 N Halsted St, +1 773 348-1010, *www.rajdarbar. com*, Su-Th 5-10PM, F-Sa 5-11PM. Great Indian food with an extensive menu. The service is creaky and the staff always seem to be breaking in flocks of new busboys,

but the taste and decor are worth the stop. $13-25.

Twin Anchors, 1655 N Sedgwick St, +1 312 266-1616, *www.twinanchorsribs.com*, M-Th 5PM-11PM, F 5PM-12AM, Sa Noon-Midnight, Su Noon-10:30PM. Impress your friends with your knowledge of Chicago by "stumbling across" this hidden neighborhood joint. Once Frank Sinatra's favorite restaurant in Chicago, it's best known for its ribs, although they also have decent steak. $12-25.

Splurge

It's no accident that the most fashionable (and expensive) restaurants are situated near Steppenwolf and the surrounding theaters on Halsted. The ease of getting a reservation will be inversely proportional to the number of shows on around that time!

Each one of these restaurants offers a memorable, world-class dining experience, and will give you a great story to tell. Don't lose track of your budget, though — spending $500 on a meal for two is not unheard of.

Alinea, 1723 N Halsted St (*North/Clybourn Red Line*), +1 312 867-0110, *www.alinea-restaurant.com*. Ranked #1 in 2006 on Gourmet Magazine's "America's Top 50 Restaurants," Alinea is just two blocks from Charlie Trotter's, where the head chef started his career. The meal is served as either a 12-course tasting menu or 24-course "tour" menu, so plan

LINCOLN PARK DRINK

your evening with plenty of time.
Tasting: $135, Tour: $195.

Boka, 1729 N Halsted St
(*North/Clybourn Red Line*), +1 312
337-6070, *www.bokachicago.com*,
Su-F 5PM-2AM, Sa 5PM-3AM.
Another Charlie Trotter's alum
runs this popular, trendy restaurant. You won't need formal
dress, but you will need a reservation. The menu mixes Japanese,
Mediterranean, European, and
dang ol' Midwestern food without apparent self-consciousness.
Plenty of seafood and a raw bar,
too. Dinners are satisfying but
light, making it the perfect place
for a pre-show meal. $50+.

Charlie Trotter's, 816 W Armitage
Ave (*North/Clybourn Red Line*), +1
773 248-6228, *www.charlietrotters.
com*, Tu-Th 6-10PM, F-Sa 5:30-
10PM, M variable (call ahead).
One of the finest restaurants in the
world, this contemporary American establishment has set the
standard by which all others are
judged for the past 20 years. Even
if the menu is a bit dated now, nobody does a wine-and-food pair-
ing as well as Charlie Trotter's.
$125-200.

Drink

If there's a college sports game
that you can't miss while you're in
town, make tracks to Lincoln Park.
Most of the alumni associations
(especially for Big Ten schools)
have a bar staked out for themselves.

3rd Coast Cafe, 1260 N Dearborn St, +1 312 649-0730,
www.3rdcoastcafe.com, 7AM-

midnight daily. Once known
as the Chicago meet-up spot
for 2600, the computer hackers
quarterly, 3rd Coast is an upscale
late-night oasis amid blocks of
impressive, silent Old Town row
houses. Evenings feature jazz and
solo guitarists, and the food is far
above average for a cafe.

B.L.U.E.S. (B.L.U.E.S. on Halsted St), 2519 N Halsted St
(*Fullerton Red/Brown/Purple Line*),
www.chicagobluesbar.com, Su-F
8PM-2AM, Sa 8PM-3AM. Small
but dedicated blues bar. On
Sundays, one cover charge gets
you into B.L.U.E.S. and Kingston
Mines across the road.

Delilah's, 2770 N Lincoln Ave, +1
773 472-2771, *www.delilahschicago.
com*, Su-F 4PM-2AM, Sa 4PM-
3AM. This is the joint where Kurt
(Cobain) met Courtney (Love).
No kidding. The booze selection
is unbeatable and recent almost-
rock-stars spin the records.

Kingston Mines, 2548 N Halsted St (*Fullerton Red/Brown/Purple
Line*), *www.kingstonmines.com*, Su-
F 8PM-4AM, Sa 8PM-5AM. The
larger of the blues bars on Halsted. Has a great set-up with two
stages and two bands every night.
One band plays for an hour on
one stage then the other band
takes over on the second stage for
an hour — continuous music all
night from 9:30PM.

Liar's Club, 1665 W Fullerton Ave
(*74 Fullerton bus*), +1 773 665-
1110, Su-F 8PM-2AM, Sa 8PM-
3AM. Good place to dance on the
weekend — the DJs play the hits
and know how to take the mea-

sure of the frat-free crowd. The round wood track-lit dance floor is a stand-out, too. If your friends don't dance, they can wait at the bar upstairs. $5 cover on weekends.

Neo, 2350 N Clark St (*Fullerton Red/Brown/Purple Line*), +1 773 528-2622, *neo-chicago.com*, Su-F 10PM-4AM, Sa 10PM-5AM. A Goth dance fortress in the heart of Lincoln Park. Music varies by night, mostly industrial and electro, with metal on Mondays and '80s/new wave on Thursdays. Drinks are reasonably priced, and include cheap beer. Th-Sa Cover $5.

Old Town Ale House, 219 W North Ave (*Sedgwick Brown Line*), +1 312 944-7020, *www.oldtownalehouse.net*, M-F 8AM-4AM, Sa 8AM-5AM, Su noon-4AM. An old-time Old Town dive, decorated with photos and newspaper clippings to show its history and favored status among famous Second City alums. Note the *very* late hours.

Red Lion Pub, 2446 Lincoln Ave (*Fullerton Red/Brown/Purple Line*), +1 773 348-2695, *www.redlionchicago.com*, 12PM-1:30AM. Great English pub with two comfortable floors across the street from the Biograph. (And like the Biograph, it's rumored to be haunted.) A few literary clubs meet here for readings.

Webster's Wine Bar, 1480 W Webster Ave (*Fullerton Red/Brown/Purple Line*), +1 773 868-0608, *www.websterwinebar.com*. Web-

ster's has wine tastings/classes twice a month, and all of the expertise to satisfy a sophisticate.

Sleep

Arlington House Hostel, 616 W Arlington Pl (*Fullerton Red/Brown/Purple Line*), +1 773 929-5380, +1 800 467-8355, *www.arlingtonhouse.com*. Hostel kitchen, laundry, games, guitars. Dorm beds from $23, private rooms from $57.

Belair Hotel, 424 W Diversey Pkwy (*Diversey Brown Line*), +1 773 248-4000. Caters to travelers on long-term stays — amenities are spare, but it's a cheap backup option. Close to the lakefront. Rooms from $208/week.

The Belden-Stratford Hotel, 2300 Lincoln Park West (*Fullerton Red Line*), +1 773 281-2900, *www.beldenstratford.com*. Gorgeous building across from Lincoln Park Zoo, overlooking the lake. It's primarily an apartment building, but there are 40 hotel rooms across its 17 floors. Rooms from $139.

Days Inn - Lincoln Park North, 644 W Diversey Pkwy (*Diversey Brown Line*), +1 888 576-3297, *www.lpndaysinn.com*. Frequented by touring bands in town to play at one of the many big clubs on the north side. $98-$130.

The Inn at Lincoln Park, 601 W Diversey Pkwy (*Diversey Brown Line*), +1 773 348-2810, *www.innlp. com*. A short walk to the Lincoln Park Zoo and the lakefront. Rooms from $148.

Contact

Lincoln Park Branch Library, 1150 W Fullerton Ave (*Fullerton Red/Brown/Purple Line*), +1 312 744-1926, *www.chipublib.org*, M-Th 9AM-9PM, F-Sa 9AM-5PM. Public library with free internet access. Two blocks west of the train station.

Screenz, 2717 N Clark St, +1 773 348-9300, *www.screenz.com/screenz*, M-Th 8AM-midnight, F 8AM-1AM, Sa 9AM-1AM, Su 9AM-midnight. Full-service internet cafe.

Get out

If you are in the mood for exploration, and would like to evade the sports bar scene in Lincoln Park, consider heading west across the river to Wicker Park *p.229* or Bucktown *p.247* for some more colorful nightlife and shopping.

L akeview has the lion's share of Chicago nightlife, starting with **Wrigleyville**, home of the Chicago Cubs and major players in the city's theater and music scenes, and **Boystown**, one of the largest and most vibrant GLBT communities in the United States. Down the street from both is the Belmont strip, where teen punks flock to shop and show off in the Dunkin' Donuts parking lot.

Further west are the neighborhoods of **North Center**, **Roscoe Village** and **St. Ben's**, which have fun, laid-back bars and restaurants.

Understand

For many years, Lakeview was so far away from the action that opening a saloon on Clark Street was a considered a peaceful retirement for convicted ex-politicians in Chicago. With the expansion of the elevated train system, however, that changed rapidly, and with the 1914 construction of Weeghman Park, later to be known as **Wrigley Field**, Lakeview became the capital of the North Side. The Chicago Cubs, also known as the most dominant baseball franchise of the 19th century, took up residence at Wrigley and commenced the relentless lack of success that has made them famous. Other teams have slumps, but the Cubs are beyond compare, tormenting their fans a hundred years of near-misses, late collapses, and abject futility unrivaled in American professional sports. So why is Game Day still a joy in Wrigleyville? As the last franchise in baseball to install stadium lights for night games, the

Cubs' schedule still features more early afternoon starts than any other team in the league, and the sun-soaked ivy walls of Wrigley Field are a pleasure no matter what the score. Today, it's a rare thing in America: a genuine neighborhood ballpark, surrounded by streets that amplify the Cubs fandom into frenzy on game day. As a nightlife destination, Wrigleyville also supports the **Metro**, one of Chicago's foremost rock venues, and other great ones like **Schuba's** and **The Vic**. The storefront theater scene also thrives here.

But there's more to Lakeview than Wrigleyville. A short walk east is **Boystown**, home of a cheerful, lively GLBT community and a great destination for anyone who enjoys high-energy nightlife. It's also home to the massive annual **Pride Parade** in June. **Roscoe Village** is west of Wrigley, and is popular with older gay couples and young people lured in by fashionable boutiques and the promise of a sunny day at one of the many sidewalk cafes on Southport, not to mention Chicago's premier movie revival house, the **Music Box**. And Lakeview embraces its inner dive bar in **North Center**, full of converted warehouses, quality bowling alleys and cheap beer without the jocks.

Get in

By train

The CTA **Red Line** makes stops in Lakeview (Belmont) and Wrigleyville (Addison, Sheridan). The **Brown Line**, further west,

connects with the Red Line at Belmont, and makes additional stops in Lakeview (Diversey, Wellington, Southport), Roscoe Village (Paulina), and North Center (Addison, Irving Park). All but Belmont and Sheridan are wheelchair accessible. The **Purple Line** from the Loop *p.47* and Evanston also stops at Belmont during weekday rush hours.

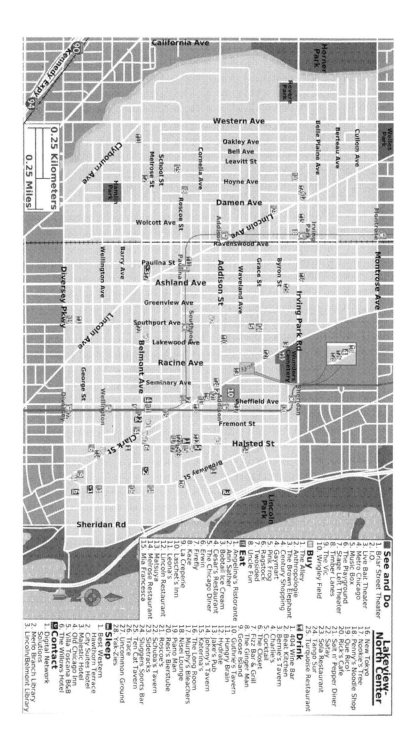

Lakeview–North Center

■ See and Do
1. Briar Street Theater
2. I.O.
3. Live Bait Theater
4. Metro Chicago
5. Music Box
6. The Playground
7. Stage Left Theater
8. Timber Lanes
9. The Vic
10. Wrigley Field

◆ Buy
1. The Alley
2. Anthropologie
3. The Brown Elephant
4. Century Shopping
5. Gaymart
6. Pink Frog
7. Ragstock
8. Twosided
9. Uncle Fun

■ Eat
1. Angelina's Ristorante
2. Ann Sather
3. Bobtail Ice Cream
4. Century Shopping
5. Tea's Restaurant
6. Chicago Diner
7. Erwin
8. Firefly
9. Kaze
10. La Creperie
11. Laschet's Inn
12. Leona's
13. Lincoln Restaurant
14. Matsuya
15. Melrose Restaurant
16. Mia Francesca

16. New Tokyo
17. Nookie's Tree
18. Penny's Noodle Shop
19. Que Rico!
20. Rick's Cafe
21. Salt n' Pepper Diner
22. Sala Restaurant
23. Tango Sur
24. Turquoise Restaurant

◼ Drink
1. 404 Wine Bar
2. Bar Kitchen
3. Bernie's Tavern
4. Charlie's
5. Cocktail
6. The Closet
7. Fizz Bar & Grill
8. The Ginger Man
9. Goose Island
10. Guthrie's Tavern
11. Hungry Brain
12. Hydrate
13. Jake's Pub
14. Johnny's Tavern
15. Katerina's
16. The Long Room
17. Murphy's Bleachers
18. Nisei Lounge
19. Piano Man
20. Resi's Bierstube
21. Roscoe's
22. Schuba's Tavern
23. Sidetracks
24. Sluggers Sports Bar
25. Ten Cat Tavern
26. Trace
27. Uncommon Ground
28. Yak-Zies

■ Sleep
1. Best Western Hawthorn Terrace
2. City Suites Hotel
3. Majestic Hotel
4. Old Chicago Inn
5. Villa Toscana B&B
6. The Willows Hotel

Contact
1. Digital Network Solutions
2. Merlo Branch Library
3. Lincoln/Belmont Library

LAKEVIEW SEE

By bus

8 Halsted travels through Boystown. Be warned, though, that a recent poll named this the worst bus route in the city. It's late when it shows up and goes nowhere fast.

9 Ashland is an all-night route.

11 Lincoln runs from Lincoln Park through some nice parts of Roscoe Village and North Center, connecting with the Brown Line at Paulina, and on to Lincoln Square *p.313.*

22 Clark runs the length of the north side, but it slows to a crawl through Wrigleyville, particularly on weekends and on days of Cubs games. It runs all night long.

36 Broadway comes in from Uptown *p.273* and carries on to the Loop *p.47.*

49 Western runs all night through most of the city and hits the Belmont/Western intersection, near which is the best of the Roscoe Village nightlife.

76 Diversey runs east/west on Diversey, the border between Lincoln Park and Lakeview, and continues to Logan Square.

77 Belmont runs all night and connects Roscoe Village with the Belmont Red/Brown Line stop and Boystown.

80 Irving Park runs most of the east/west length of the city, connecting with the Brown Line in North Center and the Sheriden Red Line.

152 Addison travels east/west through the edge of Boystown, Wrigleyville, and on to North Center.

By car

Lake Shore Drive has exits at Belmont and Addison. Beware of driving on Clark Street on weekends and during Cubs games, though. The taxis are a menace and the drunks are drawn to the middle of the street like flies to lights. You'll go nowhere fast and see Chicago at its worst in slowmotion.

See

Horner Park, 2741 W Montrose Ave, +1 773 478-3499, *www.chicagoparkdistrict.com*. Great big wonderful park with plenty of softball fields, football and soccer fields, basketball and tennis courts, trees, and a nice walking path. The leafy surroundings make it a great place for the annual pumpkin patch in the fall.

Wunders Cemetery, 3963 N Clark St (*Sheridan Red Line*), +1 773 525-4038. Overshadowed by the magnificent Graceland Cemetery across the street in Uptown, the smaller, slightly overgrown Wunders was established in 1859 and features some intriguing monuments, with more of a forgotten-by-time atmosphere than its more famous neighbor. A third cemetery, **Jewish Graceland**, is directly south. Free.

Do

Music Box, 3733 N Southport Ave (*Southport Brown Line*), +1 773 871-6604, *www.musicboxtheatre.com*, Evening shows on weekdays, matinees and midnight movies on weekends. Chicago's foremost source of cinematic delight, with two screens for classic and world-premiere independent movies and the occasional mini-festival. Tickets $8.25-$9.25.

Timber Lanes, 1851 W Irving Park Rd (*Irving Park Brown Line*), +1 773 549-9770, *www.timberlanesbowl.com*, M-F 11AM-2AM, Sa 3PM-3AM, Su 1PM-2AM. If you like to sample the bowling culture of any city you visit, this is a fine choice; there are eight well-kept lanes, a cash bar, a good jukebox, and a few references to *The Big Lebowski*. Might be wise to call ahead for availability in the early evening, though, as there are a few leagues. $2-$2.50 per game, except F-Sa at night, when it's $20/hour per lane.

Wrigley Field, 1060 W Addison St (*Addison Red Line*), +1 773 404-2827, *chicago.cubs.mlb.com*. Ernie Banks, Harry Caray, that damned billy goat, and the 1908 champs; yes, this is the home of the **Chicago Cubs**, the North Side's beloved, diabolically unsuccessful baseball team. Among ballparks, only Fenway in Boston can match the old-time beauty of Wrigley and its famous ivy-covered walls. If you'd like to see Wrigley without attending a game, **tours** *chicago.cubs.mlb.com* are occasionally offered ($25). Tickets can be as low as $8 for 'value dates', but the prize seats in the bleachers are usually $32, and certain dates wind up in scalpers' hands long before regular folks get a shot at them. 'Associations' host 'guests' on the rooftops around Wrigley, usually with unlimited beer and burgers, for upwards of $100.

Take me out(side) to the ball game

Cubs games can sell out months in advance, especially for weekend games and battles with their crosstown rivals, the White Sox. But if that's the only time you have to visit, don't despair. Show up early and inquire at the Day Of Game ticket windows at Clark and Addison. If they turn you away, walk around outside and see if the scalpers are offering anything within your budget. (If you're feeling really confident, slip into one of the long lines for the rooftop parties on Sheffield or Waveland and claim to be with whatever party the guy two spots ahead of you claims to be with. IDs are not always checked, and once you're in, security is nil.) Still no luck? Relax outside the sidewalk-level fence on Sheffield to get a decent view of the game. There are always a few people watching it there for free. Scalpers will get desperate by the fourth inning and approach you with offers. If you have no money at all to spend, head down to Waveland Avenue and join the die-hards camped out there to chase out-of-the-park home run balls. Somebody usually has a radio tuned to the game action, and you might come away with a souvenir.

LAKEVIEW◖◗

Music

A few great venues are also listed under Drink as well.

Metro, 3730 N Clark St (*Addison Red Line*), +1 773 549-0203, *www.metrochicago.com*. Chicago's foremost rock venue, although other genres like electronic and hip hop figure in the lineup as well. If a band is on the verge of stardom and they're on their way through Chicago, the Metro has a knack for booking them. Many shows are all ages, and are generally affordable. Tickets general admission (e.g. standing room only), so be prepared to stand, and press forward for your right to see a guitarist's nostrils. **Smart Bar**, next door, is owned by the Metro and features good DJs most nights of the week. Tickets vary by event.

Schuba's, 3159 N Southport Ave, +1 773 525-2508, *www.schubas.com*, Shows start 9-10:30PM. One of Chicago's landmark venues for cool music. The building was built over a hundred years ago by the Schlitz beer company, a heritage that is acknowledged by countless plastic cups serving that and other cheap beers for indie rock fans. Tickets $10-$18.

The Vic, 3145 N Sheffield Ave (*Belmont CTA*), +1 773 472-0449, *www.victheatre.com*, Check website for movie showtimes; usually two shows, 8PM/10:30PM. The Vic hosts the **Brew and View** *www.brewview.com*, a second-run movie theater with cheap Miller beer, and turns into a good concert venue on other nights — not dissimilar to the Metro in size or sound quality, but there are seats. Concert prices vary; movies are $5, plus $1.50 for cheap beers.

Theaters

Briar Street Theater, 3133 N Halsted St (*Belmont CTA*), +1 773 348-4000, *www.blueman.com*, Box office M-F 9AM-9PM, Sa 9AM-10PM, Su 12-4PM. The Chicago home of the nationally famed performance art Blue Man Group. Shows in the evenings, with matinees included on weekends. (Be advised, though: if you've seen them elsewhere, you're not likely to see anything new here.) Tickets from $49.

iO (formerly ImprovOlympic), 3541 N Clark St (*Addison Red Line*), +1 773 880-0199, *www.iochicago.net*, Usually two shows a night, around 8PM/10:30PM, with midnight shows F-Sa. iO is the puppy mill of improv comedy: its training center churns out graduates at a rapid pace, and most are given the brief honor of performing unpaid on its two stages (both of which have bars) until there are more grads to rotate in. Shows are generally solid, if lacking the artistic direction that makes the other major comedy theaters great. However, when veterans and visiting luminaries take the stage on Monday nights for the **Armando Diaz Experience** or Wednesdays for *TJ & Dave*, the results can be exhilarating. W 8PM and midnight shows free; other shows $5-$14.

Live Bait Theater, 3914 N Clark St (*Sheridan Red Line*), +1 773 871-

1212, *www.livebaittheater.org*. Live Bait is a good venue for small theater companies such as current residents **The Artistic Home** *www.theartistichome.org* and solo performers to debut original plays or adaptations — no bad seats, and reliably interesting shows. Tickets usually $10-20.

The Playground, 3209 N Halsted St (*Belmont CTA*), +1 773 871-3793, *www.the-playground.com*, Usually two shows a night, around 8PM/10PM, with occasional midnight shows F-Sa. The Playground has a few things going for it: the perfect location for beginning or ending the night with a show, a BYOB liquor license, and a non-profit co-op structure that makes the performers here some of the most enthusiastic and committed you'll find. Quality will vary by ensemble, but long-timers Homey Loves Chachi and The Fling are exceptional, and the **Big Yellow Bus** on Thursday nights assembles the best the theater has to offer. $8-$12.

Stage Left Theater, 3408 N Sheffield Ave (*Addison Red Line*), +1 773 883-8830, *www.stagelefttheatre.com*, Shows usually 8PM. One of the mainstays of Chicago's storefront theater since 1982, Stage Left hosts everything: new works of social, political, intently serious drama are balanced out by manic rough drafts of new comedies by guest ensembles and the "R-rated improv" of the pH company *www.whatisph.com* late Friday and Saturday nights. Tickets $10-20.

Events & Festivals

Pride Parade, 3712 N Broadway St, +1 773 348-8243, *www.chicagopridecalendar.org*, Last weekend of June. The annual celebration of Chicago's gay community, led by a parade down Halsted with floats and foam rubber contraptions that are not for the faint-of-heart. It's *crowded*, but it's a favorite of people from all over the city, and always high-energy. Most Boystown bars, clubs, and restaurants hold special events along with it.

Buy

There are a few shopping areas of note. The Southport Corridor (3300 N to 3800 N) has a row of independent boutiques along with a few specialty stores. Lincoln Avenue in Roscoe Village also has some worthwhile shops, particularly near the Paulina Brown Line stop. Clark Street near Diversey has a few chain retailers like Marshall's, and a number of upscale boutiques are crammed alongside resale behemoths on Belmont, near the train station.

On game days, the streets of Wrigleyville are packed with vendors selling cheap Cubs gear.

The Alley, 3228 N Clark St (*Belmont CTA*), +1 773 883-1800, *www. thealley.com*, M-Th 1PM-9PM, F-Sa 1PM-11PM, Su 12PM-8PM. *The* rock 'n roll shop in Chicago. Styles extend into punk, mod, emo, rockabilly, and goth; offerings range from clothes, shoes, and jewelry to bondage gear. It's the kind of edgy that is loved by no one as much as teenagers. Look for the skull and crossbones logo.

Anthropologie, 3532 N Southport Ave (*Southport Brown Line*), +1 773 935-2693, *www.anthropologie. com*, M-Sa 10AM-7PM, Su 12-5PM. Librarian chic clothes boutique.

The Brown Elephant, 3645 N Halsted St., +1 773 549-5943 , 11AM-6PM daily. Find bargains on a large selection of second hand merchandise, including many upscale brands. All proceeds support HIV/AIDS care and gay and lesbian services.

Century Shopping Centre, 2828 N Clark St, +1 773 929-8100, Most stores M-F 10:30AM-9PM, Sa 10:30AM-6PM, Su 12-6PM; open later for movies. A vertical mall headlined by the **Landmark's Century Centre** multiplex *www.landmarktheatres.com* showing independent and foreign movies, and several floors of stores from fashion chains like **The Express**.

Gaymart, 3457 N Halsted St (*Belmont CTA*), +1 773 929-4272, M,W-Sa 11AM-7PM, Su 12-6PM. With a large variety of gay-themed items — from sex toys to mouse pads and greeting cards — Gaymart is a must visit for Boystown shoppers.

Pink Frog, 3201 N Clark St, +1 773 525-2680, M-Sa 11AM-7:30PM, Su 12-5PM. One of the best places in Chicago for cute and stylish shoes for women, and a selection of jackets and skirts to match. If you can't find the shoes you want here, the DSW Warehouse at 3131 N Clark is huge and might have them.

Ragstock, 812 W Belmont Ave (*Belmont CTA*), +1 773 868-9263, *www.ragstock.com*, M-Th 10AM-9PM, F-Sa 10AM-10PM, Su 12-7PM. Cheap re-sale clothes shop. They also have a location in Wicker Park, but this one is open later (for those impulse fedoras) and has two floors.

Twosided, 2958 N Clark St (*Wellington Brown Line*), +1 773 244-6431, *www.twosided.net*, M-Sa 11AM-7PM, Su 11AM-6PM. Excellent selection of letterpress cards and other artful items, antiques, and one-of-a-kind objects. They also have a framing gallery in Andersonville, Foursided, but this one is a true gem.

Uncle Fun, 1338 W Belmont Ave (*Belmont CTA*), +1 773 477-8223, *www.unclefunchicago.com*, Tu-F 12-7PM, Sa 11AM-7PM, Su 11AM-5PM. Somewhere between a treasure hunt, a toy store, and a state of derangement — all designed, in their own words, to Restore your Whimsical Nature.

Eat

It's not until you reach the high-end that Lakeview dining becomes especially memorable, but there are plenty of quick, reliable places. Most importantly, a lot of them are **open late** — this is probably the best place in the city to grab a bite after midnight.

Budget

Bobtail Ice Cream Company, 2951 N Broadway St, 3425 N Southport Ave, +1 773 880-7372

(Broadway), 773-248-6104 (South-port), *www.bobtailicecream.com*, Oct-Mar Su-Th 11AM-10PM, F-Sa 11AM-11PM; Apr-Sept Su-Th 11AM-11PM, F-Sa 11AM-midnight. Terrific locally-made ice cream at half the price of Cold Stone. The Broadway location has a small, retro soda fountain ambiance, while the Southport is roomier and more modern.

Lincoln Restaurant, 4008 N Lincoln Ave (*Irving Park Brown Line*), +1 773 248-1820, M-F 6AM-10:30PM, Sa-Su 6AM-11PM. The food is average/above average diner fare, and the decor hasn't changed for decades, but a certain kind of person will feel compelled to enter by the giant head of Abraham Lincoln hanging out front, and perhaps you are that person. There's no accounting for the Civil War-themed menus, though. Good stand-up comedy shows are sometimes held in the **Lincoln Lodge** *www.thelincolnlodge.com* side-room, and there's a bar as well. $8-13.

Melrose Restaurant, 3233 N Broadway St, +1 773 327-2060, 24 hours. Open around the clock and always busy, the Melrose is a diner of modest culinary aspirations (burgers, omelettes) but it's right at the center of Boystown whether it's time for brunch or long past time to sleep. $7-9.

Nookie's Tree, 3334 N Halsted St, +1 773 248-9888, *www.nookiesrestaurants.net*, M-Th, Su 7AM-12AM, F-Sa all night. Casual, unpretentious diner that has been in Boystown for a long time. It's great for brunch,

late-nights on weekends, and people-watching. $9-14.

Penny's Noodle Shop, 3400 N Sheffield Ave, +1 773 281-8222, *www.pennysnoodleshop.com*, Su,Tu-Th 11AM-10PM, F-Sa 11AM-10:30PM, M closed. The original location and always busy. If you're looking for fast food, Penny's serves delicious Thai/Asian food and charges less than McDonald's. $4-8.

Salt n' Pepper Diner, 3537 N Clark St (*Addison Red Line*), +1 773 883-9800, M-Th 7AM-10PM, F-Sa 7AM-midnight, Su 7AM-4PM. This Wrigleyville greasy spoon has typical diner fare, but done in a way that makes it uniquely Chicago. The burgers are excellent, and so is the service. Lunch under $9.

Satay, 936 W Diversey Ave (*Diversey Brown Line*), +1 773 477-0100, Tu-Th 11AM-10PM, F-Sa 11AM-11PM, Su-M 4PM-10PM. Decent Thai, Chinese, and Japanese food directly under the Diversey station. (It's never too loud, though.) The menu is surprisingly long for the size of the place, and they tend to do tofu notably well. $7-11.

Mid-range

Angelina's Ristorante, 3561 N Broadway St, +1 773 935-5933, *www.angelinaristorante.com*, M-Th 5:30-10PM, F-Sa 5:30-11PM, Su brunch 10:30AM-3PM, 5:30-10PM. High-end Italian cuisine with a charming, intimate vibe. The pumpkin ravioli is a knockout. $14-25.

Ann Sather, 929 W Belmont Ave (*Belmont CTA*), +1 773 348-2378, *www.annsather.com*, M-F 7AM-3PM, Sa-Su 7AM-4PM. This Swedish standby is a can't-miss for one of the city's best breakfasts, served all day, including warm, fresh-baked cinnamon rolls dripping with sugary icing. Now a bona-fide chainlet with five locations around Chicago, but try the nicely renovated 50-year-old Belmont branch. $10-14.

Cesar's Restaurant, 3166 N Clark St (*Belmont CTA*), +1 773 248-2835, *www.killermargaritas.com*, M-Th 11AM-11PM, F-Sa 11AM-midnight, Su 1-8PM. Mind-blowing margaritas and Mexican food at a price that practically demands over-indulgence. There's another location nearby at 2924 N Broadway. $9-14 for a meal, although the sky's the limit with the margaritas.

The Chicago Diner, 3411 N Halsted St, +1 773 935-6696, *www.veggiediner.com*, M-Th 11AM-10PM, F 11AM-10:30PM, Sa 10AM-10:30PM, Su 10AM-10PM. A restaurant serving vegetarian-only food on Chicago's north side, the Diner's emphasis on quality — and its vegan shakes, which it proudly describes as "the shiznit" — has kept it around for more than 20 years. $11-16, but $5.99 veggie brunch is offered until 3:30PM.

La Creperie, 2845 N Clark St (*Diversey Brown Line*), +1 773 528-9050, *www.lacreperieusa.com*, Tu-F 11:30AM-11PM, Sa 11AM-11PM, Su 11AM-9:30PM. Big, tasty crepes for breakfast, dinner, and dessert, with plenty of wine and beer. The outdoor seating is especially nice. $8-14.

Laschet's Inn, 2119 W Irving Park Rd (*Irving Park Brown Line*), +1 773 478-7915, M-F 2PM-10:30PM, Sa-Su noon-10:30PM; tavern to 2AM Su-F, to 3AM Sa. Originally a tavern, Laschet's now has a full kitchen for mighty German food and meaty dinner specials. $7-20.

Leona's, 3215 N Sheffield Ave (*Belmont CTA*), +1 773 327-8861, *www.leonas.com*, Su-Th 11:30AM-11PM, F-Sa 11:30AM-12:30AM. The original location of the Chicago chainlet, serving good Italian and American fare. They serve plenty of meat, but the menu is friendly to vegetarians. Also notable for their fried mozzarella sticks, which are huge enough that they must be ordered individually. $12-18.

Matsuya, 3469 N Clark St (*Addison Red Line*), +1 773 248-2677, M-F 5-11:30PM, Sa-Su noon-11:30PM. Not to be confused the beef bowl chain in Japan, but this Matsuya serves good, reliable sushi and tempura platters, and earns points for being an oasis amid the otherwise greasy food near Wrigley. $11-$17.

New Tokyo, 3139 N Broadway St, +1 773 248-1193, 2-10PM. A small, unpretentious sushi joint at the edge of Boystown, and BYOB as a bonus. The menu has a good variety for budget and taste. $10-16.

Que Rico!, 2814 N Southport Ave, +1 773 975-7436, M-Th 5-11PM, F-Su 12-10PM. Great Mexican/Argentinean food with comfortable indoor and outdoor seating that can turns one hour into three before you ever think to look at your watch. There's a second location at 2301 W Roscoe (tel. 773-248-7426) in Roscoe Village. $14-22.

Splurge

Erwin, 2925 N Halsted St, +1 773 528-7200, *www.erwincafe.com*, Tu-Th 5:30-9:30PM, F-Sa 5:30-10:30PM, Su 10:30AM-2PM (brunch), 5-9PM (dinner). Billed as "an American cafe," Erwin has a short menu of original creations and a few stand-bys, supported by a sizable bar and cute, family-friendly decor. Their burgers tend to score well in local food lists. Valet parking available ($8). $20-27.

Firefly, 3335 N Halsted St, +1 773 525-2505, M-Sa 5:30PM-1:30AM (closed Tu), Su 5:30PM-midnight. Fine dining and a fine atmosphere in the midst of Boystown, with a mostly carnivorous French-accented menu. Just an all-around nice place for a good evening with a friend, a date, or anyone visiting Boystown for the first time. $18-27.

Kaze, 2032 W Roscoe St (*Addison Brown Line*), +1 773 327-4860, *www.kazesushi.com*, 5-11PM. Top-of-the-line fresh sushi. Tuesday nights feature a four-course (plus sake) tasting menu for $45 per person.

Mia Francesca, 3311 N Clark St (*Belmont CTA*), +1 773 281-3310, *www.miafrancesca.com*, Dinner Su-Th 5-10PM, F-Sa 5-11PM; brunch

Sa-Su 11:30AM-2PM. The original location for Mia Francesca's fine Italian dining, and the best — it's noisy, crowded, and *not* the place for an intimate meal, but Mia's has great pasta & fish, and offers a very Chicago atmosphere of hustle & bustle. $18-30.

Rick's Cafe, 3915 N Sheridan Rd (*Sheridan Red Line*), +1 773 327-1972, Tu-Su 6-10:30PM, M closed. The food is made with love at this great little restaurant, run by a husband and wife. "Casablanca" is the perfect metaphor for the menu here, which surrounds colonial powers like Spanish, French, and Italian food with elements from Moroccan and Mediterranean. It's BYOB, and there's a liquor store across the street. $20-30.

Sola, 3868 N Lincoln Ave (*Irving Park Brown Line*), +1 773 327-3868, *www.sola-restaurant.com*, Lunch Th-F 11:30AM-2PM, Sa-Su 10AM-2PM; Dinner Su-Th 5:30-10PM, F-Sa 5:30-11PM. Chef Carol Wallack was Jack Nicholson's personal chef, which is about as fine a qualification as anyone could have. The menu covers contemporary American cuisine with Hawaiian, Asian, and Polynesian accents. $15-28.

Tango Sur, 3763 N Southport Ave (*Southport Brown Line*), +1 773 477-5466, M-Th 5-10:30PM, F-Sa 5-11:30PM, Su noon-10:30PM. Argentinean steakhouse with *fantastic* beef. There are a few side dishes like empanadas and a good dessert menu, but the beef is the star attraction. It's BYOB. $20-30.

LAKEVIEW DRINK

Turquoise Restaurant, 2147 W Roscoe St, +1 773 549-3523, *www.turquoisedining.com*, M-Th 11:30AM-11PM, F-Su 11AM-midnight. Extensive menu of fresh seafood, Mediterranean, and vegetarian specialties. Plenty of fruity and exotic drinks and lounging space on offer, too. $18-26.

Drink

Boystown

The nightlife in Boystown may be the best in Chicago. It's wild, uninhibited and just plain fun, regardless of sexual orientation. Most of the action is on Halsted/Broadway between Addison and Belmont.

Charlie's, 3726 N Broadway St, +1 773 871-8887, *www.charlieschicago. com*, Su-F 3PM-4AM, Sa 3PM-5AM. Late night dance bar and a great place for the after hours party, although they play country for the early crowd before midnight on weeknights or 2AM on the weekends. Karaoke hits on Sunday and Thursday.

The Closet, 3325 N Broadway St, +1 773 477-8533, *www.theclosetchicago.com*, M-F 2PM-4AM, Sa 12PM-5AM, Su 12PM-4AM. Forgive the pun if you can — this lesbian dive bar is another great after hours destination and *the* place to go for hook-up attempts that drag late into the night. It's open a lot earlier in the day than most Boystown spots and usually has sports or music videos on by day.

Cocktail, 3359 N Halsted St, +1 773 477-1420, Su-F 4PM-2AM, Sa 4PM-3AM. A small, fashionable bar that anyone can walk right into for a drink at the bar or a dance among the eye candy at the back.

Hydrate, 3458 N Halsted St, +1 773 975-9244, *www.hydratechicago. com*, Su-F 8PM-4AM, Sa 8PM-5AM. Inheritor of the space formerly owned by the infamous Manhole, Hydrate is now the ultimate dance club to See-and-Be-Seen on Halsted. On a night out in Boystown, everybody winds up here at one point or another. Cover $10-20, depending on DJ and event.

Roscoe's, 3356 N Halsted St, +1 773 281-3355, *www.roscoes.com*, M-Th 3PM-2AM, F 2PM-2AM, Sa 1PM-3AM, Su 1PM-2AM. Roscoe's is a multi-purpose bar — by night, there are good drink specials and a great dance floor, but by day, you'll find a relaxed neighborhood bar with artwork by local artists and a sidewalk cafe (in the summer) for lunch.

Sidetracks, 3349 N Halsted St, +1 773 477-9189, *www.sidetrackchicago.com*, Su-F 3PM-2AM, Sa 3PM-3AM. A large, stylish, multi-room bar that makes a great place to start the night, with slushy drinks and showtunes on a big screen. (Sundays are sing-along nights.) Gay or straight, this is one of the best bars in Chicago.

Wrigleyville

There is a watering hole for just about every personality type in Wrigleyville, particularly if you venture off the Clark Street drag near the ballpark. If you're here for a Cubs home game, rest assured that you'll be surrounded by thousands of merry Cubs fans and a world that desires nothing more than to put beer in your hands; on the downside, you'll be surrounded by thousands of Cubs fans and a world that desires nothing more than to spill beer on you, so get comfortable with sharing personal space with strangers. If you're drinking well into the night, choose wisely; as the evening wears on, a few of the bars on Clark turn into half-eaten piles of rancid nachos and the city's ripest gathering ground for date rape statistics.

Bernie's Tavern, 3664 N Clark St, +1 773 525-1898, Su-F 10AM-2AM, Sa 8AM-3AM. One of the most popular bars with locals and out-of-towners alike. The rather small inside bar opens to a large back patio. Crowd has gotten younger the past few years, but you'll still find fans from ages 20 to 90 having a good time.

The Ginger Man, 3740 N Clark St (*Addison Red Line*), +1 773 549-2050, M-F 3PM-2AM, 12PM-3AM, Su 12PM-2AM. Guaranteed the only bar in Wrigleyville with Joy Division and Public Enemy on the jukebox. If you want a beer after a Cubs game and you don't want to be surrounded by frat boys, this is the place. Next to the Metro and Smart Bar.

Goose Island, 3535 N Clark St, +1 773 832-9040, M-W 4-11PM, Th 4PM-12AM, F 4PM-2AM, Sa 11AM-2AM, Su 11AM-11PM. As the name suggests, you can drink the full range of the local Goose Island microbrews here, and it's reasonably spacious by Wrigleyville standards. Tasty food, too.

Guthrie's Tavern, 1300 W Addison Ave, +1 773 477-2900, M-Th 5PM-2AM, F 4PM-2AM, Sa 2PM-3PM, Su 2PM-2AM. Cozy neighborhood bar known for its extensive collection of board games and bottled wines. It's a local favorite that escapes most of the obnoxious behavior found down the street.

Murphy's Bleachers, 3655 N Sheffield Ave, +1 773 281-5356, *www.murphysbleachers.com*, Su-F 9AM-2PM, Sa 9AM-3AM. Granddaddy bar for all bleacher bums. Get there early if you want one of the coveted outside tables. It's always packed on game days; expect to pay $5 for a can of domestic beer. In the off-season, Murphy's turns into a rather cozy neighborhood bar.

Nisei Lounge, 3439 N Sheffield Ave, +1 773 525-0557, Su,T-F 11AM-2AM, Sa 11AM-3AM, M 6PM-2AM; open at 11AM on game days. Local cult favorite with an interesting Japanese backstory. No sushi here; just a great bar with a few pool tables.

Piano Man, 3801 N Clark St, +1 773 868-9611, Su-F 11AM-2AM, Sa 8AM-3AM; may be sporadically closed during the week in the off season. Popular local bar that has no piano, just a jukebox. Neighbors want to keep this place a secret, but the word has gotten out.

Sluggers Sports Bar & Dueling Pianos, 3540 N Clark St, +1 773 248-0055, 10AM-2AM on all Cubs home game days, otherwise: M-Th 3PM-2AM, F,Su 11AM-2AM, Sa 11AM-3AM; Piano Bar F 8PM-2AM, Sa 8PM-3AM. Home away from home for suburbanites. Packed on game days; some say too packed. Sing to your heart's content with the piano guys upstairs or get out your pent-up aggression from another Cubs' heartbreaking loss in the batting cages.

Trace, 3714 N Clark St, +1 773 477-3400, Su-F 5PM-4AM, Sa 5PM-4AM; 4PM-4AM for all Cubs night games; open two hours prior to home games. Less overtly sports-focused than its neighbors. Great place if you are thirsty at 3AM.

Uncommon Ground, 3800 N Clark St, +1 773 929-3680, *www.uncommonground.com*, Su-Th 9AM-11PM, F-Sa 9AM-midnight. It's almost unbelievable that such a lovely, relaxed bar/cafe is this close to Wrigley, but there it is. Evenings see a full schedule of acoustic music with a full bar of beer, cocktails, and wine, while organic breakfast, lunch and dinner are served all day, and two fireplaces await in the winter. Uncommon Ground also hosts the annual **Jeff Buckley Festival**, now in its tenth year, in honor of the singer's legendary 1994 performance there.

Yak-Zies Bar & Grill, 3710 N Clark St, +1 773 525-9200, Su-F 11AM-2AM; Sa 11AM-3AM. Surprisingly good food at this cash-only joint. Owners will put just about any sport that's televised anywhere on at least one TV if asked. Cornell vs. Harvard Men's Ice Hockey anyone?

> **Yes, Elwood, the address is correct**
> *The Captain Morgan Club, at 1060 W Addison, is attached to Wrigley Field. Non-ticket holders may enter and imbibe to their hearts' content while watching the game on TV. Ticket holders will find a separate entrance to the ballpark inside the bar that circumvents the chaotic Sheffield entrance right next door. It's open 10AM-10PM Su-Th; 10AM-11PM F-Sa.*

Others

Lakeview bars may get a bad name from the roiling mess on Clark Street, but there are actually several great places to drink within range of Wrigley.

404 Wine Bar, 2852 N Southport Ave, +1 773 404-5886, M-F 5PM-2AM, Sa 5PM-3AM. Comfortable atmosphere and a wide variety of wines. It may not be the first thing you think of when you think about a wine bar, but they serve a chicken pot pie that is *delicious*. It's connected to **Jack's** next door, which is more of a sports bar.

Beat Kitchen, 2100 W Belmont Ave, +1 773 281-4444, *www.beatkitchen.com*, M-Th 4PM-2AM, F 11:30AM-2AM, Sa 11:30AM-3AM, Su 11:30AM-2AM.

There's beer and late-night food in the quiet front room, but the Beat Kitchen is worthy of recognition as one of the best venues in the city outside of Wicker Park for double or triple bills of excellent, little-known local and touring bands. Tuesdays are set aside for the Chicago Underground Comedy stand-up showcase.

Fizz Bar & Grill, 3220 N Lincoln Ave (*Paulina Brown Line*), +1 773 348-6000, *fizzchicago.com*, M-F 5PM-2AM, Sa 12PM-3AM, Su 11AM-1AM. Nothing exceptional — just a bar on the classy side of things with a good beer garden, upscale food menu, and a dance floor that occasionally gets going.

Hungry Brain, 2319 W Belmont Ave, +1 773 935-2118, *www.emergingimprovisers.org*, Tu-Su 8PM-2AM. There's a lot to like at this small Roscoe Village bar: a few pinball and arcade machines, the sense of being in someone's comfortable basement (with beer), and the Sunday night (10PM) Transmission series for improvisational and experimental jazz.

Jake's Pub, 2932 N Clark St, +1 773 248-3318, *www.jakespub.net*, M-F 3PM-2AM, Sa noon-3AM, Su noon-2AM. A good place to recover from shopping binges at the Century Shopping Centre and its neighbors (see Buy). Jake's has a good beer selection and dependable jukebox. Dogs are not only welcome — they're encouraged.

Johnny's Tavern, 3425 N Lincoln Ave (*Paulina Brown Line*), +1 773 248-3000, Hours vary. About as far

from the Wrigleyville bar scene as you can possibly get; this legendary, straight-outta-1974 tavern is owned by an old man, Johnny, who is well into his eighties. If he chooses to let you in — after you've rang the doorbell, and waited patiently for admittance — you'll enjoy cheap Czech beers and a time-warp.

Katerina's, 1920 W Irving Park Rd, +1 773 348-7592, *www.katerinas.com*, M-F 5PM-2AM, Sa 5PM-3AM. A small and intimate setting for jazz, funk, blues, and Greek music most nights, and poetry, performance and movies when there isn't music. Southern European cuisine served along with the drinks.

The Long Room, 1612 W Irving Park Rd (*Irving Park Brown Line*), +1 773 665-4500, M-F 5PM-2AM, Sa 5PM-3AM, Su 7PM-2AM. A low-lit neighborhood lounge with a casual atmosphere worth settling into for a while — and, yes, it's a very long room.

Resi's Bierstube, 2034 W Irving Park Rd (*Irving Park Brown Line*), +1 773 472-1749, 3PM-2AM daily. A fine old-fashioned brauhaus, with high marks for the music, the beer garden, and the ambiance. Food on offer from the kitchen (closed Mondays) includes sausages and schnitzel, of course.

Ten Cat Tavern, 3931 N Ashland Ave (*Irving Park Brown Line*), +1 773 935-5377, Su-F 3PM-2AM, Sa 3PM-3AM. The kitty on the sign is cradling a ten-ball because there's pool to be played here, but in most other respects, this is someone's apartment that happens to have a bar in it (and a pretty good backyard).

Hot tamales?

One man connects the many bars of Roscoe Village and North Center. His name is unknown to most, but his offer is a local legend: "Hot tamales?"

For several years, the number of places visited by the hot tamales guy in one night (roughly 9PM to close) has put Santa Claus to shame. Many of these bars serve cheap beer but no food, so five tamales for $5 can seem like a pretty good deal, and he's even got cheese-only for vegetarians. He's not long on presentation, doing a steady trade of Ziploc bags from a cooler, but damned if those tamales don't hit the spot sometimes. Bargoers tend to hold him in awe for his sheer ubiquity, even when they're not hungry.

So if you're getting hungry but you're settled into a good dive, be patient. To paraphrase Ben Franklin, the Roscoe Village and North Center bar scene, nothing is certain except death, taxes, and the hot tamales guy.

Sleep

Most visitors will feel comfortable staying here in terms of safety, and Lakeview is a better place to experience something of the real city than the retail isolation of the Near North *p.71*. Given the boozy atmosphere, though, it's probably better for singles and young couples than families with kids in tow. (You can get to Wrigley from anywhere in the city via the Red or Brown Line, after all.)

There are also a handful of budget and mid-range options just south of Boystown in Lincoln Park *p.123*. Hotels are usually booked solid for the Pride Parade in June, so make reservations early or be ready to check in other areas.

Mid-range

Old Chicago Inn, 3222 N Sheffield Ave (*Belmont CTA*), +1 773 816-2465, *www.oldchicagoinn.com*. Reasonably priced bed and breakfast in a turn-of-the-century greystone building, not far from Wrigley Field and the nightlife on Belmont. Amenities include internet access in the lobby, continental breakfast, and a complimentary lunch or dinner at Trader Todd's restaurant/karaoke bar two doors south. Rooms from $99.

Villa Toscana Bed & Breakfast, 3447 N Halsted St (*Addison Red Line*), +1 800 404-2643, *www.thevillatoscana.com*. Closest accommodations to Wrigley Field, in a turn-of-the-century building. Rooms from $99/$109 off and on-season.

Splurge

Best Western Hawthorn Terrace, 3434 N Broadway (*Addison Red Line*), +1 773 244-3434, *www.hawthorneterrace.com*. 59 rooms with wireless internet and a breakfast buffet. It's close enough to walk to Wrigley Field and the bars on Clark Street, but not close enough that you'll have to listen to them while you try to sleep. Rooms from $189.

City Suites Hotel, 933 W Belmont Ave (*Belmont CTA*), +1 800 248-9108, *www.cityinns.com*. Art Deco interiors and elegant furnishings, right next to the Belmont train station — so light sleepers may want to look elsewhere. Among the amenities are wi-fi, afternoon cookies, and access to Bally's Fitness Club. Rooms from $189.

Majestic Hotel, 528 W Brompton Ave (*Belmont CTA*), +1 800 727-5108, *www.cityinns.com/majestic*. Boutique hotel in a residential pocket, with olde worlde touches like poster beds and butler pantries. Similar amenities to the City Suites Hotel, which is under the same management. Rooms from $209.

The Willows Hotel, 555 W Surf St (*Belmont CTA*), +1 800 787-3108, *www.cityinns.com/willows*. European decor in a city-designated landmark building, two blocks from the lake. Same management as the City Suites and Majestic hotels. Rooms from $179.

Contact

Digital Network Solutions, 2917 N Broadway St (*Wellington Brown Line*), +1 773 755-5225, *www.diginetsolution.com*, M-Th 9:30AM-12:30AM, F-Sa 12:30AM-1AM, Su 10AM-12:30AM. Scanning, printing, CD-burning available. Remarkably cheap at $3/hour.

Merlo Branch Library, 644 W Belmont Ave (*Belmont CTA*), +1 312 744-1139, *www.chipublib.org*, M-Th 9AM-9PM, F-Sa 9AM-5PM, Su closed. Free public internet access.

Three blocks east of the train station, near Boystown.

Lincoln/Belmont Branch Library, 1659 W Melrose St (*Paulina Brown Line*), +1 312 744-0166, *www.chipublib.org*, M-Th 9AM-9PM, F-Sa 9AM-5PM, Su closed. Free public internet access. Three blocks south of the train station.

Get out

If it's a crosstown baseball series, you'll need to get on the Red Line and head south to Bridgeport *p.175* for the Chicago White Sox.

It would take more than one curse to put the Cubs in their current condition, but the most famous of them, the Billy Goat Curse, began with the owner of the Billy Goat Tavern in the Near North *p.71*.

Follow the theater trail in the storefront comedy direction to Uptown *p.273* or the big-name comedy/drama direction in Old Town *p.123*.

Andersonville *p.273* is a stylish neighborhood a short trip northwest of Boystown with several gay and lesbian-friendly bars and businesses.

Edgewater *p.291* has the GLBT Gerber/Hart Library and the less scholarly Leather Archives and Museum. During the summer, Chicago's gay community tans at Edgewater's Hollywood Beach.

Dedicated to original theater that explores gender and sexual identity, the **About Face Theater Company** *aboutfacetheatre.com* performs at major theaters like

Steppenwolf in Old Town *p.71*
and storefronts around Boystown.

Hyde Park is one of Chicago's most famous neighborhoods, most certainly so on the South Side, located along the south lakefront. Having played host to the White City, the University of Chicago, President Obama, the setting for Richard White's Native Son, and a host of eccentric residents from Saul Bellow to Clarence Darrow to Muhammad Ali, this part of town has more than its fair share of Chicago history.

There is more than enough for a visitor to see here, and devoting a full day to exploring Hyde Park can make for a fine itinerary. Architecture buffs will have their hands occupied by the many Victorian mansions and Prairie School houses; anyone with an intellectual bent should be delighted by Hyde Park's independent bookstores, overawed by the University of Chicago's terrifying intensity, and intrigued by the Oriental Institute; and just about everyone will enjoy a trip to the stimulating Museum of Science and Industry or taking a stroll and a swim along the Point and the beach.

Understand

The White City

Aside from Rockefeller's decision to locate the university here, the neighborhood's biggest event was without a doubt **The Chicago World's Fair** in 1893, celebrating the 400 year anniversary of Columbus' first arrival in the New World. The event was designed largely by Frederick Law Olmstead and Daniel Burnham, and brought visitors (and exhibitions) from all over the world. The magnificently landscaped parks were all Olmstead's

HYDE PARK UNDERSTAND

creation, which sparked a wave of "municipal beautification," to which Chicago owes the creation of many of its fantastic parks. Olmstead initially planned to dredge a canal along the Midway, topped by arched bridges, but costs and technical difficulties scrapped the plan (the plan was tried again in the 1920s, but was again canceled after the 1929 stock market crash).

*Exhibitions were displayed in Washington Park, Jackson Park, and the Midway Plaisance. Attractions ranged from the world's first Ferris Wheel, Buffalo Bill's Wild West Show, the "Street in Cairo," performances by Scott Joplin, Balinese gamelan, and the first East-West international gathering of religious leaders. But the the crowning glory was the **White City**, a collection of gleaming white neoclassical buildings in Jackson Park, watched over by the enormous golden Statue of the Republic.*

*The Columbian Exposition raised Chicago's international profile in spectacular fashion, and left it with some very well sculptured buildings and parks. Unfortunately, **tragedy** waited around the corner for the area. The fair provided the setting for one of the country's first serial killers, who lured victims to his "World Fair Hotel," where they met with grisly murders (Devil in the White City makes for a good read on a visit here). The fair also brought to Chicago a smallpox epidemic, and the city mayor was assassinated two days before the closing ceremony. Perhaps most cruelly, the White City burned down shortly after the fair ended, leaving only two landmarks — the still magnificent Museum of Science and*

Industry and the golden Statue of the Republic.

Neighborhoods

Kenwood developed into one of Chicago's most upscale suburbs after the Civil War, and its Kenwood Historic District between Cottage Grove & Blackstone and 47th & 51st is a treasure trove of mansions representing virtually all the fashionable architectural styles of the late 19th century (including an excellent collection of early houses by Frank Lloyd Wright). The mansion owners are of interest too — their ranks currently include Reverend Louis Farrakhan, the Obama family, and the city's oldest Jewish community. Former residents range from the infamous Leopold and Loeb, Muhammad Ali, the fictional Dalton family from *Native Son,* and the founder of the Nation of Islam, Elijah Muhammad.

The central **Hyde Park** neighborhood is the biggest draw, dominated by the rather awesome presence of the **University of Chicago**. During the 1950s, desegregation fueled extensive "white flight" from this area, transforming the racial make up of nearly the entire South Side from all white to all black. Here, however, the University of Chicago leveraged its financial power, political clout, and social engineering brainpower to muscle through the city's first "urban renewal" project. This project, unflatteringly referred to by many neighborhood residents as "urban removal," used eminent domain powers to demolish urban housing developments, to remove nightclubs and bars, and to make the neighborhood more suburban in character (and to decimate the commercial strip on 55th St west of the railroad).

The project was paternalist, classist, and evicted many if not the majority of the neighborhood's low-income residents, but the end result of the University-driven "renewal" project is that Hyde Park is to this day one of the nation's most durable mixed-income, mixed-race neighborhoods, and is home to one of the only significant white communities for miles on the South Side. Hyde Park maintains its unique characteristics in its unique isolation from the rest of the city: no convenient L service, giant Washington Park to the west, frigid-in-the-winter Midway Plaisance to the south, and persistent redevelopment projects pushing to the north through Kenwood and to the south through Woodlawn.

Today, Hyde Park is full of **amazing bookstores**, leafy streets, the siren song of cheap greasy food, great museums, and **more Nobel Prizes per square kilometer** than any other neighborhood on Earth.

Woodlawn, to the south of the Midway, south of the University, is characterized by **urban blight**. With high levels of violent crime (especially by the 63rd St Green Line stops), blocks worth of vacant lots, and lacking in commercial activity, Woodlawn is well off the beaten tourist path. But Jackson Park (as well as the areas of Woodlawn close to the park) is perfectly safe, and a beautiful place for a walk. 63rd St still has a few remaining businesses from its salad days, but is not a great place to hang out after dark.

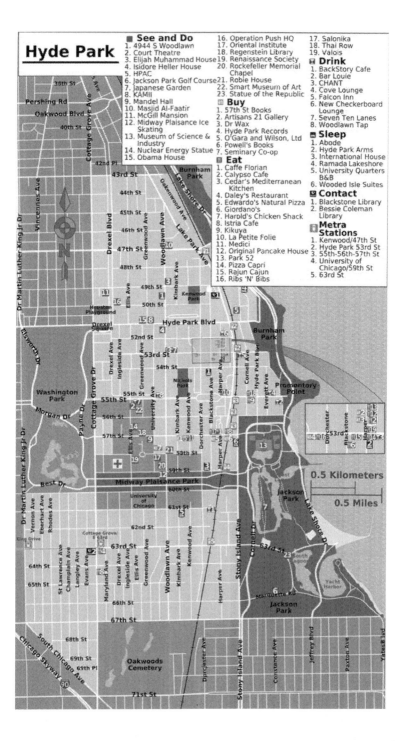

Hyde Park

■ See and Do
1. 4944 S Woodlawn
2. Court Theatre
3. Elijah Muhammad House
4. Isidore Heller House
5. HPAC
6. Jackson Park Golf Course
7. Japanese Garden
8. KAMII
9. Mandel Hall
10. Masjid Al-Faatir
11. McGill Mansion
12. Midway Plaisance Ice Skating
13. Museum of Science & Industry
14. Nuclear Energy Statue
15. Obama House
16. Operation Push HQ
17. Oriental Institute
18. Regenstein Library
19. Renaissance Society
20. Rockefeller Memorial Chapel
21. Robie House
22. Smart Museum of Art
23. Statue of the Republic

■ Buy
1. 57th St Books
2. Artisans 21 Gallery
3. Dr Wax
4. Hyde Park Records
5. O'Gara and Wilson, Ltd
6. Powell's Books
7. Seminary Co-op

■ Eat
1. Caffe Florian
2. Calypso Cafe
3. Cedar's Mediterranean Kitchen
4. Daley's Restaurant
5. Edwardo's Natural Pizza
6. Giordano's
7. Harold's Chicken Shack
8. Istria Cafe
9. Kikuya
10. La Petite Folie
11. Medici
12. Original Pancake House
13. Park 52
14. Pizza Capri
15. Rajun Cajun
16. Ribs 'N' Bibs

■ Drink
1. BackStory Cafe
2. Bar Louie
3. CHANT
4. Cove Lounge
5. Falcon Inn
6. New Checkerboard Lounge
7. Seven Ten Lanes
8. Woodlawn Tap

■ Sleep
1. Abode
2. Hyde Park Arms
3. International House
4. Ramada Lakeshore
5. University Quarters B&B
6. Wooded Isle Suites

■ Contact
1. Blackstone Library
2. Bessie Coleman Library

■ Metra Stations
1. Kenwood/47th St
2. Hyde Park 53rd St
3. 55th-56th-57th St
4. University of Chicago/59th St
5. 63rd St

17. Salonika
18. Thai Row
19. Valois

Get In

By bus

You can get to Hyde Park by taking several CTA buses from downtown Chicago. Routes #6 (Hyde Park Express) and #4 (Cottage Grove) are common choices. The 55/Garfield bus is a very cheap and efficient way to travel between Midway Airport and Hyde Park. It passes by the University of Chicago and terminates at the Museum of Science and Industry. To get from place to place within the area, CTA offers several useful neighborhood routes between the University and other points in the district, the #171 between the University and the Museum of Science and Industry being the most useful. *facilities.uchicago.edu*

By train

The **Metra Main Electric Line** is the most efficient public transport between the Loop *p.47* and Hyde Park. It is a quick, comfortable 15-20 minute ride and costs just over $2 for a one way trip. Be sure to check the train schedules *metrarail.com* ahead of time, however, because it runs infrequently during off-peak times. Key stops are at Kenwood/47th St, Hyde Park 53rd St, 55th-56th-57th St, and Univ. of Chicago/59th St.

Alternatively, the CTA **Red Line** and **Green Line** link the Loop with Garfield Avenue in Washington Park *p.191*. Although more convenient — they run more frequently, and operate 24 hours a day — the two stops are too far from Hyde Park to walk and lo-

cated in rough neighborthoods. But the very frequent 55/Garfield bus will take you straight from either of them to anywhere along 55th St.

By car

Coming south on **Lake Shore Drive**, it is most convenient to take the southbound exit at 51st St/Hyde Park Blvd for a drive, or the 57th St exit for the Museum of Science and Industry and the University. Coming from the southeast on the **Chicago Skyway**, get off early at the Stony Island Ave exit and follow it north. From the **Dan Ryan Expressway**, you'll definitely want to take the 55th St/Garfield Blvd east exit, which will take you into the heart of Hyde Park through Washington Park.

A car is not a bad way to see the Hyde Park, especially if you plan to cover a lot of territory. Free on-street parking is generally easy to find. The most difficult area to park is without question the area around the University of Chicago, where the street parking during the day is limited and policed with an iron fist by the University Police. Even in this area, however, it is usually possible (if a bit frustrating) to find metered parking, or to just pay at one of the big university or hospital lots. Try looking on the Midway, or on a less safe street to the south of the university. It can also be difficult to find free parking right by the Museum of Science and Industry during tourist season, but there is always room in the museum's pay lots.

By bicycle

Hyde Park is a fairly easy 7-mile ride from the Loop *p.47* using the **Chicago Lakefront Path**. You may cross under Lake Shore Dr at either the 51st St pedestrian bridge or the 55th or 57th St underpasses. The 57th St underpass will take you to the **Museum of Science and Industry**, of which the main body of the **University of Chicago** campus is 3 blocks west.

Hyde Park is quite accommodating to cyclists; many students and faculty at the University ride around the neighborhood, making bikes fairly visible entity.

See

Kenwood Historic District

These impressive structures are all privately owned and unfortunately closed to the public. The only exception is the Nation of Islam mosque, but you should be sensitive to the fact it is a place of worship and is *not* accustomed to tourists.

4944 S Woodlawn, 4944 S Woodlawn Ave. A gargantuan 8,000 square foot Tudor revival mansion once owned by Muhammad Ali.

Drexel Fountain, at Hyde Park Blvd & Drexel Ave. This ornate fountain that stands in the tiny Drexel Square Park is the oldest in Chicago — one of the first monuments erected in the Chicago area. Commissioned by a wealthy stockbroker by the name of Fran-

cis Drexel, who managed to get the avenue, square, and fountain all named after himself without ever setting foot in Chicago.

Elijah Muhammad House, 4855 S Woodlawn Ave. The former home of Elijah Muhammad, the founder of the Nation of Islam, and the home to the NoI's current firebrand leader, Louis Farrakhan. Check out the stained glass windows, goofy fountains, as well as all the N.O.I. security!

Isidore Heller House, 5132 S Woodlawn. One of Frank Lloyd Wright's earliest distinctive buildings (1897), often credited as the turning point in his early career when he shifted towards the Prairie School.

KAMII (KAM Isaiah Israel), 5039 S Greenwood Ave, +1 773 924-1234, *www.kamii.org*. It looks like a Byzantine style mosque, but that minaret is actually a smokestack for this synagogue. The building was built in 1924 for the reform Isaiah Israel congregation, which later merged with Chicago's oldest Jewish congregation, Kehilath Anshe Ma'ariv (KAM), which in turn moved out of its massive temple on Drexel Avenue. The interior is marvelously elaborate, if you manage to get inside — being as it is across the street from the Obama house, you are unlikely to even set foot on the block.

Masjid Al-Faatir, 1200 E 47th St, +1 773 548-3524, *masjidal-faatir. com*. Masjid Al-Faatir is the largest and most impressive of Chicago's 20 Nation of Islam mosques. It was built in 1987 by one of Elijah Muhammad's sons with generous support from local Muhammad Ali (the boxer).

McGill Mansion, 4938 S Drexel Ave. Easily mistaken for a French Castle, this mansion was built in 1893 for the Scottish McGill family, which founded the famous Montreal University of the same name. The mansion was converted into 34 condos in 2000.

Operation Push HQ, 930 E 50th St, +1 773 373-3366, *www.rainbowpush.org*. The enormous classical revival building at 50th & Drexel is the national headquarters of Jesse Jackson's RainbowPUSH organization. The building's facade might lead you to expect a Lincoln-sized statue of the reverend inside, but this was actually a Jewish synagogue founded in 1932 by the aforementioned KAM.

The Obama House, 5046 Greenwood Ave (*right across the street from KAMII*). This pretty house is home to the family of current U.S. President Barack Obama. The vacant lot to the left was the source of minor controversy in Chicago, when it came out that the Obama family had purchased it at sub-market rates from friend and criminal real estate broker Tony Rezko. You'll notice, despite the much touted media characterizations of their house as a "Hyde Park white-porticoed mansion," it's not actually in Hyde Park, and while a nice big house, it's no mansion. Good luck getting on the 5000 block of Greenwood — it's still the family house, and the block is closed off even to pedes-

trians, and crawling with police and Secret Service. You should be able to get a look up from the 51st St sidewalk, but lingering around taking photographs might draw unwelcome attention from security.

University of Chicago

Main Campus, 5801 S Ellis Ave (*Centered around the main quad between Ellis Ave and University Ave, 57th St and the Midway*), +1 773 702-1234, *www.uchicago.edu*. One of the world's great universities, the University of Chicago's Gothic campus exudes academic rigor and intellectual intensity, known to students as "the place where fun comes to die." Its imposing gray buildings make it a must-see for architecture fans. Even if you are not a prospective student, you can take advantage of its free campus tours.

Smart Museum of Art, 5550 S Greenwood Ave, +1 773 702-0200, *smartmuseum.uchicago.edu*, T W F 10AM-4PM, Th 10AM-8PM, Sa-Su 11AM-5PM. The Smart museum is small, but has an excellent collection, thoughtfully exhibited. Free.

Regenstein Library, 1100 E 57th St, +1 773 702-8740, *www.lib.uchicago.edu*. If you are not a student and are not on a tour, you can't enter the gigantic collection of over 4.5 million volumes, but you can marvel at the exterior architecture. The building is one of the world's best examples of the Brutalist movement, which emphasized the structural materials (rough concrete in this case), as well as striking repetitions and irregularities of angular forms.

Nuclear Energy Statue, 5700 S Ellis Ave. This Henry Moore statue marks the area where Enrico Fermi and his team of scientists successfully produced the first controlled nuclear chain reaction. Although possibly unintended, visitors often see a resemblance to a human skull or mushroom cloud.

Oriental Institute Museum, 1155 E 58th St, +1 773 702-9514, *oi.uchicago.edu/museum*, T,Th-Sa 10AM-6PM, W 10AM-8:30PM, Su noon-6PM. The University of Chicago Oriental Institute has one of the best collections of ancient Egyptian and Near Eastern archeology in the world, which is moreover free, small, very well exhibited, and basically started by Indiana Jones. Some highlights include: much of the Assyrian "Fortress of Sargon," a colossal statue of King Tutankhamun, and the Mummy and Coffin of Meresamun. Visitors with a strong interest may want to devote several hours to pore over the dense exhibits, but the small museum can be quickly "skimmed" in 15 minutes. Free, suggested donation $5 adult, $2 child.

The Renaissance Society, 5811 S Ellis Ave, Cobb Hall 418, +1 773 702-8670, *www.renaissancesociety.org*, T-F 10AM-5PM, Sa-Su noon-5PM. A small gallery of avant-garde painting, which will appeal greatly to aficionados, less so to casual visitors. Free.

Rockefeller Memorial Chapel, 5850 S Woodlawn Ave, +1 773 702-2100, *rockefeller.uchicago.edu*, 8AM-4PM, tours of the carillon: M-F 11:30AM and 5:30PM. This giant Gothic church is named for the University founder, John D. Rockefeller, who intended it to be the "central and dominant feature" of the University. It may not be that, but it is impressive, with a huge organ and the second largest carillon in the world. Free.

The Citadel of Science and Research

If practical, try to approach the University from the south or the Midway when visiting for the first time, so that you are confronted by the imposing stone walls of the main campus — it's an impressive sight."

Other attractions

Hyde Park Art Center (HPAC), 5020 S Cornell Ave, +1 773 324-5520, *www.hydeparkart.org*, M-Th 9AM-8PM, F-Sa 9AM-5PM, Su noon-5PM. The oldest alternative art venue in the city is dedicated to the visual arts, usually has several contemporary exhibits running at any given time, and frequent events like artist talks, poetry readings, and music performances.

Jackson Park, 6401 S Stony Island Ave, +1 773 256-0903, 7AM-11PM daily. Named for President Andrew Jackson and the site of the World's Columbian Exposition in 1893. The most prominent monument remaining from the event is the fully gilded "Statue of the Republic." Other sites include the

Osaka Garden on the Wooded Island, a series of lagoons designed by Frederick Law Olmsted, and several well-hidden bird watching trails along the water.

Osaka Garden (Japanese Garden) (*On the northeast side of Jackson Park's Wooded Island*), Sunrise-sunset, daily. The Osaka Garden grew out of the Pavilion for the Japanese Government at the 1893 World's Columbian Exposition and was planned by Olmsted as well. During WWII, the gardens suffered from repeated anti-Japanese vandalism and arson, culminating in the site's abandonment to those unsavory types who inhabit abandoned urban parkland. Chicago's sister city, Osaka (which is Japan's second city, after all), donated the money in the 1980s to restore the gardens, prompting a name change from the Japanese Garden to the Osaka Garden. Today, the gardens are one of Chicago's finest secret places and a wonderful escape from harrowing tourist adventures. Free.

Midway Park, 1130 Midway Plaisance North (*Located between 59th and 60th St*). A large, long grassy park, which mostly just serves to give visitors a good view of the University of Chicago. But the Winter/Summer reading gardens just south of the University's main quad are quite beautiful and a nice place to relax from touring.

Museum of Science and Industry, 5700 S Lake Shore Dr & E 57th St (*Take CTA buses 2, 6, 10, 28, 55, or the Metra Electric Line*), +1 773 684-1414, *www.msichicago.org*, Summer and holidays M-Sa 9:30AM-5:30PM, Su 11AM-5:30PM, other seasons M-Sa 9:30AM-4PM, Su 11AM-4PM. No tour of Chicago's museums is complete without a visit to this one. Spend hours upon hours looking at really cool stuff you never even knew you didn't know about. So much to do, so little time. You can return for free the following day if you take your ticket to "Will Call" on the way out on your first day. Great for kids, with many hands-on exhibits and the famous Coal Mine; adults will enjoy the display of the German U-boat 'U-505'. $11 adult, $5 child.

Robie House, 5757 S Woodlawn Ave, +1 708 848-1976, *www.wrightplus.org*, Tours: M-F 11AM, 1PM, 3PM; Sa-Su 11AM-3:30PM every 30 minutes. This fabulously impractical house designed by Frank Lloyd Wright is one of the world's most famous examples of the Midwestern "Prairie School" of architecture, which aimed to create buildings with prominent horizontal lines evocative of the prairie landscape. The interior is bizarre, intended to remind its inhabitants of a ship, and is surrounded by stained art glass windows. You must take an official tour to see the interior, which lasts about an hour. Tours of the surrounding historic neighborhood are offered as well — it is best to inquire by phone beforehand. Be sure to take a gander at the University of Chicago's Business School across the street, which was designed to emulate the style of the Robie

HYDE PARK◻○

House in a more modern fashion. $12 adult, $10 youth, $5 child.

◻○ Do

The University of Chicago hosts some truly world class performing arts. The U of C Presents' classical music performances are particularly excellent. If you are looking to relax, head to the huge area parks for 18 holes of golf, a sunset at Promontory Point, or ice skating on the Midway. Or if you are into film, the University's nightly Doc Films screenings and regular director visits are a treasure.

Court Theatre, 5535 S Ellis Ave, +1 773 753-4472, *www.courttheatre. org*, performances: W-Th 7:30PM, F 8PM, Sa 3PM & 8PM, Su 2:30PM & 7:30PM. Excellent dramatic theater on the University campus. Student $8-20, general $25-50, half-price tickets available one hour before the show.

Doc Films, 1212 E 59th St (*Inside Ida Noyes Hall*), Office: +1 773 702-8574 Hotline: +1 773 702-8575, *docfilms.uchicago.edu*, Check the website's calendar for screenings, nightly during the school year and W-Sa during the summer. Those zoning laws are again to "blame" for the total absence of any movie theaters in this section of Chicago. But their absence clearly benefits the longest-running student film society in the country, which puts on an impressive number of independent documentaries, art-house films, and other socially relevant movies throughout the year, all in a state-of-the-art cinema. Doc Films

attracts a very knowledgeable crowd (perhaps because the students and neighborhood residents have no other movie options!) and it is a good place to eavesdrop on some intense, intellectual conversations. $5 general admission, tickets go on sale 30 minutes before screenings and credit cards are not accepted..

Jackson Park Golf Course, 6300 S Hayes Dr, reservations: +1 312 245-0909, lessons: +1 847 480-4853, management: +1 312 755-3579, *www.cpdgolf.com*, Sunrise-sunset. 18 holes of golf and a driving range, all in the middle of Jackson Park. Golf carts available for $15. M-F $22.75, Sa-Su $25.75.

Jackson Park Beaches (*along the lake south of Promontory Point*), Memorial Day-Labor Day 9AM-9:30PM daily. There are better beaches further north and further south, but if you're here and want to get a swim in, Jackson Park's two beaches are fine — 57th St Beach is less than a ten minute walk from the Museum of Science and Industry.

Midway Plaisance Ice Skating, 1130 Midway Plaisance North (*E 59th St at Woodlawn Ave*), +1 312 745-2470, Su-Th noon-7PM, F noon-4:30PM & 5PM-7PM, Sa 1PM-9PM. Free.

Promontory Point Park (The Point), 5491 S Lake Shore Dr, +1 312 747-6620. Promontory Point is a beautiful spot to take in the great skyline view, gaze off into the blue, watch summer fireworks, or take a (technically illegal, but everybody does it) swim in its submerged beach (north side of the point). The Point was constructed under the depression era Works Progress Administration in the style of the Prairie School of park design.

University of Chicago Presents, Mandel Hall, 1131 E 57th St, +1 773 702-8068, *chicagopresents. uchicago.edu*, Performances usually on F 8PM or Su 3PM. The University of Chicago Presents hosts numerous classical music performances in Hyde Park, usually featuring big-name national and international performers for relatively low prices. Student $10, general $30-35.

Buy

The University has had a big hand in zoning regulations designed to keep chain stores, and really any stores, out of the district. Hyde Park actually lacks a single clothing store. Book lovers and collectors, on the other hand, will be thrilled with the multiple independent and used bookstores along 57th Street and the *awe-inspiring* Seminary Co-op. Aside from books, Hyde Park is now likely the world's number one destination for Barack Obama merchandise, who is becoming somewhat of a local hero figure. The convenience stores are full of dancing Obama dolls, t-shirts, etc., and other stores and restaurants are all touting "Obama eats here!" "Obama shops here!" Don't let the hype shape your choices though, it's a small neighborhood, and the Obamas have probably tried out *all* the restaurants by now.

57th St Books, 1301 E 57th St, +1 773 684-1300, *www.semcoop.com*, M-F 10AM-9PM, Sa-Su 10AM-8PM. A branch of the University's Seminary Co-op that has frequent literary events, including poetry readings, author talks, and writing workshops.

Artisans 21 gallery, 5225 S Harper St, +1 773 288-7450, *www.artisans21gallery.com*, T-F noon-6PM, Sa 10AM-6PM, Su noon-5PM. A gallery cooperative selling everything from ceramics to paintings to jewelry.

Dr Wax, 5225 S Harper Ave, +1 773 439-8696, *www.drwax.com*, M-Sa 11AM-7PM, Su noon-6PM. Used records and new and used CDs. All sorts of music.

Hyde Park Records, 1377 E 53rd St, +1 773 288-6588, *www.hydeparkrecords.net*, M-Th 11AM-7PM, F-Sa 11AM-8PM, Su noon-6PM. A huge selection of vinyl and a smaller selection of CDs.

O'Gara and Wilson, Ltd, 1448 E 57th St, +1 773 363-0993, *ogarawilsonbooksellers.blogspot.com*, M-F 11AM-7PM, Sa 11AM-8PM, Su noon-6PM. An impressively atmospheric antiquarian bookseller that has been open at this location for **120 years**, with a wide selection acquired mostly from Hyde Park estate sales, students, and professors. The staff is incredibly knowledgeable. $1-2,000.

Powell's Books, 1501 E 57th St, +1 773 955-7780, *www.powellschicago. com*, 9AM-11PM daily. Used books overflowing the shelves, all over the place.

HYDE PARKEAT

Seminary Co-op Bookstore, 5757 S University Ave, +1 773 752-4381, *www.semcoop.com*, M-F 8:30AM-9PM, Sa 10AM-6PM, Su noon-6PM. The world's largest academic bookstore has a collection covering *every* topic.

Eat

The center of dining in the Hyde Park area is along 53rd St and Harper Ct, although the University crowd packs itself into the nearer dining strip along 57th St. Accordingly, there is a significant difference in both atmosphere and price between the two dining centers (the latter being collegiate and overpriced). You can have a fine meal in Hyde Park in any price category, but there are no truly great, standout restaurants in this neighborhood, which suffers from having a captive audience — it is quite difficult to get to any other dining hot spots in the city without a car (the nearest being Chinatown *p.175* or soul food in Chatham *p.203*).

Budget

The odd "Thai Row" on 55th St deserves a mention. These are definitely not the best Thai restaurants in Chicago, but they serve tasty, greasy food in large portions on the cheap. No one seems to know why these Thai restaurants congregated in this one spot.

Daley's Restaurant, 809 E 63rd St, +1 773 643-6670, *daleysrestaurant. com*, 6AM-9PM daily. Huh? Daley worship in Woodlawn? No, that couldn't be and it isn't. Built by one *John* Daley, Chicago's oldest eatery has served as Woodlawn's neighborhood restaurant for about **120 years!** As the Irish fled to the suburbs, the menu shifted towards offering nothing but the soulest soul food around (the breakfast is a particular draw — wonderful french toast). Owing to the housing projects just north, the area around this Green Line stop is on the rough side, but Daley's will treat you to a strong dose of delicious food and friendly service with nice atmosphere. $4-12.

Harold's Chicken Shack. The great South Side fried chicken chain is cheap, usually a little dirty, and always delicious. Crowded at meal times. $2-5.

1208 E 53rd St, +1 773 725-9260, 10AM-11:30PM daily. The Hyde Park location is easy to visit, with a parking lot and rare dine-in seating, but the quality vacillates.

6419 S Cottage Grove Ave, +1 773 363-9586, *www.haroldschickenshack2.com*, Su–W 11AM-midnight, Th 11AM–3AM, F-Sa 11AM–4AM. Another hit-or-miss unreliable Harold's location, just under the Green Line stop, in a considerably less welcoming environment than the Hyde Park location!

Istria Cafe, 1520 E 57th St, +1 773 955-2556, M-F 6:30AM-7PM, Sa 7AM-7PM, Su 8AM-6PM. Premium coffee and an assortment of pricey, but well prepared panini, pastries, and gelato served right under the Metra stop. $3-5.

Original Pancake House, 1517 E Hyde Park Blvd, +1 773 288-

2322, M-F 7AM-3PM Sa-Su 7AM-5PM. Often called the best pancake house in Chicago, vindicated by the ostentatiously long line on weekends. An exhaustive pancake menu and delightful service. As you would expect, though, it is extremely crowded, and on weekends you will be packed in with strangers like sardines. $5-10.

Rajun Cajun, 1459 E 53rd St, +1 773 955-1145, M-Sa 11AM-9:30PM. A hole-in-the-wall that, interestingly enough, serves a combination of Indian and soul food. Probably the only place around where you can sip a mango lassi while eating collard greens and fried chicken. While the seating area is a little neglected, the atmosphere benefits from the waiting-in-line dancing to the Hindi club/rock music. $5-10.

Ribs 'N' Bibs, 5300 S Dorchester, +1 773 493-0400, www.hydeparkrecords.net, Su-Th 11AM-midnight, F-Sa 11AM-1AM (sometimes closes early without warning). A true Hyde Park institution serving BBQ sauce over everything, from the $2 Bronco Burger to more expensive rib plates. Food is smoked in a traditional wood-burning stove, which gives the neighborhood its salivatory smell. The BBQ here is actually pretty mediocre (at best), and there is far better cue to be had in Bronzeville and Chatham, but this one is awful convenient. Limited seating. $2-20.

Siam Thai Restaurant, 1639 E 55th St, +1 773 324-9296, 11AM-10PM daily. Choose this one over the others if you are in the mood

for pad thai. $5-12.

Snail Thai Cuisine, 1649 E 55th St, +1 773 667-5423, 11AM-10PM daily. Weird name, but this is the most popular and brightly lit of the three Thai places on Thai Row. $5-12.

Thai 55th, 1607 E 55th St, +1 773 363-7119, www.thai55restaurant.com, 11AM-10PM daily. Probably the least popular of the three Thai Row locations, but the best bet for pad see ew and bubble tea. $5-12.

Valois, 1518 E 53rd St, +1 773 667-0647, 5:30AM-10PM daily. Cash only diner/cafeteria institution for about 80 years that serves as the heart of the Hyde Park community — a favorite with lifelong Hyde Parkers, bleary eyed graduate students, police officers, tweed-jacket sporting professors, and a certain U.S. President. Breakfast served until 4PM. $5-8.

Mid-range

Caffe Florian, 1450 E 57th St, +1 773 752-4100, Su-Th 11AM-11PM, F-Sa 11AM-midnight. An Italian cafe popular with the students. Most of the menu at the Florian is uninspired, but their deep-dish pizza is a true neighborhood favorite. $5-8.

Calypso Cafe, 5211 S Harper Ave, +1 773 955-0229, www.thecalypsocafe.com, Su-Th 11AM-10PM, F-Sa 11AM-11PM. All sorts of Caribbean food in what is widely considered Hyde Park's best restaurant. Has a full

HYDE PARKEAT

bar. $10-15.

Edwardo's Natural Pizza Restaurant, 1321 E 57th St, +1 773 241-7960, M-Th 11AM-10PM, F-Sa 11AM-11PM, Su 11AM-10PM. Come here specifically for its famous stuffed spinach pizza and you won't regret it — well, you may regret the weight-gaining aftermath, but you won't regret the immediate experience. $8-15.

Giordano's, 5309 S Blackstone Ave, +1 773 947-0200, *www.giordanos.com*, Su-Th 11AM-11PM, F-Sa 11AM-midnight. Not all Giordano's are created equal, but this is the original location and one of the better places in the city to try Chicago stuffed pizza. If some in your party are afraid to face the behemoth, there are plenty of non-pizza options on the menu. $10-23.

Kikuya, 1601 E 55th St, +1 773 667-3727, *kikuyaonline.com*, T-Sa Noon-10PM, Su 4:30PM-9PM. Hyde Park's oldest and most traditional Japanese restaurant serves tempura, sushi, sashimi. $10-15.

Medici, 1327 E 57th St, +1 773 667-7394, M-Th 11AM-11PM, F 11AM-12PM, Sa 9AM-12PM, Su 9AM-11PM. An Italian place *very* popular with the students, that can lay claim to above average baked goods, fine thin-crust pizza, Italian dishes, and a fun ambiance in their downstairs seating area (a separate door to the west of the street-level bakery). Also serves excellent floats with flavors like almond and grenadine. If you ask the admissions office to recommend a nice place nearby to take your kid, they'll point you in this direction. $8-18.

Pizza Capri, 1501 E 53rd St, +1 773 324-7777, M-F 10AM-11:30PM, Sa-Su 9AM-midnight. Good upscale Italian cuisine and stuffed pizza at a reliable Chicagoland chain. Try the gourmet ingredients like feta cheese and fine sausage on a stuffed pizza for a deliciously fattening night. *Great* bread. $11-20.

Salonika, 1440 E 57th St, +1 773 752-3899, 7AM-10PM daily. Adequate, but overpriced, diner fare with some Greek and Mexican entries, and a constant flow of coffee. The nice atmosphere and comfy booths are the real reason to come and lounge about. $7-14.

Splurge

Cedar's Mediterranean Kitchen, 1206 E 53rd St, +1 773 324-6227, *eatcedars.com*, Su-Th 11:30AM-10PM, F-Sa 11:30AM-11PM. Cedar's is the most stylish choice of restaurants in Hyde Park, and the Lebanese cuisine should not disappoint. $13-19.

La Petite Folie, 1504 E 55th St, +1 773 493-1394, *lapetitefolie.com*, lunch: T-F 11:30AM-2PM, dinners: T-Su 5PM. A very good, unpretentious French restaurant on the south end of the Lake Shore shopping center. The U of C alumnae who own the place apparently tired of scientific research and moved to France for a while to graduate with honors from the prestigious Cordon Bleu Paris school of gastronomy. And Hyde Park rejoices. Prix fixe menu available daily 5PM-6:30PM. $15-25.

Park 52, 5201 S Harper Ave (*in the same building as the New Checkerboard Lounge*), +1 773 241-5200, *www.park52chicago.com*, Su-Th 5PM-10PM, F-Sa 5PM-11PM. Jerry Kleiner's new restaurant, distinguishing itself by being the only truly upmarket fine dining in the neighborhood. New American cuisine, fancy offbeat decor, and right next to the Checkerboard Lounge. Reservations recommended. $22-40.

Drink

One of the University's many powerful Hyde Park legacies is the general lack of nightclubs and bars, which once covered the now desolate stretch of 55th St west of the Metra tracks. Ask any student, **Jimmy's** (a.k.a. Woodlawn Tap) is really *the* place to go for a beer. Live music in the past was just about absent in the neighborhood, but there are a couple good options nowadays. The most obvious is the newly relocated, legendary blues club, the **Checkerboard Lounge**. But you can also catch some good smooth jazz F-Sa nights (usually) at **CHANT** or the restaurant <eat name="Mellow Yellow" alt="" address="1508 E 53rd St" directions="" phone="+1 773 667-2000" email="" fax="" url="" hours="" price=""></eat> Or you could listen to some of the student jazz combos at Jimmy's, Su afternoon-evening.

BackStory Cafe, 6100 S Blackstone, +1 773 324-9987, *backstorycafe.com*, 8AM-8PM daily. Chicago's most hidden gem is nearly impossible to find, but may be Chicago's finest cafe. Run by Woodlawn's artsy/social-cause-chasing Experimentation Station, this extraordinarily laid-back cafe serves incredible fresh coffee (details like the measurement of coffee beans really pay off) and whole pots (for 2-4 people) of quality loose leaf teas for just $4.50. And they have free WiFi. And they screen free indie films/documentaries on Sunday nights. And open mic on Friday nights. To find the place, which is located in an odd industrial/construction zone, with minimal signage, head south from the Midway on Dorchester to take a left on 61st St. It's just around the corner at the dead end on what barely passes for a street. Lastly, don't worry about the location, the streets around the cafe are perfectly safe. Food: $3-6.

Bar Louie, 5550 S South Shore Dr, +1 773 363-5300, *www.barlouieamerica.com*, 11AM-2AM daily. A chain bar & grill, with unexciting food, and very slow service, but… stiff mojitos, outdoor seating, and location right by the beach makes for a great time in the summer. That the clientele is very diverse is another plus.

CHANT, 1509 East 53rd St, 773-324-1999, *www.chantchicago.com*, Su-M noon-10PM, Tu-Th 11:30AM-midnight, F-Sa 11:30AM-1AM. CHANT is a restaurant and bar, but skip the food and go straight to the bar.

(The food is fine, but the service is not.) The decor is extraordinarily chic for Hyde Park, and there's live entertainment (often jazz) F-Sa starting at 9:30PM.

Cove Lounge (The Cove), 1750 E 55th St , +1 773 684-1013, Su-Th 10:30AM-2AM, F 11AM-2AM, Sa 11AM-3AM. A loud, upbeat dive bar that's way more eclectic than whatever bars you've been to in the past. Its got a weird 70's nautical theme, interesting music on the jukebox, and cheap drinks. Unfortunately, it's also a tiny space and can get overcrowded.

Falcon Inn, 1601 E 53rd St, M-F 10:30AM-2AM, Sa 11AM-3AM, Su noon-2AM. The sleeper dive bar in Hyde Park, largely unknown to the student crowd. It's tucked away on a quiet section of 53rd Street, and serves an eclectic crowd of friendly locals, who come to relax, enjoy the very cheap beer, and the pizza through the window to Cholie's next door. (Cholie's pizza is a Chicago travesty, but hey, you're drinking $1.50 beer.)

New Checkerboard Lounge, 5201 S Harper Ct, +1 773 684-1472, 11AM-2AM daily, live music usually starts after 9:30PM. The old Checkerboard Lounge in Bronzeville was perhaps the nation's most legendary venue for the blues, owned by none other than Buddy Guy. In a real blow to the Chicago blues, it closed in 2003. In search of a new home, Checkerboard moved to Hyde Park—a move quite controversial, in that had moved into the most well-to-do neighborhood in the

area. Indeed, the Checkerboard is no longer the tiny, smoke-filled juke joint that played host to blues legends like Howlin' Wolf, Muddy Waters, Junior Wells, as well as some blues worshippers like the Rolling Stones and Led Zeppelin. Don't worry, though, it might be impossible to fill those giant shoes, but it's still a great blues club, and you'll get a real taste of blues on the South Side. Cover $3-20.

Seven Ten Lanes, 1055 E 55th St, +1 773 347-2695, M-Th 11:30AM-1AM, F-Sa 11:30AM-2AM, Su 11:30AM-midnight. Beer, bowling, shuffleboard, and an art deco ambiance. Its proximity to the University allows it to be overpriced, but it's the only place around to satisfy bowling urges, or to have a good beer outside. They also happen to have some very good foreign beers on tap.

Woodlawn Tap (Jimmy's), 1172 E 55th St, +1 773 643-5516, Su-F 10:30AM-2AM, Sa 10:30AM-3AM. From the University perspective, this is the one and only real bar in Hyde Park (and accordingly, the only establishment that was saved from the University-driven "urban removal"). A good place to be served beer by PhDs and to listen in on the intense intellectual debates about topics you didn't know existed. Some famous writers used to frequent the bar, including Saul Bellow and Dylan Thomas. Live jazz on Sunday nights and you might catch a University improv comedy group during the week. But above all, the dark cavernous atmosphere, the low-key vibe, and the greasy burgers make this one of the best dives in the city. While it's a university favorite, *don't* expect a rowdy singles scene here—it's the U of C, folks. Cover $3-20.

Sleep

Considering the hordes of university-affiliated visitors Hyde Park is oddly devoid of hotels. Most visitors stay downtown; the Loop *p.47* along Michigan Avenue is the best bet, since the southbound Metra stops are just outside the hotels. There are some nice quiet options, though, if you know where to look.

Abode, 5412 S Blackstone Ave, +1 312-576-4299, *theabodechicago.com*, Checkin: 3PM, Checkout: noon. Short term apartment rentals located near Hyde Park's "downtown" area. 15-20 minute walk to the University. Kitchens fully stocked. $150/night.

Hyde Park Arms Hotel, 5316 S Harper Ave, +1 773 493-3500. If Kerouac and the Blues Brothers have interested you in checking into a transient hotel, the Hyde Park Arms is the place for you, as it is far cleaner and safer than its peers elsewhere. Hotel rooms leased weekly, bi-weekly, or monthly. The 70 rooms include standard hotel furnishings and a fridge, but no stove or microwave; all utilities are paid by the building, unless you want cable. Per week $145-$155.

International House, 1414 E 59th St, +1 773 753-2270, *ihouse.uchicago.edu*, Checkin: 3PM, Checkout: noon. A student dormitory, which provides budget short-term accommodations to those "affiliated with either the University of Chicago or another cultural, educational or professional institution" (and their guests). They do their reservations (and information requests) by email. The rooms are mostly dorm rooms, but there are a couple nicer ones with private baths available (at significantly higher rates). Discounted weekly rates ares also available. $60-128.

Ramada Lakeshore Chicago, 4900 S Lakeshore Dr, +1 773 288-5800, *www.ramada-chicago.com*, Checkin: noon, Checkout: 3PM. This is the only major hotel in the area. It is unfortunately far from anything in the area of interest, but its rates are low and it has plenty of free parking and a downtown shuttle. $125-140.

University Quarters B&B, 6137 S Kimbark Ave, +1 773 855-8349, *www.universityquarters.net*. Comfy and close to the University, albeit awkwardly south of the Midway. Rest assured the owners will take good care of you. $150-165.

Wooded Isle Suites, 5750 S Stony Island Ave, +1 800 290-6844 , *woodedisle.com*. A pretty fantastic option for staying in Hyde Park, the Wooded Isle suites are right next to the Museum of Science and Industry, Jackson Park, the 57th St Metra station, and the 57th St dining strip. All rooms include a fully equipped kitchen and housekeeping service every other day. It's a bit of a walk to the University (0.8 miles), but make your student come visit you *here* — it's also just a couple blocks from the beach. $180-217 (can go as low as $60 off-season).

Contact

The following public libraries offer free public internet access:

Blackstone Branch Library, 4904 S Lake Park Ave, +1 312 747-0511, M-Th 9AM-9PM, F-Sa 9AM-5PM. This particular library is not just a free internet joint, it's a beautiful work of art, filled with marble and murals. It was created as a charitable work by Timothy Blackstone, a 19th century railroad baron who also founded the Union Stockyards on the Southwest Side.

Bessie Coleman Branch Library, 731 E 63rd St, +1 312 747-7760, M-Th 9AM-8PM, F-Sa 9AM-5PM.

Stay safe

Many University students seem to live in fear of their neighborhood, and the University takes pains to explain to visitors that it is not unsafe, and that they have appropriate security measures to keep their students safe. Nonetheless, the fear persists. Know that this is **wholly irrational**. Hyde Park and to a somewhat lesser degree Kenwood are some of the safest inner neighborhoods in Chicago, with *very* low violent crime rates. Moreover, the University famously fields the third largest police force in Illinois, and the second largest private police force in the world (the first being the Pope's), with full police powers. That means there are twice as

many police in Hyde Park than any other neighborhood around. Feel safe walking down the street at night, because you are. The only places you should actively worry about crime are in Woodlawn (south of 61st St), where there is a good deal of violent and drug-related crime, which categorically does not spill over across the Midway.

Get out

The famous **Museum Campus** and McCormick Center are just north in Chicago's Near South *p.95*.

Chicago's Bronzeville *p.191*, the historic **Black Metropolis**, is just a stone's throw away from Hyde Park, and well worth a visit for its huge role in African-American history. In particular the **DuSable Museum of African-American History** (which is just across the street from the University of Chicago Hospital) is very easy to visit when in the University area and should not be missed.

Oak Woods Cemetery, outstanding Memphis-style **barbecue**, and some of the best **blues** in the city are located a few miles south on Cottage Grove in Chatham and Greater Grand *p.203*.

If you are up for a little drive, head south to the historic planned industrial community of Pullman, on the Far Southeast Side *p.377*, and afterward grab some incredible smoked shrimp at the 95th St bridge.

Bridgeport-Chinatown is the South Side at its most dynamic, as the old South Side Irish neighborhood of the Daleys increasingly blends with the old Chinese immigrant community to the north. Enormous cathedrals now stand next to Buddhist temples, and Old Style washes down lo mein. If you are a visitor, though, you only need to keep in mind two things: **Chinese food** and **baseball**.

Understand

Chicago's Chinatown is pleasantly authentic. At the many restaurants in the area, local Chinese customers are joined by Chicagoans from all over the city "going Chinese" for the night. Chicago's Chinatown is the third largest in the United States, the Midwestern business center for Chinese-Americans, and home to large populations of Cantonese and Taiwanese. The main street, Wentworth Ave, is a great place for dining out and rummaging through eccentric stores, looking for gifts. US Cellular Field, better known as Comiskey Park, is several blocks south of Chinatown and is home to the South Side's favorite baseball team, the Chicago White Sox.

Bridgeport is a large Irish-American enclave that has produced some of Chicago's most famous South Side Irish, such as Finley Peter Dunne and the two mayors Daley. Being the birthplace of the city's power brokers has been good to Bridgeport. The first Daley remembered playing in the streets as a child, dodging fetid puddles filled with carcasses from the local slaughterhouses. Bungalows and other single-family homes

are more the norm these days.
Bridgeport is now seeing a large
influx of Mexican immigrants,
which means more good food
options are springing up left and
right, and has even seen a wave
of North Siders priced out of hip
neighborhoods like Wicker Park
p.229 and Lincoln Park *p.123*. The
most interesting "immigrants" of
late are certainly the Zhou brothers Da Huang and Shan Zuo, who
are both internationally acclaimed
painters, and who have bought
five large buildings along Morgan
Street for the ostensible purpose
of building a serious artist colony
in Bridgeport. Regardless of what
brings you to the neighborhood,
it is full of gritty character (and
characters) and is quite possibly
haunted — Bridgeport is always
an interesting place for a walk.

Bridgeport-Chinatown

■ See and Do
1. Co-prosperity Sphere
*2. Daley Residence
2. mn Gallery
3. Saint Barbara Church
4. Saint Mary of Perpetual Help
5. Zhou B Art Center

▨ Buy
1. Augustine's Eternal Gifts
2. Grandstand
3. Let's Boogie

0.5 Kilometers

0.5 Miles

▥ Eat
1. Gio's
2. Ed's Potstickers
3. Kevin's Hamburger Heaven
4. Han 202
5. Healthy Food Lithuanian
6. Maxwell St Depot
7. Morrie O'Malley's Hot Dogs
8. Pancho Pistola's
9. Polo Cafe
10. Ramova Grill
11. Ricobene's
12. Scoops

▨ Drink
1. Bernice & John's
2. Bridgeport Coffeehouse
3. First Base
4. Mitchell's Tap
5. Schaller's Pump

▦ Sleep
1. Benedictine Bed
   & Breakfast

▨ Contact
1. Daley Library

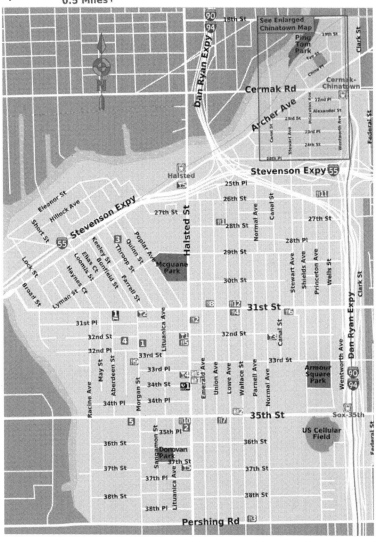

Chinatown

■ See and Do
1. Chinatown Mural
2. Chinese-American Museum
3. Chinese Cultural Institute
4. Dr Sun Yat Sen Museum
5. Nine Dragon Wall
6. Pui Tak
7. Sun Yat Sen Park
7. Veterans Memorial

■ Buy
1. Chinatown Bazaar
2. CW Mei's Gift Shop
3. Evergreen Jewelry

4. Golden Dragon Fortune
   Cookies
5. Hoypoloi Gallery
6. Mei Wah Co Inc
7. Ten Ren Tea & Ginseng Co

■ Eat
1. Bertucci's Corner
2. Cantonesia
3. Feida
4. Ken-Kee Restaurant
5. Lao Sze Chuan
6. Lawrence's Fisheries
7. Little Three Happiness
8. Mandarin Kitchen

9. The Noodle Vietnamese
   Cuisine
10. Penang
11. Phoenix
12. Saint's Alp Teahouse
13. Seven Treasures
14. Shui Wah
15. Spring World
16. Yee Heung Seafood House

■ Sleep
1. Chinatown Hotel

■ Contact
1. Chinatown Library

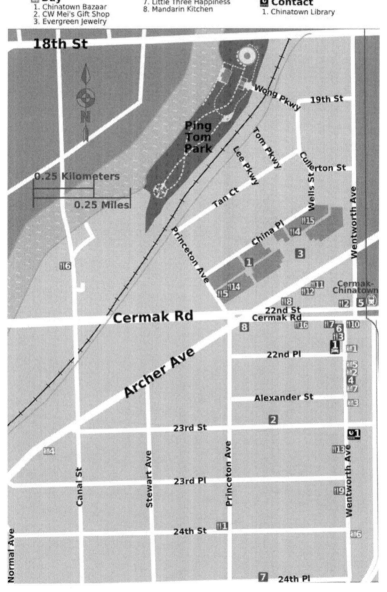

Get in

By train

The main L stations are on the CTA **Red Line** at Cermak-Chinatown and Sox-35th for visiting Chinatown and US Cellular Field respectively. Other options include Halsted and Ashland on the **Orange Line**, which are on the northern and western outskirts of Bridgeport, and 35-Bronzeville-IIT on the **Green Line**, which is a block and a half east of the Sox-35th station.

By bus

The main routes into Bridgeport-Chinatown from the Loop *p.47* are #62, which runs the length of Archer Ave from State St, and the #24, which runs from Clark St to Wentworth Ave through the center of Chinatown and next to US Cellular Field. Route #8 is also useful, as it runs north-south along Halsted St, which runs through the Near West Side *p.215* and Near North *p.71* neighborhoods as well as the middle of Bridgeport.

By car

Parking is always plentiful in Bridgeport, and you can usually find spaces right by your destination, though you should check to make sure you're not on a permit parking only residential street. On game days, however, watch out — though no signs go up, you can be ticketed for parking in the neighborhood. Take the L instead to avoid the bad game day traffic and pricey parking lots.

Chinatown is more crowded, but you should still have little trouble finding on-street metered parking around Cermak/Archer on weekdays or on off-hours.

The **Dan Ryan** and **Stevenson Expressway** cut across the east and north of the district. From the Dan Ryan, take either of the 31st or 35th Street exits; from the Stevenson, take the Cermak Avenue/Chinatown exit for Chinatown and the Damen Avenue exit via Archer or 35th Street for Bridgeport. The main city streets are Halsted Street (north-south), and 31st St, 35th St, and Pershing Rd (east-west).

Get around

The easiest way to get around Bridgeport by public transport is on the two main east-west bus routes #35 and #39, which run along 35th St and Pershing Rd, as well as the aforementioned #8 running north-south on Halsted St. Bus routes are not terribly convenient between the two neighborhoods, but #62 Archer does run along the north of Bridgeport from the Chinatown L stop, from which you can hop on the Halsted route. Chinatown itself is very compact and easily covered on foot.

See

You can cover Chinatown's sites easily in an hour or two on foot, but if you are interested in art, set aside some real time to explore the new Bridgeport galleries that fly under the popular radar, but are quite important to the contemporary art world in Chicago.

Chinatown

Chinatown Square, 2100 S Wentworth Ave, +1 312 225-0088. This main square is a Chinatown landmark, with some cheesy pagoda-like structures as well as animal sculptures of the Chinese zodiac. Be sure to check out the Chinatown Mural — a mosaic of painted tiles depicting the migration of Chinese-Americans from China to, ultimately, Chicago's Chinatown. Ultimately, though, the reason to come here is to wander into the surrounding Chinatown Marketplace, full of narrow alleys packed with shops and restaurants, which occasionally threaten to transport you back to Taipei.

Chinese American Veterans Memorial, 2169 S Archer Ave. A small memorial to Chicago Chinatown residents who served the United States in foreign wars.

Dr Sun Yat Sen Museum, 2245 S Wentworth Ave (*3rd floor, above the Chicago Food Market*), +1 312 842-5462, Sa-Su noon-5PM, M-F by appointment only. A one-room museum good for some Kuomintang nostalgia. Free admission.

Nine Dragon Wall (*just across Wentworth Ave from 200 W Cermak Rd*). A smaller semblance of the ancient glazed tile Nine Dragon Wall located in Beijing's Behai Park.

Ping Tom Memorial Park, 300 W 19th St (*phone=+1 312 746-5962*), *www.chicagoparkdistrict.com*. A riverside park with a Chi-

nese touch, including a riverside Chinese pavilion and a bamboo garden. On a clear day the park has nice southwest side views of the Chicago skyline. The park offers many summertime events from movie screenings to the very popular dragon boat races. Check the Chinatown Chamber of Commerce's website *www.chicagochinatown.org* for details.

Pui Tak, 2214 S Wentworth Ave, +1 312 328-1188, *www.puitak.org*. A historical landmark building notable for its traditional Chinese architecture now houses a Christian community center.

Bridgeport

Co-Prosperity Sphere, 3219-21 S Morgan St, +1 773 837-0145, *www.lumpen.com*, Sa noon-5PM & by appointment. Bridgeport's (and possibly Chicago's) most radical and experimental artistic space is huge, full of artists and their art, and is an ever-expanding force in the neighborhood — they plan to host live music in the near future. A very interesting place to browse!

Daley Residence, 3536 S Lowe Ave. Life-long home of the famous, the infamous, Richard J. Daley, and the place where his sons, current Mayor Richard M. Daley and state congressman John P. Daley, grew up. There isn't much at all to be seen here aside from the nice prairie-style brick one story, and don't bother the current residents.

mn Gallery, 3524 S Halsted, +1 773 847-0573, *www.mngallery.net*, Sa-Su noon-5PM during exhibitions. Run by a local couple, this three-story building houses exhibitions of contemporary art by Chicago and regional-based artists. Be sure to check ahead to make sure that they have an open exhibition.

Saint Barbara Church, 2859 S Throop St, +1 312 842-7979. Built in 1914 to house overflow from Saint Mary of Perpetual Help, in the so-called "Polish Cathedral Style." Dominates the Bridgeport skyline along with St Mary's.

Saint Mary of Perpetual Help, 1039 W 32nd St, +1 773 927-6646, *www.stmaryofperpetualhelp.com*. Another massive, opulent church of the Polish Cathedral Style, built in 1882.

Zhou B Art Center, 1029 W 35th St, +1 773 523-0200, *www.zbcenter. org*, M-Sa 11AM-5PM. A big arts center in the heart of Bridgeport hosting three contemporary painting galleries: Oskar Friedl, 33 Collective, and the Zhou Brothers Art Foundation, as well as the eerie abstracts and mixed-media experiments of 4Art. The Oskar Friedl Gallery in particular really warrants a visit as it is one of the city's better spots for avant-garde works. The cafe/bar inside is also pretty fantastic. Check ahead to make sure the gallery that interests you is open. The whole huge place is open to wander around on the 3rd Friday of each month.

DO

Armour Square Park, 3309 S Shields Ave, +1 312 747-6012, *www.chicagoparkdistrict.com*, M-F 9AM-10PM, Sa-Su 9AM-5PM. A good place to play some baseball, soccer, volleyball, basketball, or take a dip in the pool. Occasional events include outdoor movie screenings.

Chicago Chinese Cultural Institute, 2145 S China Pl (*2nd floor*), +1 312 842-1988, *www.chicagocci.com*. Offers an assortment of services and events, such as: neighborhood tours, film screenings, language instruction, and cooking classes.

Chinatown Summer Fair, 10AM-8PM, 19 July 2009. A fun neighborhood festival, with a Lion Dance procession along Wentworth at 12:30PM, and performances starting at 1PM, 23rd & Wentworth.

Dragon Boat Race (*Ping Tom Memorial Park*), 9AM-4PM, 25 July 2009. Dragon Boats along the South Branch of the Chicago River.

Sun Yat Sen Park, 251 West 24th Pl. A little out of the way, but a nice small park and a great place to relax in the shade on a hot summer day.

U.S. Cellular Field (Comiskey Park) (*Sox-35th Red Line*), *chicago. whitesox.mlb.com*. Formerly known as New Comiskey Park, this is the home of the White Sox — or, as the name is properly phrased in the company of Cubs fans, The 2005 World Champion White Sox. The stadium itself was a notorious dud when it opened in 1991, but recent renovations have helped tremendously. If you just want to see a Chicago ball game and don't care who is playing, the stately charm of Wrigley Field might be the better option. But Sox tickets are easier to get, the fans are no less loyal, and the fireworks shows after Saturday night home games (win or lose) are worth the price of admission by themselves. For a nifty ballpark treat not offered at Wrigley, try the *elotes*, corn-off-the-cob with your choice of salt, butter, cheese, lime, and/or red pepper.

Good Guys wore red

For baseball, the North Side has the Cubs, and the South Side has the White Sox. But the city used to be split for football as well: the Chicago Bears played up north, at Wrigley Field, and the Chicago Cardinals represented the south side at Comiskey. Both were charter franchises of the NFL; in fact, founded in 1898, the Cardinals were the first professional football club in America.

Although they had a good run in the 1920s, by then resident at Comiskey Park, and although the "Million-Dollar Backfield" of 1947 brought a championship to the South Side, the Cardinals couldn't defend their territory against the more successful Bears, and the Bidwill family moved them to St. Louis in 1960 (and later to Arizona). Still, if you're talking sports with an older crowd in Bridgeport, don't be shy about sneering at the Pottsville Maroons and their foiled claim to the South Siders' rightful 1925 title, and Ernie Nevers' obvious superiority to that overhyped Red Grange.

Buy

The Chinatown shops are very fun, especially for gifts, but if you tire of knicknacks and knockoffs, Bridgeport has a handful of very eccentric and interesting offerings.

Chinatown

Chinatown Bazaar, 2221 S Wentworth Ave, +1 312 225-1088, 10AM-10PM daily. An odd gift shop with just about anything you could expect to be at a "Chinatown bazaar." It has a particularly good collection of cloth posters.

CW Mei's Gift & Jewelry Co., 2241 S Wentworth Ave, +1 312 225-1933, 10AM-9PM daily. Kung fu outfitters: swords, knives, outfits.

Evergreen Jewelry, 2263 S Wentworth Ave, +1 312 808-0730, 10AM-5:30PM daily. Just what the name would suggest, the store sells jewelry.

Golden Dragon Fortune Cookies, 2323 S Archer Ave, +1 312 842-8199. Yes, the man who writes the fortunes is in this factory. Buy fortune cookies fresh out of the oven, or get them in bulk until you can't carry any more.

Hoypoloi Gallery, 2235 S Wentworth Ave, +1 312 225-6477, *www.hoypoloi.com*, Su-Th 11AM-8PM, F-Sa 11AM-9PM. Probably Chicago's strangest upscale boutique with all sorts of interesting artwork and furnishings for interior decorators and gift shoppers.

Ten Ren Tea and Ginseng Co of Chicago Ltd, 2247 S Wentworth

Ave, +1 312 842-1171, 9:30AM-7PM daily. Wide selection of teas and tea accessories in a store for serious tea drinkers (if you use bags, that doesn't include you). Worth a visit just for the free samples! $2-50.

Bridgeport

Augustine's Eternal Gifts, 3327 S Halsted St, +1 773 843-1933 email augustines@sbcglobal.net, M-F 11AM-7PM, Sa 11AM-6PM. A store full of everything spiritual: from a rosary and cross collection to occult tomes and voodoo powders. Knowledgeable and helpful staff.

Grandstand, 600 W 35th St, +1 312 927-1984, *www.grandstandsox.com*, M-F noon-7PM, Sa 10AM-6PM, Su 11AM-5PM. A store with extensive inventory of sports memorabilia. A good place to pick up a reproduction Negro League jersey or rare baseball cards.

Let's Boogie, 3321 S Halsted St, +1 773 254-0139, M-Sa 11AM-6PM, Su 11AM-3PM. A big vinyl store specializing in dance music from house to hip hop. No used records around, only new. A popular shop with Chicago DJs.

Eat

Chinatown is a wonderful and popular place for foodies, with lots of options, great authentic food, and reasonable prices. The flip side is the curt "Chinatown service," but if you've got a good attitude about it, that merely adds to the authenticity. The two most

acclaimed restaurants here are Ken Kee and Lao Sze Chuan, but there are plenty of less known gems to seek out as well. For dim sum, the great rivalry is between heavyweights Shui Wah, Little Three Happiness, and The Phoenix. One big thing to watch out for are the scores of inferior dishes on those long menus. Most restaurants specialize in a limited range of dishes, and you need to know which to get a good meal—order a specialty listed below, or ask the server what the specialties are (if he directs you to the Kung Pao, *insist* on an authentic recommendation).

Bridgeport is far further off the beaten foodie path, but it's a quirky neighborhood with some excellent options. Ed's Potstickers and Healthy Food Lithuanian are the standout destination restaurants that really warrant a trip.

Budget

Chinatown

Feida Bakery, 2228 S Wentworth Ave, +1 312 808-1113, 7AM-9PM daily, Dim Sum offered 7AM-noon daily. A small, reliable bakery, where the baked goods can warm your stomach for less than a dollar. Dim sum is not as good as you can get elsewhere, but it is dirt cheap. Items vary in quality, but the seafood dumplings and desserts are excellent. All items: $0.50-3.

Lawrence's Fisheries, 2120 S Canal St, +1 312 225-2113, *www.lawrencesfisheries.com*, 24 hours. It's amazing that this place exists so close to downtown. It's fried fish heaven with frogs legs, $1.45 clam strips, fried oysters, scallops, and boiled shrimp. All that with views of the skyline, intriguing industrial and river bridge panoramas, and of a good sized hanging shark. $2-12.

The Noodle Vietnamese Cuisine, 2336 S Wentworth Ave, +1 312 674-1168, Su-Th 10AM-10PM, F-Sa 10AM-11PM. A solid Vietnamese pho (noodle soup with beef) joint, which qualifies as "ethnic food" for Chinatown residents — this is one of the few places around where you'll likely see only Chinatown residents, even on weekends. $3-6.

Saint's Alp Teahouse, 2131 S Archer Ave, +1 312 842-1886, 11AM-midnight daily. A Hong Kong teahouse chain with a very long beverage list also serves entrees. *Young* crowd that enjoys the all-ages hangout. $5-12.

Seven Treasures, 2312 S Wentworth Ave, +1 312 225-2668, *www.seventreasures.com*, Su-Th 11AM-2AM, F-Sa 11AM-2:30AM. Seven Treasures has a huge, if uninteresting, interior and late hours, but the reason to come here is for Cantonese noodle soup. Anyone who has spent time in China, and hankers for the noodle soup they had there will not be disappointed. The Hong Kong-style barbecue menu is worthwhile. $3.50-10.

Spring World Restaurant, 2109 S China Pl, +1 312 326-9966, 10:30AM-10PM daily. Yunannese cuisine in the Midwest is Spring World — a specialty quite rare this side of the Pacific, so foodies should take note. Food-wise, this is one of the best options in Chinatown (try the tea smoked duck, cold noodles, or any of the lamb or mushroom dishes), and it's very cheap to boot: 4$ lunch and $5 appetizer bar! $4-10.

Bridgeport

Kevin's Hamburger Heaven, 554 W Pershing Rd, +1 773 924-5771, 24 hours daily. Chicago, for all that it takes fast food so seriously, tends to fail in the hamburger category. *Not here.* Kevin's serves what is likely the best down-to-earth hamburger in the city, as well as classic malts, shakes, and floats. As far as atmosphere goes, think industrial wasteland truck stop. $3-6.

Maxwell St Depot, 411 W 31st St, +1 312 326-3514, 24 hours daily. Insomniacs take note! Chicago fare is the whole menu: Maxwell Street Polishes, pork chop sandwiches, hot dogs, and hamburgers. This spot serves what might be the world's *fastest* food — served usually before you can complete your order — but it's magically piping hot fresh of the grill. The crowd can get pretty weird around F-Sa 4AM, and the food is of extraordinarily low quality, but at that hour (after drinks) few things are more satisfying than a hot off the grill pork chop sandwich with a heaped mass of grilled onions and mustard. $2-5.

Morrie O'Malley's Hot Dogs,

3501 S Union Ave, +1 773 247-2700, M-F 10:30AM-8PM, Sa 11AM-6PM, closed Dec-March. Since US Cellular Field can't seem to do them right, get your real Chicago hot dogs here. Also, if you want any good insider information about the neighborhood, ask Morrie — he's helpful, friendly, and knows the area as well as anybody. If Morrie's is closed and you need a hot dog, you can get a fine one up at 35th Red Hots, closer to the stadium. $3-6.

Ramova Grill, 3510 S Halsted St, +1 773 847-9058, 5AM-8PM daily. A diner that's been around forever, serving breakfast all day and locally renowned chili. It is the quintessential dirt cheap greasy spoon and easily one of Chicago's best diners. $3-5.

Ricobene's, 250 W 26th St, +1 773 225-5555, *www.ricobenesfamoussteaks.com*, M-Th 11AM-midnight, F-Sa 11AM-1:30AM, Su 11AM-11:30PM. With one exception the food here is uninspired, but the atmosphere is extreme Bridgeport, and it's a great place to bring kids. The exception is the Italian breaded steak sandwich, yet another neighborhood "delicacy," which it does better than anyone. There's nothing subtle about it—a big ol' breaded steak on chewy Italian bread, optionally drenched in red sauce, plus cheese, and hot or sweet giardinera. Don't order the king size unless you like to view your meal as a challenge. $4-12.

Scoops, 608 W 31st St, +1 312 842-3300, *www.scoops1.com*, 11AM-11PM daily. A deceptively old fashioned neighborhood ice cream parlor offering homemade ice cream in a non-old fashioned variety of flavors. They also happen to have free WiFi and homemade cannoli. $2-5.

Mid-range

Chinatown

Bertucci's Corner, 300 W 24th St, +1 312 225-2848, M-Th 11AM-10PM, F-Sa 11AM-11PM, Su 3PM-9PM. This family-run Italian joint exudes so much Chicago character, you will feel like you just stepped off the Chinatown street into a 1930s gangster movie. Scruffy, no-nonsense Italian-American food. The fact that it's in Chinatown only attests to its hidden gem status. Full bar. $6-12.

Cantonesia, 204 W Cermak Rd, +1 312 225-0100, *www.cantonesia.com*, Su-Th 11:30AM-11PM, F-Su 11:30AM-midnight. An 60-year-old establishment offering serving adequate Cantonese cuisine and much trumpeted Mai Tais. Stick to the noodle dishes and the hot and sour soup. $8-15.

Ken-Kee Restaurant, 2129 S China Pl, +1 312 326-2088, 11AM-1AM daily. One of the best bets in the Chinatown Marketplace with an extraordinarily long menu offering Cantonese preparations of virtually any creature or vegetable. It's hard to get a table on weekend nights. $6-18.

Mandarin Kitchen, 2143 S Archer St, +1 312 328-0228, M W Th 11AM-10:30PM, T 3AM-10:30PM,

F-Su 9AM-11PM. As the name might lead you to expect, Mandarin Kitchen is one of the few restaurants around serving northern Chinese cuisine, which is generally drier and heartier than the other cuisines you can sample in Chinatown. Hot pots, where you cook the meat on your table, are the house specialty, and great for groups. Otherwise the lamb cumin and noodle dishes are very good bets. $10-16.

***Little* Three Happiness**, 209 W Cermak Rd, 842-1964, 9AM-2AM daily, dim sum until 3PM. There are two "Three Happinesses" right across the street from each other, and as you might guess, the small dingy looking one on the south side of the street is far superior. LTH is so beloved, the city's most knowledgeable foodie website is *named after it.* Specialties are many, including pan-fried rice noodles, spare ribs, crispy duck and chicken, and most famously the heads-on salt and pepper shrimp. The dim sum is excellent, and the cheapest of the big three (by a good margin). $5-25.

Shui Wah, 2162 S Archer Ave, +1 312 225-8811, Dim Sum: 8AM-3PM daily, Dinner 5PM-2AM daily. Skip dinner, served by a different management and staff — you can do better. But the dim sum, always great, is quite possibly the best in the city when it's really on. Sadly, once a hidden gem, Shui Wah was recently exposed by rave reviews in popular Chicago magazines, so getting there early or late is wise to avoid the crowds on weekends. $8-20.

Yee Heung Seafood House, 225 W Cermak Rd, +1 312 326-3171, M-Th 5PM-4AM, F-Sa 5PM-5AM, Su 5PM-11PM. Feeling peckish for authentic food in the wee hours of the morning? This is the place, and may be the best place after most close. $8-16.

Bridgeport

Ed's Potsticker House (Potsticker House), 3139 S Halsted St, +1 312 326-6898, Su-Th 10AM-10PM, F-Sa 10AM-11PM. One of Chicago's great neighborhood restaurants, though you would never know it from the inauthentic sounding name. Chicago's Chinese community more and more bleeds across neighborhood boundaries into Bridgeport proper, and this restaurant is the showcase of the culinary possibilities this creates for the area. It's a mom and pop run Chinese restaurant specializing in Northern Chinese cuisine. There are a lot of great dishes on the menu (hint, not the ones you've heard of before) — aim for the lamb cumin, soup dumplings, or the whole Szechuan style tilapia.

Gio's Cafe & Deli, 2724 S Lowe Ave, +1 312 225-6368, *www.gioscafe.com*, M-Sa 8AM-9PM. Some of Chicago's best Italian is hidden in a tiny checkerboard tablecloth deli, more resembling a grocery store than a restaurant, hidden further still in the residential streets of Bridgeport. It's also, as you might expect, a steal of a bargain. Delicious Italian pastas, chicken, and panini. $5-25.

Healthy Food Lithuanian, 3236 S Halsted St, +1 312 326-2724, *www. healthyfoodlithuanian-chicago.com*, T-W 8AM-4PM, Th-Sa 8AM-8PM, Su 8AM-5PM. Where else are you going to go for Lithuanian? Fortunately, the one option is a *very* good one and has been serving grandma's Lithuanian favorites since 1938, making it the oldest Lithuanian restaurant *in the world*. Don't miss the blynai (Lithuanian crepes). The "healthy" name comes from the fact that this restaurant only uses organic ingredients and serves a fair amount of breakfast foods made from buckwheat. It does not come from the heavy portions nor the generous sour cream. It's also an intriguing option for souvenirs, with Baltic amber jewelry and t-shirts boasting kugelis as the "breakfast of champions." $8-14.

Pancho Pistola's, 700 W 31st St, +1 312 225-8808, *www.panchopistolas.com*, M-Th 11AM-11PM, F-Sa 11AM-midnight, Su 11AM-10PM. Authentic and very solid food in a nice sit-down family owned Mexican restaurant notable for its great margaritas. One of Bridgeport's trendiest restaurants (there aren't a lot of those). $8-15.

Splurge

Han 202, 605 W 31st St, +1 312 949-1314, *www.han202restaurant.com*, 4PM-10PM daily. High class, trendy dining on the cheap! The ethnic makeup of this section of town might fool you, but "Asian Fusion" is about as unlikely as a Utah brewpub. Bridgeport is a decidedly non-trendy neighborhood. But the neighborhood's new Han 202 has taken off, and its chef's cooking has attracted favorable comparisons to some of the flashiest and most esteemed in the city. The rave reviews are no doubt reinforced by the extraordinary deal—$20 for a fixed price five-course meal, plus BYOB with no corkage fee.

Lao Sze Chuan, 2172 S Archer Ave, +1 312 326-5040, *www.laoszechuan.com*, 11:30AM-midnight daily. Often considered the best Chinese in the Chicagoland area, Lao Sze Chuan serves up fiery Szechuan cuisine. Not only is the food excellent, the service is as well, and it even has a nice ambiance. As is often the case in Chinatown, sometimes the most inauthentic sounding names hide the best dishes; Tony's Chicken is the restaurant's rightly famous dish, served with three types of chili sauce. Other famous dishes include their very unusual cumin lamb, as well as the tea duck. If what you want isn't on the menu, tell them what you want and how you want it cooked — they'll likely invent the dish on the spot! $10-17.

Phoenix, 2131 S Archer Ave, +1 312 328-0848, *www.chinatownphoenix.com*, Dim Sum: M-F 9AM-3PM, Sa-Su 8AM-3PM; Dinner Su-Th 5PM-9:30PM, Sa-Su 5PM-10:30PM. The Phoenix is the gold standard in Chicago dim sum, and with good reason. It's the one of the three top dim sum establishments that actually has nice decor, which, naturally, you pay for. Unlike the other good dim sum options, Phoenix uses the ever-popular wheeled cart method of delivery. The one downside to Phoenix is that it is better known, and therefore a good deal more crowded (and expensive) than most Chinatown restaurants — it pays to arrive either early or late to avoid the crowd. $18-30.

Polo Cafe & Catering Bridgeport USA, 3322 S Morgan St, +1 773 927-7656, *www.polocafe.com*, lunch: M-F 11AM-3PM, dinner: W 6PM-8PM, F-Sa 5PM-9PM, brunch: Sa 9AM-2PM. A fine Bridgeport steakhouse decked with Mayor Daley-worship decor. Show up early on Saturday for the "Bloody Mary Brunch" and try "The Mayor's Steak and Eggs." $15-40.

Drink

As you might expect from such an Irish neighborhood, drinking is an established tradition in Bridgeport. If Chicago machine politics and general intrigue are your cup of tea, finish a tour of Bridgeport with a cold beer at the birthplace of many a corrupt scheme, Schaller's Pump. In Chinatown, some of the nicer sit-down restaurants serve alcohol, and the bar at nearby Bertucci's Corner is very pleasant. If you're up for a weirder Chinatown experience, head to the nameless, haunted, union man's bar at 26th and Wentworth.

For tea, you're in luck. In addi-

tion to dedicated teahouses, every sit down restaurant in Chinatown will serve you endless, free looseleaf oolong tea with your meal. If you care more about the tea than the meal, Mandarin Kitchen's standard oolong is the finest.

Bernice & John's, 3238 S Halsted St. A laid back and particularly friendly Bridgeport bar with Thursday open mic nights that have caught on well with local artists.

Bridgeport Coffeehouse, 3101 S Morgan St, +1 773 247-9950, *www.bridgeportcoffeecompany.com*, M-F 6AM-8PM, Sa 7AM-8PM, Su 8AM-7PM. Starbucks doesn't exist in Bridgeport and in this coffeehouse, the staff knows their customers by name. Features original blends roasted in house and some excellent loose-leaf teas. Free wireless, live jazz on Sundays, and live blues on Wednesdays.

First Base, 3201 S Normal Ave, +1 312 791-1239, 11AM-2AM daily. A lively bar with some good Irish stout on tap. It gets raucous when the Sox are playing.

Mitchell's Tap, 3356 S Halsted St, +1 773 927-6073, *www.mitchellstap. com*, Su-F 11AM-2AM, Sa 11AM-3AM. Lots of different kinds of beer, bowling, golf machines, and frequent live music. cover on Sa only: $3-5.

Schaller's Pump, 3714 S Halsted St, +1 773 376-6332, M-F 11AM-2AM, Sa 4PM-3AM, Su 3PM-9PM. This family-owned Irish-American bar is the oldest in the city — founded in 1881.

The former speakeasy gets really crowded during and after Sox games, but it's always a good place to spot local power-brokers — it's just across the street from the Democratic Ward office. Regardless of whether you're here after a Sox game or you're just hatching political plots, you can enjoy a mighty fine corned beef and cabbage sandwich.

Zhou Brothers Cafe, 1029 W 35th St (*Just inside the Zhou B Art Center*), +1 773 523-7777, *www. zhoubcafe.com*. Certainly the most stylish hang-out in Bridgeport, the cafe/lounge is a nice place to relax on the couches, surf the free WiFi, and have a glass of wine. food: $5-10.

Sleep

If you want to get out of the touristy areas and get a real Chicago neighborhood experience, the three options below are excellent. The Chinatown experience is, as is appropriate, budget and poor, while the Bridgeport options are upscale and full of South Side character.

Chinatown Hotel, 214 W 22nd Pl (*located at Cermak/Chinatown on the Red Line*), +1 312 225-8888, *www. chinatownhotel.net*, Checkin: 3PM, Checkout: noon. Free wired internet and computers. One of the best budget options anywhere near downtown Chicago. And to top it off, its right by all sorts of delicious and cheap Chinese restaurants. But do remember that it is a budget spot — staff speaks limited English and accommodations are

pretty spare (might remind backpackers of China travels). from $67.

Benedictine Bed & Breakfast, 3111 S Aberdeen St, +1 773 927-7424, *www.chicagomonk.org*. Cozy spacious rooms within an urban Benedictine monastery. The price is *way* lower than what you would spend in a downtown hotel, but the accommodations actually blow those hotels out of the water (multiple rooms, private gardens!), and the monastery and the surrounding neighborhood have much more character. The monks are quite good cooks, and very quiet hosts — you won't even see them leave you a different breakfast each morning. Definitely make your reservations well in advance, as the two apartments often are booked solid as far as three months. $165 for 1-2 adults.

Bridgeport Bed and Breakfast, 3322 S Morgan St (*Above the Polo Cafe*), +1 773 927-1122, *www. bridgeportbedandbreakfast.com*. Run by the owner of the Polo Cafe, offering meeting space for 100 people, and suites for 4-6 visitors, the Bridgeport B&B is an unusual neighborhood B&B. One significant plus of staying here is enjoying the big gift certificates and discounts at the Polo Cafe downstairs. $200-450.

Contact

The most pleasant spots to check your email have got to be the Bridgeport Coffeehouse, Scoops, and the cafe/bar inside the Zhou

B Art Center (See above for details). But for those without a laptop, there is also free internet access also at the following two public libraries:

Chinatown Public Library, 2353 S Wentworth Ave, +1 312 747-8013, M-Th 9AM-9PM, F-Sa 9AM-5PM. Free public internet access. Also, the library manages to be a bit of an attraction in and of itself for its indoor koi pond, China-related displays, and collection of books in Chinese.

Richard J Daley Public Library, 3400 S Halsted St, +1 312 747-8990, M-Th 9AM-9PM, F-Sa 9AM-5PM. WiFi in the house of his honor.

Get out

Chicago's **Southeast Asian Strip** is located in Uptown *p.273* around Argyle Street, at the CTA Red Line stop of the same name. It is a better bet for Thai, Vietnamese, Laotian, and other Southeast Asian regional cuisines. It is also far less touristed than Chinatown.

If you came here after reading Upton Sinclair's *The Jungle* and are feeling disappointed in the general lack of hog butchery, head due southwest to visit the few remaining monuments to the once vast Chicago meatpacking district, around the Union Stockyard gate in Chicago's Southwest Side *p.347*.

For those in search of the perfect Irish pub in Chicago, you may have better luck in the Far Southwest Side *p.389*.

Bronzeville, the **Black Metropolis**, is a mecca of African-American History on Chicago's South Side, just miles south of downtown. Gwendolyn Brooks published poetry in the Chicago Defender, Andrew Rube Foster created Negro League Baseball, and Louis Armstrong kept his trumpet singing at the Sunset Cafe to keep Al Capone off his back. Long in disrepair, the neighborhood is coming back, with new residents refurbishing historic homes, and with new dining and nightlife scenes beginning to take root.

Understand

Bronzeville was the site of Chicago's version of the Harlem Renaissance, and was home to many famous African-Americans, including Gwendolyn Brooks, Richard Wright, Louis Armstrong, Bessie Coleman, Ida B Wells, Andrew Foster, and many more. The neighborhood was from the 1920s to the 1940s one of the premiere centers of African-American culture and was fairly affluent and middle class. The Great Depression hit the area hard, bankrupting black-owned businesses, but the neighborhood's worst enemy proved to be the neglectful and segregationist city government. Because black Chicagoans were restricted (unofficially) from renting and buying property outside of the "Black Belt," rents were actually higher in the district's run-down, ill-maintained buildings, owned by white absentee landlords than in the adjacent, wealthy, white neighborhoods. In 1941, the city built the infamous and gigantic Ida B Wells housing projects in Bronzeville, which produced devastating and unintended results. Because of segregation, many low-income

African-Americans were unable to find housing anywhere else and the projects quickly became overcrowded, while crime and urban blight expanded throughout the neighborhood.

Today, the neighborhood is seeing major community-driven revitalization efforts, mostly by wealthy and entrepreneurial African-Americans who value the neighborhood's historic importance. Historic clubs are reopening, and there are a handful of nice coffee shops and restaurants that have opened in recent years. More so than the present, however, the principal attraction remains the neighborhood's rich history. As a rule, the revitalization efforts have not extended below 47th Street or west of the Dan Ryan Expressway into the Washington Park and Fuller Park neighborhoods, which remain very blighted, with an extraordinary amount of vacant lots and the highest violent crime levels in the city. Unfortunately, this means that 47th Street, which has some major draws, can be a little edgy after dark. But don't worry about Washington Park the park (as opposed to the neighborhood) — it's perfectly safe during the day.

Get in

By train

The best way to reach Bronzeville by public transport is definitely the CTA **Green Line**, which runs along State and Indiana, with key stops at 35-Bronzeville-IIT, 43rd St, 47th St (Jackson), and Garfield (Jackson). The **Red Line** runs along Bronzeville's western border by the Dan Ryan Espressway — a bit further away from most Bronzeville attractions, but convenient nonetheless.

The **Metra Main Line** has a stop at 27th St, which is conveniently located near the "Walk of Fame" and Michael Reese Hospital, but not near much else.

By bus

Many CTA bus lines travel throughout Bronzeville. A few key routes are the #4 and #3, which run north-south along Michigan Ave and Martin Luther King Jr Dr respectively and will take you to Bronzeville from the Loop *p.47*. The #55 Garfield route is useful for travel between Bronzeville and Midway Airport, in the Southwest Side *p.347*.

Bronzeville

See and Do
1. Chicago Bee Building
2. Chicago Defender Building
3. Eighth Regiment Armory
4. Overton Hygienic Building
5. Sunset Cafe
6. Supreme Life Building
7. Unity Hall
8. Victory Monument
9. Wabash Avenue YMCA
10. Bronzeville Information Center
11. Dusable Museum
12. Ida B Wells House
13. Kemper Room Art Gallery
14. S.R. Crown Hall
15. King Drive Gateway
16. SSCAC
17. Stephen A Douglas Tomb & Memorial
18. 31st St Beach
19. Harold Washington Cultural Center

Buy
1. Afrocentric Bookstore/ Steelelife Gallery
2. Gallery Guichard
3. Steelelife Gallery

Eat
1. Alice's Bar-B-Que
2. Blu 47
3. Chicken & Waffles
4. Harold's Chicken Shack
5. Mississippi Rick's
6. Ms Biscuit
7. Pearl's Place
8. Richard's Jamaica Club and Restaurant

Drink
1. Bronzeville Coffee House, Inc.
2. Jokes and Notes
3. Room 43
4. Spoken Word Cafe

Sleep
1. Central Arms Hotel
2. Eagle Inn/Motel
3. Long Hotel
4. Helena House
5. Hudson Hotel
6. Amber Inn

Contact
1. Chicago Bee Library (See Chicago Bee Building above)
2. Hall Library

0.5 Kilometers

0.5 Miles

BRONZEVILLE

By car

Bronzeville is one of the few neighborhoods close to the Chicago center that is actually best seen by car. Free on-street parking is in ample supply pretty much everywhere throughout the neighborhood — owing to the relatively low population density of the district. There are many exits leading into Bronzeville from the **Dan Ryan Expressway**, although you might enjoy the ride better if you take a more northerly exit (like 35th or 31st Streets) and then explore the area from Martin Luther King Drive — some of the areas further south around the expressway are a bit run down. If coming from the Loop *p.47*, the best way is probably to just head south on Martin Luther King Drive, which serves as the main drag for most of the district.

Black Metropolis landmarks

The following buildings are the city-designated, remaining landmarks from Bronzeville's golden age, from the "Black Metropolis" city within a city where blacks could find employment serving their own community.

Chicago Bee Building, 3647-3655 State St, +1 312 747-6872, M-Th 9AM-8PM, F-Sa 9AM-5PM. The home of the Chicago Bee Newspaper, which was founded by Anthony Overton to promote black businesses and issues. The art-deco building has an elegant terra cotta facade and today houses the Chicago Bee Branch Library. Free.

Chicago Defender Building, 3435 Indiana Ave. Initially built in 1899 as a Jewish synagogue, this building housed the Chicago Defender (the **nation's foremost African-American newspaper** through World War I) from 1920-1960. The Chicago Defender published works by Langston Hughes and Gwendolyn Brooks, and is largely credited for starting the Great Migration in its exhortations to southern blacks to move to the North for greater economic opportunities and freedom. The building is oddly vacant and neglected at present and may be available for sale.

Eighth Regiment Armory (Bronzeville Military Academy), 3533 Giles Ave, +1 773 534-9750 . This was the first armory for an African-American regiment, serving the "Fighting 8th," which fought in the Spanish-American War and served with distinction in World War I. After years of disuse, this grandiose building has been restored and now houses the nation's first public college-prep military school, which is unfortunately not open for visitors.

Overton Hygienic Building, 3619-27 State St. Built by the wildly successful African-American entrepreneur Anthony Overton to house the headquarters of his nation-wide cosmetics franchise. The building housed several of his other businesses, including Victory Life Insurance Company and Douglass National Bank, America's first national African-American bank. The building is now owned by the Mid-South Planning and Development Commission. Just across the street from the now demolished, notorious Ida B Wells projects, the formerly beautiful art-deco building is in a sad state of disrepair.

Sunset Cafe (Ace Meyers Hardware Store), 315 35th St, +1 312 225-5687, M-Sa 9AM-6PM, Su 11AM-2PM. Countless jazz legends played at this legendary jazz club, including: Bix Beiderbecke, Jimmy Dorsey, Benny Goodman, Earl Hines, Fletcher Henderson, Count Basie, and of course, Louis Armstrong. The club was run by unsavory mafia types and the musicians often had no choice but to keep playing here! Disjointed as it may be, the legendary club no longer exists and the building houses a hardware store. Nonetheless, the Sunset Cafe is Chicago's **number one jazz history site** and should not be missed by anyone traveling along The Jazz Track. In recent years, there has been talk of resurrecting the club, but plans remain embryonic. Feel free to stop in if you'd like — the owner is used to all sorts of foreign jazz aficionados wandering in.

Supreme Life Building, 3501 Martin Luther King Jr Dr. Built to house the first African-American insurance company, which was one of the few Black Metropolis businesses to survive the Great Depression. The building houses the brand new Bronzeville Visitor Information Center and is finally undergoing a proper restoration which will restore the 1920 classical facade.

Unity Hall, 3140 Indiana Ave. Built in 1887 to house a Jewish social organization, this building became famous as the headquarters of the Peoples Movement Club, founded by Oscar Stanton De Priest (1871-1951), the first African-American on Chicago's City Council and the first northern black delegate to the US House of Representatives.

Victory Monument, 35th St and Martin Luther King Jr Dr. This monument was built in 1928 to honor the service of the African-American Eighth Regiment of the Illinois National Guard in France during World War I.

Wabash Avenue YMCA, 3763 Wabash Ave, +1 773 285-0020. Bronzeville's YMCA, housed in a huge 1913 brown-pressed brick building, was a major social and cultural center for the neighborhood in its heyday, providing job training and housing for recent arrivals in addition to its more common functions. A painstaking restoration was completed in 2000 and the YMCA once again is open to the community. Free.

Other sights

Bronzeville Visitor Information Center, 3501 S Martin Luther King Jr Dr, Suite 1 (*Located in the old Supreme Life Building*), +1 773 373-2842, M-F 10AM-5PM, Sa 10AM-2PM, and by appointment. The Bronzeville Visitor Information Center seeks to provide visitors with orientation and offers tours, exhibits, and a small gift shop.

BRONZEVILLE SEE

DuSable Museum of African-American History, 740 E 56th Pl (*in Washington Park, just across Cottage Grove Ave from the University of Chicago*), +1 773 947-0600, *www.dusablemuseum.org*, M-Sa 10AM-5PM, Su noon-5PM. Chicago's museum of African-American history is named after the first settler of Chicago, a Haitian named Jean Baptiste Point du Sable. The museum often has excellent and moving temporary exhibits. $3 adult, $1 child, free on Su.

Ida B. Wells House, 3624 S Martin Luther King Jr Dr, *www.nps.gov*. The home of **Ida B Wells**, prominent African-American civil rights activist and suffragette, founder of the Black Womens' movement, and founding member of the NAACP, lived here from 1919–1929. Today it is a private residence and is closed to the public.

Illinois Institute of Technology, 3300 S Federal St, +1 312 567-3000.

Kemper Room Art Gallery (art@IIT), 35 W 33rd St, +1 312 567-5293, *art.iit.edu*, M-F noon-5PM, Sa 8:30AM-5PM, Su 2PM-6PM. An art museum specializing in late-modern and contemporary art.

S.R. Crown Hall, 3360 S State St, +1 312 567-3104 (IIT Public Relations), Locked on weekends, tours available by appointment. A major architectural landmark, designed by none other than **Mies van der Rohe.**

King Drive Gateway, S Martin Luther King Jr Dr between 24th St & 35th St. A 1.5 mile stretch of Martin Luther King Jr Dr full of plaques and monuments to the neighborhood's culture and history. Highlights include Alison Saar's statue at 24th St, "Monument to the Great Northern Migration," and at the 35th St intersection, Gregg LeFevre's 14 ft bronze map of the neighborhood's history and the "Victory Monument" to the African-American 8th Regiment of the Illinois State Guard (which served in France during WWI). Additionally, look for Geraldine McCullough's "Walk of Fame," a public art installation spread throughout the median and sidewalks along the boulevard, decorated with plaques bearing the names of Bronzeville's numerous famous residents. Keep an eye out for the public benches, also designed by local artists, which range from the subtly interesting to the wildly fantastic. Since it's more than a mile long, taking a "King Drive Gateway walk" isn't really practical—it's not meant to be seen in one visit, so just check out the main sites and appreciate what you do catch.

South Side Community Art Center (SSCAC), 3831 S Michigan Ave, +1 773 373-1026, *www.southsidecommunityartscenter.com*, W-F noon-5PM, Sa 9AM-5PM, Su 1PM-5PM. A community arts center open since 1940, which was for long the only place around where minority artists could exhibit there work. Today, the center focuses primarily on **African-American art**, especially art related to the South Side. The arts center offers exhibits, occasional poetry readings, and neighborhood gallery tours (see "Do" section).

Stephen A Douglas Tomb and Memorial, 636 E 35th St, +1 312 744-6630, 9AM-5PM daily. A 46 ft tall column marks the mausoleum of one of the most prominent senators in US history (a prominent resident from whom the Douglas neighborhood gets its name), who ran and lost against Abraham Lincoln for the US presidency in a race where debate over slavery dominated the discussion.

Do

The one activity offering in which Bronzeville excels is anything involving a big open field — If you are in the center of Washington Park tossing a football around or just lying in the grass, the big city feels miles away.

31st St Beach, 3100 S Lake Shore Dr, Summers: 9AM-9:30PM. While small, 31st St Beach is one of the nicest places for a swim on the South Side. It's family-friendly, never crowded, and always has stunning views of the Chicago skyline.

Fuller Park, 331 E 45th St, +1 312 747-6144. Some very serious basketball players hit the pavement here on weekends and the courts are worth a visit to watch the local players, but keep in mind that the park is in one of Chicago's roughest areas.

Harold Washington Cultural Center, 4701 S Martin Luther King Jr Dr, +1 773 373-1900, *www.*

haroldwashingtonculturalcenter. com. This major Bronzeville landmark is a performance venue showing movies, live jazz, blues, and more.

Bronzeville Art District Trolley Tour, 3521 S Martin Luther King Jr Dr (*begins at Gallery Guichard*), +1 773 272-8000 (Gallery Guichard), +1 773 373-1026 (SSCAC), +1 773 538-4773 (Steelelife Gallery), *www. southsidecommunityartcenter.com*. The South Side Community Art Center offers a free trolley tour between the SSCAC, Guichard, and Steelelife art galleries for anyone interested in buying or just browsing. The trolley first departs from Gallery Guichard and then loops around until 9PM. free.

Washington Park. A very big park designed by Frederick Law Olmsted. The park has big open fields, which host numerous festivals, sporting events, and performances throughout the summer. Be sure to check out the DuSable Museum of African-American History and the "Fountain of Time" sculpture.

Buy

Bronzeville is an excellent spot to shop for African-American-related books and art. There are other similar galleries and bookstores throughout the South Side, but the best are here.

Afrocentric Bookstore, 4655 S Martin Luther King Jr Dr (*inside the 47th St Marketplace*), +1 773 924-3966, *www.afrobookstore. com*, M-F 10:30AM-6:30PM, Sa

10AM-6PM. A bookstore dealing mostly in African-American literature, which gets some very big-name authors to come in now and then for guest readings.

Gallery Guichard, 3521 S Martin Luther King Jr Dr, +1 773 373-8000, *www.galleryguichard.com*, T-Sa 11AM-6PM, Su noon-4PM. A Bronzeville art gallery dealing in fine art, especially related to Africa and the African diaspora.

Steelelife Gallery, 4655 S Martin Luther King Jr Dr (*inside the 47th St Marketplace*), +1 773 538-4773, T-Sa 11AM-5:30PM, Su noon-5PM. Yet another contemporary art gallery featuring works of the African diaspora.

Eat

For a long time, this area's restaurant selection has been poor, aside from a bunch of tasty fast-food take-out joints. This is changing and nothing indicates this more clearly than the first-class new addition of Blu 47.

Budget

Alice's Bar-B-Que, 65 E 43rd St, +1 773 924-3843, M-Th 11:30AM-2:30AM, F-Sa 11:30AM-5AM, Su 2PM-2AM. Open very late and offering some of the best cue in the city, Alice's would be a great take-out stop if there were fewer people inside bumming for money. Ignore them, though, and you'll be treated to a fantastic meal. $5-12.

Harold's Chicken Shack. The great South Side fried chicken chain is cheap, usually a lit-

tle dirty, and always delicious. Harold's was born right near here on 47th street, by the way, in north Kenwood, although the original location (at Greenwood) closed long ago. $2-5.

307 E 51st St, +1 773 373-9016, 10AM-2AM daily.

108 E 47th St, +1 773 285-8362, 10AM-2AM daily.

Richard's Jamaica Club and Restaurant, 301 E 61st St, +1 773 363-0471, 9AM-midnight, when open at all. Good family-friendly Jamaican restaurant/night club, but owing to the downward spiral in the neighborhood, it's not always open. $3-8.

Mid-range

Chicago's Home of Chicken & Waffles (Rosscoe's), 3947 S Martin Luther King Jr Dr, +1 773 536-3300, Su-Th 9AM-9PM, F-Sa 9AM-11PM. A great little place serving all sorts of different combinations of, as you might expect, chicken and waffles, as well as your standard soul food menu, expertly executed. The neighborhood is underserved by such nice establishments, though, and given the small space that means there's a significant wait to be seated virtually any time of the week. Oh, and the extra "s" in Rosscoe's is to forestall lawsuits from the L.A. chain. The pretty building the place inhabits was a hotel back in the days when blacks could not stay at "white hotels" around the city, so this one played host to some big African-American celebrities, including local Muhammad Ali. $10-15.

Mississippi Rick's, 3351 S Martin Luther King Jr Dr, +1 773 791-0090, M-Th 10AM-10PM, F-Sa 10AM-midnight, Su noon-8PM. The South Side is full of barbecue and Jamaican take out establishments, but this is the only to try to combine the two. Jerk rib tips are the local favorite, although you can avoid the fusion by getting the standard jerk chicken, or a fried perch dinner. But the specialty is the jerk rib tips platter — rib tips slathered with a mixed jerk-BBQ sauce. The barbecue is nothing to write home about, truth be told, but if taken as a South Side twist on Jamaican food, it's very enjoyable. $5-10.

Ms Biscuit, 5431 S Wabash Ave, +1 202 268-8088, 5AM-2PM daily. A great soul food breakfast spot, where the biscuits can't be missed and the pancakes are delicious. It's in a dicey area, but you should have no trouble parking right in front, and the place itself is friendly, bright, and cheery. And the food is really heads and shoulders above the competition throughout much of the South Side. $4-10.

Pearl's Place, 3901 S Michigan Ave, +1 773 285-1700, M-Sa 7AM-8PM, Su 8AM-6PM. A nice sit down soul food eatery right in the heart of Bronzeville and adorned with pictures of famous historical Bronzeville residents (and adjacent to the Amber Inn). Brunch/breakfast is where they really shine, with famous sausage, belgian waffles, and of course sweet potato pie. Very friendly

staff. $6-15, brunch buffet: $12.

Blu 47, 4655 S Martin Luther King Jr Dr (*inside the 47th St Marketplace*), +1 773 536-6000, Tu-Sa 11AM-3PM, 5PM-10:30PM; Su 10AM-3PM, 5PM-10:30PM. A rather upscale, but casual Cajun/Creole restaurant with an inventive menu. Live jazz on Thursday nights. The clientele tend to be fashionably dressed, due to the nice bar/lounge inside, but the place is pretty empty on weekdays. entrees $30-$50.

Drink

47th St was once the blues capital of the world. That was before the 1968 riots — now aside from the promotional statues and commemorative signs, the once legendary strip is now full of shuttered buildings and looks a bit like it got hit by a tornado. Nightlife offerings remain fairly limited, but the area around 47th St has a few gems as the neighborhood is making a comeback. Jokes and Notes is a bit more expensive, but often well worth the cover — it is as hip as a comedy club can get and some big names (like Dave Chappelle) pop in unexpectedly.

Bronzeville Coffee House, Inc., 528 E 43rd St, +1 773 536-0494, *www.bronzevillecoffee.com*, M-F 7AM-6PM, Sa 8AM-4PM. Coffee, smoothies, tea, and snacks. A comfy spot with some books to read. Has occasional live music performances. Perhaps the most interesting thing about the place,

BRONZEVILLE SLEEP

though, is just how such a nice hangout sprung up on such a desolate street.

Jokes and Notes, 4641 S Martin Luther King Jr Dr, +1 773 373-3390, *www.jokesandnotes.com*, showtimes: W-Th 7:30PM, F-Sa 8PM & 10:30PM, Su 4PM. A small and cozy comedy/smooth jazz club primarily featuring African-American stand-up comedians. $10 W-Th,Su, $20 F-Sa; 2 drink minimum.

Room 43, 1043 E 43rd St, +1 773 285-2222, +1 773 265-6197, *www.hydeparkjazzsociety.org*, Su 7:30-11:30. The Hyde Park Jazz Society's **Sunday Jazz** has moved north out of Hyde Park to a little known bar/venue, which is a small, more intimate space. The performances are going strong, and the laid back Hyde Park crowd makes for great company. Drinks and food are served throughout the performances. Cover: $10, $5 w/ student ID.

Spoken Word Cafe, 4655 S Martin Luther King Jr Dr (*inside the 47th St Marketplace*), +1 773 373-2233, M-F 7AM-6PM, Sa noon-4PM & 7PM-midnight. A coffee house that often has poetry readings and live blues and jazz.

Sleep

If you are visiting Chicago and have a strong interest in Bronzeville, you may want to stay here, as the accommodations are far cheaper than those you would find downtown *p.71*. The cheapest options are not the nicest, but bargains are there to be had. The

downside, of course, is that you may find yourself taking a lot of taxis back and forth from the city center.

Budget

Central Arms Hotel, 520 E 47th St, +1 773 624-6500. Rents rooms in eight or twelve hour increments. $32.93 for eight hours, $34.08 for twelve hours with a shared bathroom, $37.09 for a private bathroom.

Eagle Inn/Motel, 453 E Pershing Rd, +1 773 373-6100, Checkout: noon. Friendly staff, with a slogan of "the best for less." Parking available. $35 for a ten hour stay, $43 overnight, plus a refundable $3 key deposit.

Long Hotel, 5615 S. Prairie Ave (*just south of 55th St*), +1 773 288-6973. Transient hotel, very close to Washington Park. Rooms have a TV, bed, and dresser, but no a/c or remote for the TV. Rough neighborhood. $140 for the week or $500 for the month.

Mid-range

Helena House, 5020 S Michigan Ave, +1 773 536-1640. In a classic Chicago-style brick apartment building. $63 for 24 hours, plus a refundable $3 key deposit.

Hudson Hotel, 5522 S Indiana Ave (*just south of 55th St*), +1 773 493-5028, Checkout: noon. Old-fashioned Bronzeville hotel, in business for "a good while." Before 7pm $70, after 7pm $65.

200

Splurge

Amber Inn, 3901 S Michigan Ave, +1 773 285-1000. One of the few nice places to stay in the area. Much cheaper and infinitely less pretentious than the big hotels downtown, with a fine, southern Sunday brunch. Just off I-90. $110.

Contact

The following libraries offer free public internet access:

Chicago Bee Branch Library, 3647-3655 State St, +1 312 747-6872, M-Th 9AM-8PM, F-Sa 9AM-5PM.

Hall Branch Library, 4801 S Michigan Ave, +1 312 747-2541, M,W noon-8PM, T,Th-Sa 9AM-5PM.

Get out

Chicago's Museum Campus in the Near South *p.95* is a short ride by cab or on the Red and Green Lines from Bronzeville; just beyond is the downtown Loop district *p.47*.

Bronzeville's history is inextricably linked with the wealthier neighborhoods in and around Hyde Park *p.157* to the east, which have a lot to see, including the University of Chicago, numerous mansions, great bookstores, and several great museums.

Bronzeville is where Chicago's African-American history was made, Chatham-South Shore *p.203* is where Chicago's African-American history comes to eat. Martin Luther King's favorite diner, Jesse Owens' gravestone, Harold Washington's old house, and the Obama's wedding reception hall are all here, as are some *incredible* blues clubs.

Chatham-South Shore is a district at the heart of Chicago's South Side, home to the *real* Chicago blues, some mind-blowing BBQ, and the best soul food in town.

Understand

This side of Chicago does not feature in many travel plans. If you ask a hotel concierge in the Near North *p.71* to make arrangements for a trip here, the reaction — whether incredulous or simply bewildered — should be a sight to behold. Don't be fooled, though; Chatham and Greater Grand could be the highlight of your trip to Chicago. The best **blues clubs** *are all here.*

Greater Chatham (Chatham, Avalon Park, Calumet Heights, Burnside) is a residential stronghold of middle and up-per class African-American Chicagoans. No sightseeing to be done, but Chatham boasts some of the best food on the South Side (including *the ultimate Harold's*), as well as two of the city's best blues clubs.

Greater Grand rivals Chatham for soul food, BBQ, and blues club supremacy. It also has the **Oak Woods Cemetery**, which is both beautifully laid out and resting place to some of the the most famous residents of the South Side's past.

South Shore is home to a lively arts scene, largely thanks to the ETA Creative Arts Foundation and the magnificent **South Shore Cultural Center**. It is also home to one of the city's best and least known beaches, Rainbow Beach. Incidentally, many of Chicago's most prominent black politicians call this community home. Its main commercial strip runs alongside Metra's Electric Line on 71st St and is literally lined with kids hanging out when school's not in session.

Get in

By car

If you are traveling by car, it is very easy to get into the district — the two major highways on the South Side cut right through it. From the **Chicago Skyway** (I-90), heading northbound, there are exits at 73rd, Stony Island Ave, 87th, and 95th *(there are no exits heading southbound from the Dan Ryan junction to 92nd St, past the tollbooth)*. Off the **Dan Ryan** (I-94), the principal exits are at 67th, 71st, 76th, 79th, and 87th. The major relevant east-west routes within the area occur every mile, at 71st, 79th, and 87th. For north-south travel within the district, the most useful routes are Cottage Grove Ave, Stony Island Ave (by far the widest route), and to a lesser extent South Chicago Ave.

Parking is widely available in each neighborhood. It is a relatively poor section of the city, and is far enough away from the city center that on-street parking should be easy to find. The only main streets lacking on street parking are in South Shore, along 71st and Exchange.

By rail

Rail is not the best way to visit this section of the city, as you will need to take bus transfers wherever you want to go.

The one relevant CTA line, the **Red Line**, passes through the western side of Greater Grand and Chatham, right in the center of the Dan Ryan.

The **Metra Electric Main Line** runs straight from Millenium Station downtown *p.47* through the heart of the district and, while the trains run less regularly, can be more convenient than the CTA.

For visiting South Shore, on the other hand, Metra is the best way to go, as the **Electric South Chicago Branch** runs right on top of the main strip the entire way through the neighborhood, with a very convenient stop right by the South Shore Cultural Center.

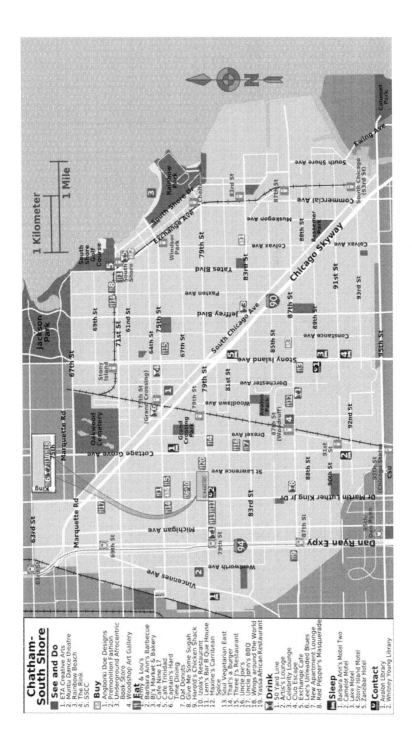

Chatham–South Shore

See and Do
1. ETA Creative Arts
2. Muntu Dance theatre
3. Rainbow Beach
4. The Rink
5. SSCC

Buy
1. Angibarki Doe Designs
2. Premonition Fashion
3. Underground Afrocentric Book Store
4. Woodshop Art Gallery

Eat
1. B & Lou's
2. Barbara Ann's Barbecue
3. BJ's Market & Bakery
4. Cafe Nine 17
5. Cafe Trinidad
6. Captain's Hard Time Dining
7. Dat Donut
8. Give Me Some Sugah
9. Harold's Chicken Snack
10. Izola's Restaurant
11. Lem's Bar B Que House
12. Maxine's Carribean Spice
13. Soul Vegetarian East
14. That's a Burger
15. Three J's Restaurant
16. Uncle Joe's
17. Uncle John's BBQ
18. Wings around the World
19. Yassa African Restaurant

Drink
1. 50 Yard Line
2. Aris's Lounge
3. Celebrity Lounge
4. Club Escape
5. Exchange Cafe
6. Lee's Unleaded Blues
7. New Apartment Lounge
8. Red Pepper's Masquerade

Sleep
1. Barbara Ann's Motel Two
2. Camelot Motel
3. Lake Motel
4. Stony Island Motel
5. Zanzibar Hotel

Contact
1. Avalon Library
2. Whitney Young Library

CHATHAM-SOUTH SHORE

By bus

Bus, while certainly less convenient than driving, is the most widely used mode of transport throughout most of the district. Route #4 runs the length of Cottage Grove Ave from Chicago State University through Hyde Park *p.157*, and all the way to Michigan Ave in the Loop *p.47*. #28 runs along Stony Island Ave from eastern Hyde Park all the way to 103rd St on the Far Southeast Side *p.377*.

For traveling east-west, the routes are simple, following the main roads: #71 along 71st St, #75 along 75th, and #87 along 87th.

See

Oak Woods Cemetery, 1035 E 67th Street, +1 773 288-3800. Were it not for the somber atmosphere, Oak Woods would probably be one of Chicago's favorite parks as it is beautifully laid out and has four attractive elongated ponds. The cemetery is the final resting place of many of the South Side's most famous residents, including Olympian runner Jesse Owens, nuclear physicist Enrico Fermi, civil rights leader Ida B. Wells, Mayor William Hale Thompson (perhaps Chicago's most eccentric leader), and the first black mayor of Chicago, Harold Washington Jr. One of the more striking monuments is the memorial to the overwhelming 6,000 Confederate prisoners of war who died at Camp Douglas (on the site of the present day Illinois Institute of Technology in Bronzeville).

The mayors' graves are located along the northwest shore of the largest lake (Symphony Lake). If Illinois' ugly political world interests you, you can find "Senator" Roland Burris' ostentatious monument/grave prepared in advance, with a list of his "achievements."

South Shore Cultural Center (SSCC), 7059 S Shore Dr, +1 773 256-0149, *www.hydepark.org*, M-Sa 10AM-6PM. An enormous South Side landmark, which once served as the private golf clubhouse — closed to African-Americans. Times have changed. The country club went bankrupt, and the golf course and tremendous building were bought by the Chicago Park District, and then converted into a beautiful and extravagant community center with large chandeliers and floor to ceiling windows. The SSCC hosts plays, live music, and dance performances. It's no stranger to fame, having hosted the wedding receptions of countless South Side notables, including the Obamas; the exterior also served as the "Palace Hotel Ballroom" for the Blues Brothers' big gig.

Do

ETA Creative Arts Foundation, 7558 S South Chicago Ave, +1 773 752-3955, *www.etacreativearts.org*, Box office: M-W 10AM-6PM Th-Su 10AM-10PM, ETA Gallery: M-W 11AM-6PM, Th-F 11AM-10PM, Sa 7AM-10PM, Su 2PM-10PM. A community center housing one top-notch African-American theater company, which puts on an extraordinary number of plays, nearly all of them world premieres. The theater itself is very nice and the community center includes two art galleries featuring mostly local African-American artists. Live music on Music Mondays (second Monday of the month). Admission to the main stage: $25.

Muntu Dance Theatre of Chicago, 6800 S Wentworth Ave, +1 773 602-1135, *www.muntu.com*, Check website for performance times. Muntu is an innovative and highly acclaimed Chicago dance company, which performs energetic interpretations of African and African-American dances and music. This location, their headquarters, is comprised of offices and a stage, although they regularly travel around Chicago's performance venues.

Rainbow Beach, 7600 South Shore Dr, +1 312 747-0832, Summers (Memorial Day-Labor Day): 9AM-9:30PM. One of the best and biggest beaches in Chicago, boasting a magnificent South Side view of the Chicago skyline, *and* it has a free parking lot! Free outdoor movies are often held in the adjacent Rainbow Park. Free.

The Rink, 1122 E 87th St, +1 773 221-3290, *www.therinkchicago.com*, T 10AM-2PM (30+) 8PM-midnight (21+), W 5:30-8:30 (families), Th 8PM-midnight (30+), F 7PM-11PM, Sa noon-3PM (pre-teen) 7PM-11PM (teen) midnight-4AM (18+), Su 5-9PM (30+) 9:30PM-1:30AM (18+). Ok, this place is cool. A roller rink oozing with South Side character and home

to not a few serious skaters who flaunt their moves to smooth R&B and old school. It has shown up a bit in pop culture, from the movies "Soul Food" and "Roll Bounce" to several nationally-aired music videos. If you are intimidated by the pros on the rink but want to check the place out, there are also arcade games and pool/ping-pong tables. It is open to different age groups at different times, so make sure to double-check the hours before coming here. Usually $7, but varies.

South Shore Country Club, 7059 South Shore Drive, +1 312 747-6250, *www.southshorecc.com*, Sunrise-sunset. Nine holes of golf maintained (somewhat) by the Chicago Park Administration. Great skyline views over Lake Michigan from the course. Weekdays: $11, Weekends: $12.50.

Buy

Angborki Doe Designs, 2650 E 83rd St, +1 773 731-2650, *angborkidoedesign.samsbiz.com*, Tu-Sa 11AM-7PM. African imports, aimed at home decor from jewelry and artwork to sofas.

Premonition Fashion, 8159 S Stony Island Ave, +1 773 374-4472, *premfash.com*, M-Sa 11AM-7PM, Su by appointment. A boutique specializing in trendy, very fashionable clothes by local designers for women of all sizes. The prices are outrageously low. All items $10-50.

The Underground Afrocentric Book Store, 1727 E 87th St, +1 773

EAT

768-8869, M-Sa 11AM-7PM. Books by and about African-Americans. Prides itself on distributing new and controversial publications. Also sells recordings of speeches by African-American leaders, African clothing, and other odds and ends.

The Woodshop Art Gallery, 441 E 75th St, +1 773 994-6666, M,W-Sa 9AM-6PM. Offers paintings and contemporary furniture by African-American artists as well as Haitian art, all at quite reasonable prices.

Eat

This section of the city is spoiled for terrific neighborhood restaurants. The majority of the city's most renowned soul food is served up here at famous locations like Army & Lou's and Izola's, both of which have served just about every prominent African-American figure who has set foot in Chicago. The city's best Memphis-style BBQ is here, too. Greater Grand is home to the city's best donuts; Chatham to the city's best fried chicken.

Now, if you are looking for something that resembles healthy food, your options are limited. Soul Vegetarian is a very good option, and the various ethnic restaurants are not quite so heart attack-inducing (mostly Jamaican, but with the odd Trinidadian and Senegalese restaurant tossed in for good measure).

South Side BBQ
Follow these rules, and you'll get some

great cue: Get your sauce on the side! There's no reason not to, and it allows you to control just how drenched the meat gets.

Follow the guide. You can easily go astray in these parts with sub-par BBQ — you cannot with the ones listed below.

Order sparingly. One combo can easily feed two, so if you're solo, plan to either make it two meals or get one of the small dishes.

Make sure they've got your order right, as communication through bulletproof glass is difficult.

Take your cue somewhere else. Good options include the Midway in Hyde Park p.157, or better still the 63rd St Pier east of Jackson Park p.157.

This is the real deal, dig in with those fingers and make a mess!

Budget

Cafe Nine 17, 917 E 79th St, +1 773 723-2222, T-W 11AM-9PM, Th-Sa 11AM-10PM, Su noon-9PM. A sandwich shop/eatery with open mic poetry nights T-W. The owner is openly gay and markets the cafe as a safe spot for the South Side LGBT community. $4-8.

Cafe Trinidad, 557 E 75th St, +1 773 846-8081, M-Th 11AM-8PM, F-Sa 11AM-9PM, Su 12:30PM-7PM. This is one of the only places to get Trinidadian cuisine in Chicago, and it knows what it is doing with its long list of curries. $3-8.

Dat Donuts, 8249 S Cottage Grove Ave, +1 773 723-1002, 24 hours daily, except Su 10PM-4AM. A must for serious donut eaters as it is home to the legendary "Big Dat" — the mother of all donuts. In addition to quantity (i.e., size), the quality attracts devoted foodies from all over the Chicagoland area. $0.25-2.50.

Harold's Chicken Shack, 100 W 87th St, +1 773 224-3314, Su-Th 10AM-2AM, F-Sa 10AM-3AM. A restaurant reviewer for the *Chicago Reader* took on the immense and grave task of finding which Harold's is the best, visiting each and every one of the 50 or so odd locations, and reviewing them on a ten point scale across twelve categories. And he found this location to be the best of them all! While the chicken should be fabulous, it's worth noting that there are more fights going on in that parking lot than is normal — usually between people who know each other, though. $2-5.

Give Me Some Sugah, 2234 E 71st St, +1 773 363-9330, *givemesomesugah.com*, Tu-Sa 10AM-7:30PM. A wonderful South Shore bakery, where everything is made from scratch (the high prices reflect this). $1.50-6.

That's a Burger, 2134 E 71st St, +1 773 493-2080, M-Th 11AM-7PM, F-Sa 11AM-9PM. *Big* to-order burgers at a local favorite. Take-out only, and *call ahead* well in advance to avoid a long wait. The house specials are the Whammy Burger, which comes with a split Polish on top, and the T.a.B Special, topped with chili, cheese, bacon and egg. Beef or turkey. $4-6.

Mid-range

Army & Lou's, 422 E 75th St, +1 773 483-3100, *www.armyandlous.com*, W-M 9AM-10PM. Former city mayor Harold Washington's favorite soul food restaurant is still a good place to spot prominent black Chicago politicians and anyone else who likes their soul food done right in a tuxedoed-waiter environment. If you enjoy your food here, you're in good company — other devotees have included Martin Luther King, Jesse Jackson, Sammy Davis Jr, Muhammad Ali, Cab Calloway, and the most honorable Richard Daley. $10-15.

Barbara Ann's Barbecue, 7617 S Cottage Grove Ave, +1 773 651-5300, Tu-Th noon-midnight, F-Sa noon-3AM. All Barbara Ann's offerings are great, but the links stand out — coarse, fatty, spicy — incredible. She also offers *beef* tips, which you would have trouble finding elsewhere in the city. Order the sauce on the side if you don't want your links to drown. $8-16.

BJ's Market & Bakery, 8734 S Stony Island Ave, +1 773 374-4700, M-Th 11AM-9PM, F-Sa 11AM-10PM, Su 11AM-8PM. This dining-hall like eatery offers some of the best soul food in a city full of great southern cooking. Moreover, the chef prides himself on cooking soul food for the *heart*, meaning that the food is actually healthy and won't sit so heavy in your stomach. $8-15.

Captain's Hard Time Dining, 436 E 79th St, +1 773 487-2900,

CHATHAM-SOUTH SHORE EAT

hardtimedining.com, S,T-Th 8AM-11PM, F-Sa 8AM-midnight. Fine dining on the cheap, soul food, steaks, and seafood. Offers a $15 Sunday "Gospel buffet" from 11AM-6PM with Gospel singers performing after 2:30PM. $9-14.

Izola's Restaurant, 522 E 79th St, +1 773 846-1484, Th-T 24 hrs. Legend has it that former Mayor Harold Washington began his mayoral campaign at this friendly landmark restaurant serving quality down-home-cookin'. Be sure to sit in the nice back room, which is more comfortable and has more seating than the front room (unless, that is, you're in a hurry). And check out all the huge photos of the famous people who have dined here (the Obama portrait is wall-sized). $8-14.

Lem's Bar-B-Que House, 311 E 75th St, +1 773 994-2428, W-M 2PM-4AM. Lem's sets the standard against which all Chicago cue must be judged. That's not to say it is the best — Uncle John's could certainly give Lem's a run for its money on a good day. But it serves the most reliably excellent tips and (charred) links you'll find in the city. Open late, and with a *crowded* parking lot. $5-13.

Maxine's Caribbean Spice, 1232 E 87th St, +1 773 933-0540, M-Th noon-10PM, F-Sa noon-midnight, Su noon-9PM. One of the best Jamaican restaurants in town. Features a weekend Caribbean breakfast which comes with sides of fried dumplings and boiled bananas. Note though, like all South Side Jamaican places, service is *s l o w*. $7-15.

Soul Vegetarian East Restaurant, 205 E 75th St, +1 773 224-0104, *www.kingdomofyah.com*, M-Th 7AM-10PM, F 7AM-11PM, Sa 8AM-11PM, Su 8AM-9PM. This is at once one of the best vegetarian and the best soul food restaurants in town. Occasional events range from spoken word to hip hop DJs. $8-14.

Three J's Restaurant, 1713 E 75th St, +1 773 667-1360, M-Th 8AM-11PM, F-Sa 8AM-11:45PM, Su 8AM-10PM. South Side is the place for Jamaican, and this local South Shore establishment gets five stars for the jerk chicken alone. Inside it's a nice, clean, diner-like eatery, with friendly service. Even if you never set foot in the neighborhood, you can indulge in this fine food by delivery as far as the Loop! Just know that it's cash-only, order minimum $15, you will have to step outside your hotel to get it, and call Joseph at +1 773 746-9615 for the delivery (tip him well for that drive!). $6-12.

Uncle Joe's, 8211 S Cottage Grove Ave, +1 773 962-9935, Sa-Th 11AM-10PM, F 11AM-11PM. The South Side's legendary Jamaican restaurant serving great jerk meats. It has developed into a local chain, but this is the original, and widely considered the best. $7-13.

Uncle John's BBQ, 339 E 69th St, +1 773 892-1233, M-Th 11AM-11PM, F-Sa 11AM-midnight. Uncle John's BBQ is simply the best. The tips and links are perfect, and the spare-ribs (unlike most Chicago ribs) are wonderful. If you make it out here, this place

210

CHATHAM-SOUTH SHORE DRINK

will dispel any notions you previously carried about BBQ north of the Mason-Dixon. $3.50-14.

Wings around the World, 510 E 75th St, +1 773 483-9120, M-W 11:30AM-10:30PM, Th-Sa 11:30AM-5AM, Su noon-7PM. Wings are the specialty, and they come in several flavors per nation: Canadian maple, Jamaican honey jerk, U.S. buffalo style, Japanese kamikaze, Greek lemon-garlic, etc. The sauces are rant & rave worthy and there's enough diversity to make a large order very worth it — if you're feeling splurgy, try an order of 1000 wings for $450 (call that one in first). All food is cooked to order, and the wings are big, juicy, & meaty. A note about that spicy kamikaze sauce is in order, though, it's aptly named. $7-20.

Yassa African Restaurant, 716 E 79th St, +1 773 488-9630, *www.yassaafricanrestaurant.com*, Su-Th 11AM-10PM, F-Sa 11AM-11PM. An authentic Senegalese Restaurant, which has made quite a name for itself (having been featured on the popular foodie TV show "Check Please"). But it remains a low-key, friendly hub for Chicago's Senegalese community. Don't miss the W,F dinner special: cow foot?! $9-12.

Splurge

The Parrot Cage, 7059 South Shore Dr, +1 773 602-5333, *kennedyking.ccc.edu*, W-Sa reservations accepted 5:30PM-8:30PM. An upscale restaurant at the South Shore Cultural Center that offers fine seasonal American cuisine

at impressively low prices, nice views of Lake Michigan, and is a great excuse to come admire the SSCC. $16-25.

Drink

Don't be fooled. There are plenty of **blues clubs** throughout the city, but none hold a candle to the following. Blues clubs are undoubtedly a matter of taste — you could have a great or a bad experience at any one of these, but the risk is worth it. Lee's Unleaded is probably the flagship club. **Jazz** lovers spending much time in the city should not miss a Tuesday night **Von Freeman** gig at the New Apartment Lounge.

South Side blues clubs, though, constitute a fragile ecosystem. Try not to descend en masse. The music and atmosphere will adapt to you; you won't get the real experience. Come in couples or trios instead, and immerse yourself in the culture of the **real Chicago blues**.

50 Yard Line Bar and Grille, 69 E 75th St, +1 773 846-0005, Su-F 11AM-2AM, Sa 11AM-3AM. A cool bar and a South Side steppers' lounge, where people *dance like adults*. Despite the name, this is about as far from being a sports bar as possible.

Artis's Lounge, 1249 E 87th St, +1 773 734-0491, 10AM-2AM daily. Written up in the paper as one of Chicago's coolest "dive bars," although one might wonder whether a local "dive bar" really appreciates such attention. In any rate, that review is dead on; everyone will know your name

211

CHATHAM-SOUTH SHORE DRINK

by the end of the night, and it has fantastic live blues Sunday and Monday nights from around 10PM-2AM. Drink prices are a bit steep, and there's a rule that no one may be inside without a drink—you'll be leaving drunk, so plan accordingly. No cover, accepts credit cards.

Celebrity Lounge, 2020 E 83rd St, +1 773 375-1348, Su-F noon-2AM, Sa noon-3AM. A 30+ club, but they'll probably let you in as long as you're polite. Right under the Skyway, soaked in neon, with nightly blues. Music *officially* starts at 9PM, but don't count on that, and show up after 10PM. Covers F-Sa $5-10.

Club Escape, 1530 E 75th St, +1 773 667-6454, *www.clubescapechicago.com*, Su-F 5PM-2AM, Sa 5PM-3AM. South Side gay bars are rare creatures. This is a very laid back and exceptionally welcoming bar/lounge frequented mostly by men and women in their 30s and 40s, dancing mostly to soul, house, and smooth jazz.

My Soul Cafe, 7201 S Exchange Ave, +1 773 336-8592, M-F 6AM-8PM, Sa 8AM-8PM, Su 8AM-5PM. This airy, attractive, comfortable, stay-as-long-as-you-want cafe is impossible to miss, and you wouldn't want to. Much of the menu is shoddy, but the wraps are worth ordering. The free WiFi should keep you occupied while you sip.

Lee's Unleaded Blues, 7401 S South Chicago Ave, +1 773 493-3477, T-F 8PM-2AM, Sa-Su 8PM-

3AM, M noon-2AM. Lee's is one of the best reasons to visit the Greater Grand Crossing neighborhood as it is a fabulous South Side blues club — definitely one of the best in Chicago. On top of that, this is one of the safer sections of the district *and* there's a Metra stop one block away. Blue Mondays feature a monster jam session from noon until 2AM. Be careful with the drink orders, as the club does serve a few very expensive brews. No cover, two-drink minimum.

New Apartment Lounge, 504 E 75th St, +1 773 483-7728, M-F 3PM-4AM, Sa 3PM-5AM, Su 3PM-4AM. This jazz club is simply extraordinary. It is small, has no cover, and hosts perhaps the best regular jazz show in Chicago. Not all nights see performances, but every Tuesday night Chicago jazz legend Von Freeman shows up with his quartet and enchants those who make it out to this small club from 10:30PM until a few hours before the sun comes up. His show attracts people from all walks of life from all over the city. If you want to sit at the bar, expect to pay for a few drinks. No cover, two-drink minimum.

Red Pepper's Masquerade, 428 E 87th St, +1 773 873-5700, *www.redpepperslounge.com*, M 3PM-2AM, T-F 10AM-2AM, Sa noon-3AM, Su noon-2AM. A Mardi Gras styled bar/restaurant serving Cajun cuisine. There's blues on Wednesdays and stand-up comedy Tuesdays and Thursdays. F-Sa usually see live DJs and lots of dancing. The entertainment is in the back room past the front bar. Dinners $5-8.

Sleep

Know what you're getting into if you are thinking of staying here. The options are pay-by-the-hour **flop houses** and run-down motels, with all the shady characters, **dubious mattresses**, and loose security that entails. And, well, cabs might be reluctant to pick you up if you give them one of these addresses. If staying here, though, know that the motels on Stony Island are the most secure.

Barbara Ann's Motel Two, 7621 S Cottage Grove Ave, +1 773 487-5800. Offers a bed, dresser, TV, and private bathroom. Attached to Barbara Ann's BBQ, which serves excellent rib tips. Rooms from $40 for 4 hours, $45 for 10 hours, $60 all night.

Camelot Motel, 9118 S Cottage Grove Ave, +1 773 488-3100. Rooms have a dresser, table, and television. $40 for ten hours, $55 overnight.

Lake Motel, 9101 S Stony Island Ave, +1 773 731-6600. Not far from Chicago State University and the Chicago Skyway/I-90 to Indiana. $40 for eight hours, $60 overnight, plus $2 key deposit.

Stony Island Motel, 9201 S Stony Island Ave, +1 773 731-8817. The friendliest looking option in the area, with standard rooms, also close to the Skyway. $55 for eight hours, $70 overnight.

Zanzibar Motel, 8101 S Stony Island Ave, +1 773 768-1430. Offers cable television and air conditioning. $40 for ten hours, $55 overnight.

Contact

There are two public libraries offering free wifi and public terminals. The Exchange Cafe above is another good option.

Avalon Branch Library, 8148 S Stony Island Ave, +1 312 747-5234, M-F 9AM-8PM, Sa-Su 9AM-5PM.

Whitney Young Branch Library, 7901 S Dr Martin Luther King Jr Dr, +1 312 747-0039, M-F 9AM-8PM, Sa 9AM-5PM.

Stay safe

The South Side experiences here can potentially outshine those you could have anywhere else in Chicago. There's one hitch though, and that's **violent crime**. Alas, the levels of violent crime in this area, especially in the northwest neighborhood of Greater Grand Crossing, are higher than you'd find traveling in much of the world; travel here is *not* for everyone, and many travelers will find visiting this area of the city to be beyond their comfort level.

Nonetheless, a casual visitor is very unlikely to be the target of crime; you just are not spending enough time here, so the odds are you'll be fine. Avoid side streets, where you can run into unabashed drug trade. On main streets, you might get mildly harassed if you look lost, insecure, or unfamiliar with your surroundings — if it happens, avoid eye contact, and keep walking.

It's a hassle to deal with public transport, especially if you're not staying here, and waiting around in the wee hours of the night at a bus stop, having stumbled out of a bar, is not a great idea. If you're going to be at a club, you're going to have some booze, and you'll need a ride. Arranging a point-to-point taxi ride is a good idea if you are coming from downtown. *Arrange that in advance;* residents rightly complain about the difficulty of getting a cab at night.

Get out

The South Side's Bronzeville *p.191* and Hyde Park *p.157* are just to the north and have a lot to offer a visitor interested in African-American history and culture. They also have far better hotel options, so if you are interested in basing yourself South Side, it may make sense to get a room near a Metra stop near Hyde Park.

Chatham is often considered part of the Far Southeast Side *p.377*, and there is ample reason to head further south. More soul food awaits, more blues brothers' filming locations, as well as a host of other South Side attractions like Historic Pullman.

The **Near West Side** of Chicago has two of Chicago's premiere culinary strips, **Little Italy** and **Greektown**, and basketball legend Michael Jordan's old stomping grounds with the **Chicago Bulls**.

Understand

Near West Side created many of Chicago's most beloved cultural landmarks: among others, the Chicago-style hot dog, the deep dish pizza, the immigrant port of entry, the blues, the Blues Brothers, the labor movement, "Cheat You Fair," Jane Addams and the modern concept of social justice — all were born or have roots here. You wouldn't know it from the place today, though, which is dominated the charmless campus of the University of Illinois at Chicago (UIC); outside of those areas, seen from the L tracks, stray pieces of the old neighborhoods sit like the last few teeth in the mouth of a punch-drunk prizefighter.

Close to the rail yards and factory jobs, this was Chicago's major port of entry throughout the 1800s and early 1900s. Central to everything was the **Maxwell Street Market**, which was founded by Jewish immigrants and joined by African-Americans during the Great Migration. Maxwell Street evolved from an open-air market of stalls and pushcarts to become the place where people from *everywhere* brought discount *everything* in the quest to make a fortune — and, as the saying went, Cheat You Fair. The deals, the scams, the cheap food and the street performances by future blues legends created a signature Chicago atmosphere for more than 120 years.

However, the desire of Chicago's business community to have a buffer zone between the Loop *p.47* and the West Side housing projects led to severe changes: first, the new Eisenhower Expressway cut off a slice of the east side, and then the construction of UIC destroyed the homes of more than 5,000 people. The years since have seen the university continue its path of wanton destruction, enabled by the city in every urge. In 1994, they finally managed to raze the market, which was relocated a few blocks east in reduced form.

Still, there are a few prime attractions on the Near West Side. The Chicago Bulls play on without Michael Jordan at the **United Center**, but Oprah Winfrey is still in residence at **Harpo Studios**. The small restaurant strips of **Little Italy** on Taylor Street and **Greektown** on Halsted Street have good food and tourist-friendly charm. UIC's **University Village** is rather like Hyde Park *p.157* recast by pod people, but the **West Loop** (sometimes known as the Warehouse District) features the city's most expensive restaurants, a thriving gallery scene, and several hot clubs-of-the-moment.

Get in

By train

There are several train stations on the Near West Side, but they're not very well-placed for destinations other than UIC. Buses are a more direct alternative from most of the city, including the Loop *p.47*.

The **Forest Park** branch of the CTA **Blue Line** has stops near Maxwell Street, Little Italy and Greektown (UIC-Halsted, Racine), UIC (Illinois Medical District) and the Tri-Taylor area (Western). The CTA **Green Line** and **Pink Line** have stops within a hike of the West Loop (Clinton/Lake) and the United Center (Ashland/Lake), while the Pink Line branches off to the center of UIC and near the edge of Little Italy (Polk).

The city's two regional train hubs, **Union Station** and **Ogilvie/Northwestern Station**, are right on the edge of the West Loop. They're generally used by travelers going east over the river to the Loop, but there's no reason you can't walk west instead. See the Loop *p.47* article for arrival and departure information.

By bus

The CTA runs several bus routes through the West Side:

8 Halsted can be caught as far north as Lakeview *p.139*. It runs through Greektown and hits the old Maxwell Street.

9 Ashland also runs from far north and on to the south, passing within walking distance of Little Italy and the United Center. It's an all-night route.

12 Roosevelt runs from the Near South *p.95* to walking distance of Little Italy (exit Halsted, walk south) and Greektown (exit Halsted, walk north).

19 United Center Express runs on game nights for the Bulls and Blackhawks from Michigan & Chicago in the Near North *p.71* to Madison in the Loop *p.47*, and express to the UC once it's west of the river. Service starts 90 minutes prior to game time and ends 15 minutes prior to game time, and buses will be waiting to travel the route in reverse after the game.

20 Madison runs all night from the Loop *p.47*, passing through Greektown and by the United Center.

38 Ogden/Taylor reaches UIC, Maxwell Street, and Little Italy. It will soon become the **157 Streeterville/Taylor**, extending into the Near North *p.71*.

50 Damen runs from Ukrainian Village *p.229* and passes by the United Center.

By car

For Greektown, exit I-90/94 east at Adams, or west at Monroe. From the Eisenhower Expressway, exit at Racine, and turn left. Halsted & Adams is three blocks north and six blocks east. If driving in the area in the evening, avoid the blocks around United Center at all costs, as the event traffic is horrendous.

Near West Side

See and Do
1. Bucket Rider Gallery
2. Donald Young Gallery
3. EC Gallery
4. F2 Gallery
5. GARDENfresh
6. Harpo Studios
7. Haymarket Square
8. Hellenic Museum
9. House Museum
10. Johnny's Ice House
11. Kavi Gupta Gallery
12. Museum of Holography
13. National Italian American Sports Hall of Fame
14. Primitive Art Works
15. St Ignatius College Prep
16. South Union Arts
17. Supreme Frame & Art
18. Uprise
19. United Center

Buy
1. Athenian Candle Co.
2. Barbara's Bookstore
3. Bennett Wine Studio
4. Greektown Gift & Music
5. Lissa on Maxwell
6. Maxwell Street Market
7. Pivot

Eat
1. Al's #1 Italian Beef
2. Artopolis Bakery
3. Athena Restaurant
4. Carnivale
5. Conte Di Savoia
6. Costa's
7. Dine
8. Francesca's
9. Greek Islands
10. Greektown Gyros
11. Harold's Chicken Shack
12. Jim's Original Hot Dog
13. La Lira
14. Manny's Cafe & Juice Bar
15. Mario Italian Lemonade
16. Nial Cafe & Juice Bar
17. Mr Greek Gyros
18. one sixtyblue
19. Pan Hellenic Pastry Shop
20. The Parthenon
21. Pegasus Restaurant
22. Rodity's
23. RoSal's Italian Cucina
24. Santorini
25. The Soupbox
26. Tufano's
27. Tuscany
28. Venus
29. White Palace Grill
30. Wishbone
31. Zeus Inc

Drink
1. 9 Muses
2. Cavanaugh's
3. Gennaro's
4. Jaks Tap
5. Spectrum Bar & Grill

Sleep
1. Chicago Marriott
2. Crowne Plaza
3. Metro
4. Holiday Inn Hotel

Contact
1. Mabel Manning Library
2. Theodore Roosevelt Library

See

Harpo Studios, 1058 W Washington Ave (*20 Madison bus*), +1 312 633-0808, *www.oprah.com*, Morning taping 7AM-11AM, Afternoon taping 11AM-3PM. 'Harpo' is backward for the first name of she who tapes her shows here, Oprah Winfrey. The only way to enter the court of Her Majesty is to be in an audience; reservations are necessary and tickets are hot, so call *well* in advance of your visit, ideally more than a month before, and be prepared to be flexible. Audience members must be over the age of 18. Programs are taped on weekdays from August through November and then January through May, generally two shows a day. Last-minute reservations *may* be possible; check the website *www2.oprah.com*.

Hellenic Museum and Cultural Center, 801 W Adams Ave, 4th Floor (*UIC-Halsted Blue Line*), +1 312 655-1234, *www.hellenicmuseum.org*, Tu-F 10AM-4PM, Sa 11AM-4PM. Programs and galleries celebrating Hellenic culture in the heart of Greektown. Admission $5.

Jane Addams Hull House Museum, 800 S Halsted St (*UIC-Halsted Blue Line*), +1 312 413-5353, *www.hullhousemuseum.org*, Tu-F 10AM-4PM, Su 12-4PM, M,Sa closed. UIC was built on top of the original Hull House, where the prolific writer and reformer Jane Addams lived and worked to help people in need. This museum is dedicated to her memory in two surviving buildings from the complex, now absorbed into the UIC campus, and features exhibits on local history and social justice throughout the world. Free.

Museum of Holography, 1134 W Washington Ave (*20 Madison bus*), +1 312 226-1007, *holographiccenter. com*, W-Su 12:30-5PM. "America's only museum of holography," at least according to the curator. It'll only take you 20 minutes to visit, but it's kind of interesting. (It's more like 25 minutes if you pet the cat.) Make sure to check out the holographic projection of a three-foot-long, crawling tarantula. Officially, it's $4 for adults, and $3 for children, but the cat has a habit of appearing at the donation box, so you might find yourself giving more than you counted on.

National Italian American Sports Hall of Fame, 1431 W Taylor St, +1 312 226-5566, *www.niashf.org*, M-F 9AM-5PM, Sa-Su 11AM-4PM. Exactly what the name says; this is a glittering, big-budget facility, moved here from the suburbs a few years ago. The collection pays tribute to more than 200 inductees from many professional sports, with Joe DiMaggio held in highest esteem. Space for event rentals (like fundraisers for Italian-American politicians) outstrips the space for exhibits, though. $5.

Saint Ignatius College Prep, 1076 W Roosevelt Rd, +1 312 421-5900, *www.ignatius.org*. Opened in 1869, two years prior to the Chicago Fire, this impressive building is still a working high school. No tours are offered of the interior, but pieces of famous Chicago buildings from the past have been installed around the campus, including murals from the old Chicago Stadium and intriguing ornament from lost Adler & Sullivan and Burnham & Root masterworks. (Next door, **Holy Family Church** dates from 1857.) Free, though you might call ahead if school is in session.

The Haymarket Affair(s)

*For years before and after, the Haymarket Square at Randolph St and Desplaines St was a bustling market, but on May 4, 1886, police marched on a labor rally, and someone threw a bomb from the crowd, killing seven police officers; for lack of a suspect, the organizer and speakers at the rally were arrested and charged with murder, and four were executed. The case became a seminal moment for the labor movement and free speech in the United States, giving cause to the May Day labor holiday. A statue of a policeman was erected in the square in 1889, but it became a target for anger over the trial, and was moved for safe-keeping after a streetcar rammed into it. By the 1960s, the market was gone, so the statue was returned — bringing the Chicago Police and the Weather Underground together in a tradition of blowing the thing up, repairing it, and blowing it up again. Eventually, it was moved for good. A carefully-worded bronze plaque was installed by the city in 1992, and an abstract sculpture has been in the square since 2004. For a more meaningful memorial, take I-290 west to Des Plaines Avenue in the nearby suburb of Forest Park and **Waldheim Cemetery** www.waldheimcemetery.com.*

Galleries

The West Loop has a thriving contemporary art gallery scene that's easy to explore on foot. Start at the corner of Peoria and Washington. The two most prominent galleries are the Donald Young and Kavi Gupta galleries, but the adventurous will be rewarded here — there is a wealth of smaller gallery spaces to be explored even beyond this list.

Bucket Rider Gallery, 835 W Washington Blvd (*2nd floor (yes, through the door marked Kavi Gupta Gallery)*), +1 312 421-6993, *bucketridergallery.com*, Tu-F noon-6PM, Sa noon-5PM. Contemporary art (mostly painting and photography) by international artists (like Joe Sola).

Donald Young Gallery, 933 W Washington Blvd, +1 312 455-0100, *www.donaldyoung.com*, Tu-F 10AM-5:30PM, Sa 11AM-5:30PM. Donald Young's gallery is *the* place to experience video/film art in Chicago, and the member artists include such big-names as Sol Lewitt, Richard Serra, Jeff Koons, Don Flavin, and Bruce Nauman. Exhibits tend towards the very experimental and are often neither for the fainthearted nor the easily outraged, but keep in mind that they also often rival exhibits at the world's top contemporary art museums.

EC Gallery, 215 N Aberdeen, +1 312 850-0924, *www.ec-gallery.com*, Sat 11AM-4PM or by appointment. Contemporary art. The primary focus at EC Gallery is the introduction and representation of emerging and mid-career artists whose practices traverse painting, drawing, mixed media and photo media.

F2 Lab, 840 W Washington Blvd (*2nd floor, above GARDENfresh*), +1 312 371-1391, *www.f2.cc*, Sa noon-5PM, or by appointment. A contemporary art gallery focused (refreshingly) on mouth-blown glass sculpture in the service of quirky concept art.

GARDENfresh, 840 W Washington Blvd, +1 312 235-2246, *www.gardenfresh.org*, Th-Sa noon-6PM, or by appointment. An artists' collective featuring contemporary art with a heavier-than-usual focus on concept art.

Kavi Gupta Gallery, 835 W Washington Blvd (*2nd floor*), +1 312 432-0708, Tu-F 10AM-6PM, Sa 11AM-5PM. Kavi Gupta's gallery is generally understood to have been the pioneer of the West Loop gallery phenomenon. Today his collection is still one of the area's most important and features new works from emerging international artists. If you're here, you might as well check out the Bucket Rider Gallery on the same floor or any of the other, smaller galleries in the building.

Primitive Art Works Gallery, 130 N Jefferson St, +1 312 575-9600, *www.beprimitive.com*, M-Sa 10AM-6PM. A large store/gallery packed with so-called "Primitive Art" from around the world. The selection is *wide*, including (among others): East African jewelry, Native American costumes, old-style Chinese beds, Eastern European

stained glass, etc.

Supreme Frame & Art Gallery, 652 W Randolph St, +1 312 930-9056, M-Th 8AM-4PM, Sa 9AM-3PM. Several large-sized portraits of contemporary figures. It also sells some antique art and limited editions. Supreme has a large collection of art posters, serigraphs and prints, many with a distinctly Chicago flavor

Do ◯

Johnny's Ice House, 1350 W Madison St, +1 312 226-5555, *www.johnnysicehouse.com*. If one of the local hockey teams inspires you to strap on skates, Johnny's Ice House offers ice skating year-round for people of all experience levels.

South Union Arts, 1352 S Union, *www.southunionarts.com*. This is a church that has been converted into a space for concerts and art exhibits — there's a big neon cross above the stage as a reminder. Shows are irregular, so check the website for schedules, but they're usually good, if a bit chaotic.

UIC Pavilion, 525 S Racine (*Racine Blue Line*), +1 312 413-5740, *www.uicpavilion.com*, Box office Th-F 9AM-6PM, 2-3 hours before events. UIC's campus stadium is remarkably adaptable, hosting college sports like basketball and the school's stand-out ice hockey team (the Flames), Chicago's WNBA team (the Sky), and as concerts for mid-sized to major touring bands. Tickets usually $15-35.

NEAR WEST SIDE BUY

United Center, 1901 W Madison Ave (*20 Madison bus*), +1 312 455-4500, *www.unitedcenter.com*. Home of the NBA **Chicago Bulls**. The United Center is too big to get raucously loud, but the sightlines are great from anywhere in the house, and fans of Michael Jordan will enjoy seeing his jersey in the rafters and his statue outside (check the statue details — he's wearing stone Air Jordans!). Current Bulls rookie Derrick Rose has the city buzzing, but it's usually possible to find tickets at or near face value. The city's resurgent hockey team, the Blackhawks, also plays here. On off-nights, this is Chicago's second-largest concert venue for big touring bands, the circus (in November), and other random events. Most games start at $38 for upper level seats, concerts closer to $50.

Buy

The **New Maxwell Street Market** still runs from 7AM-3PM every Sunday (tel. +1 312 922-3100), regardless of season. The much smaller size and higher vendor fees ensure that the original flavor of the world's greatest outdoor market is now only a piece of history, but the New Market has a truly awe-inspiring number of cheap Mexican food along with discount jewelry, t-shirts, random vintage items, suspicious electronics, and other flea market classics, and is a lot of fun.

More traditional retail has been slow to develop for the rest of the Near West Side, with college students being the only relatively af-

fluent consumer group in the area. Even after the spate of expensive residential developments in the West Loop and University Village, it's still under-served for shopping purposes. However, there are a few places worthy of note:

Athenian Candle Co, 300 S Halsted St, +1 312 332-6988, M,T,Th,F 9:30AM-6PM, Sa 9:30AM-5PM. It's worth a visit just to gawk at their wall of candles, but the fun in browsing begins with their extensive and eclectic collection of religious/spiritual items, from the Christian to the arcane. Ponder to which category the "Pope holograms" belong.

Barbara's Bookstore, 1218 S Halsted St, +1 312 413-2665, *www. barbarasbookstore.com*, M-F 10AM-10PM, Sa 10AM-10PM, Su 10AM-8PM. UIC students couldn't ask for better from their campus bookstore. Barbara's is run by book lovers who keep the big, comfortable store well-stocked with titles of all sorts, and this store sees an impressive list of author appearances.

Bennett Wine Studio, 802 W Washington Blvd, +1 312 666-4417, T-F noon-7PM, Sa noon-6PM, Su noon-5PM. Bennett has a strong and established reputation in Chicago for stocking her store with only the most tasteful wines, most of them from small estates and with very reasonable price tags. $10-15.

Erin Gallagher, 1017 W Lake St, +1 312 492-7548, *www.egjewelry.com*, M-F 11AM-7PM, Sa noon-7PM, Su noon-5PM.

Boutique and custom jewelry by one of Chicago's most reputable designers, although you have a chance to compete a bit by designing your own pieces.

Greektown Gift & Music Shop, 330 S Halsted St, +1 312 263-6342, M-Sa 10AM-8PM, Su noon-4PM. One stop shop for everything Greek, from kitsch to language instruction to a big collection of CDs.

Lissa on Maxwell, 729 W Maxwell St, +1 312 563-9470, *www.lissaonmaxwell.com*, M-F 11AM-7PM, Sa 10AM-6PM, Su 11AM-5PM. $250 for a dress on Maxwell Street? If you can get over that historical incongruity, you'll discover that this is a pretty cool operation, with talented designers not yet featured in places like Michigan Avenue, and biographies provided for each so you can investigate further.

Pivot, 1101 W Fulton Market, +1 312 243-4754, *www.pivotboutique. com*, M noon-6, Tu-F 11AM-7PM, Sa 10AM-6PM, Su noon-5PM. Perhaps the world's first purveyor of hemp clothing that can honestly claim the title of stylish, Pivot's mission is to introduce the word eco-smart to the world of high fashion, be it in the form of bamboo skirts or sweaters made of cashmere bought straight from Mongolian nomadic herders.

Eat

Cuisine is a major attraction for the West Side, with two of the city's most celebrated strips: **Little Italy** (Racine Blue Line) and

Greektown (UIC-Halsted Blue Line). Restaurants are almost all that remain of the communities that were there before the bulldozers and redevelopment of the 1960s. Culinary preferences will presumably guide your decision, but all things being equal, Greektown is the better choice, because UIC has more of a presence in the Little Italy area.

Budget

Greek

Also see Drink — the bars in Greektown can be good dinner options, too, unless you're looking for family dining.

Artopolis Bakery & Cafe, 306 S Halsted St, +1 312 559-9000, *www.artopolischicago.com*, Cafe M-Th 9AM-midnight, F-Sa 9AM-1AM, Su 10AM-11PM; Kitchen Su-Th 11AM-11PM, F-Sa 11AM-midnight. Greek artisan breads provide the foundation for bakery treats, sandwiches, and wood-fired pizzas. There's a full bar and wine list as well. $8-$16.

Greektown Gyros, 239 S Halsted St, +1 312 236-9310, 24 hours. There's the dinner scene in Greektown, and then there's the long-after-dinner scene. Few places in Chicago will treat you better after you leave a bar at 2AM. $6.

Meli Cafe & Juice Bar, 301 S Halsted St, +1 312 454-0748, *www.melicafe.com*, M-Sa 6AM-4PM. A bright and relaxed brunch option, with cage-free eggs and Mediterranean-influenced soups and sandwiches. $9.

Mr. Greek Gyros, 234 S Halsted St, +1 312 906-8731, 24 hours. Another solid option for greasy late-night gyros. $5.

Pan Hellenic Pastry Shop, 322 S Halsted St, +1 312 454-1886, M-Th 9AM-8PM, F-Sa 9AM-9PM, Su 12-6PM. Confront, if you dare, the incredible power of fresh *baklava*. This is a true family institution in Greektown.

Zeus Inc., 806 W Jackson Blvd, +1 312 258-8789, M-Th 7:30AM-9PM, F-Sa 11AM-9PM. A popular lunch joint.

Other

The new **University Village**, near Little Italy, has a plenty of sandwich shops and pleasant, undistinguished Thai, sushi, and other fast food restaurants catering to UIC students.

Harold's Chicken Shack #39, 518 W Harrison St, +1 312 662-9000. Harold's is here to give UIC students a graduate seminar in the art of cheap, delicious chicken. $2-5.

Jim's Original Hot Dog, 1250 S Union St (*UIC-Halsted Blue Line*), +1 312 733-7820, *www.jimsoriginal. com*, 24 hours. Established in 1939, this long-time purveyor of the Maxwell Street Polish was able to move a few blocks away when the last hold-outs were evicted in 2001. Whether it's as good as it used to be is purely academic; it's an original, and it's good. $3-5.

Mario's Italian Lemonade, 1068 W Taylor St (*Racine Blue Line*), Open May to September only; 11 AM-midnight. If you're dining in Little Italy in the summer, skip dessert at your restaurant and come here instead. Mario's has been selling *delicious* Italian ice all over Chicago for more than 50 years. There are several flavors, but lemon is the staple. $1-3.

The Patio, 1503 W Taylor St, +1 312 829-0454, Su-Th 10:30AM-11PM, F-Sa 11:30AM-midnight. Another one of the few places serving the fast food classics like Chicago-style hot dogs and Italian beef sandwiches here, in the area where they were born. $4-6.

The Soupbox, 500 W Madison Ave, +1 312 993-1019, *www.thesoupbox.com*, M-F 10AM-9PM, Sa-Su 10:30AM-7PM. Ten soups of the day, listed in advance on their website, ranging from original creations to old standbys like Clam Chowder and Cream of Mushroom; sizes include 16oz breadbowls. $5-6.

White Palace Grill, 1159 S Canal St, +1 312 939-7167, 24 hours. A good and reliable all-night diner near Little Italy and the university. Since 1939, and fortunate enough to have avoided displacement.

Mid-range

Greek

Most of the restaurants in Greektown offer free valet parking. You should be able to enjoy a meal for less than $25 at any of these restaurants, although if you'd like to splurge, most of the menus have seafood or lamb options to make that possible.

Athena Restaurant, 212 S Halsted St, +1 312 655-0000, *www.athenarestaurant.com*, Su-Th 11AM-midnight, F-Sa 11AM-1AM. Lots of hot and cold appetizers to accompany the entrees, which are a little cheaper and a little less plentiful than the other Greektown restaurants. Nice indoor and outdoor seating. $10-18, family dinners $20 per person.

Costa's, 340 S Halsted St, +1 312 263-9700, *www.costasdining.com*, M-Th 11AM-11PM, F-Sa 11AM-midnight, Su closed. Casual, welcoming Greektown restaurant. Note the coupons on their website.

Greek Islands, 200 S Halsted St, +1 312 782-9855, *www.greekislands. net*, Su-Th 11AM-midnight, F-Sa 11AM-1AM. One of the best and probably the biggest Greek restaurant in the city, with about 400 seats. Good standard Greek food: seafood, lamb, and chicken.

The Parthenon, 314 S Halsted St, +1 312 726-2407, *www.theparthenon.com*, 11AM-midnight. The *saganaki* burns brightest at the mighty Parthenon. Great family-style dinners with Greek classics are offered, and vegetarians will eat better here than anywhere else in Greektown (or almost anywhere else in Chicago). Multi-course family-style dinners $20-22 per person.

Pegasus Restaurant, 130 S Halsted St, +1 312 226-3377, *www. pegasuschicago.com*, Su 12-11PM, M-Th 11AM-11PM, F 11AM-1AM, Sa 12-1AM. Sister restaurant to the Artopolis Bakery (above). They're also at the Midway food court. Entrees $14-22, family dinners $22 per person.

Roditys, 222 S Halsted St, +1 312 454-0800, *www.roditys.com*, Su-Th 11AM-midnight, F-Sa 11AM-1AM. A long-standing Greektown restaurant (since 1973), with the braised, broiled, and roasted classics and a few more besides. $10-17.

Santorini, 800 W Adams St, +1 312 829-8820, *www.santorinichicago.com*, Su-Th 11AM-midnight, F-Sa 11AM-1AM. Santorini specializes in seafood. Excellent for the real Chicago Greek experience. Reservations usually not necessary. Family-style dinners $20-30 per person.

Venus, 820 W Jackson Blvd, +1 312 714-1001, *www.venuschicago. com*, M-Th 4-11PM, F 4PM-1AM, Sa 4PM-2AM, Su noon-11PM. Greek-Cypriot cuisine, including *mezas*, the Mediterranean version of *tapas*. There's an extensive meat and seafood menu, but vegetarians can manage. Free valet parking. $14-$20.

Italian

Valet parking is usually available at sit-down Little Italy restaurants for a nominal fee ($2-6).

Conte Di Savoia European Specialties, 1438 W Taylor St (*Racine Blue Line*), +1 312 666-3471, M-F 9AM-7PM, Sa 9AM-6PM, Su 9AM-4PM. Cheap, good Italian deli sandwiches amidst an enormous range of imported wine and groceries.

Francesca's on Taylor, 1400 W Taylor St, +1 312 829-2828, *www.miafrancesca.com*, M-F 11:30AM-2:30PM; M 5-9PM, Tu-Th 5-10PM, F-Sa 5-11PM, Su 4-9PM. Excellent Italian restaurant, and probably the busiest in Little Italy — reservations are a good idea on weekends. Moderately priced and normally provides excellent service for large parties. $18-28.

La Vita, 1349 W Taylor St, +1 312 491–1414, *www.lavitarestaurant.com*, M-Th 11AM-10PM, F 11AM-11PM, Sa 5-11PM, Su 4-10PM. Colorful, modern Italian restaurant celebrating "The Life." The decor suggests they'd like patrons to dress nicely, but a look around the dining area will reveal plenty of hooded sweatshirts. $14-26.

RoSal's Italian Cucina, 1154 W Taylor St, +1 312 243-2357, *www.rosals.com*, M-Th 4-9PM, F-Sa 4-11PM, Su closed. For the "Family" atmosphere in Italian food. Entrees $13-22. On the last Tuesday of the month (or any time with a group of 15), you can have a Big Night dinner for $65 per person..

Tufano's, 1073 Vernon Park Pl, +1 312 733-3393, Tu-Th 11AM-10PM, F 11AM-11PM, Sa 4-11PM, Su 3-9PM. Tricky to find on a residential block behind Taylor Street, but Tufano's is a nice, relaxed Italian place to eat before a night at the United Center.

Tuscany, 1014 W Taylor St, +1 312 829-1990, *www.stefanirestaurants.com*. A mainstay of the Little Italy scene. $12-20.

Other

Dine, 733 W Madison St (*20 Madison bus*), +1 312 602-2100, *www.dinerestaurant.com*, Su-Th 6AM-10PM, F-Sa 6AM-11PM. West Loop restaurant designed to be a *really nice* 1940s diner. It's next to the Crowne Plaza Hotel (see Sleep). Sandwiches $8-10, Other entrees $12-28.

Wishbone, 1001 W Washington Blvd, +1 312 850-2663, *www.wishbonechicago.com*. "Southern Reconstruction Cooking." Breakfast, Lunch, Dinner. Some nice vegetarian options, seafood, chicken, burgers, and a large variety of great Southern sides. $7-15.

Splurge

The city's most trendy and expensive restaurants are to be found in the West Loop.

Carnivale, 702 W Fulton Market (*Clinton/Lake Green/Pink Line*), +1 312 850-5005, *www.carnivalechicago.com*, M-Th 11:30AM-10:30PM (bar to midnight), F 11:30AM-11:30PM (bar to 1:30AM), Sa 5PM-11:30PM (bar to 1:30AM), Su 5PM-10PM. This chic Nuevo-Latino club has a great wait-staff and nice, colorful yet understated decor. Needless to say, they're always ready with a margarita, but only the (delicious) appetizers are available in the afternoon hours.

one sixtyblue, 1400 W Randolph/160 N Loomis St, +1 312 850-0303, *www.onesixtyblue.com*, M-Th 5:30-10PM, 5:30-11PM. Elegant surroundings with experienced French chefs, and highly acclaimed in Chicago; gentlemen are asked to leave their capital letters at the door, though. Cheese fans will delight in the cheese menu. Entrees $29-38.

Drink

Oh Maxwell Street, what have you become? A few generic, upscale sports bars catering to university students and owners of new townhomes oozed in once the blues were gone.

9 Muses, 315 S Halsted St, +1 312 902-9922, *www.9museschicago.com*, M-F 11AM-2AM, Sa 12PM-3AM, Su 12PM-2AM. More of a modern style than the other Greektown bars and restaurants, but with plentiful portions of food, good outdoor seating, and an enthusiastic late-night dance scene. $13.

Byzantium, 232 S Halsted St, +1 312 454-1227, 6PM-4AM. Another popular bar in Greektown, with plenty of Greek bar food. Scores points for great live music, which may incur a cover of $5-7.

Gennaro's, 1352 W Taylor St, +1 312 243-1035, Th 5-9PM, F-Sa 5-10PM, Su 4-9PM. This is about the only place to drink on Taylor Street that looks like it's more than ten years old. Gennaro's has a full menu of sauce-heavy dishes, but it's best enjoyed for a beer in the great atmosphere of the old,

wood-paneled bar.

Jaks Tap, 901 W Jackson Blvd, +1 312 666-1700, *jakstap.com*, M-W 11AM-midnight, Th-F 11AM-2AM, Sa noon-2AM, Su noon-11PM. A good stop after a game at the United Center. Jaks takes pride in their baby-back BBQ ribs and has more than 40 beers on tap.

Spectrum Bar & Grill, 233 S Halsted St, +1 312 715-0770, M-F 11AM-4AM, Sa 5PM-5AM, Su 5PM-4AM. The Greektown location means that *ouzo* and *saganaki* have a place among the usual bar & grill fare.

Sleep

There are many more hotels in the Loop *p.47*, close to the Blue Line, and a few places in the Near South *p.95* will also be fine if you'd like quick access to the West Side.

Chicago Marriott at Medical District/UIC, 625 S Ashland Ave, +1 312 491-1234, *www.marriott.com*. As the name implies, this hotel is close to UIC and Rush University Medical Center, and also to Little Italy. A free shuttle service to the Loop and the usual business amenities are available. Rooms from $209.

Crowne Plaza Metro, 733 W Madison St (*20 Madison bus*), +1 312 829-5000, *www.crowneplaza.com*. Just west of the Loop. Rooms from $175.

Holiday Inn Hotel and Suites Downtown Chicago, 506 W Harrison St, +1 312 957-9100, *www.hihdowntown.com*. Very close to the

Near South and the Loop as well. Rooms from $269.

Contact

The following libraries offer free public internet access:

Mabel Manning Branch, 6 S Hoyne Ave (*20 Madison bus*), +1 312 746-6800, *www.chipublib.org*, M-Th 9AM-7PM, F-Sa 9AM-5PM, Su closed. Two blocks east of the United Center.

Theodore Roosevelt Branch, 1101 W Taylor St (*UIC-Halsted Blue Line*), +1 312 746-5656, *www.chipublib.org*, M-Tu,Th 9AM-8PM, W,F-Sa 9AM-5PM, Su closed. Close to UIC.

Stay safe

Know where you're going, especially at night. Aside from the few major thoroughfares, the Near West Side has long, deserted stretches where help will be difficult to find. On the UIC campus, keep an eye out for kiosks with help phones. Also, while eating in Little Italy, don't fill up on bread; you will be unable to properly enjoy your main dish. (The same risk applies to making pre-emptive grabs for saganaki in Greektown.)

Get out

If you were here for the Blues legacy of Maxwell Street, carry on to Willie Dixon's Blues Heaven in the Near South *p.95* and the Black Metropolis of Bronzeville *p.191*, then consider moving on further south to today's home of the Chicago Blues in Chatham-South Shore *p.203*.

If you prefer a Northern Italian take on pasta or you *still* aren't full, head to the smaller but more atmospheric "Heart of Italy" near Pilsen *p.259*.

Wicker Park is the vanguard of music, nightlife, and fashion in Chicago. This article also includes the sly, enjoyable **Ukrainian Village**, immediately south, and pieces of the greater **West Town** area.

Understand

Among the most pointless topics of debate in Chicago life is whether Wicker Park has changed, is full of yuppies now, isn't what it used to be, etc. The answers are simple: yes, maybe, and who cares? Just like the Velvet Underground would have been playing stadiums if everybody who claimed to have seen them in 1967 actually did, if everybody who claims to have been there when Wicker Park was cool actually *was* there, it would be a city roughly the size of Cleveland.

Wicker Park was founded by the Wicker brothers in the 1870s, and it became part of the row of prosperous immigrant neighborhoods on the West Side of Chicago — the German and Polish beer barons of Wicker Park were neighbored by the farmers of Bucktown *p.247*, the Ukrainians in their titular Village, the Greeks and Italians of the Near West Side *p.215*, and the Czechs of Pilsen *p.259*. The brewery fortunes left two legacies that survive today: gorgeous, European-style mansions and apartment buildings, and a truly world-class set of dive bars. Wicker Park is uniquely well-served by transportation among West Side neighborhoods, with the CTA's Blue Line elevated train and the major arteries of North, Milwaukee, and Damen all converging upon the center of the area.

After the economic decline of the West Side, Puerto Ricans became the majority population in Wicker Park. With them came the other two elements that would turn the neighborhood's commercial fortunes around: low rents in those great buildings, and an art scene that became known for exciting new work. Artists and musicians from outside the area moved in, finding cheap studios in places like the **Flatiron Arts Building** and good venues to exhibit and perform like the **Double Door** and the excellent **Empty Bottle**. Among many others, the Smashing Pumpkins were formed in the area, and Liz Phair's album *Exile in Guyville* re-cast the Rolling Stones' Main Street in Wicker Park; on the visual arts side, the long-running **Around the Coyote festival** continues as an annual gathering of the neighborhood's artistic highlights. (Years later, the John Cusack film *High Fidelity* attempted to capture Wicker Park in all of its elitist, obnoxious, trend-setting glory, and was generally well-received. However, when MTV's *The Real World* arrived in 2001, it sparked off a memorable neighborhood-wide fit.)

Of course, all vinyl pants must split in the end, and by the mid-90s, real estate prices were on the rise, and bar stools were colonized by conversations about who had been priced out (the Puerto Rican artists, for one) and where the next hot scene would be (opinions vary). Demand for housing in proximity to Wicker

Park turned its neighbors Bucktown and Ukrainian Village into hot residential properties, and the boundaries between neighborhoods have become less meaningful with time. There are still a few Ukrainians in what's affectionately known as The Uke, but there are only a few places where their paths cross with the condo conversion kids: aside from the sidewalks in front of the astonishing churches in the area and in line at the terrific old bakeries, all style becomes equal at the historic **Division Street Bath House**.

Today, a few national chains have settled in among the independent fashion boutiques in Wicker Park, but it still raises a righteous middle finger to the glossy shopping on the Magnificent Mile *p.71*, still offers the best places to get a cheap beer, and still has residents who, per capita, care more about quality music and restaurants than anywhere else in the city.

Get in

By train

The O'Hare branch of the CTA **Blue Line** has stops in West Town (Chicago, Grand), Ukrainian Village (Division) and Wicker Park (Damen). The Damen stop is particularly useful, as it's right at the epicenter of Wicker Park and the border of Bucktown *p.247*, and a short walk south to Ukrainian Village and the nightlife on Division.

If you're going further afield in Ukrainian Village than Division — say, to the Empty Bottle (see Drink) — get to know the relevant bus routes, as the CTA trains don't run particularly close.

By bus

9 Ashland is an all-nighter that runs within walking distance of the shops and bars in Wicker Park (on Milwaukee) and the nightlife on Division.

49 Western runs down Western Avenue for nearly the full length of the city, passing through the western edge of Ukrainian Village. It's an all-night route.

50 Damen runs through the heart of Wicker Park and Ukrainian Village, but lacks night-owl service.

56 Milwaukee is the king of the West Side, running through the center of Wicker Park and along the eastern fringe of Ukrainian Village.

65 Grand runs from downtown to West Town, connecting with the Grand Blue Line stop, and the southern fringe of Ukrainian Village.

66 Chicago runs from the Near North *p.71* through West Town (connecting with the Chicago Blue Line stop) and Ukrainian Village, and onward to Austin *p.331*. It's also an all-night route.

70 Division is vital for the nightlife on Division, connecting to the Blue Line at the Division Blue Line stop.

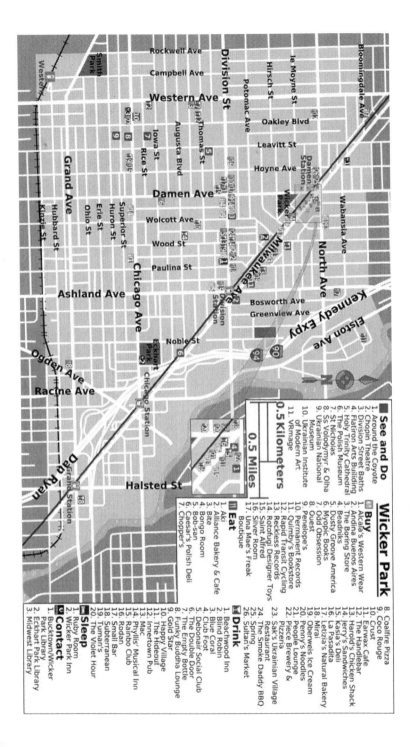

By car

I-90/94, that shining exemplar of Chicago gridlock, runs close to Ukrainian Village — exit at Division and head straight west, or make a right off Division on Milwaukee to reach Wicker Park.

This isn't one of the worst parts of the city for parking, but it can still be a challenge, and there are no public lots or garages in the area. Be patient and circle the side streets. Many upscale restaurants offer valet parking for $10 or so. Permit-only parking is in place on many side streets, so check street signs. Damen in particular has some oddball no-parking hours.

 See

While the art scene has largely moved on from Wicker Park, there are a few opportunities to explore the remaining galleries. The **Wicker Park/Bucktown Gallery Association** *www.wpbga.com* hosts Second Saturday Gallery Walks each month (meet at Around the Coyote, 6-10PM), while many of the galleries in the Flatiron Arts Building have First Friday open hours (6-9PM).

Around the Coyote Gallery, 1935 1/2 W North Ave (*Damen Blue Line*), +1 773 342-6777, *www.aroundthecoyote.org*, Tu-F 10AM-6PM, Sa 12-6PM. One of the few galleries in Wicker Park to keep regular weekday hours, Around the Coyote is partly affiliated with the festival of the same name (see below). A board of directors selects applicants among emerging artists from around the

country for short-term exhibits here.

Flatiron Arts Building, 1579 N Milwaukee Ave (*Damen Blue Line*), +1 312 335-3000, *www.flatiron.tv*. This triangular behemoth was built in 1913 by the great Holabird & Roche, one of their few major products outside the Loop. The first floor is all retail, but the second and third floors have small art studios. Aside from the First Friday open hours (above), a few galleries also have Saturday afternoon hours.

Holy Trinity Cathedral, 1121 N Leavitt, +1 773 486-6064, *www.holytrinitycathedral.net*, Open for visits Sa 11AM-4PM. Orthodox church in Ukrainian Village, designed by Louis Sullivan in 1903. It was funded in part by Czar Nicholas II; today, it thrives as a neighborhood parish.

The Polish Museum of America, 984 N Milwaukee Ave (*Division Blue Line*), +1 773 384-3352, *pma.prcua.org/homeen.html*, F-W 11AM-4PM, Th closed. Library and exhibitions on Polish heritage, both in Chicago and in Poland. $5 adults, $4 children.

St Nicholas Ukrainian Catholic Church, 2238 W Rice St, +1 773 276-4537, *www.stnicholascathedralukrcath.org*. No shortage of magnificent Ukrainian churches in this part of town — this soaring example was built in 1913 on the model of St Sophia's in Kiev. The eye-catching thirteen onion domes stand for Christ and the 12 apostles. The one weekly English-language

WICKER PARK 🔾

mass is at 11:30AM on Sundays.

Ss Volodymyr & Olha Ukrainian Catholic Church, 2247 W Chicago Ave, +1 312 455-0178, *www.stsvo. org.* This huge, golden-domed, Ukrainian Catholic church has been a local landmark since its construction in 1973. The church was built during a brief neighborhood schism over a move to use the Gregorian instead of the Julian calendar. How to upstage a church modeled after Kiev's St Sophia's? Build one modeled after Istanbul's Hagia Sophia! It is well worth a visit to marvel at the magnificent interior and iconostasis. Even if you come by when it's closed, you can appreciate at the mosaic over the entrance depicting the baptism of the Ukrainians by the parish's namesake saints. Most masses in Ukrainian.

Ukrainian Institute of Modern Art, 2320 W Chicago Ave (*66 Chicago bus*), +1 773 227-5522, *www.uima-chicago.org*, W-Su 12-4PM. This is a superb, lovingly curated collection of abstract and minimalist art by major Ukrainian and Ukrainian-American artists. The three permanent galleries represent not only Ukrainian heritage, but also one of Chicago's best and most underrated experiences for art lovers of any ethnicity. Free.

Ukrainian National Museum, 2249 W Superior St, +1 312 421-8020, *www.ukrainiannationalmuseum.org*, M-W by appointment, Th-Su 11AM-4PM. Chicago's Ukrainian museum is almost certainly the best collection of Ukrainian

ethnographic exhibits (musical instruments, traditional costumes, folk art, etc.) in the United States, as well as historical exhibits covering issues such as the incredible famines under Stalin and the fallout after the Chernobyl meltdown. The museum also hosts an impressive library and archives for researchers, as well as occasional Ukrainian-related art exhibitions. free, suggested donation: $5.

🔾o

Music venues are the main attraction here, particularly the **Double Door** and the **Empty Bottle** (see below).

Chopin Theatre, 1543 W Division St (*Division Blue Line*), +1 773 278-1500, *www.chopintheatre.com.* An experimental theater complex encompassing two stages, a cafe, and a gallery. Many works in translation from Eastern Europe have made their US debut here, although the theater keeps strong ties to Wicker Park and local history as well. $12-22.

Division Street Russian and Turkish Baths, 1914 W Division St (*Division Blue Line*), +1 773 384-9671, M-F 8AM-9PM, Sa 7AM-9PM, Su 6AM-8PM. Quoth Saul Bellow: "And down in the super-heated subcellars these Slavonic cavemen and wood demons with hanging laps of fat and legs of stone and lichen boil themselves and splash water on their heads by the bucket. There may be no village in the Carpathians where such practices still prevail." In other words, it's a good time. Facilities include a *hot* steam room, showers, cold plunge, and a lounge area. $20 entry includes two towels and soap; massage $30/$60 half-hour/hour.

VRmage, 1242 N Milwaukee Ave (*Division Blue Line*), +1 312 265-6666, *www.myspace/com/vrmage*, M-Th 9AM-10PM, F-Sa 9AM-midnight, Su closed. PCs with internet access are available, but they're something of an afterthought to the LAN gaming parties and stand-in virtual reality "pods." The staff are eager to help the uninitiated. $10/game, $5/hour internet.

Events & Festivals

Around the Coyote Festival, Flatiron Arts Building at 1935 1/2 N Milwaukee Ave, and buildings nearby (*Damen Blue Line*), +1 773 342-6777, *www.aroundthecoyote.org*, Twice per year, winter and fall. Once *the* independent art festival in Chicago and now more hit-and-miss, but it's still a huge collection of new visual art, music, theater (on stages and streets), film and video, jewelry for sale, and Wicker Park eclectica, curated by artists from around the city. Plenty of food and beer are around (especially beer). Day Passes cost $10 and cover admission to most venues, although some tours cost an extra $10; All-Access Weekend Festival Passes are $40, which include the Opening Night Party and all venues.

Buy

The intersection of Milwaukee, North, and Damen is the indie Magnificent Mile. Start at the six corners and explore from there — you'll find plenty of cutting-edge fashion boutiques heading north on Damen, and more in both directions on Milwaukee, along with national chains like American Apparel and the Levi Store.

You're also liable to do well searching for vinyl records here, both in Wicker Park and Ukrainian Village.

Books

The Boring Store, 1331 N Milwaukee Ave (*Division Blue Line*), +1 773 772-8108, *www.826chi.org*, 12-6PM daily. Most certainly *not* a secret-agent supply store, as the Chris Ware signs take pains to stress. Inside, proceeds from the sale of *perfectly normal* items like cough silencers support a non-profit writing/tutoring center for kids founded by Dave Eggers of McSweeney's fame.

Myopic Books, 1564 N Milwaukee Ave (*Damen Blue Line*), +1 773 862-4882, *myopicbookstore.com*, M-Sa 11AM-1AM, Su 11AM-10PM. Justly beloved used book store with cats, clutter (80,000 books worth), and *great* hours. They occasionally host Experimental Music Mondays and poetry readings on Sundays, but with three floors, there's always a quiet corner.

Quimby's Bookstore, 1854 W North Ave (*Damen Blue Line*), +1 773 342-0910, *www.quimbys.com*,

WICKER PARK BUY

M-F 12-10PM, Sa 11AM-10PM, Su 12-6PM. Lots of edgy books, indie comix, and hip zines (hand-stapled and well-polished alike). If somebody out there is publishing about it, Quimby's probably has it.

Clothes

Alcala's Western Wear, 1733 W Chicago Ave, +1 312 226-0152, *www.alcalas.com*, M,Th-F 9:30AM-8PM, Tu-W,Sa 9:30AM-7PM, Su 9:30AM-5PM. One perfectly reasonable reaction to the trendy fashion in Wicker Park is to go country. Alcala's has been in the neighborhood for a long time, back when the Mexican cowboy look ruled the local scene. The big, family-owned store has a *ton* of leather boots & jackets, not to mention 5,000 hats.

Andina Buenos Aires, 1740 W Division St (*Division Blue Line*), +1 773 227-6225, *www.shopandina.com*, Tu-Sa 11AM-7PM, Su 11AM-5PM, M closed. Small boutique featuring stylish, sturdy Argentine leather handbags and accessories.

Beadniks, 1937 W Division St (*Damen Blue Line*), +1 773 276-2323, *www.beadniks.com*, M-F 11AM-9PM, Sa 11AM-10PM, Su 11AM-7PM. Beads for the true bead fiend, both ready-made and ready to be made. There are classes for beginners on Tuesday nights (7-9PM, $60), and occasional workshops — check the calendar.

Ouest, 1751 W Division St, +1 312 421-2799, *www.shopouest.com*, T-F 11AM-7PM, Sa 11AM-6PM, Su noon-5PM. An upmarket women's clothing boutique focused on classic French designs.

Penelope's, 1913 W Division St, +1 773 395-2351, *www.penelopeschicago.com*, M-Sa 11AM-7PM, Su 12-6PM. Good-looking clothes — Penelope's carries younger, hip brands for men and women, but it's quality stuff, made to last. They have some good handbags, messenger bags, and cool gifts as well.

Saint Alfred, 1531 N Milwaukee Ave (*Damen Blue Line*), +1 773 486-7159, *www.stalfred.com*, M-Sa 12-8PM, Su 12-6PM. Collectible sneakers both classic and modern are sold here, along with cool kicks and other gear by local designers.

Silver Room, 1442 N Milwaukee Ave (*Damen Blue Line*), +1 773 278-7130, *www.thesilverroom.com*, M-Th 11AM-8PM, F-Sa 11AM-9PM, Su 11AM-6PM. Need a great gift for someone back home (or yourself)? Silver Room has cool stuff for men and women — good purses, hats, jewelry and accessories. The staff make shopping here a pleasure.

Una Mae's Freak Boutique, 1528 N Milwaukee Ave (*Damen Blue Line*), +1 773 276-7002, *www.unamaesclothing.com*, M-F 12-7PM, Sa 11AM-8PM, Su 11AM-6PM. Vintage clothing store run by nice people. Una Mae's has been around for a while, and they have great items for men and women, particularly from the 1960s and 70s.

Music

Dusty Groove America, 1120 N Ashland Ave (*Division Blue Line*), +1 773 342-5800, *www.dustygroove.com*, 10AM-8PM. This record store is regarded as one of the best in the country for R&B, soul, and jazz.

Permanent Records, 1914 W Chicago Ave, +1 773 278-1744, *www.permanentrecordschicago.com*, Su-Th 11AM-8PM, F-Sa 11AM-9PM. This may be the friendliest, most down-to-earth record store in Chicago. They stock mostly vinyl and used CDs, but will order anything on request, and have a rack of vintage clothes at the back of the store.

Reckless Records, 1532 N Milwaukee Ave (*Damen Blue Line*), +1 773 235-3727, *www.reckless.com*, M-Sa 10AM-10PM, Su 10AM-8PM. Hipster music shop with plenty to sell and no particular interest in selling it to you (there's a reason *High Fidelity* was set here). Zines and vinyl spruce up the CDs and DVDs.

Others

Odd Obsession, 1822 N Milwaukee (*Damen Blue Line*), +1 773 276-0894, *www.oddobsession.com*, M-Sa 12-10PM, Su 12-9PM. Ultra-eccentric video rental store. YouTube pales, cuts its hair and goes to law school next to the rarities found here. It's cheap, too.

Rapid Transit Cycling Shop, 1900 W North Ave, +1 773 227-2288, *www.rapidtransitcycles.com*, M-Th 10AM-8PM, F 10AM-5PM, Sa 10AM-6PM, Su 12-5PM. Plenty of streets in the area have nice, wide bike lanes, and considering the state of parking, this is a great place to have a bike. Rapid Transit is a family-owned shop that sells equipment and can do quick repairs.

Rotofugi Designer Toy Store & Gallery, 1953 W Chicago Ave, +1 312 491-9501, *rotofugi.com*, M-Sa 12-8PM, Su 12-5PM. Now is battle coming tofu robot, plush ninja, Glow Kaiju Eyezon. It is the proposal of bad weather for justice. CAN YOU DO NO LESS?! Right here to bring you.

Eat

Hipsters: A field guide

Residents of other neighborhoods in Chicago know Wicker Park by one word: "hipsters." Nearly every review of a bar or restaurant in the area will mention these dread creatures, who are known to viciously hang out at places in Wicker Park, relentlessly passing judgment on passers-by, possessing terrifying quantities of concentrated scorn that can destroy the self-esteem of anyone who crosses their path without a sufficiently ironic second-hand t-shirt. Their secret knowledge of music and the blue ribbons won by the Pabst brewery makes them effectively invincible on this, their home ground. Should you encounter one, retreat to the nearest bar with a fake-Irish name. Alternatively, just relax — as it turns out, hipsters come to these places to have a good time just like everyone else.

WICKER PARKEAT

Budget

The twin low-price culinary delights around here are the bakeries of Wicker Park and the delis of Ukrainian Village, many of which have been in business for several decades. The Uke also has some great Ukrainian grocers, particularly on Iowa.

Alliance Bakery & Cafe, 1736 W Division St (*Division Blue Line*), +1 773 278-0366, *www.alliance-bakery.com*, M-Sa 6AM-9PM, Su 7AM-9PM. Just a look at the whirls of frosting and gingerbread fortresses in the window tends to bring a smile. The tarts, cupcakes, and coffee back that up. Alliance has been here for more than 80 years. There's a pleasant, inviting cafe next door with free wi-fi. $3-7.

Caesar's Polish Deli, 901 N Damen Ave (*66 Chicago bus*), +1 773 486-6190, Tu-F 10AM-6PM, Sa 8AM-noon, Su,M closed. A great place for self-catering, Caesar's has a wide selection of homemade pirogies, with both savory and sweet fillings, as well as a good selection of fresh foods, and prepared products imported from Poland. $4-8.

Chopper's, 1659 N Ashland Ave, +1 773 227-7800, *www.choppers-chicago.com*, 7AM-10PM daily. A great hot dog and burger place with what may be the best milkshakes in Chicago. $3-7.

Earwax Cafe, 1561 N Milwaukee Ave (*Damen Blue Line*), +1 773 772-4019, *www.earwaxcafe.com*, M-Th 9AM-11PM, Sa-Su 8AM-midnight. A mostly-vegetarian restaurant and coffee shop with funky decor and a classic Wicker Park atmosphere. Also has movie rentals in the basement. Most lunch and dinner items fall in the $6.95-$8.95 range, with breakfast items being a couple bucks cheaper.

Harold's Chicken Shack #36, 1361 N Milwaukee Ave (*Damen Blue Line*), +1 773 252-2424. Westward the course of the fried chicken empire makes its way, to Wicker Park. Some say this outpost makes compromises for the upscale surroundings — wheat bread, moist towelettes, a general lack of bulletproof glass — but even if they do, it's still the best cheap fried chicken you'll find here or anywhere north. $3-6.

Kasia's Deli, 2101 W Chicago Ave (*66 Chicago bus*), +1 773 486-6163, *www.kasiasdeli.com*, M-F 9AM-7PM, Sa 9AM-6PM, Su 10AM-2PM. Some call these the best pierogies in Chicago — high praise, indeed. The cabbage rolls are also highly recommended. If you like what you eat but live out of state, take comfort: Kasia's will deliver the good stuff anywhere in the USA. $3-$8.

Letizia's Natural Bakery, 2144 W Division St (*Damen Blue Line*), +1 773 342-1011, *www.superyummy.com*, Su-W 6AM-5PM, Th-Sa 6AM-5PM. Breakfast sandwiches, espresso and baked goods with good, healthy cooking. If you enjoy Letizia's, come back later for **Enoteca**, the wine bar under the same management next door.

$4-12.

La Pasadita, 1132, 1140, and 1141 N Ashland Ave (*Division Blue Line*), +1 773 278-0384, *www.pasadita.com*, 9AM-3AM daily. Gradual expansion over the past thirty years has led to the curious appearance of three identically-named establishments within the same half-block of Ashland. All three are family-owned and make tasty Mexican tacos and burritos, with slight variations in the menus. The newest location at 1132 N Ashland is somewhat Americanized compared to the other two. $3-6.

Penny's Noodle Shop, 1542 N Damen Ave (*Damen Blue Line*), +1 773 394-0100, *www.pennysnoodleshop.com*, Su, Tu-Th 11AM-10PM, F-Sa 11AM-10:30PM, M closed. Excellent Southeast Asian dishes and cheap for such large portions. $6-8.

Sak's Ukrainian Village Restaurant, 2301 W Chicago Ave (*66 Chicago bus*), +1 773 278-4445, Tu-Sa 11:30AM-10PM, M closed. A cheap, long-standing diner with Ukrainian food, with a bar (to 2AM Su-F, to 3AM Sa) that's a popular first stop of the neighborhood's remaining Ukrainians on a night out.

Sultan's Market, 2057 W North Ave (*Damen Blue Line*), +1 773 235-3072, *chicagofalafel.com*, M-Sa 10AM-10PM, Su 10AM-9PM. Few restaurants *smell* as good as Sultan's Market, and the prices are absurdly low for the amount of satisfaction you'll get. Cheese and egg pitas make a nice complement to any falafel sandwich, and they also do a fine shawerma. Cash only, ATM in the back. $3.50-8.

Mid-range

Sushi is everywhere in Wicker Park — there's no shortage of style, but only a few places offer substance to match.

Aki, 2015 W Division St (*Damen Blue Line*), +1 773 227-8080, M-Th 4:30-11:30PM, F-Sa 4:30PM-midnight, Su 4:30-11PM. Good, traditional sushi in a humble, trend-free setting. You're paying for the food here, not the design. There are a few chicken options on the menu as well. $12-17.

Bite, 1035 N Western Ave (*49 Western bus*), +1 773 395-2483, *www.emptybottle.com*, M-F 7:30AM-11PM, Sa 8AM-midnight, Su 8AM-10:30PM. The food is all right (and vegan-friendly), but Bite is right next door to the Empty Bottle, perfect for a pre-show meal. (There will be lines, but they're never as bad as they look.) Alcohol can be brought over from the Empty Bottle's bar. $9-14.

Bob-san, 1805 W Division St (*Division Blue Line*), +1 773 235-8888, *www.bob-san.com*, M-Th 4:30-11:30PM, F-Sa 4:30PM-12:30AM, Su 3:30-10:30PM. Bob-san has the best and most festive sushi around, along with a menu of Japanese fusion dishes. For a dose of pure energy, try the oyster shooters: oyster, quail egg, hot sauce, and sake. $12-22.

WICKER PARKEAT

Bongo Room, 1470 N Milwaukee Ave (*Damen Blue Line*), +1 773 489-0690, *www.bongoroom.com*, M-F 8AM-2:30PM, Sa-Su 9AM-2PM. Great breakfast, with two stars: the design-your-own omelets and the big, delicious praline banana pancakes.

Coalfire Pizza, 1321 W Grand Ave, +1 312 226-2625, *www.coalfirechicago.com*, Tu-Th 5PM-10PM, F 5PM-11PM, Sa noon-11PM, Su noon-10PM. In the pizza wars between Chicago-style, Brooklyn, Naples, and gourmet-trendy, Chicago of course wins. But the pizza wars are truly a fraud, overlooking pizza (more precisely, apizza) from the humbler city of New Haven, which may indeed may be the best of them all. Chicago's new coal-fired pizza oven serves some of the best apizza outside New Haven, and while it may seem irreverent to eat pizza from Connecticut while in Chicago, you'd honestly be hard pressed to do better. Pizzas $13-18.

Crust, 2056-58 W Division St (*Damen Blue Line*), +1 773 235-5511, *www.crusteatreal.org*, Su-W 11AM-10PM, Th-Sa 11AM-1AM. Great pizza on artisan flatbreads. All ingredients are locally-grown and 100% organic — the first to be certified as such in the Midwest. $13-24.

The Handlebar, 2311 W North Ave (*On a bike, preferably*), +1 773 384-9546, *www.handlebarchicago.com*, M-W 11AM-midnight, Th-F 11AM-2AM, Sa 10AM-2AM, Su 10AM-midnight. A vegetarian friendly restaurant and beer garden in Wicker Park, and a home to Chi-town's bicycle culture. $9-12.

Jerry's Sandwiches, 1938 W Division St (*Damen Blue Line*), +1 773 235-1006, *www.jerryssandwiches.com*, Su-Th 10:30AM-10:30PM, F-Sa 10:30AM-11:30PM. Indecisive beware: there are 100 sandwiches on the menu at Jerry's, and you're welcome to customize even further. The seating is comfortable, and there's beer, too. $12.

Oberweis Ice Cream and Dairy Store, 1293 N Milwaukee Ave (*Division Blue Line*), +1 773 276-9006, *www.oberweisdairy.com*, 11AM-10PM daily. The ice cream and milkshakes aren't cheap…but they're made from milk that's all natural, hormone-free, and *really* good — and that is an understatement. $2.50-5.

People Lounge, 1560 N Milwaukee Ave, +1 773 227-9339, *www.peoplechicago.com*, Su-F 5PM-2AM, Sa 5PM-3AM. Spanish tapas restaurant with friendly staff and DJs spinning world music most nights. You can travel the whole of Spain and you'll still be blown away by the flan here. $8-15.

Piece Brewery & Pizzeria, 1927 W North Ave, +1 773 772-4422, *www.piecechicago.com*, M-Th 11:30AM-1:30AM, F 11:30AM-2AM, Sa 11AM-3AM, Su 11AM-1AM. Thin-crust pizza and micro-brews. Live music most Fridays, karaoke on Thursdays at 9PM, and a recent sensation — live band karaoke on Saturdays at 11PM. The kitchen usually isn't open past 11:30PM or so, though.

The Smoke Daddy BBQ, 1804 W Division St (*Division Blue Line*), +1 773 772-6656, *www.thesmokedaddy. com*, Su-W 11:30AM-11PM, Th-Sa 11:30AM-1AM. Jazz, swing, bluegrass and BBQ on Division. Smoke Daddy has live music seven nights a week, with big sandwiches and huge rib platters. They offer a BBQ Veggie sandwich if you're trying to coerce a vegetarian friend to come along. $12-24.

Splurge

A few of the places named above, particularly People Lounge and the sushi restaurants, could easily become Splurge affairs depending on how many drinks accompany your meal.

Coco Rouge, 1940 W Division St (*Damen Blue Line*), +1 773 772-2626, *www.cocorouge.com*, M-Sa 12-10PM, Su 12-8PM. Gourmet chocolate behind tall glass walls, with plenty of impressive creations you won't find anywhere else. If you're just passing by, take note: their hot chocolate is excellent. $7-14.

Mirai, 2020 W Division St (*Damen Blue Line*), +1 773 862-8500, *www. miraisushi.com*, M-W 5-10:30PM, Th-Sa 5-11:30PM. Future style and fresh sushi in formidable amounts, with a second-floor sake lounge. If price is no concern, Mirai is the place to revel in pure atmosphere (and raw food). $30-60.

Spring, 2039 W North Ave (*Damen Blue Line*), +1 773 395-7100, *springrestaurant.net*, Tu-Th

5:30-10PM, F-Sa 5:30-10:30PM, Su 5:30-9PM. Head chef Shawn McClain won the James Beard 2006 Best Chef of the Midwest award. Spring offers tasteful minimalism, North American cuisine with Asian influences, and water marks on the walls from the old Russian bath house that used to be here. $30-50.

Drink

Other parts of the city have their charms, but when it comes to drinking in Chicago, there's no contest: this is the place. And while there are plenty of places left for those-in-the-know, Division Street may have taken over from the more touristed (and generally obnoxious) Rush Street in the Near North *p.71* for sheer numbers in nightlife.

Anyone on the wander in Ukrainian Village should be advised: "Zimne Piwo" is Ukrainian for "cold beer." Plenty of apparently nameless bars make themselves known with those words under an Old Style sign.

Dive bars

Beachwood Inn, 1415 N Wood St, +1 773 486-9806, M-F 4PM-2AM, Sa 3PM-3AM, Su 3PM-2AM. A good, down-to-earth dive bar — dark, kind of dirty, offering cheap beer and a solid jukebox. Nothing trendy here, just the kind of neighborhood bar that brought people to Wicker Park in the first place.

Club Foot, 1824 W Augusta, +1 773 489-0379, Su-F 8PM-

2AM, Sa 8PM-3AM. Friendly punk/rock/ska hipster bar with games and pop knick-knacks in Ukrainian Village.

Gold Star, 1755 W Division St (*Division Blue Line*), +1 773 227-8700, Su-Th 4PM-2AM, Sa 4PM-3AM. An old, speakeasy-era bar among the Division nightlife that now caters to a younger crowd, but hits all the marks: cheap beer, a good jukebox, pool, and cheap beer. (Also cheap beer.)

Happy Village, 1059 N Wolcott Ave (*Division Blue Line*), +1 773 486-1512, M-F 4PM-2AM, Sa-Su noon-2AM. Yeah, it's a ping-pong dive bar. God bless America, and the beer garden too, which is the best on (well, off) Division — like walking into a backyard family reunion.

Innertown Pub, 1935 W Thomas St, +1 773 235-9795, Su-F 3PM-2AM, Sa 3PM-3AM. It's hard to say exactly what sets it apart, but with the fall of Tuman's, any survey of Ukrainian Village residents would place the Innertown first among dive bars. (Excepting the neighbors, that is, who are trying to get it closed down.) It's not easy to find but it's a landmark, so follow the noise or spend the cheap-beer savings on a cab.

Phyllis' Musical Inn, 1800 W Division St, +1 773 486-9862, Su-F 3PM-2AM, Sa 3PM-3AM. Everyone feels welcome at the Musical Inn. Outdoor seating is packed on Division in the summer, which is why this is one to know — few people are aware that a great beer garden lurks behind the tall stone fence next door to Phyllis', which looks like a garden variety dive bar at first glance. (Befitting the name, there are bands here sometimes.)

Rainbo Club, 1150 N Damen Ave (*Damen Blue Line*), +1 773 489-5999, Su-F 4PM-2AM, Sa 4PM-3AM. An old bar — the classic neon sign tips that right away — with a few literary references in its history. In a neighborhood of hipster dives, this is *the* hipster dive, but at least you can say you've been.

Music venues

Debonair Social Club, 1575 N Milwaukee Ave (*Damen Blue Line*), +1 773 227-7990, www.debonairsocialclub.com, Tu-F 9PM-2AM, Sa 9PM-3AM, Su closed. The emo-rap electro kids like it here. There are two floors of video walls, color lightboxes, ferocious deployments of lacquer, and DJs who fly around the room. It's all a little stressful, but perhaps you're into that sort of thing.

Double Door, 1572 N Milwaukee Ave (*Damen Blue Line*), +1 773 489-3160, www.doubledoor.com, M-F 8PM-2AM, Sa 8PM-3AM. No music venue in Chicago has a better location than the Double Door, right at the six corners of Wicker Park and the Damen train stop. The sound system is good, too. It's run by the owners of the Metro in Lakeview, which means that the roster of bands can seem like the Metro's leftovers — jam bands, local bands, and the occasional 90s alt-rock refugee. $3-20.

Empty Bottle, 1035 N Western Ave (*Western Blue Line, transfer to 49 Western bus going south*), +1 773 276-3600, *www.emptybottle. com*, M-W 5PM-2AM, Th-F 3PM-3AM, Sa-12PM-3AM, Su 12PM-2AM. To Chicago as the Knitting Factory is to NYC, the Empty Bottle hosts a mix of touring indie-rock veterans, local bands, and occasional appearances by American and Dutch avant-garde jazz. The sound and the room are OK at best, but the people who work here (and their great taste in music) make it exceptional. They also program events in Logan Square and Portage Park, among others. If you're hungry before a show, step next door to **Bite** (see Eat). $10-15, Mondays free.

Funky Buddha Lounge, 728 W Grand Ave (*Grand Blue Line*), +1 312 666-1695, *www.funkybuddha. com*, M-F 9PM-2AM, Sa 9PM-3AM, Su 8PM-2AM. There's a little bit of everything at this ever-changing West Town dance lounge, with trendy Asian-ish decor surrounding poetry slams, live jazz, comedy, rock, chill-out DJs, and the inevitable VIP room. There's no dress code, but if you've got fashion, this is the place to wear it. Cover usually $15-20.

The Hideout, 1354 W Wabansia Ave (*Just east of Elston, just north of North Avenue*), +1 773 227-4433, *www.hideoutchicago.com*, Tu 7PM-2AM, W-F 4PM-2AM, Sa 7PM-3AM. One of the finest drinking and hollering establishments in the US, the Hideout hosts the best in alt-folk, bluegrass, Americana and just plain hillbilly mu-

sic. The place is a bit hard to find, hidden as it is next to the city's main north-side refueling station for garbage trucks, but it's more than worth the trouble. Of special interest to old-timey fans is the regular Tuesday night appearance of **Devil in a Woodpile**.

Rodan, 1530 N Milwaukee Ave (*Damen Blue Line*), +1 773 276-7036, *www.rodan.ws*, Su-F 5PM-2AM, Sa 5PM-3AM. Upscale club with a younger, artsy crowd — yes, that's a reference to the flying Japanese monster. Good DJs spin throughout the week with video art projected on the wall, and there's a fusion menu of bar food. It's stylish, but laid-back and worth the visit.

Subterranean, 2011 W North Ave, *www.subt.net*, M 7PM-2AM, Tu-F 6PM-2AM, Sa 7PM-3AM, Su 8PM-2AM. A laid-back club with diverse music and crowd. DJs spin in the lounge and indie rock appears in the Cabaret. Drinks are worth the price, and there's a bonus: once you stumble outside, you're surrounded by great after-hours dive eateries. Cover usually $5.

Others

Blind Robin, 853 N Western Ave (*49 Western bus*), +1 773 395-3002, *theblindrobin.com*, M-F 4PM-2AM, Sa noon-3AM, Su noon-2AM. Just a couple blocks south of the Empty Bottle, this is a good place to chill after a show — good beer selection, friendly bartenders, and plenty of board games. The same owners run Lemmings and Green Eye Lounge in Bucktown.

WICKER PARKSLEEP

Blu Coral, 1265 N Milwaukee Ave, +1 773 252-2020, *www.blucoralchicago.com*, Su-F 5PM-2AM, Sa 5PM-3AM. This sleek, industrial themed sushi spot features an extensive sushi and maki menu as well as contemporary Japanese entrees. Live music on weekends 9PM-1AM.

Mac's, 1801 W Division St (*Division Blue Line*), +1 773 782-4400. A sports bar, but not in a meathead sort of way, and not at all like the post-fraternity college sports bars in Lincoln Park. Good food, TVs, and beer.

Small Bar, 2049 W Division St (*Division Blue Line*), +1 773 772-2727, *www.thesmallbar.com*, M-F 3PM-2AM, Sa 11AM-3AM, Su 11AM-2AM. The biggest beer selection in the area, save for the Map Room in Bucktown. The staff are friendly, and soccer is almost always on television.

Tuman's, 2159 W Chicago Ave (*66 Chicago bus*), +1 773 782-1400, M-F 3PM-2AM, Sa 12PM-3AM, Su 11AM-2AM. No longer the Alcohol Abuse Center that defined an era in the Ukrainian Village, but the new owners have kept the name and overcome local resentment with food, flatscreen TVs, and an all-around decent neighborhood bar.

The Violet Hour, 1520 N Damen Ave (*Damen Blue Line*), +1 773 252-1500, *www.theviolethour.com*, Su-F 6PM-2AM, Sa 6PM-3AM. Named after a T.S. Eliot poem, The Violet Hour is hidden away — there's no sign, and no name on the door. Inside, though, is a marvelous, decadent, Alice-in-Wonderland plus speakeasy vibe. It's a *great* place for a date. The cocktails are $11-12, but they won't disappoint — certified mixologists take up to four minutes to make them. And if you've never had a banana peanut-butter-and-jelly sandwich deep fried and dusted with bacon crumbs, here's your chance.

Sleep

Ruby Room, 1743-45 W Division St (*Division Blue Line*), +1 773 235-2323, *www.rubyroom.com*. A handful of B&B-style rooms above a rejuvenation spa in an 1896 building, with amenities geared toward relaxation — lush, comfortable decor, but no television or telephones. But it's right in the midst of the lively Wicker Park scene, so you won't miss them…much. Two-night minimum stay on weekends. Rooms from $155.

Wicker Park Inn, 1329 N Wicker Park Ave (*Damen Blue Line*), +1 773 486-2743, *www.wickerparkinn.com*. Bed and Breakfast, offers five beautiful rooms on-site and two apartments across the street for nightly rentals. Close to restaurants and entertainment, friendly staff can help you get the lay of the neighborhood or offer ideas on restaurants or bars to hit. Rooms from $125.

Stay safe

Wicker Park keeps a slightly rough appearance, but that's mainly for the enjoyment of the younger residents. Use common

WICKER PARKGET OUT

sense while drinking and you'll have nothing to worry about. (Don't leave valuables in cars, though.) Ukrainian Village is much the same, but stay alert around alleys while walking on side streets. In that distinctly Chicago fashion of invisible barriers respected on both sides of the law, crime stays almost exclusively on the west side of Western Avenue. But if you parked on the west side of Western, take care while walking back to your car after dark.

Contact

VRmage (see above) also offers internet access at $5/hour.

The following libraries provide free internet access:

Bucktown/Wicker Park Branch Library, 1701 N Milwaukee Ave (*Damen Blue Line*), +1 312 744-6022, *www.chipublib.org*, M-Th 9AM-9PM, F-Sa 9AM-5PM, Su closed. Brand new library one block north of the North/Milwaukee/Damen intersection.

Eckhart Park Library, 1330 W Chicago Ave (*Chicago Blue Line*), +1 312 746-6069, *www.chipublib. org*, M,W 10AM-6PM, Tu-Th 12-8PM, F-Sa 9AM-5PM, Su closed. In the Eckhart Park field house.

Midwest Branch Library, 2335 W Chicago Ave (*66 Chicago bus*), +1 312 744-7788, *www.chipublib. org*, M,W 12-8PM, Tu,Th-Sa 9AM-5PM, Su closed. Near Ukrainian Village.

Get out

Pilsen *p.259* is the most-quoted inheritor of Wicker Park's original bohemian mantle, and makes for an interesting contrast.

If, on the other hand, it is the demise of Wicker Park's Puerto Rican community that you are lamenting, retrace its migration west along Division Street into Humboldt Park on the Far West Side *p.331* — the best Puerto Rican food in the city awaits.

Logan Square is an expansive neighborhood with sweeping boulevards on Chicago's West Side. It shares a wealth of dive bars and cheap rock venues with **Bucktown**, which becomes a high-fashion destination when close to Wicker Park *p.229*.

Understand

The area now known as **Logan Square** was born in the boomtown days of the 1830s, when schoolteacher Martin Kimbell rejected a plot in the obviously going-nowhere Loop *p.47* in favor of good, solid farmland about five miles northwest. The area remained independent from the city until temptations like water and fire departments became too much to resist, and in 1889, Chicago took over. (The streets were upgraded, but they were also renamed — most cruelly, "Kimbell" became "Kimball".)

And if you were a goat farmer in the city around that time, **Bucktown** was the place to be. You knew that you were in a place that understood the importance of goats, and that any goats you owned would be in good company. As home to farms, factories, and immigrants who were employed by them, Bucktown never developed any major tourist attractions, but it did support plenty of bars for discussions of issues both goat-related and non-goat-related, and that preponderance of cheap bars is still intact.

Logan Square, on the other hand, was named for the Civil War hero Gen. John A. Logan, and its tree-lined boulevards — one of which bears his name — are what really

LOGAN-BUCKTOWN UNDERSTAND

set the neighborhood apart from
its neighbors, offering wide-open
spaces for leisurely trawls by cars,
bikes, and pedestrians alike. (Fit-
tingly, Ignaz Schwinn, founder of
the Schwinn bicycle company, settled in Logan Square.) The neighborhood became a destination for
immigrants who'd struck it rich
in Chicago, and they helped build
the beautiful housing stock that
survives today, even after the
business district collapsed in the
1950s.

It's those magnificent graystones
and richly detailed brick classics that draw waves of new residents to Logan Square today.
Right now, it's the best of both
worlds: murals and community
gardens decorate the streets, and
new residents kick portions of
their salaries to businesses run
by older ones, enjoying authentic
taquerias on wide, sunny boulevards that are (mostly) rich with
gritty, urban character and (generally) safe.

Despite the critical shortage of
goats at present, the chameleon-
like Bucktown prospers from
proximity to Wicker Park *p.229*,
with retail and restaurants that
take their cues from the hipster
paradise to its south, rough-and-
tumble spots that resemble Logan
on the other side, and new condos
not dissimilar to Lincoln Park
p.123 to the east. Bucktown is
less notable than Logan Square
in terms of looks, with a lot of
same-y new construction hurried
up to meet housing demand,
but it also has some great bars
and essential music venues with
nightly bills of jazz, scuzz and

genius.

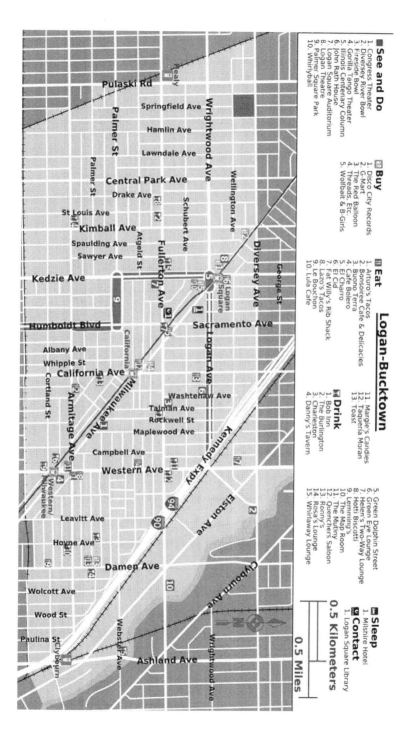

Logan-Bucktown

See and Do

1. Congress Theater
2. Diversey River Bowl
3. Fireside Bowl
4. Gorilla Tango Theater
5. Illinois Centenary Column
6. John Rath House
7. Logan Square Auditorium
8. Logan Theatre
9. Palmer Square Park
10. Whirlyball

Buy

1. Disco City Records
2. G-Mart
3. The Red Balloon
4. Threads, Etc.
5. Wolfbait & B-Girls

Eat

1. Arturo's Tacos
2. Bonsoiree Cafe & Delicacies
3. Buono Terra
4. Cafe Bolero
5. El Charro
6. El Cid
7. Fat Willy's Rib Shack
8. Lazo's Tacos
9. Le Bouchon
10. Lula Cafe
11. Margie's Candies
12. Taqueria Moran
13. Toast

Drink

1. Bob Inn
2. The Burlington
3. Charleston
4. Danny's Tavern
5. Green Dolphin Street
6. Green Eye Lounge
7. Helen's Two-Way Lounge
8. Hotti Biscotti
9. Lemming's
10. The Map Room
11. The Mutiny
12. Quenchers Saloon
13. Ronny's
14. Rosa's Lounge
15. Whirlaway Lounge

Sleep

1. Milshire Hotel

Contact

1. Logan Square Library

0.5 Kilometers

0.5 Miles

LOGAN-BUCKTOWN SEE

Get in

By train

The O'Hare branch of the CTA **Blue Line** has stops in Bucktown (Damen, Western) and Logan Square (California, Logan Square). It runs all night.

By bus

49 Western runs through Bucktown all night, connecting with the Blue Line at Western and Armitage.

52 Kedzie/California travels on California through both neighborhoods, connecting with the Blue Line at the California station, and on to the Far West Side *p.331*.

56 Milwaukee is the key route, running from Wicker Park *p.229*, through Bucktown and Logan, and on to the Far Northwest Side *p.363*. It connects near the Blue Line at Damen and again at California.

Three buses connect Bucktown with Lincoln Park *p.123*, Old Town, and the lakefront, not to mention the Red, Purple, and Brown Lines:

72 North runs a quick route between the Brown/Purple (Sedgwick) and Red (North/Clybourn) Lines and the Blue Line (Damen) at the center of the Wicker Park/Bucktown shopping district.

73 Armitage connects with the Blue Line at Western.

74 Fullerton connects with the Blue Line at California.

76 Diversey connects with the Blue Line at Logan Square.

By car

I-90/94, also known as the Kennedy Expressway, runs close to Logan Square and Bucktown. Diversey Avenue is the main exit for the neighborhood. Street parking is usually not a problem in Logan Square, but check for permit-only parking on side streets — the posted hours are a bit weird, and cops go on ticket binges every once in a while. Logan Boulevard itself usually offers plentiful open parking, though.

See

One of Logan Square's most celebrated features is **Logan Boulevard** itself, which is lined with century-old, show-of-wealth mansions. For an easy walking tour, start west of the I-90/94 underpass, and walk west to the Illinois Centenary Memorial Column, veering off to walk south on Kedzie for a few more blocks of the same. They're enjoyable by sight alone on a sunny day, but community groups like Logan Square Preservation *www.logansquarepreservation.org* hold occasional guided tours and garden walks.

Illinois Centenary Memorial Column, Milwaukee Ave, Logan Blvd, and Kedzie Ave (*Logan Square Blue Line*). Not a sight to seek out, but it's hard to miss — this column was erected in 1918 to celebrate the hundredth anniversary of Illinois' statehood, and topped with an eagle to show the committee members weren't messing around. It's out of step with the rest of the neighborhood now, but hey, only a few more years until it's time for an update!

John Rath House, 2703 W Logan Blvd, *www.ci.chi.il.us*. Nestled among the mansions of Logan Boulevard, this 1907 Prairie School house by George Maher makes a nice contrast with its elegant lines and lack of Euro mishmash.

Palmer Square Park, 3100 W Palmer Blvd (*Kedzie Ave, Humboldt Blvd, and Palmer St*), +1 773 227-3535. Designed by William LeBaron Jenney, designer to the (Victorian) stars, and a lovely job at that — with plenty of trees, shade, and green space. When New Belgium brewery finally decided to bring its Tour de Fat to Chicago in 2008, it chose beautiful Palmer Square.

Our Lady of the Underpass

Few drivers would consider the Kennedy Expressway sacred ground, but in 2005, what many believed to be an image of the Virgin Mary appeared on the wall of the Fullerton Avenue underpass. Divine revelation or water damage, the image attracted fervent devotion from local Catholics, who have diligently protected it from defacement attempts in the years since. If you'd like to decide for yourself, the spot is easy to find — look for the flowers, candles, and a few worshipers lost in prayer, especially in the morning.

Do

Logan Square Skate Park, 2430 W Logan Blvd (*Western Blue Line*). The **Logan Square Skate Park**, under the I/90-94 overpass, has ten ramps and half-pipes, benches, an asphalt surface and a drinking fountain. There is some parking on Logan Blvd itself.

Whirlyball, 1880 W Fullerton Ave (*74 Fullerton bus*), +1 773 486-7777, *www.whirlyball.com*, M-F 10AM-2AM, Sa noon-3AM, Su noon-2AM. An entertainment center with two fine ways to burn off steam: the title game, which adds the bumper cars that Native Americans always meant lacrosse to have, and **laser tag**. Packages are available with beer and bar food. Walk-ins $10 for 30 minutes (minimum four people) for whirlyball, $6 per person per 15 minutes for laser tag.

The best reason to visit Bucktown and Logan Square is the music scene, which includes several bars — see also the below.

Congress Theater, 2135 N Milwaukee Ave (*Western Blue Line*), +1 312 458-9668, *www.congresschicago.com*. Opened in 1926 and still adorned with gorgeous terra cotta, the Congress Theater is now home to the twin powers of Mexican wrestling and indie rock of an occasionally exceptional caliber. Most music events are general admission (standing room only). Shows $10-25.

Diversey River Bowl, 2211 W Diversey Ave (*76 Diversey bus from Logan Square Blue Line or Di-*

versey Brown Line), +1 773 227-5800, *www.drbowl.com*, Su-F 12PM-2AM, Sa Sept-May 9AM-3AM, summer 12PM-3AM. Never mind the bollocks, it's the Rock 'n Bowl. 36 lanes ensure that you won't be crowded out by league play, although there can be a long wait on weekends. The music and staff are great, pitchers of beer (cheap and classy) and pizza (greasy and, uh, greasy) are available, and old-school arcade games and photobooths help pass the wait, and it's smoke-free. M-Th $19/hr per lane, but only $1 per game 12-5PM; F-Sa $32/hr per lane, $39/hr 6PM-close.

Fireside Bowl, 2648 W Fullerton Ave, +1 773 486-2700, *www.firesidebowl.com*, M-F 4PM-2AM, Sa 2PM-3AM, Su 2PM-midnight. Shows on Sunday nights.. There are better places to bowl and much better places to see live music, but this is hallowed ground for the teen punk of the '80s and '90s, when the Fireside was a cheap, all-ages venue punk, hardcore, emo, and more. It's definitely *not* that any more — not surprisingly, neighborhood residents were never fond of the noise and the youth, and the owner found it easier to survive as a straight bowling alley. Lanes $3.50 a game/$20 per hour.

Gorilla Tango Theater, 1919 N Milwaukee Ave (*Western Blue Line*), +1 773 598-4549, *www.gorillatango.com*. Not many places in Chicago can match Gorilla Tango for sheer quantity — even on cold, quiet Wednesday nights, you'll find two unknown theater companies do-

ing low-budget comedies at this Bucktown storefront theater. The end results may be scattershot, but the energy is usually high and the titles alone will liven up any story about what you did on your trip. $10-18.

Logan Square Auditorium, 2359 N Kedzie Ave (*Logan Square Blue Line*), +1 773 252-6179, *www.lsachicago.com*. It's underutilized on weeknights, but this ballroom-with-a-liquor-license hosts weekend rock shows and the occasional label showcase for mainstays of Chicago music like Thrill Jockey. Tickets $10-20.

Logan Theatre, 2646 N Milwaukee Ave (*Logan Square Blue Line*), +1 773 252-0627. Opened in 1915 with 975 seats and still showing movies today, although it has since been carved up into four screens for second-run Hollywood fare. $4.

Buy

Bucktown

There are two main shopping areas in Bucktown. The first is near the intersection of Milwaukee, Damen, and North Avenue, right at the border of Wicker Park, where you'll find small, independent stores and boutiques. However, for the big-box experience, drive up to Damen and Elston, where a couple of strip malls offer major retailers and plenty of parking.

The Red Balloon, 2060 N Damen Ave, +1 773 489-9800, *www.theredballoon.com*, M-Sa

10AM-6PM, Th 10AM-7PM, Su 12-5PM. Fun, original clothes, furniture, and toys for kids — if you'd like to get your child's life started right, you'll know the value of a magnetized wooden pirate ship (complete with crew and monkey).

Logan Square

The six corners of Diversey, Milwaukee, and Kimball mark the center of the old retail district in Logan Square. It's an odd sight to see national chains like The Gap shoehorned into old art deco facades. The nearby **Mega Mall** (2500 N Milwaukee Ave) is gigantic, and when it's open, it's home to a dense jumble of stalls that has been compared to a third-world bazaar, chock full of cheap, shady merchandise. Health-code violations kept it closed for a while, and recently a fire brought commerce (as it was) to a halt.

Disco City Records, 2630 N Milwaukee Ave, +1 773 486-1495. One of the premier Latin music stores in Chicago, with a long rack of new releases, DVDs, and Spanish musical instruments (mainly bongos).

G-Mart, 2641 N Kedzie Ave, +1 773 384-0400, *www.g-mart.com*, M-F 12-7PM, Sa 12-6PM. If you need a comic book fix, G-Mart is the place. They carry titles from major and indie publishers alike, sold by a gonzo sales crew.

Threads, Etc., 2327 N Milwaukee Ave (*California Blue Line*), +1 773 276-6411, M-Sa 11AM-7PM, Su 11AM-5PM. A nearly warehouse-sized resale store, covering two floors. There's more furniture than anything else, but there should be some good finds on any given day amid the intriguing clutter.

Wolfbait & B-Girls, 3131 W Logan Blvd (*Logan Square Blue Line*), +1 312 698-8685, *www.wolfbaitchicago.com*, Tu-Th 12-7PM, F-Sa 10AM-7PM, Su usually 10AM-5PM. Clothes and jewelry for women, with everything designed, handmade, and sold in Chicago.

Eat

Logan Square covers a lot of culinary ground — stray off the beaten path and you'll find places serving Argentinean, Colombian, Cuban, Ecuadorian, El Savadorian, and regional Mexican specialties.

Budget

Arturo's Tacos, 2001 N Western Ave (*Western Blue Line*), +1 773 772-4944, *www.arturos-tacos. com*, 24 hours daily. The cheap late-night food of choice among trendy chefs and bar-goers alike in Bucktown, right outside the Blue Line. (Or is it Lazo's? See below.)

El Charro, 2410 N Milwaukee Ave (*California Blue Line*), +1 773 278-2514, 24 hours daily. There is no reason to seek out El Charro during the day, but if you're drinking in Logan Square, you need to know where the all-night Mexican food can be found. The soothing aqua walls and the steadfast Ms. Pac-Man machine don't hurt, either.

Lazo's Tacos, 2009 N Western Ave (*Western Blue Line*), +1 773 486-3303, 24 hours daily. If you're not one to stay neutral in a hotly-debated issue, you'll want to declare a loyalty between Lazo's and Arturo's for taco supremacy of this street. Both are cheap, but consider carefully: locals take this question very seriously.

Margie's Candies, 1960 N Western Ave (*Western Blue Line*), +1 773 384-1035, Su-Th 9AM-midnight, F-Sa 9AM-1AM. There's an argument to be made for putting Margie's at the top of the list of things to do and see in this article; thankfully, the Blue Line and two bus lines converge at this holy ice cream shop, founded in 1921. There's diner food as well if you need "dinner" to justify the frenzy. $3-6.

Mid-range

Buono Terra, 2535 N California Ave (*California Blue Line*), +1 773 289-3800, *www.buona-terra. com*, Tu-Th 5-10PM, F-Sa 5-11PM, Su 4-9PM. Great Italian restaurant in Logan Square. $14-20; Thursday night prix fixe dinner for $20.

Cafe Bolero, 2252 N Western Ave (*Western Blue Line*), +1 773 227-9000, *www.cafebolero.com*, Su-Th 11AM-11PM, F-Sa 11AM-midnight. Cuban restaurant that excels in both food and style, with appetizers that complement the main dishes quite well. There's live Latin jazz a couple of nights each week, and an upstairs bar for mojitos. $12-20.

El Cid, 2645 N Kedzie Ave (*Logan Square Blue Line*), +1 773 395-0505, Su-Th 9AM-midnight; F-Sa 9AM-2AM. Pretty good Mexican food in Logan Square. The outdoor seating is especially nice, well away from the street rather like sitting in someone's backyard.

Fat Willy's Rib Shack, 2416 W Schubert Ave, +1 773 782-1800, *www.fatwillysribshack.com*, Sun-Thu 11:30am-10pm, Fri-Sat 11:30am-11pm. Pulled pork sandwiches and southern-style BBQ in Logan Square. Sandwiches about $10, half-orders of ribs about $16.

Taqueria Moran, 2226 N California Ave (*California Blue Line*), +1 773 235-2663, 5AM-10PM daily. Easy to find, this taqueria is roomy and has a bit of old-style diner class, perfect for breakfast chilaquiles and solid for Mexican lunch and dinner standards. $9-17.

Toast, 2046 N Damen Ave (*Damen Blue Line*), +1 773 772-5600, M-F 8AM-2:30PM, Sa-Su 8AM-3:30PM. Popular Bucktown brunch spot. There are some clever and unique creations on the menu alongside breakfast standards, best topped with a tall glass of their tasty orange juice. $12-16.

Splurge

Bonsoiree Cafe and Delicacies, 2728 W Armitage Ave, +1 773 486-7511, *www.bon-soiree.com/cafe*, Tu-Th 5-10PM, F 5-11PM, Su 5-9PM. A French inspired restaurant/cafe/deli hybrid in Logan Square prepares astounding gourmet food you would normally find at a five star restaurant.

Deli case provides options for carryout and a fabulous brunch is served on weekends. $24 three-course prix fixe dinner.

Le Bouchon, 1858 N Damen Ave, +1 773 862-6600, *www.lebouchonofchicago.com*, M-Th 5:30-11PM, F-Sa 5PM-midnight. In Bucktown. Small, funky bistro with a limited but excellent menu of standard French fare. For peak dining hours you will need a reservation. Reasonably priced. Monday is 1/2-price wine night, and on Tuesday the entire menu is prix fixe – your choice of appetizer, main course, and dessert for $22.

Lula Cafe, 2537 N Kedzie Ave (*Logan Square Blue Line*), +1 773 489-9554, *www.lulacafe.com*, Su-M,W-Th 9AM-10PM, F-Sa 9AM-11PM. A very popular neighborhood restaurant, serving an eclectic mix of new inventions and creatively remixed standards. Because of its popularity, lines can be *really* long on Friday and Saturday nights. $16-30; Monday Night Farm Dinner $24 per person.

Drink

Bars

Bob Inn, 2609 W Fullerton Ave, +1 773 342-2309, Su-F 11AM-2AM, Sa 11AM-3AM. Good place to watch a baseball game with a cheap beer…as long as you're a White Sox fan. Otherwise, it's a good place to relax and wish you were a regular.

The Burlington, 3425 W Fullerton Ave, +1 773 384-3243, *www.theburlingtonbar.com*, 7PM-2AM daily. This, on the other hand, is definitely a Cubs bar, with plasma screens for the games and lovingly engineered old-man ambiance. When baseball isn't on, music becomes the foremost concern; it's too crowded for a dance floor, but DJs are usually on by 10PM.

Green Eye Lounge, 2403 W Homer St (*Western Blue Line*), +1 773 227-8851, *greeneyelounge.com*, M-F 3PM-2AM, Sa 12PM-3AM, Su 12PM-2AM. Just off Western and Milwaukee. The owners of the Green Eye Lounge are experts in the art of the neighborhood bar — see also Lemming's below and the Blind Robin in Ukrainian Village. There's no stress, the beer selection is good, and there are board games.

Helen's Two-Way Lounge, 2988 W Fullerton Ave (*California Blue Line*), +1 773 227-5676. An exemplary dive bar in the fine tradition of such; cheap beer, wood-paneled walls, and regulars who are settled in for the night and have been for the last couple of decades. With the changing demographics of the area, it's possible that hipsters might outnumber the men with more tenured mustaches on any given night, but it's still a fine neighborhood dive.

Lemming's, 1850 N Damen Ave (*Damen Blue Line*), +1 773 862-1688, *www.lemmingstavern.com*, M-F 4PM-2AM, Sa noon-3AM, Su noon-2AM. Comfortable neighborhood bar with local art to be seen and games (board & video) to be played. Look for the "Lemming's" sign by day and the "Schlitz" by night.

The Map Room, 1949 N Hoyne Ave, +1 773 252-7636, *www.maproom.com*, M-F 6:30AM-2AM, Sa 7:30AM-3AM, Su 11AM-2AM. Their motto is "Don't be lost," but you may as well give in to their disorienting collection of exotic beers. Their tap selection is one of the more extensive in the city, with surprises for even the most jaded beer drinker: extensive draught and bottle menu, including a cask-conditioned selection, but occasionally unfriendly management.

Whirlaway Lounge, 3224 W Fullerton Ave, +1 773 276-6809, *www.whirlaway.net*, Su-F 4PM-2AM, Sa 4PM-3AM. Whirlaway is run by the much-adored Maria, with decor that makes you feel as though you're drinking in the basement of Logan Square's collective unconsciousness's dad's house. (In less abstract terms, that's cheap beer, free popcorn, close quarters, and rock on the jukebox.)

Bars with music

Not far away, although a little difficult to find, the **The Hideout** (just east of Wicker Park *p.229*) is definitely worth seeking out for live music.

Charleston, 2076 N Hoyne Ave, +1 773 489-4757, *www.charlestonchicago.com*, M-F 3PM-2AM, Sa-Su 2PM-2AM. An old-time Bucktown joint with a big selection of reasonably priced beer and an impressive antique wood bar. There's a Jazz Jam every Tuesday night, and rock/folk/jazz shows most Fridays, Saturdays, and Sundays.

Danny's Tavern, 1951 W Dickens Ave, +1 773 489-6457, Su-F 7PM-2AM, Sa 7PM-3AM. This is a good place to dance for most of the week, thanks to a talented group of DJs who spin pop, hip-hop, jazz and soul (including the occasional all-Smiths night). Wednesday nights (once a month, 7:30PM) go literary with Danny's Reading Series and the **No Slander** poetry and fiction nights *www.noslander.com.*

Green Dolphin Street, 2200 N Ashland Ave, +1 773 395-0066, *www.jazzitup.com*, Tu-Th 9PM-2AM, F-Sa 8:30PM-3AM, Su 8PM-12AM. It's out of the way, but you have to earn a classy joint like this by finding it. Live jazz in a swanky atmosphere is the hook, with cocktails $9 and up; the jazz tends toward dance-friendly big-band, and sometimes salsa. Arrive any time after 5:30PM if you'd like dinner. Cover free or $10-20.

Hotti Biscotti, 3545 W Fullerton Ave, +1 773 772-9970, Tu-Sa 10AM-2AM. You just want coffee, but your friend wants a $2 beer; there are some issues the two of you need to settle via Scrabble, but you'd like to hear some live music. Happily, there is a place in Logan Square for you. Rock, films, and performance art figure into the schedule; Tuesdays are jazz nights.

The Mutiny, 2428 N Western Ave (*Western Blue Line*), +1 773 486-7774, *themutinychicago.com*, M 1PM-2AM, Tu-F,Su 11AM-2AM, Sa 9AM-3AM. A cavernous dive that hosts a lot of three/four band punk and rock shows, with occasional comedy nights as well. Check out the ceiling tiles painted by regulars. No cover, even for bands, and the frosty pitchers of beer are cheap.

Quenchers Saloon, 2401 N Western Ave, +1 773 276-9730, *www.quenchers.com*, Su-F 11AM-2AM, Sa 11AM-3AM. 200 different beers from around the world, 60 different whiskeys, and a decent bar menu. Everyone drinks together at this comfortable neighborhood bar. There's live music every night except Sunday, mostly jazz with some rock and DJs on the weekends.

Ronny's, 2101 N California Ave (*California Blue Line*), +1 773 278-7170, *www.mpshows.com*. In some ways, Ronny's is the heir to the Fireside's punk mantle — shows are dirt cheap, the management don't care, and two of the four bands will be asking around for a place to sleep after the show. It's not all-ages, though. Most shows $5.

Rosa's Lounge, 3420 W Armitage Ave, +1 773 342-0452, *www.rosaslounge.com*, Shows Tu-Sa 9:30PM. A rare blues outlet in this part of the city, Rosa's was reportedly founded by an Italian who met Junior Wells in Milan and was inspired to study the classic lounges of the South Side. It's considered the North Side's most authentic blues club (and also happened to be the Czech Republic's philosopher king Vaclav Havel's favorite). Today, Rosa's does modern and traditional blues almost as cheaply as the rest of the neighborhood does punk rock, but watch out for the absurd drink prices—order water and tell them what you think of $15 shots of whiskey. Watch for a chance to take the **Midnight Blues Cruise**. Most shows $5-15.

Sleep

If you're only here for a show and the options in Wicker Park *p.229* are too steep, you could commute from the hotel cluster by O'Hare Airport *p.397* on the Blue Line.

Milshire Hotel, 2525 N Milwaukee Ave (*California Blue Line*), +1 773 384-7611. Make no mistake — this is a dive. It's also a very cheap one, and deceptively well-located (a few minutes' walk from the Blue Line in Logan Square, right on the Milwaukee bus line). Don't hand over any money until you see the room, but if you're on a budget and up for a Lou Reed hotel experience, this could work for a night. Rooms with shared bath $30-$43, private bath $48, no children permitted.

Contact

The following libraries provide free internet access:

Bucktown/Wicker Park Branch Library, 1701 N Milwaukee Ave (*Damen Blue Line*), +1 312 744-6022, *www.chipublib.org*, M-Th

9AM-9PM, F-Sa 9AM-5PM. Brand new library one block north of the North/Milwaukee/Damen intersection.

Logan Square Branch Library, 3030 W Fullerton Ave (*California Blue Line*), +1 312 744-5295, *www. chipublib.org*, M-Th 9AM-9PM, F-Sa 9AM-5PM.

Stay safe

Both neighborhoods are reasonably safe, with standard precautions taken for an urban environment. Stay close to the bright lights after dark, and if you've had a lot to drink, use the money you saved on cheap beer for a taxi back to your hotel.

Get out

As fashion follows the path of Polish migration, Avondale *p.363* is often mentioned as the next place to receive the "hot neighborhood" treatment after Logan Square.

Humboldt Park on the Far West Side *p.331* has a major Puerto Rican community and a few cultural institutions that share an audience with Logan Square residents.

PILSENUNDERSTAND

Pilsen is a neighborhood on the Lower West Side of Chicago. Murals of Mexican cowboys notwithstanding, Pilsen is a lot like the Wild West: only a few minutes from the Loop *p.47* by train, this working-class area is thick with riches in art and historic architecture, encircled by developers and speculators in search of the next hot neighborhood, and occupied by a community that's fiercely proud of where they live.

Understand

Pilsen was originally settled by Irish and German immigrants, who came to work at the factories and stockyards nearby. Those industries attracted Czech immigrants next, and in the late 1800s, the neighborhood was named in honor of the city back home in Bohemia. The streets of Pilsen still bear their mark — weathered stone castles like **St. Adalbert's** and **Thalia Hall** loom over buildings with colorful turrets and dashes of ornamentation completely absent of the Prairie School influence found elsewhere in Chicago.

When the communities of the Near West Side *p.215* were shattered and scattered by the construction of the University of Illinois at Chicago, Pilsen's population shifted as well to absorb newcomers. With the city's once-thriving West Side Italian community mostly wiped out, the small **Heart of Italy** in the industrial **Heart of Chicago** neighborhood drew new focus as one place where it survived, remaining today as an alternative to the more heavily touristed Little Italy in the Near West.

259

PILSENUNDERSTAND

The construction also displaced a community of Mexicans, many of whom resettled in Pilsen. Within a few years, they became the demographic majority. Never prosperous, the area had been in economic decline for several years, its fate tied to the transition of Chicago's economy away from cattle and manufacturing; poverty remains a serious issue in Pilsen today. Nevertheless, its residents have built a set of cultural institutions that far outpace many wealthier neighborhoods, crowned by the excellent **National Museum of Mexican Art**.

Fears of gentrification began several years ago when the Podmajersky company began converting the old warehouses of East Pilsen into cheap studios for artists from outside the community. Depending on who you ask, this was either intended to:

a) Revitalize the nearly vacant eastern half of an economically depressed neighborhood by creating spaces where exciting young artists could live, work, and exhibit, a "SoHo in Chicago";

b) Jump-start the process of gentrification that happened in Wicker Park several years earlier, driving up property values by exchanging low-income residents for wealthier ones looking to trade on that artistic "cool."

The exciting artists have arrived, and now people are waiting to see what happens. There is a sense that Pilsen could be the next big thing, but there is also a concern that few of the current residents will be there when that happens. Already, some businesses seem compelled to take sides: whether to appeal to the working-class Mexican community already here, or the affluent community that might be coming. Whatever direction Pilsen may be headed, what's there now is a neighborhood with a long history of re-inventing itself, rough in places and full of inspiration, and palpably on the edge of greatness.

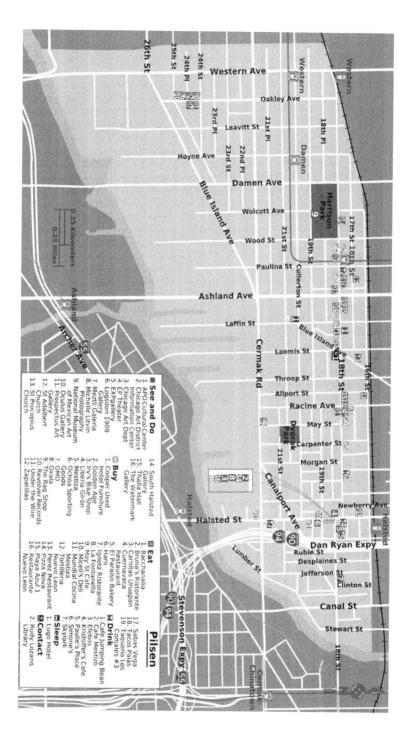

Pilsen

See and Do
1. Chicago Art District
2. Apollo Cultural Center Gallery
3. Information Center
4. Chicago Art Dept.
5. EP Theater
6. EXPgallery
7. Logsdon 1909 Gallery
8. Mestizo Gallery
9. National Museum of Mexican Art
10. Oculus Gallery
11. Prospectus Art Gallery
12. St. Adalbert Church
13. St. Procopius Church
14. South Halsted Gallery
15. Thalia Hall
16. The Watermark Gallery

Buy
1. Cooper Used Hotel Furniture
2. Golden Age
3. Knee Deep Vintage
4. Live's Bike Shop
5. May St. Cafe
6. Modern Cooperative
7. OMD
8. Oxala
9. The Rag Shop
10. Revolver Records
11. Under the Wire
12. Zapatillas

Eat
1. Bacchanalia
2. Bruna's Ristorante
3. Carnitas Uruapan
4. Cuernavaca Restaurant
5. El Paraiso Bakery
6. Haro
7. Ignotz Ristorante
8. La Fontanella
9. May St. Cafe
10. Miceli's Deli
11. Mundial Cocina Mestiza
12. Nuevo Leon
13. Perez Restaurant
14. Pizza Nova
15. Playa Azul 1
16. Restaurante Nuevo Leon
17. Sabas Vega
18. Tacos Palas
19. Taqueria Los Comales #3

Drink
1. Cafe Jumping Bean
2. Cafe Maestro
3. Efebos
4. Kristoffer's Cafe
5. Paulie's Place
6. Simone's
7. Skylark

Sleep
1. Lugo Hotel

Contact
2. Rudy Lozano Library

Get in

By train

Pilsen is very easy to reach by train from the Loop *p.47*. The key is to know which part you'd like to visit first: the arts district in East Pilsen, which is centered at 18th and Halsted, and the commercial center in West Pilsen, which is near 18th and Ashland. It's a long but manageable walk between the two areas, with a quiet zone in-between.

For the arts district, take the CTA **Orange Line** to Halsted, which is on the border of Bridgeport *p.175*, and walk a few blocks north on Halsted (the street), crossing over the river almost immediately.

For the rest of the neighborhood, including the National Museum of Mexican Art, take the CTA **Pink Line** to 18th, which is right at the commercial center of Pilsen. (Even if you're just passing through, the astonishing murals at the 18th station are worth a look.) The Pink Line also stops in the Heart of Chicago neighborhood (Damen, Western) and then on to the Far West Side *p.331*.

By bus

In the winter, knowing the transit options between East and West Pilsen is vital. The streets of Pilsen don't get the same tender, loving care from the snowplows as some other parts of the city, so the wind and the drifts can make walk between the two areas considerably more difficult.

8 Halsted runs the length of the arts district, coming from Bridgeport *p.175* to the south and the Near West Side *p.215* to the north. It connects with the Orange Line at the Halsted station.

9 Ashland will drop you at 18th and Ashland, near the taquerías and the Pink Line. It runs all night.

18 16th 18th runs, appropriately enough, down 18th street, connecting with the Pink Line at the 18th station.

49 Western runs down Western Avenue for nearly the full length of the city, passing near Pilsen and Heart of Chicago. It's an all-night route.

60 Blue Island/26th runs from the Chicago/Loop *p.47* through the Near West Side *p.215*, Pilsen, Little Village *p.331* and South Lawndale all night long.

N62 Archer branches off to cover the same ground as the 8 Halsted while passing through the arts district. Note that the plain 62 Archer only stops within walking distance back at the Halsted Orange Line stop.

By car

If you're traveling within the city, the wide expanses of Western Avenue are always the fastest way to reach Pilsen. Otherwise, use the **I-55** exit at Damen Avenue for Pilsen, and the Canalport left exit off of **I-90/94** to get to the arts district on Halsted.

See

Monday is the only day to avoid when visiting Pilsen, with both the National Museum of Mexican Art and the few non-appointment art galleries closed. Both halves of the neighborhood have annual open-doors festivals — see below.

West Pilsen

If you're walking down 18th Street from East Pilsen, it's at 18th and Racine that you'll begin to notice the change. Stores have cheerful skeletons in their windows, and inevitably some Spanish-language dance music is bumping off in the distance. By the time you reach 18th and Blue Island, take a break to enjoy the scene. Those are the speakers of community radio **WRTE** *www.wrte.org* broadcasting from the corner, across the street from the Rudy Lozano Library (see Contact). Welcome to West Pilsen.

Quite a lot of artists have studios in West Pilsen, but only the excellent **Prospectus Art Gallery** and the **A.P.O. Cultural Center** have regular open hours. Check there and at the cafes for information on exhibit openings.

A.P.O. Cultural Center, 1436 W 18th St (*18th Pink Line*), +1 773 780-1495, Hours vary. The enormous, foreboding stone edifice of the A.P.O. Building houses some worthwhile art exhibitions and the occasional concert along with community programs (such as the pool downstairs). Exhibits are usually free and open to all, but stern old ladies will keep you from wandering elsewhere.

CTA 18th Station, 1710 W 18th St (*18th Pink Line*), 4AM-1AM daily. Art and the CTA have had a bad relationship over the years, with relentlessly awful results nearly every time the CTA commissions a mural for a station or subway wall. This one, however, is a gem. The youth outreach efforts of the Museum of Mexican Art (below) and other community programs have borne fruit here, creating a walk from the station house to the platforms is nothing short of awe-inspiring (albeit distracting if you're in a hurry to catch a train). $2 to ride the train, free to view if getting off/back on a train.

National Museum of Mexican Art, 1852 W 19th St (*18th Pink Line*), +1 312 738-1503, *www.nationalmuseumofmexicanart.org*, Tu-Su 10AM-5PM, M closed. The National Museum of Mexican Art is a lovely, small gallery full of vibrant colors and well exhibited installations focused on understanding Mexican as well as Mexican-American history and culture through art. The museum serves as Pilsen's ground zero for the annual **Day of the Dead** celebration in the fall — this is a great time to visit to see all the brightly painted, skull-filled, and often humorous Ofrendas. Free.

Prospectus Art Gallery, 1210 W 18th St, +1 312 733-6132, W-Su 12-5PM. Fascinating exhibitions of modern and traditional Latin American art, about halfway between the East Pilsen galleries and the Mexican swing of West Pilsen. Free.

PILSEN SEE

St. Adalbert Church, 1650 W 17th St, +1 312 226-0340. Built in 1914 for the area's Polish community, St. Adalbert's still features murals of rousing crowd favorites like Queen Jadwiga's wedding and the time Our Lady of Czestochowa beat the hell out of some invading Swedes. It now includes a shrine in honor of Our Lady of San Juan de los Lagos and a few other touches for the Mexican Catholics who live in the neighborhood today.

St. Procopius Church, 1641 S Allport St, +1 312 226-7887, *www.stprocopius.com*. This towering stone church overlooking 18th Street was built in 1883 for the Czech Catholics in the area. Today, it's impressively weathered and gloomy from the street, but bright and austere if you manage a peek inside. Masses are held in English, Spanish, and Croatian.

Thalia Hall, 1215-25 W 18th St, +1 773 342-7430. This ornate former theater was built as a replica of an old opera house in Prague, and in its heyday served as the epicenter of Chicago Bohemian culture. Plays and operas were performed here, and much of the constitution of Czechoslovakia was drafted within these walls as well (at the end of World War I). Nearly a century later, after having served mainly as a residence for the local homeless, things seem to be looking up for Thalia Hall, with the hotly-anticipated **Ristorante Al Teatro** moving in.

East Pilsen

There's a DIY spirit in the East Pilsen art scene — almost everyone has a day job, so there are only a few galleries that can be visited without an appointment. The best time to visit is during the **2nd Fridays** (free, second Friday of each month, 6-10PM), when everyone opens up for browsing. The night often winds up at Skylark (see Bars).

Otherwise, Saturdays find plenty of galleries open — although some are listed as appointment only, there's a pretty good chance the owner will be there if he or she isn't working elsewhere.

The **Chicago Art District** *www.chicagoartsdistrict.org*, a subsidiary of the Podmajersky company, maintains a directory of the dozens of galleries in the area and their event openings. The building at 1932 South Halsted Street has the highest concentration of galleries, but only 4Art is at street level; for the others, you'll need to call up to the gallery for access.

Information Center, 1821 S Halsted St, +1 312 377-4444, *www.chicagoartsdistrict.org*, Open during 2nd Fridays, 6-10PM. This information center is located in the midst of things at 18th and Halsted, but it's only open to coincide with the 2nd Fridays Art Walk, so a stop to gather event cards at Kristoffer's Cafe (see Cafes) or in the lobby of the Pilsen East Center (1945 S Halsted) will be more informative on other days. Free.

Chicago Art Department, 1837

PILSEN

S Halsted St, +1 312 226-8601, *www.chicagoartdepartment.org*, By appointment. A showcase for eye-catching work by young and emerging artists, including students from local outreach programs. Video installations are a regular feature here. Free.

EXPgallery, 726 W 18th St, +1 847 217-7520, *www.expgallery.com*, Sa 12-4PM. Interactive exhibits in 2-D, 3-D, and 4-D media, with lots of color and perspective twists. Free.

Logsdon 1909 Gallery, 1909 S Halsted St, +1 312 666-8966, *www.logsdon1909.com*, Sa 12-5PM. Thought-provoking painting and sculpture on body images and abstract shapes, both by guest artists and the talented proprietor himself. Free.

Michelle Litvin Photography, 1827 S Halsted St, +1 312 421-9242, *www.michellelitvin.com*, By appointment. It's not easy to find this gallery open aside from the 2nd Fridays, but it's worth checking out if possible, as Litvin's images of eyes and inventive word-posters are some of the most striking work on Halsted. Free.

Oculus Gallery, 1900 S Halsted St, +1 312 226-3742, By appointment. Whether or not the gallery is open, the wide storefront windows ensure you'll be able to see an interesting collection of art here — sure, you might not be able to read the labels, but bowls of fruit literally bursting out of paintings tend to speak for themselves. Free.

The Watermark Gallery, 1839 S Halsted St, +1 312 455-9696, By ap-

pointment. As friendly a gallery as you'll find on Halsted — walk in and some jazz will be quickly cued up to accompany your visit. Exhibits focus mostly on photography, with some interesting sculpture as well. Hours are officially by appointment, but the owner is here whenever possible, so the doors are often open during the week. Free.

Do

EP Theater, 1820 S Halsted St (*Halsted Orange Line*), +1 312 850-4299, *www.eptheater.com*, Check website for schedule. Not easy to reach — the address says Halsted, but the entrance is behind the building, where the ramshackle exterior reveals a lovingly renovated theater space. Alone amid the row of art galleries, the EP Theater is an intimate (fifty seats), risk-taking showcase for new work by Chicago playwrights. The Tuesday Night Reading Series (7PM) is free. Most shows $15.

Harrison Park, 1824 S Wood St (*18th Pink Line*), +1 312 746-5491, *www.chicagoparkdistrict.com*. If you have kids in tow and they've been patient through the National Museum of Mexican Art (or they need to burn off some energy before going in), you might reward them with some monkey time right next door at Harrison Park, which has a big playlot with swings, slides, jungle gyms and more.

Meztli Galeria y Organizacion Cultural, 556 W 18th St, +1 312 738-0860, *www.meztli.net*, Hours vary. Home to art exhibitions and a performance space for several theater companies, both English and Spanish-language. Prices vary, $6-15.

South Halsted Gallery, 1825 South Halsted, 312-804-8962, *www.sohachicago.com*, by appointment. Exhibiting visionary works of art and connecting people with artists and their work. Open every Second Friday and by appointment.

Events & Festivals

Don't forget the **Second Fridays** every month in East Pilsen (above).

Mole de Mayo, 1800-1820 S Paulina, +1 312 733-2287, *www.eighteenthstreet.org*, 11AM-7PM. An annual *mole* cook-off and outdoor festival at the beginning of May. $1.

Pilsen East Artists Open House, Halsted, around 18th and 19th (*Halsted Orange Line*), +1 312 738-0786, *www.chicagoartsdistrict.org*, Last weekend of September. For more than 35 years, the Podmajersky properties in East Pilsen have opened their doors for an annual weekend-long festival of exploring galleries both open and nestled around hidden inner courtyards and sunken gardens.

Pilsen Open Studios, 18th, between Leavitt and Carpenter (*18th Pink Line*), +1 312 733-6132, *www.pilsenopenstudios.com*, Second weekend of October. West Pilsen's art studios open up for all to see, including many that aren't open any other time of year. Local

cafes and businesses get involved, and there's a free trolley on call for the route, too. A similar arts fest is often held in Little Village the same weekend.

Buy

Pilsen is a highly underrated shopping destination in Chicago, with several affordable and intriguing vintage stores on 18th.

Cooper Used Hotel Furniture, 1929 S Halsted St, +1 312 226-2299, M-Sa 8AM-6PM, Su 10AM-5PM. Only in the Pilsen arts district could you find a store this weird. While it has the trappings of a Situationist prank, this warehouse actually is in the business of selling used furniture and furnishings from old hotels. Beyond the beds, tables, and couches, you'll find stacks of identical cheap-ornate lamps and those familiar vague watercolor paintings. It's eerie, amazing, and quite often a great deal.

Golden Age, 1744 W 18th St (*18th Pink Line*), +1 312 850-2574, *www.goldenagestore.com*, Th-Su 12-6PM. Small-press art books & zines, both Pilsen-centric and otherwise.

Irv's Bike Shop, 1725 S Racine Ave, +1 312 226-6330, M-Tu,Th-F 10AM-7PM, Sa 10AM-6PM, W,Su closed. Pilsen is a serious bicycle neighborhood, and Irv's is a good place for repairs and accessories.

Liberia Girón, 1443 W 18th St (*18th Pink Line*), +1 312 226-2086, M-Sa 9AM-8PM, Su 10AM-6PM. A good collection of Spanish-language books, magazines, newspapers, and more, with occasional appearances by Spanish-speaking authors like Cubs pitcher Carlos Zambrano.

Mestiza, 1010 W 18th St, +1 312 563-0132, *www.mestizachicago.com*, Tu-Sa 11:30AM-7PM, Su 11:30AM-4:30PM, M closed. Nuevo Latino style boutique, mostly new and vintage clothing for women with some nifty accessories (including a special focus on Frida Kahlo jewelry) and a nice selection of Mexican wrestling masks for men.

Ochoa Sporting Goods, 1749 W 18th St (*18th Pink Line*), +1 312 829-9310, M-F 11AM-7PM, Sa 10AM-6PM, Su 10AM-3PM. There's Chicago-centric sports gear, too, but if you have a specific futbol jersey in mind, this is your best bet.

OMD, 1419 W 18th St (*18th Pink Line*), +1 312 563-9663, *www. omdchicago.com*, Tu-Sa 12-7PM, Su 12-5PM, M closed. Designer apparel, fragrances and style accessories for hipsters of the male and female persuasions, with t-shirts by local designers **Sharp Chicago** *www.sharp-chicago.com*.

Oxala, 1651 W 18th St (*18th Pink Line*), +1 312 850-1655, M-Sa 11AM-8PM, Su 11AM-2PM. Oxala is a botanica shop, selling herbs and religious items, but they also have stylish jewelry and artwork for sale — as well as a side trade in *consulte destinos*, for those who can't wait to find out.

The Rag Shop, 1112 W 18th St, +1 312 243-1724, M-Sa 11AM-8PM, Su sometimes open, sometimes closed. A small but colorful, happy-go-lucky vintage clothes boutique, with some curious eclectica toward the back.

Revolver Records, 1524 W 18th St, +1 312 226-4211, *www.myspace. com*, 12:30-8PM daily. Get your vinyl here. Revolver sells new and used records with a passion for soul, jazz, and old-skool & independent hip-hop. The screen-printed shirts are also worth checking out.

Under the Wire, 2210 S Halsted St, +1 312 733-9350, *www. underthewire.biz*, W-F 11AM-6PM, Sa 10AM-5PM. Intriguing jewelry and ceramics a couple blocks south of the East Pilsen galleries, worth a browse even if you're not planning to buy anything.

Zapatillas, 1421 W 18th St (*18th Pink Line*), +1 312 226-4040, M-F 10AM-8PM, Sa 10AM-6PM, Su 11AM-5PM. Upscale designer shoes and boots for women, with prices ranging from $50 to $500.

Eat

Pilsen restaurants aren't long for variety — there are cheap Mexican taquerías and bakeries, slightly more expensive taquerías, and dirt-cheap pizza joints. But they're authentic, cheap, and *really* good. (The taquerías, that is, not necessarily the pizza joints.)

Equally memorable Italian restaurants can be found a little west in the "Heart of Italy" block of Heart of Chicago.

PILSEN EAT

Budget

Carnitas Uruapan, 1725 W 18th St
(*18th Pink Line*), +1 312 226-2654,
M-W,F 8:30AM-5PM, Sa-Su 7AM-
6PM. The best carnitas (stewed
pork) around. (Kids will love the
cartoon pigs on the wall as long as
they don't connect them to what
they're eating.) The cactus salad
comes highly recommended, too,
but runs out early in the day. As
for the rest of the menu, well, you
either want a big sheet of fried
pork rinds or you don't, and nothing this guide tells you is going to
change your mind one way or the
other. $6.

El Paraiso Bakery, 1156 W 18th St,
+1 312 733-8616, 4AM-9PM daily.
Take-out only — that's because
walking into El Paraiso is like entering a huge, busy kitchen, with
towering stacks and tray after tray
of bread, buns, and cookies of all
kinds there for the taking. You'll
see determined local mothers and
grandmothers loading up in here,
so be careful not to get in their
way.

**Panaderia Tortilleria Nuevo Leon
Bakery**, 1634 W 18th St, +1 312
243-5977 , M-F 5:30AM-9PM, Sa-
Su 6AM-9PM. Tasty bakery run by
the Nuevo Leon family, who run
the fine restaurant a block down.
They serve Mexican bread, pastries, coffee, and other early morning essentials under the watchful
eye of a 1986-87 Chicago Bears
team poster. $1-4.

Sabas Vega, 1808 S Ashland Ave,
+1 312 666-5180, M-F 8AM-5PM,
Sa-Su 6AM-5PM. Another good
option for carnitas, with more

seating than Uruapan. If it's cold
outside, take note: they brag that
their cauldron runs at 266 degrees
Fahrenheit! $6.

Tacos Palas, 1700 S Halsted St, +1
312 733-0433, 7AM-8:30PM daily.
Tacos Palas is perhaps the best
taquería in Pilsen, so if you don't
intend to have a sit-down multi-
course meal, head straight here to
grab some dirt cheap, incredible
tacos. $1.50-4.

Taquería Los Comales #3, 1544 W
18th St (*18th Pink Line*), +1 312
666-2251, *www.loscomales.com*, Su-
Th 7:30AM-1AM, F-Sa 7AM-3AM.
A local chain that's almost certainly the quickest draw among
Pilsen taquerías, with food made
fresh and *very* fast, and served by
a friendly waitstaff. $5-8.

Mid-range

Cuernavaca Restaurant, 1160 W
18th St, +1 312 829-1147, 10AM-
midnight daily. One of the more
authentic Mexican restaurants in
Pilsen, with dishes ranging from
basic combination burrito platters to more interesting, obscure
dishes and great moles. The leafy
decor manages to be festive and
elaborate, without descending
into over-the-top Mexican camp
(even the Virgin Mary shrine).
There's a full bar for the latest
futbol. $10-15.

May St. Cafe, 1146 W Cermak Rd
(*18th Pink Line*), +1 312 421-4442,
www.maystcafe.com, Tu-Th 5PM-
10PM, F-Sa 5PM-11PM, Su 5PM-
9PM. This recent sensation offers Mexican, Cuban, Puerto Rican, and "traditional American"

fusion cuisine, served to a lively BYOB crowd. It's out of the way, but still within walking distance from the Pink Line. $12-32.

Mundial Cocina Mestiza, 1640 W 18th St, +1 312 491-9908, *www.mundialcocinamestiza.com*, 11AM-10:30PM. A lovely dining room for delicious, Mexican/Mediterranean-influenced cooking — one of the highlights of Pilsen cuisine. $12-38.

Perez Restaurant, 1163 W 18th St, +1 312 421-3631, M-Sa 6AM-8PM. Heaping plates of Mexican food and powerful margaritas, with outdoor seating when the weather permits. Not to mention easy parking; hard to come by with restaurants in the area. Get the Lime (limon) Margarita. You won't regret. $10-25.

Pizza Nova, 1842 W 18th St, +1 312 666-3500, Su-Th 11AM-midnight, F-Sa 11AM-1AM. Great stuffed pizza just across the park from the Museum of Mexican Art. $5-20.

Playa Azul 1, 1514 W 18th St (*18th Pink Line*), +1 312 421-2552, M-Th 8AM-midnight, F-Su 8AM-2AM. Family-run Mexican restaurant with high quality seafood dishes at prices no one else in the city can beat, and a mermaid emerging from the wall to bless the proceedings. $10-15.

Restaurante Nuevo Leon, 1515 W 18th St (*18th Pink Line*), +1 312 421-1517, 7AM-midnight daily. A nice family-run restaurant serving good, authentic Mexican food, including some excellent fish dishes

as well as superb tacos. Even if you're not hungry, stop by to have a look at the gorgeously painted building. $6-14.

Heart of Italy

These are tricky to reach, but if you like Italian food, it's well-worth the trip. Take the Pink Line to Western, walk a few blocks blocks south and then turn right to reach the 2400 South block of Oakley. The huge variable in the price of your meal is the kind of wine you choose.

Bacchanalia, 2413 S Oakley (*Western Pink Line*), +1 773 254-6555, *www.bacchanaliachicago.com*, M-Th 11AM-10PM, F 11AM-11PM, Sa 4-11PM, Su 3:30-9PM. A warm, old world atmosphere and a busy kitchen. $14-22.

Bruna's Ristorante, 2424 S Oakley (*Western Pink Line*), +1 773 254-5550, M-Th 11AM-10PM, F-Sa 11AM-11PM, Su 1-10PM. Opened in 1933, and currently owned by an immigrant from Siena in Tuscany, who brings that influence to some of the dishes served here. $16-25.

Haro, 2436 S Oakley (*Western Pink Line*), +1 773 847-2400, *www.harotapas.com*, Tu-Th 12-11PM, F 12PM-1AM, Sa 5PM-1AM. The anomaly on Oakley — a cafe/restaurant specializing in *pinxtos*, which are the Basque version of *tapas*. Sangria and flamenco dancing complement the food. Reservations recommended. $10-16.

PILSEN DRINK

Ignotz Ristorante, 2421 S Oakley (*Western Pink Line*), +1 773 579-0300, *www.ignotzschicago.com*, Tu-Th 11AM-9:30PM, F 11AM-11PM, Sa 4-11PM, Su 3-9PM. Thin-crust pizza, veal, and the straight-outta-*The Sopranos* exterior are the specials here. $11-24.

La Fontanella, 2414 S Oakley (*Western Pink Line*), +1 773 927-5249, M-F 11:30AM-10PM, Sa-Su noon-11PM. Since 1972. Dimly lit, with traditional Italian dishes and some creations of the chef. $18-28.

Miceli's Deli & Food Mart, 2448 S Oakley (*Western Pink Line*), +1 773 847-6873, M-F 8AM-4:30PM. The Sun-Times called it one of Chicago's 10 best delis. The meatballs and clams are true Italian, but people rave about the veggie sub. $4-8.

Drink

Pilsen is slowly building on its nightlife options, though most of these options cater to local hipsters and artists moving into the area. Aside from the options listed here, a few of the restaurants listed above have bars worthy of your drinking dollar, Cuernavaca in particular. Otherwise, you might head over to the Near West Side *p.215* on the 8 Halsted bus and booze it up there.

Cafes

Cafe Jumping Bean, 1439 W 18th St (*18th Pink Line*), +1 312 455-0019, M-F 6AM-10PM, Sa-Su 8AM-8PM. Reputation has it that this is Chicago's warmest and most inviting neighborhood coffee shop. It certainly lives up to the name: tiny, and always jumping with people. $2-6.

Cafe Mestizo, 1646 W 18th St (*18th Pink Line*), +1 312 421-5920, *www.cafemestizo.com*, M,Tu,Th,F 7AM-9:30PM, W 7:30AM-10PM, Sa-Su 9AM-8PM. Seldom will you find a coffee shop that uses its space so well — the walls of Cafe Mestizo hold large-scale work by local artists, plenty of seating, a computer for internet access, and a sit-down Ms. Pac Man machine. Sunday nights feature live jazz. $2-6.

Efebos, 1640 S Blue Island Ave (*18th Pink Line*), +1 312-633-9212, M-F 8:30AM-10PM, Sa 10AM-8PM. Spacious and well lit coffee shop that offers a nice alternative to the often cramped Cafe Jumping Bean. You can buy a single cup of coffee or homemade soup and sit for hours using their wi-fi. They have a wide variety of salads and sandwiches, and plenty of couches to park yourself in. The walls double as exhibition space for local artists. $2-6.

Kristoffer's Cafe and Bakery, 1733 S Halsted St, +1 312 829-4150, *www.kristofferscafe.com*, M-F 7:30AM-7PM, Sa 8AM-6PM, Su 8AM-4PM. Clearly designed with visitors from the arts district in mind, Kristoffer's has a warm, reasonably large space with a range of sandwiches, drinks, and baked goods. (They call their seven varieties of *tres leches* cakes a family specialty.) You'll find free wifi and event cards for *every* art opening in the area. Lunch $5-8.

Bars

Paulie's Place, 1750 S Union Ave, +1 312 829-7724, M-Sa 7AM-3AM, Su 11AM-2AM. Paulie's keeps long hours to serve two crowds: second-shift workers in the early morning, and the East Pilsen art crowd at night. The beer is cheap and so are the pool tables.

Simone's, 960 W 18th St, +1 312 666-8601, *www.simonesbar.com*, Su-F 11:30AM-2AM, Sa 11:30AM-3AM. A recent arrival to the Pilsen bar scene, owned and operated (much to the chagrin of those from whom the ever-rising cries of gentrification originate) by a Lincoln Park-based owner. Good food (especially the Mexican-influenced Pilsen Burger), but go for the beer: while their mixed drinks cost more than Skylark and aren't nearly as strong, they have an absolutely spectacular collection of beers on tap and in cans/bottles. That, and the decor is done out in this bizarre steampunk-pinball machine theme. They usually have really good DJs spinning on most nights and trivia nights on Tuesdays.

Skylark, 2149 S Halsted St, +1 312 948-5275, Su-F 4PM-2AM, Sa 4PM-3AM. Wicker Park ex-pats have made this bar their own, right at the southern edge of Pilsen and the gallery scene. From the outside, it looks like an old-man bar that's been prepped for use as a bunker during World War II, but on the inside there's an excellent selection of cheap beer, pinball, a photobooth, some of the strongest $5 mixed drinks you'll find anywhere in the city, and

tater tots — oh, delicious tater tots. If you have poor taste in movies, you might be delighted to hear that Skylark was featured prominently in the 2006 movie, *The Breakup.*

Sleep

Lugo Hotel, 2008 S Blue Island Ave, +1 312 226-5818. A reasonably safe transient hotel offering single occupancy rooms with shared bathrooms, communal kitchen and television area. The owners take pride in the community feel (watching Bears games together on Sundays, for example). $100/$300 weekly/monthly.

Contact

Many of the local cafes offer internet access — see above.

Rudy Lozano Branch Library, 1805 S Loomis St (*18th Street Pink Line*), +1 312 746-4329, *www. chipublib.org*, M-Th 9AM-9PM, F-Sa 9AM-5PM. Free public internet access.

Stay safe

Smash-and-grab robberies have been reported for cars parked in East Pilsen during the 2nd Fridays art walk, so park in a well-lit area if possible and take any valuables with you (or, better, leave them at your hotel). Many Chicago residents overstate the crime rate in Pilsen, but it still has some problems. After dark, stick with other people and be aware of your surroundings.

Get out

The majority of Chicago's Mexican-Americans live in Little Village *p.331* to the west and near Marquette Park and Back of the Yards on the Southwest Side *p.347*.

The other major gallery scenes are in River North *p.71* and the West Loop *p.215*, albeit with far higher rents. Pilsen's potential antecedent Wicker Park also has some small galleries worth notice, as does Rogers Park *p.291*. You'll find a gallery scene even further off the beaten path in Bridgeport *p.175*.

U ptown is a scruffy, jazz-inflected neighborhood on the north side of Chicago. Within its boundaries, off to the side of the action, are the residential areas of Sheridan Park and Buena Park, and an exciting Southeast Asian community based around Argyle Street.

This article also includes **Andersonville**, a short walk to the west, which is an upscale, lesbian-friendly neighborhood.

Understand

Uptown is the result of a divine message received by men with a tremendous amount of money in the early 1920s. Here, by the lake, there was to be an entertainment district of such magnificence that it would shift the entire center of Chicago to the north,

and within a few years, overtake even Manhattan for supremacy in the nation. Up went canyons of Art Deco magnificence: hotels, department stores, palaces of music and the arts; all in accord with the vision. Ever see a movie where cigar-chomping gangsters escort gorgeous molls into a damn good jazz club? That's **The Green Mill**. Where thousands of earnest teens dance their hearts out for a famous live radio broadcast? That's the **Aragon Ballroom**. And the crowning achievement was the **Uptown Theatre**, where every man could see a movie like a king.

But there was the small matter of the stock market crash in 1929. Right as Uptown was reaching its peak, new construction slammed to a halt and Uptown never recovered. Needing tenants, many buildings were carved up for low-income housing, and maintenance

273

was lowered to match the rent. There was still revelry, but it was seedier, and less of a destination for the fresh-faced teens of yesteryear. Unlike other parts of the city, which were reinvented by changing fortunes across the decades to come, Uptown stayed on the mat, beaten down by poverty.

At last, though, Uptown is reaping the rewards of that heritage. Years of cheap living created a diverse community that's still resident there today, highlighted by the amazing **Southeast Asian** pocket on Argyle between Sheridan and Broadway. (It's sometimes mistakenly known as "Little Saigon" or "North Side Chinatown," but it's too diverse for one label.) For the first time in decades, the entertainment district is growing again, with the survivors holding strong and joined by some great new options. In an area where a dilapidated pancake house from the 1950s still counts as new construction, the seedy atmosphere of Uptown can be absorbing like few others in the city, and makes for a memorable night out.

Andersonville hasn't experienced the highs or the lows of Uptown, and strikes a completely different vibe. Originally a hub for Swedish immigrants, whose influence can be seen in a few restaurants and bars, it became a hub for Chicago's lesbian community, and today has a less raucous atmosphere than the younger GLBT scene in Boystown *p.139*. The stylish boutiques and inviting restaurants have made it a great place for people of all back-

grounds to live, and a laid-back destination for shopping or entertainment, particularly at the **Neo-Futurarium**, Chicago's most inventive original theater.

Get in

By train

Uptown is well-served by public transportation from the center of the city, with all of the sights and nightlife within an easy walk of the train. The CTA **Red Line** runs from the Loop *p.47* through Uptown (Wilson, Lawrence, Argyle) and near Andersonville (Berwyn). These are some of the CTA's oldest and worst-kept stations, so accessibility for handicapped travelers will be a major issue — plan to connect a bus instead. (The Addison Red Line station in Wrigleyville *p.139* is the closest fully-accessible station.)

The walk from any of the Uptown Red Line stations to Clark Street and Andersonville is no real bother except in the winter, when you're better off waiting inside the station for a bus (see below).

By bus

22 Clark also runs all night on Clark Street from Edgewater *p.291* (to the north) and on to Lakeview *p.139* (to the south).

36 Broadway also runs from Edgewater *p.291* (to the north), passing by the concert venues and the Southeast Asian stores, and from there to eastern Lakeview *p.139*. It's only a half-block walk from the Red Line stops.

50 Damen runs along Damen from the Brown Line and Ashland, north of Foster, near the western edge of Andersonville.

78 Montrose connects with the Brown Line in North Center *p.139* and the Wilson Red Line in Uptown.

80 Irving Park runs along Irving Park. Connections can be made with the Irving Park Brown Line stops as well as the Sheridan Red Line.

81 Lawrence connects with the Red Line station of the same name and operates all night. You won't need the bus to reach the concert venues, but it does run through Albany Park *p.313* and to the Jefferson Park *p.363* Blue Line station.

92 Foster connects with the Red Line at Berwyn and is the best way to reach Andersonville from the train. It also ends up west at the Jefferson Park Blue Line station.

145 Wilson/Michigan Express runs all-stops as far west as Damen, connecting with the Ravenswood *p.313* Metra station, and then runs express on Lake Shore Drive to the Near North *p.71* and the Loop *p.47*.

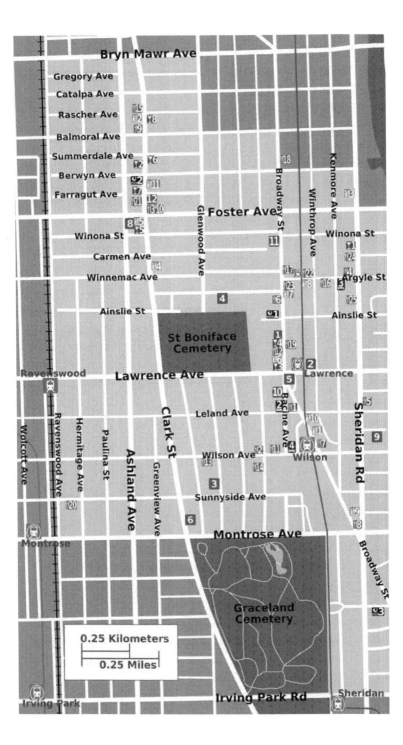

Uptown

■ See and Do

1. Annoyance Theater
2. Aragon Ballroom
3. Black Ensemble Theater
4. Essanay Studios
5. The Green Mill
6. Japanese American Service Community
7. Montrose Beach
8. The Neo-Futurarium
9. The People's Music School
10. The Riviera
11. South-east Asia Center
12. Swedish American Museum Center

▥ Buy

1. A-Z Wallis Army Navy Store
2. The Brown Elephant
3. Early to Bed
4. Foursided
5. Hip Fit

6. Shake, Rattle, & Read
7. Tai Nam Market Center
8. Tan Thana Gift Shop
9. The Tattoo Factory
10. Uptown Bikes
11. Women & Children First

▥ Eat

1. Agami
2. Alma Pita
3. Ann Sather's
4. Cafe Hoang
5. Cafe Too
6. Furama Restaurant
7. Gigio's
8. Grace African Restaurant
9. Hamburger Mary's
10. Jin Ju
11. Magnolia Cafe
12. Marigold Restaurant
13. Nigerian Kitchen
14. Palace Gate
15. Pasticceria Natalina
16. Pho 777
17. Pho Xe Tang
18. Sabai-dee
19. Silver Seafood
20. Spacca Napoli
21. Svea
22. Sun-Wah BBQ
23. Thai Avenue
24. Tweet...let's eat
25. Vinh Phat BBQ

Lake Shore Dr

Simonds Dr

Lincoln Park

Hazel St

Clarendon Ave

7

Buena Ave

Sidney R Marovitz Golf Course

▥ Drink

1. Big Chicks
2. Charlie's Ale House
3. Crew
4. Fat Cat Bar & Grill
5. Hopleaf
6. Kopi
7. Simon's Tavern
8. Star Gaze

■ Sleep

1. Chicago Lodge
2. Darlington Hotel
3. Northmere the SRO Hotel
4. Wilson Club Hotel

▣ Contact

1. Bezazian Library
2. Screenz
3. Uptown Library

UPTOWNSEE

By car

The best way to reach Uptown by car is the fabled **Lake Shore Drive**, which has exits at Wilson, Lawrence, Foster, and Bryn Mawr ending at Sheridan and Hollywood in Edgewater. Drive a few blocks west from any of these and you're at **Broadway**, the main street in Uptown.

Clark Street is the main drag for Andersonville, with a few sights on Ashland, a short walk to the west.

See

Uptown is rich with Art Deco buildings large and small, albeit in varying stages of preservation or neglect. The **Wilson Red Line** station is worth a look for the arch over the original entrance at the corner of Wilson & Broadway, into which a Popeye's Chicken has been incongruously crammed. Tourists who are crows will find this arch especially enjoyable, judging from the number of crows that spend time here. In much better shape is the **Bridgeview Bank Uptown** at Lawrence and Broadway, the tallest building in the area, with a well-kept green and white facade. The old Goldblatt's Department Store at 4718 N Broadway has been carefully renovated on the outside for a Borders bookstore. Back on the other end of the scale is the magnificent sandstone **Uptown Broadway Building** at 4707 N Broadway, crumbling and covered in netting for a possible (expensive) renovation.

Another worthy stroll for architecture enthusiasts is the **Hutchinson Street District** *www.ci.chi.il. us*, from 600-900 W Hutchinson, closer to the lake. It's the post-Mies apartment blocks that dominate the Uptown skyline from the lake, but Hutchinson has some lovely street-level Prairie School houses by George Maher.

Essanay Studios, 1333-45 W Argyle St (*Argyle Red Line*). From 1907-17, Hollywood was in Uptown. A dizzy list of silent movie giants shot films here, Charlie Chaplin and local girl Gloria

Swanson among them, and the city's awful winters played a part in shifting production to California for part of the year. When Chaplin left, the studio collapsed, and California started seeming more attractive year-round. The building is now a protected landmark, and houses the bi-lingual St Augustine College *www.staugustinecollege.edu*. No tours are available, but check out the grand name above the doorway.

Graceland Cemetery, 4001 N Clark St (*Sheridan Red Line*), +1 773 525-1105, *www.gracelandcemetery.org*, Grounds 8AM-4:30PM, office 8:30AM-4:30PM. A stunner. Chicago history lies in rest here, from the major names (Burnham, Sullivan, Field, Pullman, Mies) to the footnotes (Charles Dickens' obscure brother Augustus). Some credit Sullivan's 1890 design for the Getty Tomb as the opening act of modern architecture. (And Inez Clarke's grave is one of the most famous "haunted" spots in Chicago.) The new (and warm) office can supply a map for the grounds, which are quite large. Come with time to wander. Free.

Japanese American Service Committee, 4427 N Clark St (*22 Clark bus*), +1 773 275-0097, *www.jasc-chicago.org*, Hours vary. A social services agency for the Chicago Japanese community with occasional exhibits of interest, such as a collection of photos and art relating to internment camps during World War II. Festivals and cultural events also pop up from time to time.

South-east Asia Center, 5120 N Broadway St, 1124 W Ainslie (*Argyle Red Line*), +1 773 989-6927, *www.se-asiacenter.org*, M-F 8:30AM-5:30PM. Not a tourist sight, necessarily, but a center for the local South-east Asian community, young and old. Ten languages (besides English) are spoken by the staff. Volunteer opportunities like English teaching and elderly care abound.

Swedish American Museum Center, 5211 N Clark St (*Berwyn Red Line*), +1 773 728-8111, *www.samac.org/index1.html*, Tu-Fri 10AM-4PM, Sa-Su 11AM-4PM. Celebrates Swedish-American heritage and Swedish immigration in all its forms, including Buzz Aldrin's temporary immigration to the moon. $4 adults, $3 kids.

Do

Uptown has one of the best collections of concert venues in Chicago, most of which are renovated holdovers from the area's Roaring Twenties heyday.

One that *isn't* renovated is the huge **Uptown Theatre** *uptowntheatre.com* on Broadway. It was built by the Balaban and Katz movie kings in 1925 to be as lavish as possible, and when it opened, it was described as "an acre of seats in a magic city," second only to Radio City Music Hall in size. With the declining fortunes of the neighborhood, it was shuttered in the early 1980s, and has remained in limbo ever since; too expensive to demolish, but too expensive to fix. It could yet be restored, although it would be a difficult task, especially with the still-shaky state of the Uptown economy. Until something happens, the majestic facade and marquee will peer out over Broadway, eerie in the darkness.

Aragon Ballroom, 1106 W Lawrence Ave (*Lawrence Red Line*), +1 773 561-9500, *www.aragon.com*, Box office M-F 9AM-6PM. Built in 1926 with an interior that is meant to recreate a Spanish palace courtyard, the Aragon cost more than two million dollars at the time, and the well-preserved interior still has the otherworldly brilliance. It shifted from big-band sensation to prizefight arena and swinging mod disco, but it's been in good hands for more than thirty years now, as promoters for Latin dances and rock shows split nights of the week.

The Green Mill, 4802 N Broadway St (*Lawrence Red Line*), +1 773 878-5552, *www.greenmilljazz.com*, M-Sa noon-4AM, Su noon-4AM. Jazz and lots of it at this Uptown landmark, famously an old hangout of Al Capone (who's not, though, around as much as he used to be). Go on a Sunday evening for the **weekly poetry slam** *www.slampapi.com*. National talents Kurt Elling *www.kurtelling.com* and Patricia Barber *www.patriciabarber.com* perform on weekdays along with a few other excellent resident ensembles. Covers usually less than $10.

The Riviera, 4746 N Racine Ave (*Lawrence Red Line*), +1 773 472-

0449, *www.jamusa.com*, Box office opens when doors open for the night's show. Probably the only old Balaban and Katz movie palace that's still in full use as a nightly entertainment venue, mostly for all-ages punk and indie rock bands, but occasionally hip-hop as well. There are seats in the balcony, but the main floor is standing room only. Stay behind the rail to stay out of the mosh pit (should one begin).

Theaters

Annoyance Theater, 4840 N Broadway St (*Lawrence Red Line*), +1 773 561-4665, *www.annoyanceproductions.com*. The Annoyance began with the long-running *Co-ed Prison Sluts*, which set the tone for what followed: fun, original shows with equal parts ironic kitsch and cheerful shock, led by Mick Napier, who directed some of Second City's best shows. The Annoyance is also one of the major training centers for comedy students in Chicago. Tickets $5-$15.

Black Ensemble Theater, 4520 N Beacon St (*Wilson Red Line*), +1 773 769-4451, *www.blackensembletheater.org*, Sa 8PM, Su 3PM. Committed to building racial bridges through telling stories of African-American history to a cross-cultural audience. If that sounds stodgy, consider how they do it: recent productions have included *Memphis Soul*, a full-scale resurrection of the sound and story of Stax Records. $40.

Neo-Futurarium, 5153 N Ashland Ave (*Berwyn Red Line*), +1 773 275-5255, *www.neofuturists.org*, F-Sa 11:30PM, Su 7PM, closed last two weeks of December. Andersonville — and the second floor of the Nelson Funeral Home, to be precise — is the home of the long-running late-night show **Too Much Light Makes The Baby Go Blind** and its ever-changing menu of the funny, the profound, and the occasional tongue bath for a 20th century European ethos, intended to be accomplished within the confines of thirty plays in sixty minutes. Arrive early — people are turned away almost every week. No advance tickets; admission is $7 plus the roll of a six-sided die.

Other

Montrose Beach, 4400 N Lake Shore Dr (*Wilson Red Line*). Uptown got short-changed when it comes to beaches compared to its neighbors on the north and south, but this is what's there, a short walk east on Wilson. One bonus: it's officially Dog Friendly. The smaller **Foster Beach** is a few blocks north at 5200 N Lake Shore Drive.

The People's Music School, 931 W Eastwood Ave (*Argyle Red Line*), +1 773 784-7032, *www.peoplesmusicschool.org*, M-W,F 12-7:30PM, Th 12-8PM, Sa 9AM-3PM, Su closed. For a distinctly non-seedy music experience, try the kids-friendly classical and world music concerts at this community-based not-for-profit music school. Concerts free,

but donations welcome.

Andersonville

You'll find several cute, stylish clothes boutiques for women in Andersonville. With the number of cafes and bakeries sharing the streets, it's a great place to shop, stop, and shop again.

The Brown Elephant, 5404 N Clark St (*22 Clark bus*), +1 773 271-9382, *www.howardbrown.org*, 11AM-6PM. A thrift shop that makes a difference: All proceeds benefit the Howard Brown Health Center, a health care center that serves the needs of the LGBT community and the HIV/AIDS community in Chicago. The selection is more hit than miss, so it's worth a look.

Early to Bed, 5232 N Sheridan Rd (*Berwyn Red Line*), +1 773 271-1219, *www.early2bed.com*, Tu-Sa 12-9PM, Su noon-6PM, M closed. Lesbian-owned, female-oriented sex shop without the sleaze. They hold weekly workshops on topics ranging from erotic writing to strategies for, well, you know. Check the schedule on the website (mostly Tuesdays). Workshops are $15/$10 students, reservations required.

Foursided, 5061 N Clark St (*22 Clark bus*), +1 773 506-8300, *www.foursided.net*, M-F Noon-7PM, Sa 11AM-7PM, Sun Noon-5PM. An eclectic framing shop with a fun selection of cards, one-of-a-kind treasures, and found-art assemblages by the staff and local artists

281

UPTOWN BUY

that's worth a look.

Hip Fit, 1513 W Foster Ave (*22 Clark bus*), +1 773 878-4447, *www.hipfitandersonville.com*, Tu-F 11AM-7PM, Sa 11AM-6PM, Su 12-4PM. Denim boutique with retro and contemporary, standard and designer jeans, and an emphasis on "no attitude shopping." Plenty of accessories, too.

Shake, Rattle & Read, 4812 N Broadway St (*Lawrence Red Line*), +1 773 334-5311, 12-6PM. A pop culture emporium and a labor of love for the owners, this store has dense warrens of used paperbacks, pulp novels and vinyl records (78 and 45rpm), mostly jazz, with a sealed-in-plastic selection of memorable news magazines on the wall and porn magazines on a rack toward the back. If you want a peek into the heart of Uptown or just a paperback to last until your next stop, this is the place.

Women and Children First, 5233 N Clark St (*22 Clark bus*), +1 773 769-9299, *www.womenandchildrenfirst.com*, M-Tu 11AM-7PM, W-F 11AM-9PM, Sa 10AM-7PM, Su 11AM-6PM. This is one of the foremost feminist bookstores in the country, with more than 30,000 books and a regular schedule of events and author appearances. (Hillary Clinton is among the roster of guests.) If you have kids in tow, bring them to **Storytime** on Wednesday mornings (10:30-11AM).

Uptown

With the glory days of Goldlbatt's long past, Uptown isn't much of a destination for shopping — save, of course, for the Asian imports on and around Argyle.

A-Z Wallis Army Navy Store, 4647 N Broadway St (*Wilson Red Line*), +1 773 784-9140, *www.a1militarygear.com*, M-Th 9:30AM-5:45PM, F 9:30AM-6:45PM, Sa 9AM-5:45PM, Su 10AM-3:45PM. Has about a dozen names, but the idea remains the same: this is one of the oldest Army surplus stores in Chicago, and a pretty big one at that. It also doubles as a "discount department store," so there are some cheapster watches and the like.

Tai Nam Market Center, 4925 N Broadway St (*Argyle Red Line*), +1 773 275-5666, *www.tainammarket.com*, Hours vary by store. Under the red arch on Broadway near Argyle, this strip mall has outlets for Vietnamese, Chinese & Thai restaurants and groceries, nail & skin care, and imported jewelry, music and videos.

Tan Thana Gift Shop, 1135 W Argyle St (*Argyle Red Line*), +1 773 275-8687, M-F 9AM-6PM, Sa-Su 9:30AM-6PM. Packed to the rafters with statues, pottery, and other Asian gift items. **Trung Tin**, a block east at 1057 W Argyle, also has a big selection.

The Tattoo Factory, 4441 N Broadway St (*Wilson Red Line*), +1 773 989-4077, *www.tattoofactory.com*, 10AM-2AM. Uptown after dark is the kind of place that inspires a tattoo (or a piercing). According to the owners, this is the oldest continually operating tattoo parlor in Chicago.

Uptown Bikes, 4653 N Broadway St (*Wilson Red Line*), +1 773 728-5212, M-F 11AM-7PM, Sa-Su 11AM-5PM, W closed. If you're biking through Chicago, this is a great place for parts, accessories, or quick repair. There are some neat custom bikes for sale, but no rentals.

Eat

Budget

Asian

Argyle is the wonderland. The Red Line drops you right in the midst of it — three blocks, from Sheridan to Broadway, of cheap and delicious Asian food. If you believe in eating where the locals eat, Argyle is most certainly the place to go; this is authentic cooking, with no tourist traps to be found. Vietnamese restaurants and bakeries are the most plentiful, with various disciplines of Chinese food a respectable second, and Thai dishes included on the menus of several non-Thai restaurants. Happily, there's a Laotian option in the neighborhood as well.

Cafe Hoang, 1010 W Argyle St (*Argyle Red Line*), +1 773 878-9943, 9AM-11PM. It's at the far end of the block, but Cafe Hoang is worth the walk. The menu features several pages of Vietnamese options and a page of Thai. The

portions are generous, the food is flavorful, and it's hard to resist spending a while. They make a mean durian smoothie. $8-$12.

Dong Thanh, 4925 N Broadway St (*Located in Tai Nam Market Center*), +1 773 275-4928, M 8AM-4PM, Tu-Su 8AM-8PM. BYOB restaurant named for the city by the same name in Vietnam. They take pride in customizing spice levels to suit your taste. $6-$8.

Furama Restaurant, 4936 N Broadway St (*Argyle Red Line*), +1 773 271-1161, *www.furamachicago.net*, Su-Th 9:30AM-9:30PM, F-Sa 9:30AM-10PM. Dim sum, Mandarin, and Cantonese in comparatively palatial second-floor digs. Furama is the biggest and has the most conventional menu of the Argyle Asian restaurants, but that doesn't mean it isn't good. $8-$10.

Pho 777 (House of Noodle), 1065 W Argyle St (*Argyle Red Line*), +1 773 561-9909, M,W-Th 9:30AM-10PM, F-Su 9AM-10PM. Pho is widely available on Argyle, but it's a serious matter in the two big, green rooms of the House of Noodle. Pho supremacy between this and Tank Noodle below is a hot topic of local debate. BYOB. $5-10.

Pho Xe Tang (Tank Noodle Restaurant), 4953 N Broadway St (*Argyle Red Line*), +1 773 878-2253, M-Tu,Th-Sa 8:30AM-10PM, Su 8:30AM-9PM. Pleasant, tourist-friendly restaurant that serves a suitably wide range of variations on pho and a few other Vietnamese and Chinese dishes, right on the corner of Argyle and

Broadway. $5-$12.

Sabai-dee, 5359 N Broadway St (*Berwyn Red Line*), +1 773 506-0880, 10AM-8PM. About three blocks north of Argyle, Sabai-dee is Chicago's one and only Laotian restaurant. There are a few Chinese and Vietnamese stand-bys to fill out the menu, but it's the Lao sausage and curry that make this place special. $5-8.

Sun-Wah BBQ, 1134 W Argyle St (*Argyle Red Line*), +1 773 769-1254, Su-W 9AM-9PM, F-Sa 9AM-9:30PM. Among the top culinary treasures on Argyle. Where others might bother with plants, Sun-Wah keeps a few rows of roast birds in the front window. The duck is obviously the headliner, but the pork earns acclaim as well. Order the duck from the to-go window and get a cheaper, more delicious, option. $8-$10.

<eat name="Hon Kee" alt="" address="1064 W Argyle St" directions="Argyle Red Line" hours="W-M 9AM-9PM" is another good place for Chinese BBQ.</eat>

Thai Avenue, 4949 N Broadway St (*Argyle Red Line*), +1 773 878-2222, M-Th 11AM-9:30PM, F-Sa 11AM-10PM, Su 11AM-9PM. Features the longest Thai-language menu in the area. They have popular lunch specials. $6-8.

Thai Pastry, 4925 N Broadway St (*Located in Tai Nam Market Center*), +1 773 784-5399, *www.thaipastry.com*, Su-Th 11AM-10PM, F-Sa 11AM-11PM. Inside the Tai Nam Market Center, this is a Thai bakery with a nice sit-down

area to relax over coffee, although they do have a full lunch and dinner menu. $8-$10 (meal).

Vinh Phat BBQ, 4940 N Sheridan Rd (*Argyle Red Line*), +1 773 878-8688, 9AM-7PM daily. There are two sides to this Vietnamese BBQ: birds and bread. The baguettes are priced at a very Vietnam-like three-for-$1, while the BBQ'd birds get chopped up into *banh mi* sandwiches. $1-6.

Other

Cheap fast food can be found around the Wilson Red Line station, but there are several better options for eating well on a budget.

Alma Pita, 4600 N Magnolia Ave (*Wilson Red Line*), +1 773 561-2787, M-F 11AM-9PM, Sa 11AM-8PM, Su closed. Mom & Pop Middle Eastern, Lebanese and Indian restaurant. There's a $5 vegetarian special, and the tilapia fish curry is a house specialty. $4-9.

Gigio's, 4643 N Broadway St (*Wilson Red Line*), +1 773 271-2273, Su-Th 9AM-midnight, F-Sa 9AM-2AM. *Really* good greasy thin-crust pizza by the slice — never mind the way the place looks. It's open late in case you're hungry after a show at the Green Mill, the Aragon or the Riviera on the other side of the tracks. $2.50-13.

Grace African Restaurant, 4409 N Broadway St (*Wilson Red Line*), +1 773 271-6000, *graceafrican.com*, M-Sa 12:30PM-midnight, Su 12-10PM. The menu isn't long, but

UPTOWNEAT

this friendly, authentic Ghanaian restaurant has a great atmosphere and the best decor in the area. $8-$10.

Nigerian Kitchen, 1363 W Wilson Ave (*Wilson Red Line*), +1 773 271-4010, M-Sa 11AM-10PM, Su closed. Not much for atmosphere, with a loud television hanging over the sparsely decorated dining area, but it's one of Chicago's few sources for yam-heavy Nigerian food, and BYOB too. $4-11.

Palace Gate, 4548 N Magnolia Ave (*Wilson Red Line*), +1 773 769-1793, M-W 10AM-8PM, Th-Su 10AM-9PM. In Ghana, it's considered a taboo to eat in public without inviting others to join you, so don't come to Palace Gate looking for solitude with your *fufu* dumplings. The decor is plastic and basic, but the atmosphere is merry. $8-$10.

Svea, 5236 N Clark St (*22 Clark bus*), +1 773 275-7738, M-F 7AM-2:30PM, Sa-Su 7AM-3:30PM. Swedish breakfast spot with renowned lingonberry pancakes. $4-9.

Mid-range

Ann Sather, 5207 N Clark St (*22 Clark bus*), +1 773 271-6677, *annsather.com*, M-F 7AM-2PM, Sa-Su 7AM-4PM. Chicago's most popular Swedish chainlet has to get a mention in formerly Swedish Andersonville. The weekend brunch lines can be long, but see if you're sorry when the homemade cinnamon rolls arrive. $10-$14.

Cafe Too, 4715 N Sheridan Rd (*Berwyn Red Line*), +1 773 275-0626, *www.cafetoo.org*, M 7AM-10AM, Tu-W 7AM-3PM, Th-F 7AM-9PM, Sa 9AM-9PM, Su 9AM-3PM. Cafe Too has the longest lines you'll find in Uptown, and that's for a good reason: everything on the menu is prepared and served by former homeless people in a culinary training program. It's organized through the **Inspiration Cafe** *www.inspirationcorp.org* at 4554 N Broadway, which is a great place to volunteer for a day. $9-$17, BYOB.

Hamburger Mary's, 5400 N Clark St (*22 Clark bus*), +1 773 784-6969, *www.hamburgermaryschicago. com*, Daily 11am-11pm. Legendary burgers, fried twinkies and plenty more. $8-12.

Jin Ju, 5203 N Clark St (*22 Clark bus*), +1 773 334-6377, Su,Tu 5-10PM, W-Th 5-10:30PM, F-Sa 5-11PM. Possibly the only Korean food in Chicago outside of Seoul Drive. Seafoodies and vegetarians will do equally well; if unsure, try the *bulgogi*, and resolve all of life's other uncertainties with a round or two of *soju*. $12-$20.

Pasticceria Natalina, 5406 N Clark St (*22 Clark bus*), +1 773 989-0662, Tu-F 7AM-6PM, Sa-Su 8AM-5PM. Sicilian bakery with a devoted following. The prices are steep ($3 for a cannoli), but people leave satisfied.

Silver Seafood, 4829 N Broadway St (*Argyle Red Line*), +1 773 784-0668, 11AM-1AM. Hong Kong-style seafood, some of which comes out of the tank at the back of the banquet-style dining room. Whether this meal is a mid-range or a splurge depends on how deep into the Chinese-only menu you'd like to go. It's just down the block from the Argyle Asian restaurants. $6-58.

Tweet...let's eat, 5020 N Sheridan Rd (*Argyle Red Line*), +1 773 728-5576, *www.tweet.biz*, W-M 9AM-3PM. Brunch only, with organic materials. Try the quiche platter ($14) or the lox ($12). Free wi-fi and parking.

Splurge

Hopleaf in Andersonville (see Drink) deserves consideration for anyone looking for a terrific meal (with beer included).

Agami, 4712 N Broadway St (*Lawrence Red Line*), +1 773 506-1845, *www.agamisushi.com*, M-Th 5PM-midnight, F-S 5PM-2AM; Su 5PM-10:30PM. Sushi, maki, and cooked Japanese fare that lives up to the prices and fancy decor. There's a full bar, and a $15 corkage fee per bottle of wine will apply for BYOB. $16-$30.

Magnolia Cafe, 1224 W Wilson Ave (*Wilson Red Line*), +1 773 728-8785, *www.magnoliacafeuptown.com*, Tu-Th 5:30-10:30PM, F-Sa 5:30-11:30PM, Su 10AM-3PM, 5-9PM. Upscale bistro with the warm decor, live jazz, varied menu and valet parking worthy of stretching your budget. $14-$32.

Marigold Restaurant, 4832 N Broadway St (*Lawrence Red Line*), +1 773 293-4653, *www.marigoldrestaurant.com*, Su,Tu-Th 5:30-10PM, F-Sa 5:30-11PM. If you're in the area for a concert or a show, this stylish new Indian restaurant has earned good notices and has a great location, although it also has much higher bills than the Indian restaurants on nearby Devon Avenue in West Rogers Park. $22-$30.

Spacca Napoli, 1769 W Sunnyside Ave (*Montrose Brown Line*), +1 773 878-2420, *spaccanapolipizzeria.com*, Lunch W-Sa 11:30AM-3PM, dinner W-Th 5-9PN, F-Sa 5-10PM, Su 12-9PM, closed M-Tu. If you're weary of the pizza struggle between Chicago and NYC, side with the Sicilians at this fantastic Neapolitan restaurant and their excellent wine list. $15-25.

Drink

Cafes

Kopi, 5317 N Clark St (*Berwyn Red Line*), +1 773 989-5674, Open M-Th 8AM-11PM, F 8AM-midnight, Sa 9AM-midnight, Su 10AM-11PM. Describes itself as "a traveler's cafe." In practice, it's a relaxed coffee shop of the early 1990s vintage, with earthy decor and earnest staff.

Bars

If you're looking for a drink in Uptown, don't forget to raise a glass at the **Green Mill** (above).

Big Chicks, 5024 N Sheridan Rd (*Argyle Red Line*), *www.bigchicks.com*, Open 4PM (3PM Sa). Gay-friendly bar in Uptown, with a dance floor, plenty of food, and a

fine beer garden.

Charlie's Ale House, 5308 N Clark St (*22 Clark bus*), +1 773 751-0140, *www.charliesalehouse.com*, Su-Th 11:30AM-1AM, F-Sa to 2AM. Beer, steaks and upscale bar food in Andersonville.

Crew, 4804 N Broadway St (*Lawrence Red Line*), +1 773 784-2739, *www.worldsgreatestbar.com*, M-F 11:30AM-2AM, Sa-Su 11AM-2AM. Gay sports bar & grill — check the "I Love Tight Ends" t-shirts on the bar staff. It's a great place to watch a game, and parties are ready to erupt on Friday and Saturday nights. Good food, too.

Fat Cat Bar & Grill, 4840 N Broadway St (*Lawrence Red Line*), +1 773 506-3100, *www.fatcatbar.com*, M-F 4PM-2AM, Sa noon-3AM, Su noon-2AM. Brand new and very popular, with decor and cocktails that attempt to evoke the Art Deco class of the original Uptown.

Hopleaf, 5148 N Clark St (*Berwyn Red Line*), +1 773 334-9851, *www. hopleaf.com*, M-F 3PM-2AM, Sa noon-3AM, Su noon-2AM. Fantastic selection of beer, with a surprisingly accessible menu for delving into the world of Belgians and local microbrews. The food is great, especially the steamed mussels, but the beer is even better. It's pricey, though. Make sure to come early, The Hopleaf is popular and usually packed. The monthly **Bookslut Reading Series** *www.bookslut.com* is held upstairs.

Simon's Tavern, 5210 N Clark St (*22 Clark bus*), +1 773 878-0894, Su-F 11AM-2AM, Sa 11AM-3AM. Simon's has roots as a Prohibition-era speakeasy and a Swedish hangout (from which, rumor has it, Norwegians were barred). Today, there's cheap beer on tap and vikings among the unpretentious decor.

Star Gaze, 5419 N Clark St (*22 Clark bus*), +1 773 561-7363, *www.stargazechicago.com*, Tu-F 6PM-2AM, Sa 5PM-3AM, Su 11:30AM-2AM, M closed. Glittery lesbian & gay dance club. Fridays are salsa, Saturdays are old school hip hop, and Sundays are given for the Chicago Bears to inspire karaoke of triumph or misery.

Sleep

Don't book a room in Uptown with expectations of that old swingin' class — most of these rooms are used by transients and homeless people getting back on their feet, and should only be considered by travelers as rock-bottom budget options. Nearby Edgewater *p.291* has a few nice, gay-friendly B&Bs, though.

Budget

Darlington Hotel, 4700 N Racine Ave (*Lawrence Red Line/Wilson Red Line*), +1 773 561-1741. On a residential street, a short walk from the Green Mill, the Riviera, and other Uptown music venues. Rooms vary — some have sinks, some have baths, other have neither. $35 per night with a $30 key deposit.

Northmere the SRO Hotel, 4943 N Kenmore Ave (*Argyle Red Line*), +1 773 561-4234. Close to Uptown and the lake. Rooms are furnished and include refrigerators; no kitchen facilities, although residents are allowed to rent microwaves. Monthly rates only. $380/month with a same-sex shared bath, $415/month for a private bath.

Wilson Club Hotel, 1124 W Wilson Ave (*Wilson Red Line*), +1 773 784-0691. Nestled between storefronts in the dingy heart of Uptown, close to the CTA station, this hotel offers only a bed. It's for men only. $65 per week, $202 per month, with a $15 key deposit.

Mid-range

Chicago Lodge, 920 W Foster Ave (*Argyle Red Line*), +1 773 334-5600. Offers wireless internet and free parking. Ideal location for exploring the Southeast Asian restaurants and stores on Argyle, and close to the lake as well. $87 for one bed, $99 for two, $133 for whirlpool suites.

Contact

Libraries

Bezazian Branch Library, 1226 W Ainslie St (*Argyle Red Line*), +1 312 744-0019, *www.chipublib.org*, M-Th 9AM-8PM, F-Sa 9AM-5PM, Su closed. Just off Broadway, a quick walk from the Southeast Asian restaurants.

Uptown Branch Library, 929 W Buena Ave (*Sheridan or Wilson Red Line*), +1 312 744-8400, *www.chipublib.org*, M-Th 9AM-8PM, F-Sa 9AM-5PM, Su closed. Free public internet access.

Internet cafes

The Food Mart at the corner of Wilson and Magnolia has a few internet terminals amid the usual convenience store ambiance.

Screenz, 5212 N Clark St (*Berwyn Red Line*), +1 773 334-8600, *www.screenz.com/screenz*, Open daily, 9AM-midnight. Full-service internet cafe in Andersonville.

Stay safe

Andersonville is safe more or less around the clock, as long as you use basic city common sense. Uptown can be a risky proposition after dark, though, especially near Wilson Avenue. You'll be fine walking between the concert venues to the CTA, but save any architecture walks for earlier in the day. A lot of transients and homeless people live in Uptown, where there are some drug/alcohol rehab centers. So while the overall crime rate is not high compared to some other parts of the city, it's advisable to be aware of your surroundings, even in daylight.

Get out

If it's jazz history that brought you here, don't forget Bronzeville *p.191*, which in its day was home to Louis Armstrong and Chicago jazz in its golden age. If you care less about the history, however, and just want to hit the current top jazz clubs, head down to the Velvet Lounge in the Near South *p.95*, which should not disappoint.

For a more expensive theater experience, the prices rise as you head south through Lakeview *p.139* and Old Town *p.123*.

If the GLBT scene in Andersonville leaves you wanting more, head south on Clark and then a couple blocks east towards Boystown *p.139*.

If you had a good time on Argyle, the Red Line can take you straight to Chinatown *p.175* on the South Side.

R ogers Park is the northern border of Chicago — the wild-eyed inheritor of un-inhibited lakefront, swamps become beaches, and the beauty of Chicago bricks. There may be no better place to experience the casual riches the city has to offer, with several miles of parks and beaches, and quiet blocks of breathtaking apartments and homes.

This article also includes **Edge-water**, the more reasonable counterbalance to its neighbor (fewer calamities, and a few terrific bars), and **West Ridge**, home to several ethnic communities, including nearly a mile of great Indian restaurants and stores.

Understand

When Philip Rogers arrived in Chicago for the first time in 1834, he immediately began making plans to leave. There was mud everywhere, the narrow streets were choked and chaotic, and the winters were brutal. But he was stuck in Chicago because the waterways back to New York were frozen, so Rogers had to wait out the winter; by the spring, he had a line on a pretty good team of oxen, so he headed as far north as he could, past the limits of the city and its fringe settlements, out to wild swampland where Indian villages were still resident — and there began **Rogers Park**.

The nature of Rogers Park is calamity amid beauty and the equality of impulse toward each. In this way, many of the neighborhood's key events can be understood: the secession of the **West Ridge** area (sometimes called West Rogers Park) over whether to incorporate as a village (which they did anyway); the 1894 "Home-Made Transfer War," in which Rogers Park residents stuck it to railroad tycoon Charles Yerkes by refusing to pay extra to ride the northern extension of his streetcar line, and tried to pass off the transfers they'd made at home on the conductors; and the "Cabbage Head War" of 1896, in which a Rogers Park politician gave unsophisticated West Ridge farmers an unflattering nickname, and they proved him wrong by putting cabbages on poles and marching on his house.

With regular floods from the wild and swampy beaches to the east, annexation to Chicago and its sewage services proved a strong temptation. As the city surged north, a building boom followed, and Rogers Park was blessed with a gorgeous stock of residential and commercial buildings; West Ridge wound up with long blocks of lovely, modest Prairie-style bungalows. Only one famous name is still in the area (Frank Lloyd Wright's **Emil Bach House**), but the routine beauty of the architecture in Rogers Park and West Ridge is still incredible.

The diversity, too, is unrivaled in a notoriously segregated city. Rogers Park has always been the most beautiful place in Chicago where basically anyone could afford to live — silent Irish generations still fighting the Cabbage Head War in their sleep, and immigrants newly arrived from Ser-

bia, from Jamaica, from the Sudan. For a visitor, special mention has to go to the Indian community on **Devon Avenue**. Between roughly 2200 W and 2700 W Devon, among thriving import stores that specialize in saris, spices, and the latest Bollywood dreams, there are a number of amazing Indian and Pakistani restaurants that will almost certainly spoil you for the stuff back home (assuming "back home" is anywhere but the Indian subcontinent). The only day *not* to go is Tuesday, when many businesses and restaurants are closed.

Edgewater, on the other hand, is remarkably laid-back. It was originally demarcated as part of the Uptown *p.273* community area, but when that area went into economic decline, Edgewater residents swiftly seceded and established their own neighborhood. Today, it segues neatly into Andersonville to the south, with a few gay cultural institutions and several nice restaurants, coffee shops and bars.

Get in

By train

The CTA **Red Line** runs from the Loop *p.47* to Edgewater (Bryn Mawr, Thorndale, Granville) and Rogers Park (Loyola, Morse, Jarvis), eventually terminating at Howard Street on the border of Evanston. (There is a major bus terminal adjacent to the Howard station — see below.) The dilapidated, urine-soaked Morse and Jarvis are two of the worst stations on the CTA map. Travelers with disabilities should plan to disembark at Howard, Loyola or Granville and use a bus to cover any remaining distance to their destinations.

The CTA **Purple Line** runs from Evanston to Howard, continuing non-stop southward to the Belmont station in Lakeview *p.139* during weekday rush periods. The CTA Yellow Line from Skokie ends at Howard.

The Metra *www.metrarail.com* **Union Pacific North Line** stops in Rogers Park (at Lunt Ave) before moving on to Evanston. Not every train serves that station, though, so check signs or schedules before boarding.

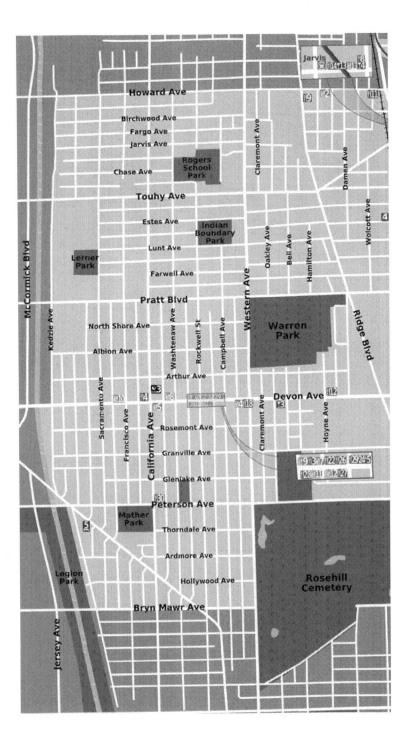

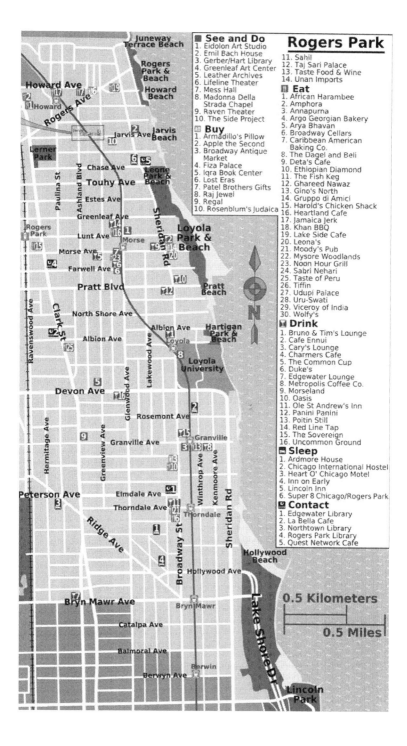

Rogers Park

■ See and Do
1. Eidolon Art Studio
2. Emil Bach House
3. Gerber/Hart Library
4. Greenleaf Art Center
5. Leather Archives
6. Lifeline Theater
7. Mess Hall
8. Madonna Della Strada Chapel
9. Raven Theater
10. The Side Project

■ Buy
1. Armadillo's Pillow
2. Apple the Second
3. Broadway Antique Market
4. Fiza Palace
5. Iqra Book Center
6. Lost Eras
7. Patel Brothers Gifts
8. Raj Jewel
9. Regal
10. Rosenblum's Judaica
11. Sahil
12. Taj Sari Palace
13. Taste Food & Wine
14. Unan Imports

■ Eat
1. African Harambee
2. Amphora
3. Annapurna
4. Argo Georgian Bakery
5. Arya Bhavan
6. Broadway Cellars
7. Caribbean American Baking Co.
8. The Dagel and Beli
9. Deta's Cafe
10. Ethiopian Diamond
11. The Fish Keg
12. Ghareeb Nawaz
13. Gino's North
14. Gruppo di Amici
15. Harold's Chicken Shack
16. Heartland Cafe
17. Jamaica Jerk
18. Khan BBQ
19. Lake Side Cafe
20. Leona's
21. Moody's Pub
22. Mysore Woodlands
23. Noon Hour Grill
24. Sabri Nehari
25. Taste of Peru
26. Tiffin
27. Udupi Palace
28. Uru-Swati
29. Viceroy of India
30. Wolfy's

■ Drink
1. Bruno & Tim's Lounge
2. Cafe Ennui
3. Cary's Lounge
4. Charmers Cafe
5. The Common Cup
6. Duke's
7. Edgewater Lounge
8. Metropolis Coffee Co.
9. Morseland
10. Oasis
11. Ole St Andrew's Inn
12. Panini Panini
13. Poitin Still
14. Red Line Tap
15. The Sovereign
16. Uncommon Ground

■ Sleep
1. Ardmore House
2. Chicago International Hostel
3. Heart O' Chicago Motel
4. Inn on Early
5. Lincoln Inn
6. Super 8 Chicago/Rogers Park

■ Contact
1. Edgewater Library
2. La Bella Cafe
3. Northtown Library
4. Rogers Park Library
5. Quest Network Cafe

0.5 Kilometers

0.5 Miles

By bus

11 Lincoln/Sedgwick travels Lincoln Avenue and then cuts over to Kedzie through West Ridge, passing by the Lincoln Village shopping mall.

22 Clark runs all night along on Clark Street through Rogers Park and Edgewater, and on to Andersonville *p.273*, Lakeview *p.139*, and the rest of the North Side.

36 Broadway runs through Edgewater and on to Uptown *p.273*, connecting with the Red Line at Granville.

49 Western stops on Devon in the midst of the Indian restaurants and stores and continues all the way up to Howard Street and the Evanston border.

96 Lunt connects with the Morse Red Line near the lake and the Rogers Park Metra station further west.

97 Skokie runs from the Howard CTA Station through south Evanston & Skokie, connecting with the CTA Yellow Line and ending at the Old Orchard Shopping Center.

147 Outer Drive Express runs express on Lake Shore Drive to and from the Magnificent Mile *p.71*, becoming all-stops for Edgewater and Rogers Park.

151 Sheridan is also an express from downtown, running all-stops down Sheridan Road. It's an all-night route.

155 Devon connects with both the Morse and Loyola Red Line stations, and travels through the length of the Indian neighborhood on Devon.

Several PACE suburban routes depart from the Howard Street bus terminal.

215 Crawford-Howard runs west down Howard Street, ending up at the Old Orchard shopping complex in Skokie.

290 Touhy travels through the Orthodox Jewish community in West Ridge, crossing into the suburbs and later back to the Far Northwest Side *p.363*.

By car

The best way to reach Edgewater and Rogers Park by car is the fabled **Lake Shore Drive**, which ends at Sheridan and Hollywood in Edgewater. The **Edens Expressway** has exits at Peterson and Touhy just west of the two neighborhoods.

The intersection of Sheridan and Devon can be confusing if you're trying to follow directions. Coming from Rogers Park, although it looks as though Sheridan continues south past Devon, that's where it becomes Broadway; Sheridan actually veers left at that point and then right along the lake. From the other direction, this is the eastern border of Devon Avenue, even though it looks like it continues further east — that's where the Sheridan name has taken over.

Parking is generally no problem in Edgewater and West Ridge, but Rogers Park is never easy. Watch for permit-only streets near Loyola University, and check street signs on Sheridan before parking overnight there. They're usually full, but there are meter parking lots near the beach at the end of Touhy and between Lunt & Greeleaf, and on the western side of the L tracks on Glenwood.

See

The **Glenwood Avenue Arts District** is a nice idea that someone had at some point, and it's still optimistically advertised by banners up and down the street (between Pratt and Touhy), but there isn't much going on. Most of the storefronts are vacant (or appear to be). Occasional group shows are held at the **Eidolon Art Studio** *www. eidolonartstudio.com* (7001 N Glenwood Ave) and the **Greenleaf Art Center** *www.greenleafartcenter.com* (1836 W Greenleaf).

For a better check on the artistic pulse of Rogers Park, check out the block-long concrete bench between Pratt Beach and Loyola Beach (facing the lake and the jogging trail), which is divided up into short segments and repainted every year by members of the community and a few local businesses, musing on the neighborhood, the city, outer space, and whatever else is on their minds — a good mix of the memorable and the inexplicable.

Emil Bach House, 7415 N Sheridan Rd (*Jarvis Red Line*). This is the only survivor of the two homes Frank Lloyd Wright built in Rogers Park, commissioned by a

local brick magnate. (And Chicago is a good place to be in the brick business.) After years of neglect, a new owner has scrupulously restored the house, but it's not open for tours — you'll have to content yourself with exterior views of the home's late Prairie School style, and the ingenuity of Wright's design that copes with the small lot and the busy street facing the house.

Gerber/Hart Library, 1127 W Granville Ave (*Granville Red Line*), +1 773 381-8030, *www.gerberhart.org*, W-Th 6-9PM, F-Su noon-4PM. A private, non-profit library spanning a couple of storefronts next to the train station, with 14,000 books, 800 periodicals, and extensive archives on GLBT issues. Reading groups for men and women are held here, as is Cinema Lesbiana and other events. Call or write ahead for access to the archives or special research requests. Free.

Leather Archives and Museum, 6418 N Greenview Ave (*Loyola Red Line*), +1 773 761-9200, *www.leatherarchives.org*, Th-F 11AM-7PM, Sa-Su 11AM-5PM. *Not* a collection of informational exhibits about making clothes from the hides of cows. This is an adults-only collection of sex and fetish-related books, with S&M artifacts and photo exhibits of gay male erotica by notable names such as Robert Mapplethorpe. $5.

Mess Hall, 6932 N Glenwood Ave (*Morse Red Line*), +1 773 465-4033, *www.messhall.org*. Sometimes busy nearly every day of the month, and other times silent for weeks on end, the Mess Hall is an "experimental cultural center" that represents a Rogers Park tradition of agitprop eclectica — art exhibits, lectures, films, and people showing up with food. There's a schedule on the website, but you might as well just stop by to see what's going on.

Madonna della Strada Chapel, 6525 N Sheridan Rd (*Loyola Red Line*), +1 773 508-2200, *www.luc.edu*, M-F 7:30AM-8PM, Sa 7:30AM-noon, Su 7:30AM-10PM; masses M-F 8AM & noon, Su 10:30AM, 5PM, 9PM. Art deco style meets religious devotion in the spectacular Madonna della Strada Chapel, built in 1938 on the grounds of Loyola University's campus. Thanks to a recent renovation, the chapel is sparkling like new, but there's still work being done on the pipe organ. Free.

The Ghost Pilot of Rogers Park

Calvary Catholic Cemetery, across Sheridan Avenue from Juneway Terrace Beach at the border between Chicago and Evanston, has a few notable names buried within, including White Sox owner Charles Comiskey (inexplicably interred on the Cubs' side of town) and "Hinky Dink" Kenna, a legendarily corrupt alderman from the former vice district who left $33,000 in his will for a mausoleum and received an $85 tombstone from his heirs instead.

But one of the best-known stories about Calvary comes from someone who isn't buried there. Legend has it that "Charlie," an Air Force pilot doing training exercises over Lake Michigan during World War II, crashed and drowned. According to one version of the story, Charlie wanted badly to get back to his plane, and would pace around near the cemetery gates, until one night a forgetful keeper left them open — and Charlie was never seen again. According to another, Charlie wants back in: his ghost "is still seen today" getting out of the lake sopping wet, covered in seaweed, and crossing Sheridan to get some rest in Calvary.

Do

Loyola University Chicago *www.luc.edu* has its flagship campus here, with 15,000 students. In 1991, it absorbed Mundelein College, a pioneering women's school. Loyola University athletics haven't been up to much since the 1963 NCAA basketball championship, but Rogers Park would still go nuts at the first signs of life from the Ramblers — Loyola basketball tickets ($5-10) are a cheap way to catch some local flavor and have fun.

This area isn't well-known for theater, but it should be — there are some exceptional companies here. The **Heartland Cafe** (see Eat) is event-happy, and there are a few great music venues to check out (see Drink).

Lifeline Theater, 6912 N Glenwood Ave (*Morse Red Line*), +1 773 761-4477, *lifelinetheatre.com*. Performs original work and adaptations of adult ("A Room With A View") and children's ("The Stinky Cheese Man") literature; their motto is "big stories, up close." $10 KidSeries, $14-26 other shows.

No Exit Cafe, 6970 N Glenwood Ave (*Morse Red Line*), +1 773 743-3355, *www.heartlandcafe.com*. The No Exit Cafe was first opened here in 1967, going through chess, jazz, Go, and other phases along the way. Today, it has a stage in regular use (mostly weekends) for performances of all kinds, including political dance, theater, and sketch comedy, some of which have been highly acclaimed. It's run by the owners of the Heartland Cafe, which means that food and coffee are available.

Raven Theatre, 6157 N Clark St (*22 Clark bus*), +1 773 338-2177, *www.raventheatre.com*. Iconoclasts by default, the resident company at the Raven has the courage to tackle classic American plays *without* putting a post-modern spin on the material or thrusting technology into the staging. It's kooky, but it works. Non-resident companies also find room to debut new works on the well-designed stage here. $15-20.

The Side Project, 1439 W Jarvis Ave (*Jarvis Red Line*), +1 773 973-2150, *www.thesideproject.net*. They're new in the neighborhood, but the Side Project is quickly becoming one of Chicago's best storefront theaters. Shows include world premiere dramas and well-chosen revivals of overlooked plays, with committed actors and innovative staging that has the audience in the midst of the action. $10-15.

Beaches

As with the rest of Chicago, the official swim season runs from Memorial Day to Labor Day, 9AM-9:30PM daily. However, the parks along the lakefront are open year-round (6AM-11PM daily), and fill up with picnics at the first sign of spring. And the piers on Pratt Beach are favorites with people taking the "polar plunge" on New Year's.

Edgewater

Hollywood Beach (Osterman Beach), 5800 N Lake Shore Dr (*Thorndale Red Line*), +1 312 747-0832, *www.chicagoparkdistrict.com*. Although the beach earned its original name (Hollywood Beach) from being at the end of Hollywood Avenue, the Lake Shore Drive high-rises in the background give this nice, long beach a slightly Miami look. It's extremely popular with Chicago's gay and lesbian community, and also with Edgewater families. There are paths for rollerblading or running near the beach. Note the huge pink Edgewater Beach Apartments building amid the skyline — they were originally part of a larger (pink) hotel, built in 1927.

Rogers Park

Rogers Park is lined with pure lakefront glory. From Loyola all the way north, nearly every block east of Sheridan ends in a public beach and park. Some are little more than a building's length wide, and others run much longer. During the summer, these are *very* popular with locals, but they're also a great place for a walk during the fall and even the winter, when most turn into moonscapes.

From south to north:

Hartigan Park & Beach, 1031 W Albion St (*Loyola Red Line*). Close to the university and the student housing. There's some picnic space here and a big, new playground with jungle gyms and slides. It's connected by a strip of sand to North Shore Beach to the north.

Pratt Beach, 1050 W Pratt Blvd (*Loyola Red Line*). Aside from the tennis courts and the jogging paths, there are lots of interesting features to be found here: weeping trees left from this area's original incarnation as a swamp, a giant concrete sculpture for climbing, tennis courts, random public art installations, and best of all, the *long* pier leading out to an old lighthouse. Pratt Beach includes North Shore Beach and Columbia Beach to the south, and it segues into Loyola Park & Beach to the north with the long art wall, making them the longest public beach in Chicago.

Loyola Park & Beach, 1230 W Greenleaf Ave (*Morse Red Line*). Wide open spaces are here: room for soccer, basketball courts, and a public field for baseball (along with one non-public field). The Heartland Cafe operates a concession stand during the summer, and there are a few small piers. It

ends in the Leone Park & Beach to the north, a training beach for Chicago lifeguards.

Jarvis and Fargo Beaches, 1208 W Jarvis (*Jarvis Red Line*). Less crowded than their neighboring beaches. Jarvis Beach is more popular with younger swimmers as they are under the watchful gaze of the Chicago Junior Life Guard program. It also offers some open space to toss a Frisbee or people-watch. Fargo Beach is a real gem with its community garden of native beach grasses, decorating the sea retaining wall that separates the beach from the property to the west. Don't miss the wonderful plantings in the "tree box" at the end of Fargo Ave. The local take ownership for this beach and it shows. Be careful; many a local "outdoorsman" has been known to illegally launch a kayak from this public beach, and the dogs off leashes can get a bit "hairy" at times. Sherwin Beach, connected to the south of Jarvis Beach, is a small sand spit that offers a chance to sneer at the adjacent private beach.

Howard Beach, 7519 N Eastlake Terrace (*Howard Red/Purple/Yellow Line*). There's a pretty good playground here, and a modestly-sized beach.

Rogers Beach, 7705 N Eastlake Terrace (*End of Rogers Ave*). The perfect size for a beach, with tennis courts and a cliff for contemplative strolls, picnic space and a modest strip of sand for swimmers.

Juneway Terrace Beach, 7800

N Eastlake Terrace (*at the curve of Sheridan*). This is it: you've reached the end of Chicago, and it's a nice one, with lots of green space and a fun jump down to the sand. Daredevils can swim for freedom to Evanston.

Events & Festivals

Glenwood Avenue Arts Fair, 6900 N Glenwood Ave (*Morse Red Line*), +1 773 262-3790, *www.rogerspark. com*. Annual festival in August to celebrate the neighborhood and throw some light on the Glenwood Avenue art galleries, food & drink, performances, and events for kids. Free.

Buy

Outside of Devon Avenue and a couple of cowboy fashion shops on Clark, there are only a few notable places to shop in this part of the city.

Apple the Second, 745 W Howard St, +1 847 424-0786, *www.applethesecond.com*, M-Sa 12-7PM. The apple represents temptation, which in this case is upscale, European-influenced fashion for women at reasonable prices. The Polish-Mexican couple who run the store have unique items and enjoy being here.

The Armadillo's Pillow, 6753 N Sheridan Rd, +1 773 761-2558, *www.abebooks.com*, Su,Tu-Th 12-8PM, F 12-10PM, Sa 10AM-8PM. This is a warm, goofy, cluttered bookstore with an unpredictable collection of used and rare books, guided by laid-back,

book-loving staff. The worn, comfortable couches and self-serve coffee make it nice to stick around for a while.

Broadway Antique Market, 6130 N Broadway St (*Granville Red Line*), +1 773 743-5444, *www.bamchicago.com*, Open M-Sa 11AM-7PM, Su 12-6PM. Two floors of antiques in Edgewater. The first floor has plenty of interesting Chicago ephemera, but the nifty full-room set-ups on the second floor are fun to explore whether or not you plan to buy anything.

Lost Eras, 1511 W Howard St (*Howard Red/Purple/Yellow Line*), +1 773 764-7400, *www.losteras.com*, M-Sa 10AM-6PM, Su 12-5PM. This cavernous costume shop can, at turns, resemble a collection of haunted antiques — this stretch of Howard Street has several dusty old Jazz Age buildings, and this is one of the few that's open without having been scrubbed clean. Their costume selection is terrific, but it's worth the visit just to have a look around.

Rosenblum's World of Judaica, 2906 W Devon Ave, +1 773 262-1700, Su 10AM-4PM, M-W 9AM-6PM, Th 9AM-7PM, F 9AM-3PM, Jewish holidays closed or limited hours. A few blocks west of the Indian shopping district, this is the premier Jewish bookstore in Chicago, with an unmatched collection of sacred Hebrew texts, books for kids, and gifts like the occasional Chanukah baseball. **Levinson's Bakery** is just a block east if you'd like to pore over your purchases with some challa.

Taste Food & Wine, 1506 W Jarvis Ave (*Jarvis Red Line*), +1 773 761-3663, *www.tastefoodandwine.com*, M,W-Sa 11AM-9PM, Su 11AM-6PM. A lovely little wine shoppe, with a nice spread of moderately-priced wines, some beers and ciders, and various tasty nibblies. (Prosciutto? Roasted figs? Cornichons? Oh, yes.) The wines don't favor any one geographical location overmuch, and tend to lean towards a pleasantly high quaffability quotient instead of veering towards either pole of self-pickling (musty snobbery on one end, and "get me loaded up on that box o'vino" on the other). The Monday and Friday tastings are a treat, as are conversations with the friendly staff.

Unan Imports, 6971 N Sheridan Rd (*Morse Red Line*), +1 773 274-4022, M-Sa 11AM-7PM. This tiny, wonderful shop stocks African imports ranging from clothing, jewelry and masks to beauty products and djembe (drums from Mali). Dr. Alphonsus Ntamere, a Nigerian studying in Evanston started this store almost twenty years ago after getting distracted from his post-doctoral studies, and it's still a highlight of shopping on the North Side.

Devon

Saris, jewelry, suitcases, phone cards, spices, Bollywood movies, and more saris — Devon Avenue is a great place to shop. Bargaining is generally welcome, so don't be shy to make a counter-offer.

Fiza Palace, 2407 W Devon Ave, +1 773 973-3492. Even if you've never seen a sari before, you'll feel welcome shopping for men's, women's, or children's Indian fashion in this friendly store. Bead-centric jewelry is also available.

Iqra Book Center, 2749 W Devon Ave, +1 773 274-2665, *www.iqra.org*. An impressive collection of books on Islam and Muslim culture, with plenty of dual-language books and toys for teaching children Arabic. There are some nice gifts, too. If they don't have what you're looking for, try the smaller **Islamic Books and Things** at 2601 W Devon.

Patel Brothers Gifts, 2600 W Devon Ave, 11AM-8PM daily. There are at least three stores by this name on Devon, so check the address. If you're at this one, you'll find a glorious clutter of Indian gifts — if these are cheap tourist statuettes, for example, they certainly don't look like it.

Raj Jewel, 2652 W Devon Ave, +1 773 465-5755. Of the many jewelry shops on Devon, Raj Jewel has the most flash and class, with uniformed employees on hand to show off a substantial collection of gold and diamond jewelry.

Regal, 2616 W Devon Ave, +1 773 973-1368. There is the requisite selection of beautiful saris, but fans of pastel men's dress shirts will fall silent with awe at the treasures to be found here.

Sahil, 2605 W Devon Ave, +1 773 338-3636, *www.sahil.com*, W-M 11AM-8PM. This is the height of retail elegance on Devon — the two sparkling floors of Sahil

ROGERS PARKEAT

wouldn't look out of place on the Magnificent Mile. They have dazzling Indian fashion and everyday wear for men, women, and children, and accessories to match. If you don't mind spending freely, you'll leave with some amazing outfits.

Taj Sari Palace, 2553 W Devon Ave, +1 773 338-0177, W-M 11AM-8PM. There are nice saris for women and juniors at this long-standing boutique, but the craft-minded will delight in the reams of colorful fabric sold here, suitable for making saris, men's suits, and home decorations. **Al-Raheem** at 2655 W Devon also sells reams of fabric.

 Eat

Budget

Annapurna, 2608 W Devon Ave, +1 773 764-1858, 11AM-9PM daily. Devon Avenue can boggle the mind of the weary vegetarian not accustomed to having this many choices. Annapurna is a hole in the wall and the menu is geared toward Hindi speakers, but this is a good place to try something new — or just ask for samosas and chaat, and you shall receive. $1-5.

Argo Georgian Bakery, 2812 W Devon Ave, +1 773 764-6322, M-Sa 9AM-7PM, Su 9AM-6PM. If you haven't had Georgian food, your culinary life has yet to begin. Drop everything you are doing and head straight to this bakery to try khachapuri, a mouth wateringly-flaky cheese-filled pastry. Try some Borjomi sparkling spring water too. The

bakery's hours seem subject to managerial whim (and the Georgians are whimsical folks), so it's wise to call ahead before visiting. Georgian is the only language spoken, so practice saying Hah-chah-poo-ree and Bohr-joh-mee. $.50-4.

Capt'n Nemo's, 7367 N Clark St (*Howard Red Line*), +1 773 973-0570, *chicagobestitalianbeefsoupscateringrestaurants.com*, M-Sa 11AM-7PM. One of Chicago's best sandwich and soup deals. Wide variety of fresh made toasted subs and soups — including their famous chili. Every person entering is immediately offered a taste sampling of any of the day's soups. $4-8.

Caribbean American Baking Company, 1547 W Howard St (*Howard Red Line*), +1 773 761-0700, *www.caribbeanamericanbakery.com*, M-Sa 8AM-9PM, Su 10AM-5PM. Take-out only, but Howard Beach is right down the block — sun, surf, Jamaican bread and Jerk chicken patties are what the north pole of Chicago is all about. (Vegetable patties are available, too.) $2-7.

The Dagel and Beli, 7400 N Greenview Ave (*Jarvis Red Line*), +1 773 743-2354, M-F 7AM-8PM, Sa-Su 6AM-8PM. Steamed bagel sandwiches with free Spoonerisms. Attached to Charmers Cafe, from which drinks can be ordered. $5-7.

Deta's Cafe, 7555 N Ridge Blvd, +1 773 973-1505, 10AM-11PM daily. The culinary diversity of

ROGERS PARKEAT

Rogers Park extends as far as Montenegro. This small, friendly cafe offers soups, salads, and burek (stuffed rolls of fried dough) that are as close to home-made as you can get — Deta loves to show customers her kitchen. $2-8.

The Fish Keg, 2233 W Howard St (*Howard Red/Purple/Yellow Line*), +1 773 262-6603, Su-Th 8AM-midnight, F-Sa 8AM-1AM. If the stomach that sits within you is no shrinking flower, the fried walleye, fried shrimp, and hush puppies at this renowned fish shack will do very well by you.

Ghareeb Nawaz, 2032 W Devon Ave, +1 773 761-5300, 7AM-2AM daily. The name, meaning "protector of the poor", is a reference to the Sufi saint Moinuddin Chishti, who was best known for feeding the hungry. This isn't the gourmet Devon experience, but how's this sound: naan or chapatis, chicken biryani, and a mango lassi to drink for less than $5. Interested? Come and carry-out, or try the family room. $2-6.

Harold's Chicken Shack #44, 6952 N Clark St (*22 Clark bus*), +1 773 465-2300, M-Th 11AM-1:30AM, F-Sa 11AM-2AM. Hark! Harold's has come to Rogers Park!

Noon Hour Grill, 6930 N Glenwood Ave (*Morse Red Line*), +1 773 338-9494, Su-M 8AM-3PM, W-Sa 8AM-7PM. It doesn't look like much from the outside, but where else are you going to have to choose between a hearty diner breakfast (bacon, sausage, eggs), Korean home cooking (bi bim bop, Yook Gue Jung soup), or the

point at which they meet (Korean spaghetti, bulgogi and kimchee omelettes)? $5-8.

Wolfy's, 2734 W Peterson Ave (*49 Western bus, 84 Peterson bus*), +1 773 743-0207, M-Sa 10:30AM-9PM, Su 11AM-8PM. Hot dogs and Polish sausages are a powerful, ancient tradition in West Ridge, and while there are still plenty of fast food shacks in the area, Wolfy's is the last of the old-school, pilgrimage-worthy hot dog proprietors. For a bit of hot dog history, sneak a peek at the hot dog sculptures behind the now-closed U Lucky Dawg (formerly Fluky's) a short distance east at 6821 N Western.

Mid-range

Devon

Most restaurants on Devon specialize in cuisine from specific regions of India, which can vary quite a bit. Southern Indian cooking will be less familiar to most, but it's also remarkably friendly to vegetarians.

Arya Bhavan, 2508 W Devon Ave, +1 773 274-5800, *www.aryabhavan. com*, M-Th 2-3PM,5-9PM, F 12-3PM,5-9:30PM, Sa-Su 12-9:30PM. The first thing you notice is the pink handkerchiefs, floating over the tables like butterflies. Arya Bhavan has a small but lovely dining room, serving mostly northern Indian food (and a weekend buffet) for vegetarians *and* vegans. As a bonus, it's open most major holidays. $6-12.

Khan BBQ, 2401 W Devon Ave, +1 773 338-2800, Sa-Th 12:30PM-11PM, F 2-11PM. If you've had it with vegetarians, this is where to get some meat on your plate. Khan BBQ serves the best kabobs on the street, charcoal-fired and caramelized, and they're busy from open to close. $8-12.

Mysore Woodlands, 2548 W Devon Ave, +1 773 338-8160, Tu-Th 11:30AM-9:30PM, F-Sa 11:30AM-10PM. Purely vegetarian Southern Indian cooking, with a spacious dining room. If you've never tried dosai, which is somewhere between a burrito, a crepe, and a horn-of-plenty, they have several cheap, filling varieties here. $8-10.

Sabri Nehari, 2502 1/2 W Devon Ave, +1 773 743-6200, *www.sabrinihari.com*, noon-midnight daily. This Pakistani restaurant is one of the busiest on Devon, filled with local families. They do wonders with chicken, especially the monumental chicken charga, in which an entire bird is deep-fried and marinated with secret spices. $9-13.

Tiffin, 2536 W Devon Ave, +1 773 338-2143, *www.tiffinrestaurant.com*, 11:30AM-3PM, 5-10PM. Possibly the fanciest restaurant on Devon, with a space-age ceiling and decor that calls to mind an expensive hotel lobby. Tandoori dishes are the specialty, and there's a lunch buffet seven days a week. $10-20.

Udupi Palace, 2543 W Devon Ave, +1 773 338-2152, *www.udupipalace. com*. This is one of the most popular restaurants with visitors on Devon, offering a Southern Indian-

style vegetarian menu that packs its fair share of spice. $9-12.

Uru-Swati, 2629 W Devon Ave, +1 773 262-5280, *www.uru-swati. net*, Su-M,W-Th 11AM-9PM, F-Sa 11AM-10PM. The aqua walls and cafe-like atmosphere make Uru-Swati a relaxing place to stay, and their vegetarian menu covers a lot of range — you can pair standbys like naan with new finds from northern and southern India. $9-12.

Viceroy of India, 2518 W Devon Ave, +1 773 743-4100, *www.viceroyofindia.com*, 11:30AM-2:30PM daily, Su-Th 5-10PM, F-Sa 5-10:30PM. It's currently covered in scaffolding with no sign, but visitors and locals still seek out the Viceroy for its mighty chicken, lunch buffet ($8-9), and long wine list. The menu is primarily northern Indian. This is a great place to go with a big party. $12-20.

Others

African Harambee, 7537 N Clark St (*Howard Red/Yellow/Purple Line*), +1 773 764-2200, Su-Th 12-10PM, F-Sa 12-11PM. Pan-African food and flavors with seafood, meat, and vegetarian options on the menu. Plenty of African beers and wines, too.

Broadway Cellars, 5900 N Broadway St (*Thorndale Red Line*), +1 773 944-1208, *www.broadwaycellars.net*, M-Th 5-10PM, F 5-11PM, Sa 11:30AM-9PM, Su 10:30AM-3PM. Neighborhood bistro in Edgewater with plenty of wine to sample, either while splashing out on dishes like the duck lasagna or keeping calm with a simple nosh platter. $10-19.

Ethiopian Diamond Restaurant & Lounge, 6120 N Broadway St (*Granville Red Line*), +1 773 338-6100, *www.ethiopiandiamond.com*, M-Th noon-10PM, F noon-10:30PM, Sa-Su 11AM-11:30PM. Ethiopian cuisine in Edgewater, equally friendly to carnivores and vegetarians and best enjoyed with a group to share a platter. $11-20.

Gino's North, 1111 W Granville Ave (*Granville Red Line*), +1 773 465-1616, 3PM-2AM bar, 4-11PM kitchen daily. Virtually unknown in the annals of Chicago pizza lore, Gino's North — not East, as in the famous city-wide chain — is, nevertheless, a great love of all who know it. The key is to confirm that Peggy is working that day; if she's in the kitchen, make tracks to enjoy the work of one of the finest pizza auteurs of our time.

Heartland Cafe, 7000 N Glenwood Ave (*Morse Red Line*), *www.heartlandcafe.com*, Kitchen M-Th 7AM-10PM, F 7AM-11PM, Sa 8AM-11PM, Su 8AM-10PM; bar M-Th 7AM-midnight, F-Sa 8AM-2AM, Su 11AM-midnight. There's almost always something going on at the hippie-friendly Heartland Cafe: open mic nights, live rock/jazz/blues, plays, and art/photo exhibits. While vegetarian-friendly, the menu is a bit overpriced — you are paying for the ambiance. The outdoor seating is a pleasure in the summer. Check out the "kozmic" bookstore (and the photobooth) while you're waiting for a table.

$10-18.

Jamaica Jerk, 1631 W Howard St (*Howard Red/Purple/Yellow Line*), +1 773 764-1546, *www.jamaicajerk-il.com*, Tu-Th 11AM-9PM, F-Sa 11AM-10PM, Su 12-8PM. Jamaican and Caribbean cuisine, with free parking and kid's menus to boot. It's right outside the Howard CTA station, fronted by the facade of the old Howard Theater. If it's too crowded, try **Good to Go** three blocks west.

Lake Side Cafe, 1418 W Howard St (*Howard Red/Purple/Yellow Line*), +1 773 262-9503, *www.lake-side-cafe.com*, Su,Tu-F 5PM-9PM, Sa 12-9PM. Close to the lake and the train, serving organic vegetarian food — things that look like meat (fake Polish dogs) and things that don't (soups, salads, pizzas).

Leona's, 6935 N Sheridan (*Morse Red Line*), +1 773 764-5757, M-Th 11AM-11PM, F 11AM-12:30AM, Sa 11:30AM-12:30PM, Su 10:30AM-10:30PM. Good all-around Italian and American fare; plenty of meat, but vegetarian-friendly as well, including the terrific big vegan burger. This location has a big, padded kids room with animated movies to keep them occupied during Sunday brunch. $12-18.

Moody's Pub, 5910 N Broadway St (*Thorndale Red Line*), 5910 N Broadway St, *www.moodyspub.com*, M-Sa 11:30AM-1AM, Su noon-1AM. An Edgewater institution since 1959, serving beer and monster

Moodyburgers. The dark, cave-like interior is a great refuge in the winter, while the sizable beer garden takes equal advantage of summer. $9-12.

Splurge

Amphora, 7547 N Clark St (*Howard Red/Purple/Yellow Line*), +1 773 262-5767, M-Sa 11AM-4PM,5PM-10:30PM,Su 4-10:30PM; bar to 1AM Tu-Th, to 2AM F-Sa, to 10PM Su. Carnivorous Mediterranean pleasures in Rogers Park, at the Evanston border. The bar attached to the restaurant features a DJ every Friday and occasional jazz. $16-28.

Gruppo di Amici, 1508 W Jarvis Ave (*Jarvis Red Line*), +1 773 508-5565, *www.gruppodiamici.com*, Tu-Sa 5PM-midnight, Su 11AM-10PM. An upscale Roman pizza restaurant with a wood-burning oven flown over from Italy and cured for nine weeks until ready. Try one of the Italian style thin pizzas with a cold micro brew, or pair one of the many great appetizers with the daily seafood special. They have a great selection of wines — let the local sommelier / master mixoligist help with selecting a bottle of wine or just sip one of several wonderful cocktails. In the summer, the outdoor seating here is some of the nicest in Rogers Park. $16-24.

Taste of Peru, 6545 N Clark St (*22 Clark bus or Granville Red Line*), +1 773 381-4540, Su-Th 11:30AM-10PM, F-Sa 11:30AM-11PM. Given the nature of Peruvian cuisine, this one is probably best enjoyed by seafood lovers. Live Peruvian mu-

sic on the weekends. Reservations recommended, although not necessary if you're willing to wait. (That'll give you a chance to hit the liquor store down the block, as Taste of Peru is BYOB.) $18-22.

Drink

Coffee shops

There's a wealth of independent coffee shops with great character (and coffee) around here, and rarely any competition for seating.

Cafe Ennui, 6981 N Sheridan Rd (*Morse Red Line*), +1 773 973-2233, M-Th 6AM-11PM, F 6AM-midnight, Sa 7AM-midnight, Su 7AM-11PM. A fine little coffee shop just down the block from the beach on Lunt. There's something about the checkered floor that eliminates the mere possibility of pretension. The back row of tables near the bookshelves is a hot-spot for chess games. There's live jazz on Sunday nights.

Charmers Cafe, 1500 W Jarvis Ave (*Jarvis Red Line*), +1 773 743-2233, M-F 6:30AM-6PM, Sa-Su 7AM-6:30PM. Coffee roasted by Metropolis, plus teas, pies and pastries, smoothies and ice cream in the summer. Sandwiches can be ordered from the Dagel and Beli next door.

The Common Cup, 1501 W Morse Ave (*Morse Red Line*), +1 773 338-0256, *www.commoncupchicago.com*, M-Th 6AM-8PM, F 6AM-8PM, Sa 7AM-8PM, Su 8AM-8PM. This is the potential of Rogers Park: a nicely rehabbed storefront in a classic, anonymous beauty of an early 1900s building, open early for commuters and full of local art, with an eclectic menu (including ice cream) and an unpretentious atmosphere for readers and conversations alike.

Metropolis Coffee Company, 1039 W Granville Ave (*Granville Red Line*), +1 773 764-0400, *www.metropoliscoffee.com*, M-F 6:30AM-8PM, Sa 7AM-8PM, Su 7:30AM-8PM. Highly acclaimed coffee roasted on-site, with other drinks, baked goods, delicious pastries for breakfast and free wi-fi as well. This is some of the best coffee in Chicago and people know it, so it can get crowded.

Panini Panini, 6764 N Sheridan Rd, +1 773 761-4110, 8AM-10PM daily. A nice cafe a block from the lake, serving good coffee, salads and sandwiches with an Eastern European accent. The laid-back atmosphere and outdoor seating make this a perfect post-beach pit stop.

Bars

Rogers Park and Edgewater have several quality dives where a good time is the one and only priority — save your fashion for another part of the city. Howard Street was a jazz hotspot several decades ago, and while there are no clubs there now, several places near Morse Avenue are picking up steam as live music venues.

If you're hungry, heading down Broadway to raise a glass over a burger at **Moody's Pub** (see above) is always a sound idea.

Bruno & Tim's Lounge, 6562 N Sheridan Rd (*Loyola Red Line*), +1 773 764-7900, M-F 9AM-2AM, Sa 9AM-3AM, Su 11AM-2AM. Bruno & Tim's is a classic Rogers Park bar, offering booze, television, and long hours for its regulars. Whatever the time of day, it's always late Saturday night inside Bruno & Tim's. There's a fairly big liquor store in the other half of the storefront.

Cary's Lounge, 2251 W Devon Ave, +1 773 743-5737, *www.caryslounge.com*, Su-F 9AM-2AM, Sa 9AM-3AM. In operation for more than 40 years, Cary's Lounge stakes a claim to the coveted title of best dive bar in Chicago. It's also a haven for serious pool players. There are bands on Fridays, DJs on Saturdays, and a good jukebox for the rest. The beers are cheap, with domestics under $3 and imports topping out at $6.

Duke's, 6920 N Glenwood Ave (*Morse Red Line*), +1 773 764-2826, Su-F 11AM-2AM, Sa 11AM-3AM. Right around the corner from the Morse station, Duke's is a first-class neighborhood bar. Beer and whiskey are cheap, and Friday, Saturday, and Sunday nights are packed year-round with live rockabilly, bluegrass, and country — and no cover charge.

Edgewater Lounge, 5600 N Ashland Ave, +1 773 878-3343, M-F, Su 12PM-2AM, Sa 12PM-3AM. A solid neighborhood bar down the street from the fancier digs in Andersonville. There's food and a good range of regional beers and microbrews, and live bluegrass occasionally pops up.

Morseland, 1218 W Morse Ave (*Morse Red Line*), +1 773 764-8900, *morseland.com*, M-F 5PM-2AM, Sa 5PM-3AM, Su 5PM-2AM. There's pure class in here. Cocktails, cheap beer, imported beer, and bar food that's good enough for delivery; DJs spin, jazz trios tromp, and a neo-soul atmosphere rules all.

Oasis, 6809 N Sheridan Rd, +1 773 973-7788, M-F 3PM-4AM, Sa noon-5AM, Su noon-4AM. Local dive with late hours. Just a block in from the lake on the busy intersection of Sheridan and Pratt. The Oasis has two rooms, darts (metal ones!), free pretzel rods, specials with time limits, and a menacing late night bouncer. Packaged goods for those that want to take their liquor to go. With many an over-served customer, mayhem is known to ensue.

Ole St Andrew's Inn, 5938 N Broadway St (*Thorndale Red Line*), +1 773 784-5540, M-F 3PM-2AM, Sa noon-3AM, Su 11AM-2AM. There's no hurry in the comfortable seating here, even though the place is supposedly haunted by the ghost of a former owner — at least he's motivated to keep you there, and the current owners oblige with a good beer and wine selection.

Poitin Stil, 1502 W Jarvis Ave. (*Jarvis Red Line*), +1 773 338-3285, M-F 3PM-2AM, Sa noon-3AM. Su noon-2AM. Irish or not, you'll feel like you're knocking 'em back in Galway at this Rogers Park's authentic Irish pub. The name (pronounced "poo-chine still") is

Gaelic for moonshine. Located in the former Charmers space, the bar was rehabbed and walls were knocked down, so look for exposed bricks and large windows, not to mention the maroon shades of Galway's home team colors. Though there's no kitchen, a free buffet is brought in to help guests cheer on the Bears on Sundays. Billiard table, good juke box, karaoke, and trivia some nights. Occasionally live music. Great bar staff.

Red Line Tap, 7006 N Glenwood Ave (*Morse Red Line*), +1 773 274-5463, M-F 4PM-2AM, Sa noon-3AM, Su 2PM-2AM. A solid place for a beer, not far from the lake. Food is available from the Heartland Cafe next door. Sometimes $5 cover for live music.

The Sovereign, 6205 N Broadway St (*Granville Red Line*), +1 773 764-8900, *www.thesovereignchicago.com*. Super friendly, comfortable establishment in Edgewater. A place where the jukebox is just the right volume and you'll never feel uncomfortable. For cheap beer and generous mixed drinks, this a friendly neighborhood bet.

Uncommon Ground, 1401 W Devon Ave (*Loyola Red Line*), +1 773 465-9801, *www.uncommonground.com*, M-Th 9AM-midnight, F-Sa 9AM-2AM, Su 9AM-10PM. A new second branch of the Lakeview bar promises great things for the Rogers Park music scene, with the former program director of the jazz landmark **The HotHouse** on board to set the schedule. There's a full menu of organic food and eco-friendly touches like solar panels on the roof.

Sleep

Budget

Chicago International Hostel, 6318 N Winthrop Ave (*Granville or Loyola Red Line*), +1 773 262-1011, *www.hostelinchicago.com*. A very basic and calm hostel with kitchen facilities, safebox rental, lockers, huge common room with internet access. The minimum age is 16 and reservations are required, but there's no curfew. It's one block from Loyola University, close to the lake. However, the rooms' walls haven't been painted forever and 70s mooses drawings are hanged above the beds. Avoid if decoration has any importance for you. What you see from the pictures on their site isn't what you get. Rooms $25.50.

Lincoln Inn, 5952 N Lincoln Ave, +1 773 784-1118. This cousin of the Sin Strip motels is missing the over-the-top neon, but it's in a sedate location within a close walk of the Indian community on Devon Avenue and a shopping center. Rooms from $42 1-10 hours, $52 all night.

Mid-range

The notorious motels of Lincoln Avenue have been listed in Lincoln Square, although some are located close to West Ridge.

Ardmore House, 1248 W Ardmore Ave, +1 773 728-5414, *www.ardmorehousebb.com*. Bed & breakfast for GLBT travelers in a century-old Victorian home,

not far from Hollywood Beach. Rooms from $99. Garage parking available for $20.

Heart O' Chicago Motel, 5990 N Ridge Ave, +1 773 271-9181, *www.heartochicago.com*, Checkout: 11am. Want to impress a local? Generations of north-siders have driven past the Heart O' Chicago's famous sign without seeing what's inside — 45 basic motel rooms, as it turns out. Continental breakfast and wireless internet are included. You'll probably want a car if you're staying here, though.. Rooms from $79.

Inn on Early, 1241 W Early Ave, +1 773 334-4666, *www.innonearly. com*. Bed & breakfast with three guest rooms in Edgewater, close to the lakefront. Rooms from $95, plus $25 for more than single occupancy.

Super 8 Chicago/Rogers Park, 7300 N Sheridan Rd (*Morse Red Line*), +1 773 973-7440, *www.super8.com*. Right down the street from the beach. Many amenities including parking, internet, and facilities for long-term stays. Rooms from $120.

Contact

Libraries

Edgewater Branch Library, 1210 W Elmdale Ave (*Thorndale Red Line*), +1 312 744-0718, *www.chipublib.org*, M-Th 9AM-9PM, F-Sa 9AM-5PM. Free public internet access at a classic 1970s branch, just off Broadway.

Northtown Branch Library, 6435 N California Ave (*155 Devon bus*), +1 312 744-2292, *www.chipublib.org*, M-Th 9AM-9PM, F-Sa 9AM-5PM. Free public internet access, near the culinary glories of Devon Avenue.

Rogers Park Branch Library, 6907 N Clark St (*Morse Red Line/22 Clark bus*), +1 312 744-0156, *www.chipublib.org*, M-Th 9AM-9PM, F-Sa 9AM-5PM. New library with free public internet access, a few blocks west of the CTA station (or east of the Metra station).

Internet cafes

La Bella Cafe & Internet, 6624 N Clark St (*22 Clark bus*), +1 773 856-7000, 10AM-10PM daily. Internet access, fax and full-service printing, and webcams/microphones for chats back home. There's coffee, tea, juice, and some basic food. $4/hour.

Quest Network Services, 7301 N Sheridan Rd (*Jarvis Red Line*), +1 773 761-3555, *www.Questpcs.com*, M-F 11AM-10PM, Sa 11AM-11PM, Su 1-9PM. Conveniently located internet cafe, just a block from the beach.

Stay safe

Edgewater and West Ridge are low crime areas, with common sense applied. Rogers Park, on the other hand, can be trouble by night. Chicagoans tend to overstate the crime rate there, largely because it's surrounded by neighborhoods where crime is comparatively unknown. By overall city standards, it's not particularly dangerous, but don't carry anything irreplaceable on your person (or in your car) if you plan to go roaming after dark. (That said, trouble by day is virtually nonexistent.)

Campus police can be relied upon to patrol the area near Loyola University around the clock, extending as far as Devon, but some visitors may feel uncomfortable walking alone on Morse, Jarvis, Glenwood, Howard, and their side-streets late at night. There are police cameras on the streetlights at Morse, so wave and say 'hello'.

Wandering the beaches and parks is fine after dark, but don't go swimming after hours, particularly at the smaller beaches — certain property owners thrive on calling the cops on late swimmers. Climbing the breakwater rocks between beaches can be a lot of fun, but is not allowed by the Chicago Park District lifeguards.

Get out

Evanston is the next city north, offering more beaches, lovely tree-lined residential areas and a thriving downtown.

Many visitors continue down Sheridan Avenue through Evanston to Wilmette in order to see the spectacular **Baha'i Temple**.

North Lincoln is a collection of neighborhoods on the north side of Chicago through which **Lincoln Avenue** wanders, remembering treasures and curiosities of the last century in Chicago life, moving along, and forgetting them all over again.

Lincoln Square, **Albany Park**, and **North Park** are much better known to residents than tourists, but anyone will feel welcome here. To paraphrase Lionel Richie, this is where Chicago is easy like a Sunday morning, all week long.

The best reasons to come here are the shopping — unquestionably cool, and completely unpretentious — and the restaurants, which serious Chicago food lovers consider some of the best in the city.

Understand

Lincoln Square was settled by German farmers in the 1860s, when the area (along with portions of the neighboring Uptown *p.273*) was known as **Ravenswood**. With the arrival of what is today known as the Brown Line elevated train in 1906, population surged, and a thriving small business community developed under the L tracks and around the network of streetcar lines. By the 1920s, the relatively affluent community had a movie palace, now known as the **Davis Theater**, and rows of attractive commercial buildings — most notably the **Krause Music Store**, whose façade was the last commission of master architect Louis Sullivan. Although the neighborhood is now culturally diverse, a few vintage businesses like the **Chicago Brauhaus** and

The Huettenbar celebrate its German heritage through, well, celebration.

Today, Lincoln Square has some of the city's best shopping (even for people who don't like shopping), and some terrific restaurants and bars; more than anything else, though, Chicago doesn't get any more pleasant than Lincoln Square for brunch on a Saturday or Sunday afternoon.

The Greater Lincoln Square area includes the smaller, residential neighborhoods of Budlong Woods, Ravenswood Gardens, and Ravenswood Manor, which is crossed by the pretty North Branch of the Chicago River — unrecognizable from the more famous sludge in the Loop *p.47*.

Also listed in this article are **Albany Park** and **North Park**, two diverse residential neighborhoods to the northwest of Lincoln Square. There's no better place in Chicago to find late-night Guatemalan dinner or Filipino dessert. Kedzie Avenue has an amazing run of authentic Middle Eastern restaurants, and a major Korean population lives and works on the stretch of Lawrence Avenue known as "Seoul Drive." The Brown Line makes it easy to skip the over-priced tourist restaurants downtown and enjoy a quick culinary tour at a fraction of the price you'll find by your hotel — unless you're staying on the Sin Strip (see Sleep).

North Lincoln

See and Do
1. Albany Park Theater Project
2. Cambodian Association of Illinois
3. Giddings Plaza
4. Marie's Golden Cue

Buy
1. Architectural Artifacts
2. Russian Books and Records

Eat
1. Al-Khaymeh
2. Apart Pizza
3. Chicago Kalbi
4. Chiyo Japanese Restaurant
5. Great Sea Chinese Restaurant
6. Il Seong Jung
7. Joy Yee
8. Kang Nam
9. Korean Noodle Restaurant
10. Midori Japanese Restaurant
11. Nazareth Sweets
12. Noon O Kabab
13. Salam
14. Semiramis
15. Shelly's Freez
16. So Gong Dong Tofu House
17. Ssyal Ginseng House
18. Tre Kronor

Drink
1. Cafe Orange
2. Lincoln Karaoke
3. Lutz Cafe & Pastry Shop
4. Montrose Saloon
5. The Perfect Cup
6. Rockwell's Neighborhood Grill
7. Schlegl's Bakery & Cafe

Sleep
1. Apache Motel
2. Diplomat Motel
3. Guest House
4. The O Mi Motel
5. The Patio
6. Summit Motel
7. Tip Top Motel

Contact
1. Albany Park Branch Library
2. Budlong Woods Branch Library
3. Mayfair Branch Library
4. Sulzer Regional Library

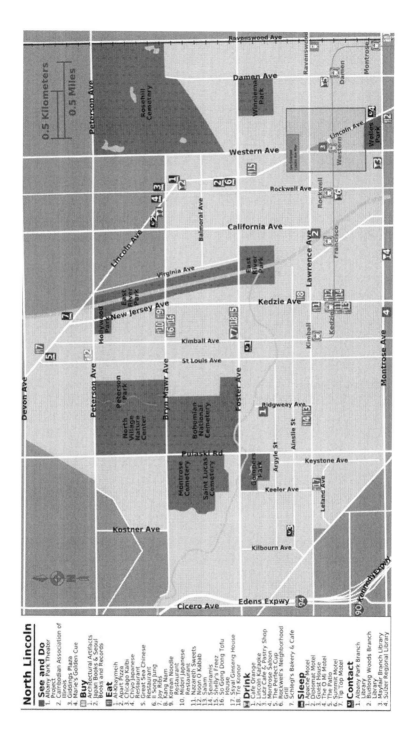

NORTH LINCOLNSEE

Get in

By train

The CTA **Brown Line** runs from the Loop *p.47*, and makes stops in Ravenswood (Montrose, Damen), Lincoln Square (Western), Ravenswood Manor (Rockwell, Francisco), and terminates in Albany Park (Kedzie, Kimball). The stations from Rockwell to Kedzie are street-level, and most have a second entrance on the other end of the platform. All stations are wheelchair accessible.

The Metra **Union Pacific North Line** stops at Ravenswood (Lawrence Avenue) before moving on to Rogers Park *p.291* and Evanston.

By bus

11 Lincoln runs down a key route down Lincoln Ave, connecting with North Center *p.139* and West Ridge *p.291*, but it stops running too early in the evening.

49 Western runs all night through most of the city, connecting to the Brown Line at the Western station in the heart of Lincoln Square.

50 Damen connects with the Brown Line at the Damen station.

78 Montrose runs along the border with Irving Park on the Far Northwest Side *p.363*, connecting with the Brown Line in North Center *p.139*.

81 Lawrence is ideal for travel on "Seoul Drive". It connects to the Red Line in Uptown *p.273*.

82 Kimball/Homan connects with the Brown Line at Kimball serving Albany & North Park heading up to Devon.

92 Foster connects with the Red Line at Berwyn and is the best way to reach Andersonville from the train. It also ends up west at the Jefferson Park Blue Line station.

By car

Lincoln Ave is the main thoroughfare for Lincoln Square. While few roads in Chicago can match Lincoln for unique shops and restaurants, it's perpetually under construction, and traffic rarely moves fast. Take Western if you are in a hurry. Accordingly, if you are coming up the **Kennedy Expressway**, take the Western Ave exit, although if you are coming from the north on the **Edens Expressway**, the Peterson Ave exit is probably the fastest way into the district.

Free parking is generally available on side streets, but keep an eye out for permit-parking zones.

See

The heart of Lincoln Square is **Giddings Plaza**, a fountain square located on a one-way stretch of Lincoln Avenue. It's a popular gathering spot, and on summer evenings, impromptu concerts from the Old Town School of Folk Music often spill out into the square. Nearby, there are a few flourishes in honor of the neighborhood's German heritage and namesake: while out and around, look for the Maypole, a few German murals, the decidedly Teutonic Thomas Jefferson Pumping Station, and the Beardless Action Lincoln statue.

The only notable sight in the neighborhood is the home of disgraced former Gov. Rod Blagojevich, but an aimless stroll on a sunny day in **Ravenswood Manor** is one of the best afternoons Chicago has to offer. Exit the Francisco Brown Line stop and you're right in the midst of several blocks of classic Chicago bungalows and brick mansions.

Cambodian Association of Illinois, 2831 W Lawrence Ave (*Francisco Brown Line*), +1 773 878-7090, *www.cambodian-association.org*, Community Center M-F 9AM-5PM, Museum & Memorial M-F 10AM-4PM, Sa-Su by appointment. In addition to their work with Cambodian immigrants and refugees, the CAI also runs a small but highly effective Heritage Museum and Killing Fields Memorial at their building near Albany Park.

DANK-HAUS German Cultural Center, 4740 N Western Ave (*Western Brown Line*), +1 773 275-1100, *www.dank.org*, Sa 11AM-3PM, and for special events such as **German Cinema Now**,

showing contemporary German films with English sub-titles, on the third Monday of every month at 7PM. D.A.N.K. is an acronym for German American National Congress, which is also on-site, a cultural and social hub for the German-American community throughout Chicago and the Midwest. The Cultural Center hosts art exhibitions in two gallery spaces. Usually free.

Krause Music Store, 4611 N Lincoln Ave (*Western Brown Line*). Built in 1922, this was the last commission of legendary architect Louis Sullivan. The beautiful terra-cotta facade was restored in 2006. It currently houses a design studio.

Rosehill Cemetery, 5800 N Ravenswood Ave, +1 773 561-5940. Rosehill doesn't have as famous a burial list as Graceland nearby in Uptown, but the mix of Chicago historical figures, Civil War soldiers, and Bohemian statuary makes it worth a look. The Gothic cemetery gate was built in 1864, one of the few remaining structures from before the Great Chicago Fire.

Do

This is a laid-back area, with plenty of opportunities to relax or pick up a new hobby.

Albany Park Theater Project, 5100 N Ridgeway Ave, +1 773 866-0875, *www.aptpchicago.org*. A community gem: experienced theater veterans guide a multi-ethnic ensemble of teenagers in creating original plays about the immigrant stories in their neighborhood.

The Chopping Block Cooking School, 4747 N Lincoln Ave (*Western Brown Line*), +1 773 472-6700, *www.thechoppingblock.net*, M-F 10AM-9PM, Sa-Su 10AM-6PM. Even if you're only going to be in town for one day, you can drop in for a class (no experience necessary) on a wide variety of culinary subjects, with plenty of hands-on experience included. Check the calendar on their website to see if anything strikes your fancy. Kids classes $20, adults $40-$75.

Davis Theater, 4614 N Lincoln Ave (*Western Brown Line*), +1 773 784-0893, *www.davistheater.com*. In the neighborhood for more than 80 years. They mostly show current Hollywood movies, but there are special features every once in a while, including Bollywood musicals for the Indian community on Devon. Tickets $8, $5.50 before 6pm.

Gompers Park, 4222 W Foster Ave (*Foster & Pulaski*), +1 773 685-3270, *www.chicagoparkdistrict.com*. A big, lovely park (39 acres) with the full range of outdoor sports activities, including a lagoon for fishing. A new statue in honor of the park's namesake, labor hero Samuel Gompers, was unveiled in 2007.

Lincoln Square Lanes, 4874 N Lincoln Ave, +1 773 561-8191, Su-F 12PM-2AM, Sa 12PM-3AM. A second-floor bowling alley, right above a hardware store, with hand-scoring and an old Midwestern lodge feel. $4 per game; cheap

beer, too.

Marie's Golden Cue, 3241 W Montrose Ave (*Kedzie Brown Line*), +1 773 478-2555, M-F 12PM-2AM, Sa-Su 11AM-2AM. A classic pool hall with eighteen well-kept tables. It's seedy enough that you can enjoy hustlers working the room, but not so rough-and-tumble that Marie can't announce her new grand-kids on the vintage marquee outside. Hot dogs and a couple of arcade machines are available. $5-9 per hour.

The Old-Town School of Folk Music, 4544 N Lincoln Ave (*Western Brown Line*), +1 773 728-6000, *www.oldtownschool.org*. If you're interested in folk music from America or anywhere else in the world you should definitely plan to spend some time at the Old-Town School. There are classes ranging from beginners' clawhammer banjo to advanced Flamenco dance. Even if you are just passing through town, consider stopping by to see a concert or just to check out the store, which features a fabulous array of banjos, fiddles, guitars, and rare folk instruments from around the world, as well as recordings of just about every sort of folk music (and early jazz) you can imagine.

Welles Park, Between Western, Lincoln, Montrose, & Sunnyside Ave (*Sunrise to sunset*), +1 312 742-7511, *www.chicagoparkdistrict.com*. One of the best neighborhood parks in the city. Welles Park is a perfect match for Lincoln Square: 15 acres of great facilities (tennis, softball, an indoor pool) that never feels remotely crowded, except when the Old Town School of Folk Music holds the free summer **Folk & Roots Festival** *www.oldtownschool.org* here.

Lincoln Square

■ See and Do

1. The Chopping Block Cooking School
2. Davis Theater
3. DANK-HAUS German Cultural Center
4. Krause Music Store
5. Lincoln Square Lanes
6. The Old-Town School of Folk Music

■ Buy

1. Book Cellar
2. Eclecticity
3. European Import Center
4. Gallimaufry Gallery
5. Hangar 18
6. Laurie's Planet of Sound
7. Merz Apothecary
8. Quake Collectibles
9. Salamander Shoes
10. Timeless Toys

■ Eat

1. Cafe Selmarie
2. Chicago Brauhaus
3. Costello Sandwich & Sides
4. Garcia's Restaurant
5. La Bocca della Verita
6. Los Nopales
7. Rosded Restaurant
8. Spoon Thai

■ Drink

1. Bad Dog Tavern
2. The Daily Bar & Grill
3. The Grafton
4. The Grind
5. Huettenbar
6. Nidersachsen Club Chicago

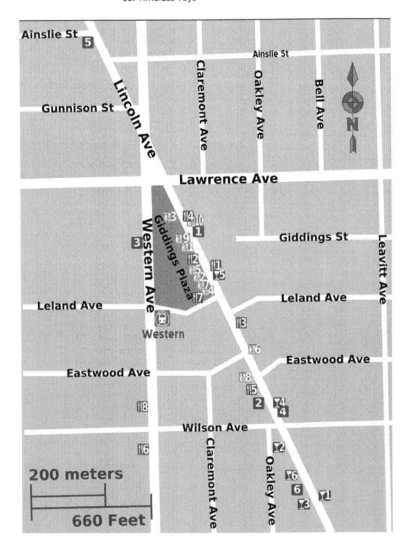

Buy

If you've come to Chicago to shop, give the designer jumble on the Magnificent Mile *p.71* its due and then come to Lincoln Square, where they have stuff you *can't* buy at the mall back home. There are several labor-of-love shops here, and they're a lot of fun to browse.

Architectural Artifacts, 4325 N Ravenswood Ave, +1 773 348-0622, *www.architecturalartifacts. com*, 10AM-5PM daily. Chicago has built many of the world's greatest buildings, and Chicago has also destroyed many of the world's greatest buildings. This is where a lot of the pieces wind up — an *enormous* warehouse full of tiles, furnishings, and exterior ornament from classic skyscrapers and bungalows. (Find the interior courtyard for the biggest pieces.) The prices befit the awe the items inspire, but it's absolutely worth a browse whether or not you plan to buy anything.

Book Cellar, 4736 N Lincoln Ave (*Western Brown Line*), +1 773 293-2665, *www.bookcellarinc.com*, M,W-Sa 10AM-10PM, Tu,Su 10AM-6PM. Splendid, comfortable book store with author events, a wide selection of Chicago books, and wine by the glass.

Eclecticity, 4718 N Lincoln Ave (*Western Brown Line*), +1 773 275-3080, *www.eclec.com*, M-Sa 11AM-9PM, Su 11AM-5:30PM. Proudly described as a "purely self-indulgent venture," Eclecticity is shopping for shopping's sake, with collectibles old and new from around the world, and a wide selection of candles.

European Import Center, 4752 N Lincoln Ave (*Western Brown Line*), +1 773 561-8281. Address the embarrassing lack of garden gnomes and authentic Black Forest cuckoo clocks in your life.

Gallimaufry Gallery, 4712 N Lincoln Ave (*Western Brown Line*), +1 773 728-3600 , *www.gallimaufry.net*, M-Sa 10AM-6PM (Th to 8PM), Su 1-6PM. A little bit of everything, and a wonderful selection thereof; jewelry, secret boxes, imported scarves, and several varieties of kaleidoscopes are among the delights you'll find here.

Hangar 18, 4726 N Lincoln Ave (*Western Brown Line*), +1 773 275-3349, *www.hanger18chicago.com*, M 11AM-6PM, Tu-F 11AM-7PM, Sa 11AM-6PM, Su 11AM-5PM. From handbags to baby slings, from toys to journals, this is where cool *stuff* is found; nothing you urgently need, and lots of things you'll realize you want.

Japan Books & Seoul Books and Records, 3450 W Peterson Ave, +1 773 463-7229, M-Sa 10AM-7PM, Su noon-5PM. Two stores at one location selling principally books and magazines, but also music, comic books, and videos. As you would expect the former store offers goods in the Japanese; the latter in Korean.

Laurie's Planet of Sound, 4639 N Lincoln Ave (*Western Brown Line*), +1 773 271-3569, *lauriesplanetofsound.tripod.com*, M-Sa 10AM-10PM, Su 11AM-7PM. Excellent neighborhood CD &

NORTH LINCOLNEAT

DVD store with staff who care about music — not infrequently is this called the best record store in the city.

Merz Apothecary, 4716 N Lincoln Ave (*Western Brown Line*), +1 773 989-0900, *www.merzapothecary.com*, M-Sa 9AM-6PM. Established in 1875 as a typical corner drug store, Merz Apothecary sold herbal medicines and traditional remedies from the Old World under several generations of the Merz family. In 1972, Abdul Quaiyum bought the store and expanded sales to include international health, body, and beauty products, and today, the thriving business doubles as a tourist destination for its classic atmosphere.

Quake Collectibles, 4628 N Lincoln Ave (*Western Brown Line*), +1 773 878-4288. If you have long yearned to re-assemble the squad of Dinobots that your mother so heartlessly sold at a garage sale, this would be a good place to start. Prices for in-original-package items vary, but the real danger lies in the several bins of loose action figures at $3 apiece or 4 for $10.

Salamander Shoes, 4740 N Lincoln (*Western Brown Line*), +1 773 784-7463, *www.salamandershoes.com*, M-W 9:30AM-6PM, Th 9:30AM-8PM, F-Sa 9:30AM-6PM, Su 12-4PM. Imported walking shoes on stylish display, with a few bigger-than-usual sizes.

Sweden Shop, 3304 W Foster Ave, +1 773 478-0327, *www.theswedenshop.com*, M-Sa 10AM-6PM, Su 10AM-3PM. Scandinavian import store in North Park, owned by the couple that runs the Tre Kronor restaurant (see Eat).

Timeless Toys, 4749 N Lincoln Ave (*Western Brown Line*), +1 773 334-4445, M-W, Sa 10AM-6PM, Thu,F 10AM-7PM, Su 11AM-5PM. Classic toy store — as in, no Disney characters or cheap movie tie-ins — with plenty to buy and plenty more to play with in the store.

Eat

Put simply, there's food in this area that's found nowhere else in Chicago, and it's *good*. Middle Eastern and Korean are the headliners, but there are also Thai, German, and Japanese places that are consistently mentioned among the city's best. With most restaurants easily accessible from the Brown Line, it's worth a trip for dinner even if you're staying elsewhere.

Budget

Apart Pizza, 2205 W. Montrose Ave (*Western Brown Line*), +1 773 588-1550, *www.apartinc.com*, M-Tu 5-11PM, W-Su 11AM-11PM. One of the best locations for Neopolitan-style pizza in Chicago, and unlike the well-known main competitor Spacca Napoli, here you won't have to wait an hour to get in the door. Makes an amazing $5 personal pizza, and features free delivery. $5-18.

Costello Sandwich & Sides, 4647 N Lincoln Ave (*Western Brown Line*), +1 773 989-7788, *www.costellosandwich.com*, Su-Th 11AM-9PM, F-Sa 11AM-10PM. Sandwich joint with more than enough options to make Subway's head spin. $6-8.

Garcia's Restaurant, 4749 N Western Ave (*Western Brown Line*), +1 773 769-5600, M-Th 10AM-1AM, F 10AM-3AM, Sa 10AM-4AM, Su 10AM-12AM. Cheap Mexican restaurant that earns loyalty for plentiful, tasty food and late-night hours. $4-12.

Korean Noodle Restaurant, 3236 W Bryn Mawr Ave, +1 773 588-0305, M-Sa 10AM-10PM. Korean noodle soup is generally similar to other East Asian noodle cuisine, but is often fiery hot, full of Korean hot sauce. $3-6.

Nazareth Sweets, 4638 N Kedzie Ave, +1 773 463-2457, M-Sa 10AM-10PM, Su 10AM-9PM. If you've had dinner on Kedzie, skip dessert there and savor this on the train back to the hotel. Nazareth has the cheap, fresh baklava and semolina cakes you so richly deserve. $2-5.

Rosded Restaurant, 2308 W Leland Ave (*Western Brown Line*), +1 773 334-9055, Tu-Sa 11:30AM-9PM, Su noon-8:30PM. Hole-in-the-wall Thai restaurant with traditional recipes and big, flavorful portions. $10-20.

Salam, 4636 N Kedzie Ave (*Kedzie Brown Line*), +1 773 583-0776, 9:30AM-9:30PM. Falafel comes no cheaper in Chicago than at this mostly Palestinian restaurant. It's a neighborhood hang-out and has

nothing in the way of decor, but anyone is welcome, and the menu changes throughout the week to keep the regulars satisfied. $3-10.

Semiramis, 4639 N Kedzie Ave (*Kedzie Brown Line*), +1 773 279-8900, M-Th 11AM-10PM, F-Sa 11AM-11PM. BYOB Lebanese food that excels even in staples like hummus. Semiramis is smack outside the Kedzie station, and its comfortable, casual dining room is a great place to pass some time. $6-13.

Shelly's Freez, 5119 N Lincoln Ave (*Western Brown Line*), +1 773 271-2783, 9AM-9:45PM daily. A giant hot dog and a giant soft-serve ice cream cone on the walls outside advertise a simple, timeless culinary truth. $2-4.

Tre Kronor, 3258 W Foster Ave, +1 773 267-9888, *www.swedishbistro.com*, Tu-Sa 7AM-10PM, Su 9AM-3PM. Along with Andersonville, North Park has a pocket of Swedish Chicago. Good for breakfast, brunch, or a quick *fika*. $5-15.

Mid-range

One of the true pleasures of Chicago dining is a weekend brunch in Lincoln Square. **Cafe Selmarie** is the best-known spot, but a few of the bars serve a worthy brunch as well — see Drink for more options.

Al-Khaymeih, 4748 N Kedzie Ave (*Kedzie Brown Line*), +1 773 583-0999, 10AM-10PM. Lebanese cuisine in Albany Park. Try a *mezza*, a set selection of twelve appetizers for your dipping pleasure. $10-22.

Cafe Selmarie, 4729 N Lincoln Ave (*Western Brown Line*), +1 773 989-5595, *www.cafeselmarie.com*, M 11AM-3PM, Tu-Th 8AM-10PM, F-Sa 8AM-11PM, Su 10AM-10PM. A favorite spot for brunch since 1983, with outdoor sitting right in the fountain square. $8-$17.

Chicago Kalbi, 3752 W Lawrence Ave, +1 773 604-8183, *www.chicago-kalbi.com*, W-M 5PM-midnight. Korean/Japanese BBQ. Reportedly has a shrine to Japanese baseball players, making it worth the trip for *pro yakyu* fans. $14-30.

Great Sea Chinese Restaurant, 3254 W Lawrence Ave, +1 773 478-9129, Su-Th 11AM-9:30PM, F-Sa 11AM-10:30PM. A nice attractive restaurant serving a wide range of Chinese and Korean foods. $8-14.

Il Song Jung, 3315 W Bryn Mawr Ave, +1 773 463-2121, 5PM-2AM daily. A Korean BBQ restaurant with an interior you would only find on "Seoul Drive." Patrons cook their own food on the table as they eat. $10-15.

Kang Nam Restaurant, 4849 N Kedzie Ave, +1 773 539-2524, 10:30AM-10:30PM. A smoky, family-run Korean BBQ with no decor, a back room for karaoke, free parking, and *lots* of food — entrees come with numerous side dishes. If two or more in your party order the same dish, you'll have the option of cooking at your table. $10-25.

Los Nopales, 4544 N Western Ave (*Western Brown Line*), +1 773 334-3149, *www.losnopalesrestaurant.com*, Tu-Su 10AM-10PM. BYOB Mexican restaurant; the name means "cactus paddle," and that's one of their signature dishes. (And there's a liquor store around the corner on Leland.) $7-18.

Midori Japanese Restaurant, 3310 W Bryn Mawr Ave, +1 773 267-9733, W-M lunch: 11:30AM-2:30PM, dinner: 5PM-11PM, karaoke: 7PM-1:30AM. This Japanese restaurant is an excellent value, offering all sorts of hard-to-find Japanese dishes and private dining rooms for up to 6 people. $10-15.

Noon O Kabab, 4661 N Kedzie Ave (*Kedzie Brown Line*), +1 773 279-8899, *www.noonokabab.com*, M-Th 11AM-10PM, F-Sa 11AM-11PM, Su 11AM-9PM. Persian food that deservedly earns rave reviews, particularly the *polo* (seasoned rice) dishes. Meals come with some tasty complimentary appetizers. It's a great take-out option, too. $7-$17.

So Gong Dong Tofu House, 3307 W Bryn Mawr Ave, +1 773 539-8377, 10AM-10PM, closed W. Serves up sizzling portions of Korean tofu stew with beef, seafood, or vegetables, and dan jang chi gae, memorably described by the Chicago Reader as "an aggressive bean paste stew." $10-15.

Spoon Thai, 4608 N Western Ave (*Western Brown Line*), +1 773 769-1173, *www.spoonthai.com*, 11AM-10PM. Authentic Thai food, with bits and pieces from other Asian cuisines. Rumor has it that a secret

Thai-only menu exists for a wider range of options. Weekday lunch specials are only $4.95.

Ssyal Ginseng House, 4201 W Lawrence Ave, +1 773 427-5296, M-Sa 10:30AM-9:30PM, Su 1-9PM. Ginseng-infused Korean soups (chicken, fish, and miso). Check out the bizarre (and perfectly natural) twisted jars of ginseng in the window. $11.

Splurge

Chicago Brauhaus, 4732 N Lincoln Ave (*Western Brown Line*), +1 773 784-4444, *www.chicagobrauhaus.com*, 11AM-12AM, closed Tuesdays. Whenever you walk into the Brauhaus, you're right on time for Oktoberfest, which has carried on for more than forty years at this authentic, family-run German restaurant. If schnitzel, brats, beer, and the Austrian Elvis sounds appealing, *mach schnell!* $16-22.

Chiyo Japanese Restaurant, 3800 W Lawrence Ave, +1 773 267-1555, *www.chiyorestaurant.com*, W-M 5PM-midnight. Shabu-shabu, nabe, Kobe beef, and other Japanese delights in Albany Park. Kaiseki (set) dinners $80, chef selections $40, a la carte $5-7 per item.

Joy Ribs, 6230 N Lincoln Ave, +1 773 509-0211. Korean BBQ, starring duck, beef, and pork, with a house specialty of pheasant. $44 for two people.

La Bocca della Verita, 4618 N Lincoln Ave (*Western Brown Line*), +1 773 784-6222, *www.laboccachicago.*

com, Su-Th 5-10PM, F-Sa 5-11PM. The Mouth of Truth is a slow-food favorite, as the owners take their sweet time in preparing these faithful Italian-from-Italy recipes. Dogs are welcome to accompany their owners on the outdoor patio, with bowls of water available for hot days. $16-22.

Drink

Cafes

The Grind, 4613 N Lincoln Ave (*Western Brown Line*), +1 773 241-4482, *www.thegrindco.com*, M-F 7AM-10PM, Sa 8AM-10PM, Su 8AM-7PM. Wi-fi and plenty of outdoor seating.

Lutz Cafe & Pastry Shop, 2458 W Montrose Ave, +1 773 478-7785, *www.lutzcafe.com*, Su-Th 7AM-7PM, F-Sa 7AM-8PM. Enjoy coffee and something sweet from this legendary bakery (est. 1948), or just stop by to gaze in awe at the amazing display case. The cafe has a nice outdoor garden (weather permitting).

The Perfect Cup, 4700 N Damen Ave (*Damen Brown Line*), +1 773 989-4177, M-F 6:30AM-9PM, Sa 7:30AM-9PM, Su 7:30AM-8PM. A quiet coffee shop near the CTA with a take-a-book leave-a-book policy.

Schlegl's Bakery & Cafe, 3334 W Foster Ave, +1 773 539-9207, *www. schlegls.com*. Sip coffee and snack on a Bavarian pastry (or two).

Bars

Not accidentally, you'll find more than a few karaoke joints on Lincoln, Western, and Lawrence, near the Korean BBQ restaurants. The rest listed here are upscale restaurant/bar combos and a few affable dives.

Bad Dog Tavern, 4535 N Lincoln Ave (*Western Brown Line*), +1 773 334-4040, *www.baddogtavern.com*, M 5PM-2AM, Tu-Th,F 12PM-2AM, Sa 11:30AM-3AM, Su 11AM-2AM. A great pub with a menu worthy of an upscale restaurant. Live music on Monday and Tuesday nights.

Cafe Orange, 5639 N Lincoln Ave, +1 773 275-5040, 5:30PM-2AM daily. Lively Korean bar with flavored *soju*, ice cream, *bi bim bop* and a dance floor.

The Daily Bar & Grill, 4560 N Lincoln Ave (*Western Brown Line*), +1 773 561-6198, *www.sparetimechicago.com*, Su-F 12PM-2AM, Sa 12PM-3AM. The perfect distillation of a stylish 50's diner and a full bar with enough screens to keep a sports fan satisfied, along with a food menu of staples done well like mac 'n cheese, pot pies, and cheesy tater tots.

The Grafton, 4530 N Lincoln Ave (*Western Brown Line*), +1 773 271-9000, *www.thegrafton.com*, M-F 5PM-2AM, Sa 11AM-3AM, Su 11AM-2AM. Cozy Irish pub with better-than-average food (and even better desserts). Live music on Wednesdays/Sundays (Irish) and Tuesdays (folk).

The Huettenbar, 4721 N Lincoln Ave (*Western Brown Line*), +1 773 561-2507, Su-F 11AM-2AM, Sa 11AM-3AM. A good neighborhood tavern with a top selection of German beers.

Lincoln Karaoke, 5526 N Lincoln Ave, +1 773 895-2299, M-Th,Su 7PM-3AM, F-Sa 7PM-5AM. Korean, Chinese, Japanese and English karaoke heaven, with private rooms, free parking, and *very* friendly staff. Rooms $25/hour, beer $3.

Montrose Saloon, 2933 W Montrose Ave (*Kedzie Brown Line*), +1 773 463-7663, *myspace.com*. A truly beautiful dive bar with games, cheap beer, and a schedule of events that includes a bluegrass jam on the second Wednesday of every month.

Niedersachsen Club Chicago, 4548 N Lincoln Ave (*Western Brown Line*), +1 773 878-1020, *www.niedersachsenclubchicago.org*. A German-American social club, open to the public on the first Saturday of every month. There's authentic German food and drink on offer, and the *Kappen Abend* — literally, "hat night" — is a showcase for "the craziest of crazy hats," not to mention the occasional outbreak of a *schunkling* circle.

Rockwell's Neighborhood Grill, 4632 N Rockwell (*Rockwell Brown Line*), +1 773 509-1871, *www.rockwellsgrill.com*, M-Th 4-10PM, F 4-11PM, Sa 10AM-11PM, Su 10AM-10PM. A neighborhood favorite at the center of a small commercial district around the

Rockwell CTA station, not far from the river. The outdoor seating is especially nice and will slip pleasant hours from your pocket.

NORTH LINCOLN SLEEP

Sin Strip slipping away

In the early days of the inter-state motorways, US-41 was the route of choice between Chicago and Milwaukee. Twelve motels sprang up on Lincoln Avenue between Peterson/Devon and Foster to accommodate road-weary travelers, with giant neon signs bearing names like Stars, Tip-Top, and Rio.

However, with the opening of the Edens Expressway (I-94), traffic dried up on US-41. The full extent of what happened next depends on who you ask; pretty much everyone will admit that, yes, some hookers did take advantage of the hourly rates offered by some motels, the name of the O Mi Motel did take on a certain irony, and the Lincoln Avenue motels did come to be known as Sin Strip. It's not a question of whether there was a cesspool; merely a debate over whether the cesspool was all-encompassing.

Over the last ten years, the city government has been using every legal maneuver in its considerable repertoire to get the Lincoln Avenue motels closed, as part of the effort to remove centers for crime and vice, and to prime a few more areas to join in Chicago's real estate boom. Several have been condemned or sold to condo developers. A handful do remain, however, and are run by owners who insist that they run respectable businesses and are fighting to stay open.

While perhaps not a place to bring a family keen on standard Chicago tourist fare, there are a few things to be said for saying on Sin Strip: the area has gentrified considerably, and it's no longer particularly dangerous

in the area. (Just a bit seedy.) The CTA Brown Line is only a short bus ride or walk away, taking you into the center of the city. The rates are a lot cheaper than what you'll see downtown, especially for long-term stays. And, of course, there are those impossibly cool signs...

Sleep

The #11 Lincoln bus runs past all of the **Sin Strip motels** (see infobox), and stops at the Western Brown Line station in Lincoln Square.

Apache Motel, 5535 N Lincoln Ave, +1 773 728-9400. Run by a friendly, eager family of Indian descent (as in India, not the yellow Native American Indian head that sits atop their sign). Close to a public library. $50 per night, plus $2 key deposit.

Diplomat Motel, 5230 N Lincoln Ave, +1 773 271-5400. The southernmost of the surviving motels, within a reasonable walk of Lincoln Square. Color TV proudly offered. $62 per night.

Guest House, 2600 W Bryn Mawr Ave, +1 773 561-6811. Right around the corner from the O Mi, but with tons (comparatively) of parking and a grand (comparatively) archway. King-size beds with television, but no cable. $67 per night.

The O Mi Motel, 5611 N Lincoln Ave, +1 773 561-6488. Other than the candy-stripe turquoise/white wall near the office, the O Mi is restrained in decor. It's across the street from the Budlong Woods public library. $40 per night.

The Patio, 6250 N Lincoln Ave, +1 773 588-8400. Famed for the blue cursive in their neon sign: "Adventures in Living!" $50 per night.

The Rio Motel, 6155 N Jersey Ave, +1 773 463-2733. Just off Lincoln, a reasonable walk from the Indian food on Devon. Television, but no cable. $52 per night.

Summit Motel, 5308 N Lincoln Ave, +1 773 561-3762. Also within a reasonable walk of Lincoln Square. $50 per night.

Tip Top Motel, 6060 N Lincoln Ave, +1 773 539-4800. Cable, kitchenettes, and air conditioning. $49 per night.

Contact

Albany Park Branch Library, 5150 N Kimball Ave (*Kimball Brown Line*), +1 312 744-1933, *www.chipublib.org*, M-Th 9AM-8PM, F-Sa 9AM-5PM. Free public internet access. Befitting its location, this library has a strong collection of Korean-language materials.

Budlong Woods Branch Library, 5630 N Lincoln Ave (*11 Lincoln bus*), +1 312 742-9590, *www.chipublib.org*, M-Th 9AM-9PM, F-Sa 9AM-5PM, Su closed. Free public internet access, walking distance from most of the motels.

Mayfair Branch Library, 4400 W Lawrence Ave (*81 Lawrence bus*), +1 312 744-1254, *www.chipublib.org*, M,W 12-8PM, Tu,Th-Sa 9AM-5PM, Su closed. Free public inter-

net access.

Sulzer Regional Library, 4455 N Lincoln Ave (*Western Brown Line*), +1 312 744-7616, *www.chipublib.org*, M-Th 9AM-9PM, F-Sa 9AM-5PM, Su 1-5PM. The regional library for the north side of Chicago, with a huge collection and free public internet access.

Get out

A short walk south down Lincoln Avenue, in North Center *p.139*, the colorful spectre of Honest Abe's giant head (at the Lincoln Restaurant) beckons all who enjoyed themselves in his Square.

Chicago's **Far West Side** is best known (somewhat unfairly) for being impoverished and crime-ridden, but it has at least one major attraction as well as some fabulous parks, vibrant immigrant communities, and blues legends. Regardless, you're definitely off the tourist map on the Far West Side.

Understand

The Far West Side represents a very large, heterodox slice of Chicago life ranging from some of Chicago's most blighted neighborhoods to the solidly middle-class bungalow belt, with some strong immigrant communities in between. The Garfield Park Conservatory is a lovely and easy excursion from downtown for any visitor to Chicago, but beyond this one attraction, the Far West Side is untrodden by the camera-wielding tourist masses of the Loop *p.47* and Near North *p.71*. Pat yourself on the back if you make it this far into Chicago — you are really seeing the city.

Neighborhoods

Garfield Park is the Far West Side's most notorious neighborhood for violent crime and visitors with low tolerance for urban grit should probably keep their distance. But on the other hand, the park from which the neighborhood derives its name is one of the city's best laid out and it contains a major attraction in the form of the Garfield Park Conservatory, in addition to a gorgeous fieldhouse. Don't be afraid to visit the park itself — there is an L stop hovering right over the conservatory and the park is quite safe.

South Lawndale is the heart of Chicago's enormous Mexican community and is a great escape from Chicago's gringo downtown. Although mostly residential, the long "downtown" strip (known as **Little Village**, or **La Villita**) along 26th Street between Sacramento and Pulaski is a vibrant, smile-filled strip jam-packed with Mexican musical instruments, weekend festivals, bars, Virgin Mary towels, media-shops, and (most importantly) taquerías. As a matter of fact, La Villita feels like not just an escape from Chicago, but from the United States generally — it's certainly as close to Mexico as you can get in the Midwest.

North Lawndale bears little resemblance to South Lawndale. Unlike its very safe neighbor, North Lawndale is still recovering from very high levels of violent crime in the 1970s–1980s. During this time, the northern section of the neighborhood, known as K-Town for its countless streets beginning with the letter K, was jokingly referred to as "Kill-Town" for its violence problem. The neighborhood has some history to its name, but fairly little remains to interest a visitor by way of shopping or sights. Sears used to have its headquarters here and you might be interested in driving by Chicago's first "Sears Tower" (and other gargantuan Sears buildings) which the city is now restoring in hopes of rejuvenating the long-impoverished community around Homan Square.

Humboldt Park sits between gentrifying Logan Square *p.247* and blighted Garfield Park and, somehow, here the twain do meet. The neighborhood has for some time been a cultural stronghold of Chicago's Puerto Rican community, centered around the long commercial strip on Division Street. The association between Division Street and Puerto Rican Chicagoans is pretty firmly cemented in the minds of most Chicagoans owing to the Division Street riots of 1966. The riots began during a Puerto Rican community parade, as a result of an economic downturn and high tensions between Chicago's Puerto Ricans and the police (and neighboring Polish-American communities) that came to a head after the Chicago Police shot a young Puerto Rican man in the neighborhood. Any legacy of violence, however, is long gone and visitors should feel comfortable visiting Division Street during the day to soak up the Puerto Rican vibes.

Humboldt Park's populace is diverse, but awkwardly un-integrated. Its Puerto Rican community now sits between the less affluent black community to the west and southwest, and a new, burgeoning white community seeking lower rents than in the neighborhoods to the east and north. The eponymous park is a lovely spot to observe the neighborhood's contrasts — between the three communities who flock there to enjoy the big lagoon, playgrounds, and fields, but never quite mix socially.

Austin is a fairly unique, albeit not terribly interesting section of the city. It is the largest single Chicago community area in terms of area and population, but it sits at the extreme periphery of Chicago life along the western border of the city, having only been annexed in 1899. The jewel in this neighborhood's crown is Columbus Park, considered the best work by Prairie School land-scape artist Jens Jensen. The park has a nice lagoon and 9 holes of golf and is just off the Eisen-hower Expressway (which was built over the southern end of the original park). The neighbor-hood is overwhelmingly African-American and middle class, and can't quite make up its mind whether it is urban or suburban.

Belmont Cragin, **Hermosa**, and **Montclare** have a somewhat mixed identity between the Far West Side and the Far Northwest Side *p.363*, as the residents of these areas are a mix of what you would find in the over-whelmingly Polish-American neighborhoods to the north and the Puerto Rican and Mexican-American neighborhoods directly to the south. The neighborhoods are experiencing a huge influx of Mexican-Americans and Puerto Ricans trading up for nicer houses from Pilsen *p.259* and Humboldt Park. For the most part, these are quiet, residential communities lacking significant tourist draws.

Far West Side

■ See and Do
1. Aguijón Theater
2. Aloft Loft
3. Apollos 2000
4. Garfield Park Conservatory
5. Laramie State Bank Building
6. Sears Tower
7. Walser House

■ Buy
1. Brickyard Mall
2. Music for You
3. Out of the Past Records

■ Eat
1. Cafe Colao
2. Edna's Restaurant
3. Feed
4. Home Run Inn Pizzeria
5. La Bruquena
6. La Palma
7. Los Dos Laredos
8. Lou Malnati's
9. MacArthur's
10. Maiz
11. Mi Tierra
12. Operetta
13. Peeples Taco Place
14. Red Ginger
15. Taquerías Atotonilco
16. Taquería Los Comales
17. Wallace's Catfish Corner

■ Drink
1. California Clipper
2. The Continental
3. Jedynka Club
4. La Justicia
5. Los Globos
6. Rooster Palace

■ Sleep
1. Fullerton Hotel
2. Grand Motel West
3. Hotel Norford
4. North Hotel

■ Contact
1. Austin Library
2. Douglass Library
3. Galewood-Montclare Library
4. Humboldt Park Library
5. Legler Branch
6. Marshall Square Library
7. North Austin Library
8. North Pulaski Library
9. Portage-Cragin Library
10. Toman Library
11. West Belmont Library
12. West Chicago Ave Library

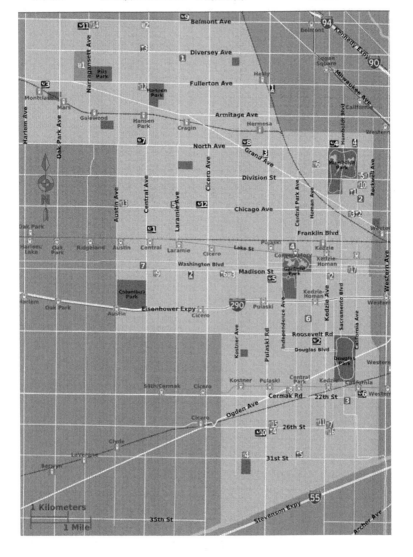

Get in

By train

The **Forest Park** branch of the CTA **Blue Line** runs from the Loop *p.47* through the Near West Side *p.215* and on into the Far West, with stops in South and North Lawndale.

The **Pink Line** runs through the Near West Side *p.215* and Pilsen *p.259* and heads to South Lawndale.

The **Green Line** runs to the Far West Side, with a stop in Garfield Park (Conservatory) and on to Oak Park across the city border. This is the oldest part of the CTA system, although the tracks and stations were renovated in the late 1990s. Looking through the window of the train gives you a picture of a different part of Chicago. On the trip from the Loop, you might also notice the gentrification spreading west from downtown — there are startlingly rapid changes from gentrified to decayed neighborhoods.

By bus

The CTA runs several bus routes through the West Side:

12 Roosevelt runs through the West Side along the edge of Garfield Park and North Lawndale.

18 16th/18th runs from the Near South Side *p.95* through Pilsen, Little Village and North Lawndale all night long.

20 Madison runs from the Loop *p.47* west through the West Side,

passing by the United Center all night long.

21 Cermak runs from the Near South Side *p.95* heading west through the Lower West Side, running parallel to the Pink Line. (Damen-54th/Cermak).

38 Ogden/Taylor runs along Ogden Avenue to California.

49 Western runs down Western Avenue for nearly the full length of the city, passing by Ukrainian Village *p.229* and Pilsen *p.259* to the east and Humboldt Park/Garfield Park to the west. It's an all-night route.

52 Kedzie/California travels on Kedzie through the Far West Side *p.331* making connections at the Green Blue and Pink Lines.

53 Pulaski covers most of the Far West Side and runs all night.

54 Cicero covers the other major north/south thoroughfare, although it's not an all-night route.

57 Laramie runs up and down Laramie Avenue.

60 Blue Island/26th runs from the Chicago/Loop *p.47* through the Near West Side, Pilsen, Little Village and South Lawndale all night long.

65 Grand runs from the Near North *p.71* through West Town *p.229*, Humboldt Park, and onward to Harlem.

66 Chicago runs from the Near North *p.71* through West Town *p.229* and Ukrainian Village, passing within a short walk of Humboldt Park, and onward to Austin. It's also an all-night route.

70 Division runs from the Near North *p.71* through West Town *p.229* and Ukrainian Village, passing within a short walk of Humboldt Park, and onward to Austin.

72 North Avenue runs from the Near North *p.71* through West Town *p.229* and Humboldt Park, and onward to Austin.

82 Kimball/Homan connects with the Blue Line at Kedzie-Homan and the Central Park Pink Line serving Humboldt Park, Garfield Park, and Lawndale.

85 Central connects with the Green Line heading up and down Central Ave.

91 Austin Runs up and down Austin Avenue along the border between Chicago and Oak Park.

94 South California Runs up and down California Avenue connecting with the Green and Pink Lines.

By car

The **Eisenhower Expressway** (I-290) is the major thoroughfare crossing the Far West Side, although travelers along the historic Route 66 will pass through the area as well, on **Ogden Avenue**, which leads from downtown. If you are going to Garfield Park or Humboldt Park, the main I-290 exits are at Pulaski, Kedzie, and Western. For Little Village, it's usually faster, though, to take the Pulaski or Kedzie Avenue exits from the **Stevenson Expressway** instead.

See

The Garfield Park Conservatory is the one real sightseeing draw on the Far West. The Sears Tower is quite interesting as well, but it's hard to get to without a car, and the old Sears buildings are *technically* not open to visitors.

Garfield Park (*Conservatory Green Line*). History-filled Chicago park a mere 15 minutes west of downtown, with some fun outdoor sculptures, plenty of green space, and a fabulous fieldhouse. It's in a rough neighborhood, though you can take the L right to the park, which is safe.

Garfield Park Conservatory, 300 N Central Park Ave, *www.garfieldconservatory.org*, F-W 9AM-5PM, Th 9AM-8PM. Amazing botanical conservatory, one of the largest indoor gardens in the world, which is often blessed with large-scale contemporary art installations as well as frequent family-oriented events. Definitely bring the kids, who will not lack for things to climb on and strange environments to run around in. Perhaps in an effort to assuage especially fearful Chicagoans, the L stop actually hovers directly above the conservatory entrance, so definitely don't pass this place over for fear of the surrounding neighborhood. There is also ample free lot and on-street parking right around the main building. Free admission, except during special exhibits and events.

Laramie State Bank Building, 5200 W Chicago Ave. Chicago's

The Original Sears Tower and Headquarters buildings

most far flung city landmark is covered with wonderfully elaborate carvings in its art deco, terra cotta exterior. The bank's construction was finished in the malapropos year of 1929.

Old Sears Tower, 900 S Homan Ave. Chicagoans can't get enough Towers of Sears. This is the original, which at a height of 250 feet served as Sears' headquarters until the move into the slightly taller building downtown. Once the largest commercial building in the world, the tower must now content itself with being the tallest in the Far West Side. A short jaunt in either direction on Arthington St will reveal more grandiose old Sears buildings, from the power plant and warehouses to the west to the headquarters building just across the street to the east.

Walser House, 42 N Central Ave, *www.cityofchicago.org*. For sake of comprehensiveness, you might want to drive by this Frank Lloyd Wright house in Austin after a tour of his numerous buildings in neighboring Oak Park. The house is a textbook example of success in applying the Prairie School design principles of strong horizontals and open interiors. Look especially for the attractive windows (not originals, unfortunately), whose patterns have inspired a line of Frank Lloyd Wright jewelry. Closed to the public.

Do

Aguijón Theater, 2707 N Laramie Ave, +1 773 637-5899, *www.aguijontheater.org*, Shows usually F,Sa,Su. A busy theater with acclaimed productions of Spanish-language and bi-lingual comedy, drama, music, and dance. $20.

Aloft Loft, 941 N California Ave (*#52 California bus*), +1 773 507-2604, *www.aloftaerialdance.com*, Check website for showtimes. A theater group comprised of... trapeze artists?! The space is run by an "aerial dance" troupe which puts on shows and runs high-flying circus training programs. If you're in town for the week and looking for something really out of the ordinary to do, consider signing up for their Two-Day Beginning Trapeze course ($65). It's in an alley and has no signs, so you'll have to really look for it.

Apollos 2000, 2875 W Cermak Rd, +1 773 247-0200. The Apollos is a major local landmark, its art deco theater facade now serving a music hall. The events calendar is dominated by live Mexican bands, but branches out into a little of everything. You'll need to swing by or check the papers to keep abreast of events, but even if you don't catch a show, take note of this beautiful building.

Wallace's Catfish Corner (See eat section for contact information), *www.catfishcorners.com*. Each summer Wallace's puts on outdoor blues concerts in East Garfield Park, and you should not pass up such an opportunity. Word has it this parking lot extravaganza may be the best blues experience known to man. Check their website for details (See below).

Events & festivals

Little Village Arts Fest, 2756 S Harding Ave, +1 773 542-9233, *lvcdc.org/artsfest*, October — see website for dates. Like the Pilsen Open Studios event in neighboring Pilsen, the annual Little Village Arts Fest opens the doors of the several art studios and participating businesses in the neighborhood for a weekend of browsing and community spirit.

Buy

For the most part, if you are out shopping in the Far West Side of Chicago, you somewhere got lost. The one exception being the endless Little Village strip along 26th St, which is after the Magnificent Mile *p.71*, the largest commercial strip in the city in terms of revenue. The miles of colorful, bargain knickknack shops along the Little Village strip make for very fun window shopping, and can produce kitschy souvenirs that look like you took a trip to a different country.

Brickyard Mall, 2554 N Narragansett Ave, +1 773 745-8838, M-Sa 10AM-9PM, Su 11AM-6PM. Aside from dominating Belmont Cragin commerce, there's nothing much special about the Brickyard Mall. But you'll find what you need here.

Music for You, 3150 N Central Ave, +1 773 745-4641, M,W-Sa 10AM-8PM, Su 11AM-5PM. Not a square inch remains unused in this store — it's fully covered in hard-to-find dance music cds from Eastern Europe, serving the two main communities of Belmont Cragin.

Out of the Past Records, 4407 W Madison St, +1 773 626-3878, M-Sa 9AM-9PM, Su 10AM-7PM. An out of the way music store selling loads of R&B, jazz, blues, and gospel LPs and tapes.

Eat

The Far West has virtually no high-end dining options, but if you are fine with spending less, a ton of great food experiences await. Little Village boasts some of the best authentic Mexican food in the city, Garfield Park and Austin have some fine down-home cooking, and Humboldt Park has a veritable monopoly on Chicago's Puerto Rican fare.

Budget

Cafe Colao, 2638 W Division St (*A block and a half east of Humboldt Park, #70 Division bus*), +1 773 276-1780, M 7AM-5PM, T-F,Su 7AM-6PM, Sa 8AM-6PM. This small, inviting cafe is one of the best options for visitors wanting a simple, yet authentic Puerto Rican lunch. One part coffee shop, one part bakery, and delicious sandwiches. If you are up early and in the neighborhood, come here for a terrific Puerto Rican breakfast. $2-5.

Edna's Restaurant, 3175 W Madison St (*Two blocks east of Garfield Park*), +1 773 638-7079, T-Su 6AM-7PM. Edna's is renowned for having some of the best soul food in Chicago's West Side. Peerless biscuits, heavenly breakfasts, and pie to die for. You are likely to be served by Edna herself. $3-8.

Feed, 2803 W Chicago Ave (*#66 Chicago bus*), +1 773 489-4600, M-Sa 11AM-10PM. This Garfield Park rotisserie chicken joint also boasts a mean pulled pork BBQ sandwich, all with a host of comfort-food side dishes — Feed pulls in a lot of business all week long. The food is garbage, of course, compared to a place like Edna's, but that's reflected in the price. $3-6.

La Palma, 1340 N Homan Ave (*Two blocks west of the park*), +1 773 862-0886, M-Sa 8AM-7PM, Su 10AM-6PM. La Palma won't catch your eye, but this cafeteria-style eatery is considered by locals to serve the best Puerto Rican food in Chicago. If authentic is what you want, this is your best bet. $4-8.

MacArthur's, 5401 W Madison Ave, +1 773 261-2316, *www.macarthursrestaurant.com*, 11AM-9PM daily. Perhaps Austin's favorite soul food kitchen, MacArthur's delights patrons with properly done comfort food in a cafeteria-style eating area. Since getting the Sen. Obama endorsement in "The Audacity of Hope," MacArthur's is now drawing foodies from all over the city — with all due respects to the Senator, he isn't right that this is the *best* soul food in the city, but it is easily the best *value*. $3-8.

Peeples Taco Place, 5944 W Chicago Ave, +1 773 626-7699, Weekdays 8AM-3AM, weekends 24 hours. The soul food taco is a rare beast, but the long lines coming out the door of this small Austin carryout joint should give confidence to the quality of its inauthentic and wildly unhealthy "Mexican" cooking. Get your tacos drenched in hot sauce and the fries in mild. $1.50-5.

Taquería Atotonilco, 3916 W 26th St (#53 *Pulaski bus*), +1 773 762-3380, M-Th 9AM-2AM, F-Su 24 hours. Tacos and tortas in a small, family run taquería. Also a good spot for fruit fanatics, as they offer fresh squeezed juices and licuados (milkshakes made with fresh fruit). $1.50-5.

Taquería Los Comales, 3141 W 26th St, +1 773 523-1689, *www.loscomales.com*, M-Th 7:30AM-3AM, F,Su 7:30AM-5AM, Sa 7:30AM-6AM. The original Los Comales is a big, family-friendly, cafeteria-style eatery with a take-out counter and even a drive-through window. Skip the combo platters in favor of the authentic, cilantro-drenched tacos. If your taco experiences have been limited to gringo chains, the ones here will leave you weak in the knees with pleasure. The "Al Pastor" pork taco is the local specialty, but all options are great. Wash your meal down with a glass of horchata and all will be right with the world. $1.50-8.

Mid-range

Home Run Inn Pizzeria, 4254 W 31st St (#53 *Pulaski bus*), +1 773 247-9696, M-Th 11AM-10PM, F 11AM-11:30PM, Sa noon-11:30PM, Su noon-10PM. If you've spent much time in Chicago at all, you've probably run into Home Run Pizza, whether you passed by a franchise or just the frozen goods aisle of a grocery store. This is the original location. Many consider its crunchy Chicago-thin-crust pizza the best in the city. $10-20.

La Bruquena, 2726 W Division St (#52 *Division bus*), +1 773 276-2915, M-Su 10AM-11PM. An excellent, very authentic, and inviting Puerto Rican-Caribbean restaurant next to the park on Division. $10-16.

Los Dos Laredos Restaurante, 3120 W 26th St, +1 773 376-3218, M-Th 6AM-midnight, F-Su 24 hours. A natural choice for dinner if you are in Little Village — you can't miss the brightly painted building under the Little Village Arch. A breakfast of chorizos and omelets will not disappoint. Later in the day try one of their signature massive grill combos. Live bands perform on Saturday nights. $10-18.

Lou Malnati's, 3859 W Ogden Ave, +1 773 762-0800, *www.loumalnatis.com*, M-Th 11AM-9PM, F-Sa 11AM-10PM, Su 12:30-4PM. Top notch deep dish pizza in Lawndale. Stick to the pizza — the other dishes are sub-par. It's actually the first sit-down restaurant in the neighborhood, staffed by mostly volunteers, & proceeds go to the local community center — eat your pizza for the children! $8-22.

Maiz, 1041 N California Ave, +1 773 276-3149, T-Su 5PM-10PM. When in Humboldt Park, Puerto Rican food really should be the choice of the day, but you might not be able to resist this particular Mexican restaurant. It serves Mexican antojitos in a manner akin to a Spanish tapas restaurant, and has an exotic selection of very traditional, but not-well-known dishes from Mexico's regions — like Tamal Oaxaqueno, a tamale wrapped in a banana leaf, stuffed with chicken or pork and green salsa and topped with cheese. The low prices make this small restaurant a rather astounding deal. $10-20 (meal).

Mi Tierra, 2528 S Kedzie Ave, +1 773 254-7722, *www.mitierrarestaurant.com*, M-Th 11AM-10:30PM, F 11AM-2AM, Sa 11AM-3:30AM, Su 11AM-2AM. Mi Tierra is an excellent Mexican restaurant that tends to get more gringo visitors than most establishments in über-Mexican Little Village. That's probably because the place is more fun for its very colorful and friendly atmosphere than for the food, which while very good, is outclassed by some of the less inviting restaurants nearby. $7-15.

Operetta, 5653 W Fullerton Ave, +1 773 622-2613, noon-10PM daily. English menus are available, but they're the secondary option at this Czech/Bohemian restaurant in Belmont-Cragin. Goulash and bread dumplings in hearty portions are the stand-bys, with food to be accompanied by a pilsner, but the waitresses will guide you through extra options. $10-15.

Red Ginger, 3103 N Narragansett Ave (#77 *Belmont bus*), +1 773 622-5606, *www.thaicuisine.com*, M-Th 11AM-10PM, F-Sa 11AM-11PM, Su 4PM-9PM. Classy, top-notch Pan-Asian dining in (surprisingly) Belmont Cragin, focusing on Thai, Japanese, Chinese, and Caribbean foods. BYOB. $10-18.

Wallace's Catfish Corner, 2800 W Madison St, +1 773 638-3474, *www.catfishcorners.com*, M-Th 11AM-midnight, F-Sa 11AM-3AM, Su 11AM-10PM. If it was good enough for Mayor Harold Washington Jr, Don King, and even Mr T, it stands to reason Wallace's soul food is good enough for you. The ribs are fabulous, but be sure to save room for the sweet potato pie. $9-13.

Drink

Most of Chicago's bar hoppers couldn't locate the Far West Side on a map, but if you are looking for something different, there are some real gems. And rest assured you will successfully evade the Lincoln Park frat-boy crowd.

California Clipper, 1002 N California Ave, +1 773 384-2547, *www.californiaclipper.com*, Su-F 8PM-2AM, Sa 8PM-3AM. Somehow the coolest, trendiest bar/lounge in this section of the city has actually been here for over 70 years. The authentic jazz-age art deco bar, serving authentic jazz-age American cocktails (and $2 PBRs) just enjoyed a thorough restoration, and the red lighting, red booths, and red bar make for a very attractive place to enjoy some drinks. Entertainment is provided in the form of live music F-Sa (jazz, blues, honky tonk, country, etc.), as well as ridiculous board games like Pretty Princess and Hungry Hungry Hippos.

The Continental, 2801 W Chicago Ave (*#70 California or #52 Chicago bus*), +1 773 292-1200, M-F 5PM-4AM, Sa 5PM-5AM, Su 6PM-4AM. Somehow the party wound up at the intersection of Garfield Park, Humboldt Park, and Ukrainian Village. Rock 'n' roll blares out the speakers into the small hours of the night. Because of the extremely long hours, it fills up with already wasted trendsters after midnight and gets extremely trashy and raucous, but that can be fun in its own way.

Jedynka Club, 5616 W Diversey Ave (*76 Diversey bus*), +1 773 889-7171, *www.jedynka.com*, W-F 8PM-2AM, Sa 8PM-3AM, Su 8PM-2AM. *The* premiere upscale dance club for the young Polish scene in Chicago. Sunday nights are Euro-retro, Wednesday nights are karaoke, and a regular crew of Polish DJs are on the job. Polski is the first language here, but anyone can manage. Dress nice (preferably something tight and shiny) and have a blast. Friday nights see such Polish offerings as mini-skirt & "buff chest" competitions. Free admission and sometimes free food/drinks before 10PM, otherwise cover usually $10.

La Justicia, 3901 W 26th St, +1 773 522-0041, M-Th 10AM-10PM, F 10AM-3AM, Sa 9AM-midnight, Su 9AM-11PM. You'll have fun here. La Villita's favorite Latin-American rock club packs in large, high energy crowds every Friday night. The place is just a mild mannered restaurant, however, the rest of the week.

Los Globos, 3059 S Central Park Ave, +1 773 277-4141, F 7PM-1:30AM, Sa 7PM-2:30AM. A giant Mexican country nightclub/dance hall with three full bars deep into the thick of La Villita. Weekends can see hundreds of visitors, seeking to replicate an experience for which you'd normally have to head to Northern Mexico. Cover: $15-20.

Rooster's Palace, 4501 W Madison Ave, +1 773 678-0739. Walk in here and you'll think you're in a movie. It's just not possible to pack more West Side blues culture into one bar, and for a good reason—it's sadly the only one left of the West Side's legendary blues clubs. A true neighborhood dive, which sees nonetheless a trickle of blues lovers from all over the city to catch the likes of Tail Dragger, a bluesman who's been sweatin' all over Chicago since the days when he played with Howlin' Wolf. Showtimes are unpredictable, so you might want to call in advance, but Tail Dragger usually plays all Saturday night

Sleep

Options are few in these parts; if you are looking for cheaper accommodations away from the city center, there are better options elsewhere. If you are looking to stay on the Far West specifically, you might also consider hotels in the neighboring suburbs of Oak Park, Berwyn and Cicero.

Fullerton Hotel, 3919 W Fullerton Ave, +1 773 227-2100. The Far West Side saw a lot of mob activity back in the day and this independent hotel can claim the dubious distinction of having put up John Dillinger on occasion. Otherwise, it's just another cheap, dingy option far from the city center. Rooms from $32 for bath shared with one other room, $135 weekly for the same.

Grand Motel West, 4925 W Madison St, +1 773 921-1900. Accommodations *really* far west, although not far from the Green Line train and the expressway. Rooms from $50.

Hotel Norford, 1508 N Pulaski Rd, +1 773 235-1202. An old, independent, somewhat run-down hotel in northwestern Humboldt Park. For those with lively 1930s gangster imaginations, George "Red" Barker caught 18 bullets from a Tommy gun right in front of the hotel steps in 1932. Rooms from $29 shared bath, $34 private.

North Hotel, 1622 N California Ave, +1 773 278-2425. By Far West Side standards, this spot has a good location — just across the intersection from the Humboldt Park Lagoon. Only weekly rates available, $125 plus $50 security deposit, pay stub and ID.

Contact

The following libraries offer free public internet access:

Austin Branch, 5615 W Race Ave (*Central Green Line*), +1 312 746-5038, *www.chipublib.org*, M,W 12-8PM, Tu,Th-Sa 9AM-5PM. In Austin.

Douglass Branch, 3353 W 13th St (*Kedzie Blue Line*), +1 312 747-3725, *www.chipublib.org*, M 12-8PM, W 10AM-6PM, Tu,Th-Sa 9AM-5PM. In North Lawndale.

Galewood-Montclare Branch, 6969 W Grand Ave (*65 Grand bus*), +1 312 746-5032, *www.chipublib.org*, M,W 12-8PM, Tu,Th-Sa 9AM-5PM. In Montclare.

Humboldt Park Branch, 1605 N Troy St (*72 North bus*), +1 312 744-2244, *www.chipublib.org*, M-Th 9AM-8PM, F-Sa 9AM-5PM. Across from Humboldt Park itself.

Legler Branch, 115 S Pulaski Rd (*Pulaski Green Line*), +1 312 746-7730, *www.chipublib.org*, M-Th 9AM-7PM, F-Sa 9AM-5PM. Five blocks south of the train station.

Marshall Square Branch, 2724 W Cermak Rd (*California Blue Like (Forest Park Branch), 21 Cermak bus*), +1 312 747-0061, *www.chipublib.org*, M,Th 12-8PM, Tu-W,F-Sa 9AM-5PM. In South Lawndale.

North Austin Branch, 5724 W North Ave (*72 North bus*), +1 312 746-4233, *www.chipublib.org*, M-Th 9AM-8PM, F-Sa 9AM-5PM. In Austin.

FAR WEST SIDE GET OUT

North Pulaski Brunch, 4300 W
North Ave (*72 North bus*), +1
312 744-9573, *www.chipublib.org*,
M,W,F-Sa 9AM-5PM, Tu,Th 12-
8PM. In Austin.

Portage-Cragin Branch, 5108 W
Belmont Ave (*77 Belmont bus*),
+1 312 744-0152, *www.chipublib.
org*, M-Th 9AM-9PM, F-Sa 9AM-
5PM. In Belmont-Cragin.

Toman Branch, 2708 S Pulaski Rd
(*53 Pulaski bus*), +1 312 745-1660,
www.chipublib.org, M-Th 9AM-
9PM, F-Sa 9AM-5PM. In South
Lawndale.

West Belmont Branch, 3104 N
Narragansett Ave (*77 Belmont bus*),
+1 312 746-5142, *www.chipublib.
org*, M-Th 9AM-9PM, F-Sa 9AM-
5PM. One block south of Belmont.

West Chicago Avenue Branch,
4856 W Chicago Ave (*66
Chicago bus*), +1 312 743-0260,
www.chipublib.org, M-Th 9AM-
9PM, F-Sa 9AM-5PM. In Garfield
Park.

Stay safe

The usual advice given by
Chicagoans for staying safe on
the Far West Side is to simply
stay away from the Far West Side,
given its notorious reputation for
violent crime. Garfield Park (the
neighborhood, not the park) and
much of North Lawndale do their
best to live up to this reputation,
but the reality across the district is
quite varied. The northern neighborhoods around Belmont-Cragin
rank among some of the safest in
the city. While certain residential
areas of South Lawndale can be a

little edgy at night, visitors should
have no worries walking 26th St,
night or day—you would be more
likely to run into trouble on Navy
Pier.

On the other hand, if you are
visiting North Lawndale, Garfield
Park, or much of Austin, usual
rules for blighted urban neighborhoods apply: know where
you're going, stick to well-lit main
streets, arrange/plan transportation in advance, and don't leave
anything visible (even trash) in a
parked car. Anything you'd want
to see in Garfield Park is fortunately located within one block
of the Conservatory L stop along
main streets, although you still
might want to avoid walking back
to the stop after dark if you are by
yourself. If you are visiting any of
the sights in North Lawndale or
Austin, it's best to travel by car.

The more traveled sections of
Humboldt Park (i.e., east of the
park) are pretty safe by big city
standards any time of the day.
Other areas, especially southwest
of the park, however, have some
rougher streets you may want to
avoid.

Get out

The Green Line is a good way to
reach Oak Park, the Frank Lloyd
Wright fiesta.

For authentic Mexican food a little closer to downtown, head to
Pilsen *p.259*.

There are some great small blues
clubs on the Far West Side, but arguably the best are in Chatham-

Greater Grand *p.203.*

SOUTHWEST SIDEUNDERSTAND

The **Southwest Side** of Chicago is far off the beaten path in Chicago. Plenty of visitors know Midway Airport, but never see anything beyond. Truth be told, there *isn't* a lot to see. But the Southwest Side does hold some interest as the former home to the infamous **Union Stockyards** as well as a few hidden culinary gems well worth the trek.

Understand

The Southwest Side is large enough where you cannot understand it without understanding its neighborhoods.

The **Back of the Yards** is a loose term encompassing the community areas of McKinley Park, Brighton Park, and New City, referring to the area's history as the home to the vast hordes of immigrant laborers in the Union Stockyards of Upton Sinclair's *The Jungle*. Though the stockyards are long gone, the blue-collar character remains. The actual stockyards themselves were located in the heart of New City between Ashland Ave and Halsted from Pershing Rd (39th St) to 47th St. Today they are marked by the **Union Stock Yard Gate** and a large industrial park. The area surrounding the industrial park is comprised of predominantly Mexican-American neighborhoods and has some good food on offer. **Canaryville** (between Halsted and Wentworth from Pershing to 49th) is an Irish-American neighborhood with a notorious reputation for violence over the past century. **McKinley Park**, on the other hand, is experiencing a rapid gentrification as younger Chicagoans

347

are priced out of "hipper" neighborhoods.

Marquette Park is an ethnically mixed neighborhood divided between mostly African-Americans, primarily concentrated to the east of the park and Mexican-Americans, primarily concentrated in the area immediately west of the park; along with some Polish and Lithuanian-Americans, centered around one very large and fabulous park. Further west, the area becomes more ethnically inclusive, with median income playing a more prominent role in residency. Aside from the park (and its golf course), the neighborhood is alluring mostly just for its great Mexican food, as well as its rare-in-America Lithuanian dining. This neighborhood was once dominated by a big, wealthy, Lithuanian-American community, but its demographic began to shift dramatically following Martin Luther King Jr's anti-segregation marches (which at the time met with violence from residents). Accompanying desegregation in this neighborhood was characteristic "white flight," which put an end to the "Lithuanian Gold Coast" and heralded a more open neighborhood which most recently has become a major destination in the United States for Mexican immigrants.

Around Midway, you'll find Chicago's second airport, surrounded by an ethnically diverse collection of neighborhoods. This section of town is home to a large, established Polish community, as well as more recently arrived Mexican communities. The neigh-

borhoods of Archer Heights, Garfield Ridge, and Clearing are important centers of Polish culture in the United States; you are likely to hear as much Polish as English while walking around these neighborhoods. Points of interest are pretty spread out, but the food and nightlife sure beats the airport hotels. And you don't have to venture *too* far to find one-in-a-million pizza, or some Croatian baked goods.

In the southeast are a couple of far-flung African-American neighborhoods. **Auburn Gresham** and **Washington Heights** have far less of interest to travelers, aside from the Obama family's now famous church, but both are nice enough neighborhoods and have some good places to eat if you find yourself in the area.

Englewood also deserves a mention, but mostly as a warning — it is a large, impoverished, and relatively violent neighborhood with just about nothing to offer a traveler. It is generally best to just roll through on one of the main roads (e.g., 55th St) or to avoid the area altogether.

The Union Stockyards
The massive meatpacking industry of the Union Stockyards developed alongside the technological innovation of the refrigerated railway car. Livestock of the agrarian Midwest were brought to the rail hub of Chicago and its stockyards to be processed and shipped off around the country. At its peak, the Union Stockyards processed about 82% of the meat consumed in the

SOUTHWEST SIDE GET IN

Get in

By plane

Midway Airport (IATA: **MDW**) plays second fiddle to the Chicago giant that is O'Hare International *p.397*, but it nonetheless services a lot of domestic flights and is a more convenient point of entry. Just about everyone coming into this part of Chicago goes through this airport, which primarily serves domestic flights on low-cost carriers — it is the hub for Southwest Airlines.

Although the rather archaic Midway website does not properly link to a high-quality, detailed set of terminal maps, they can be accessed here *www.flychicago.com*.

Parking rates Hourly Parking: $4 for the first hour and $2 for each additional hour

Daily Parking: $4 for the first hour, each day is $25.

Economy Parking: $2 for the first hour, $5 for two hours, and 12$ per day (or just over 2 hours!)

Note: parking charges are incurred after 10 minutes in all lots, save the cell phone waiting area.

By train

The CTA **Orange Line** runs from downtown through the district on its way from the Loop *p.47* to Midway Airport, providing quick and easy access to the airport, as well as some northern areas of the Southwest Side from the Loop *p.47*, but keep in mind that a bus transfer will likely be necessary to get you from the L station to anywhere other than the airport. Travel time is about 25-30 minutes from the Loop to Midway, but you may wait up to 30 minutes between trains during off peak hours.

Metra's Rock Island commuter rail line serves the southernmost neighborhoods of the district, and can get you to Auburn-Gresham or Washington Heights. But again, keep in mind that you will need to take a bus from the station to your destination. Trains depart from the downtown LaSalle Station. A ride to the Gresham station costs just over $2, to Longwood or Washington Heights, just over $3.

The **Metra Southwest Service** goes straight from Union Station in the Near West Side *p.215* to the Ashburn neighborhood, where it stops twice at "Wrightwood" and "Ashburn." Only take this train if you are going to Ashburn, not if you are going to the airport, as its stops are on the other end of the district.

Southwest Side

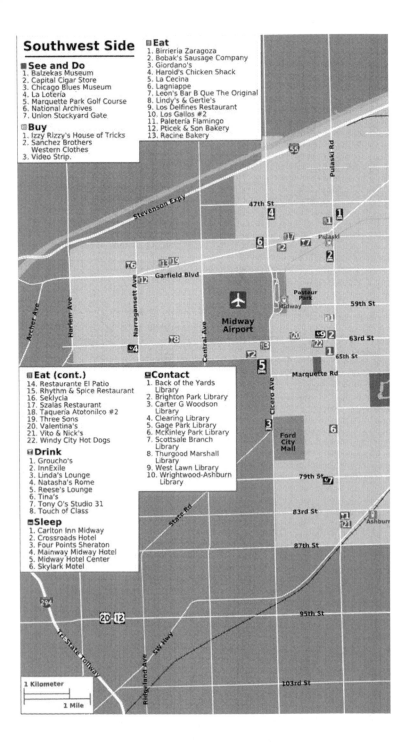

■ See and Do
1. Balzekas Museum
2. Capital Cigar Store
3. Chicago Blues Museum
4. La Lotería
5. Marquette Park Golf Course
6. National Archives
7. Union Stockyard Gate

▥ Buy
1. Izzy Rizzy's House of Tricks
2. Sanchez Brothers Western Clothes
3. Video Strip.

■ Eat
1. Birrieria Zaragoza
2. Bobak's Sausage Company
3. Giordano's
4. Harold's Chicken Shack
5. La Cecina
6. Lagniappe
7. Leon's Bar B Que The Original
8. Lindy's & Gertie's
9. Los Delfines Restaurant
10. Los Gallos #2
11. Paletería Flamingo
12. Pticek & Son Bakery
13. Racine Bakery

■ Eat (cont.)
14. Restaurante El Patio
15. Rhythm & Spice Restaurant
16. Seklycia
17. Szalas Restaurant
18. Taquería Atotonilco #2
19. Three Sons
20. Valentina's
21. Vito & Nick's
22. Windy City Hot Dogs

▥ Drink
1. Groucho's
2. InnExile
3. Linda's Lounge
4. Natasha's Rome
5. Reese's Lounge
6. Tina's
7. Tony O's Studio 31
8. Touch of Class

▥ Sleep
1. Carlton Inn Midway
2. Crossroads Hotel
3. Four Points Sheraton
4. Mainway Midway Hotel
5. Midway Hotel Center
6. Skylark Motel

▥ Contact
1. Back of the Yards Library
2. Brighton Park Library
3. Carter G Woodson Library
4. Clearing Library
5. Gage Park Library
6. McKinley Park Library
7. Scottsdale Branch Library
8. Thurgood Marshall Library
9. West Lawn Library
10. Wrightwood-Ashburn Library

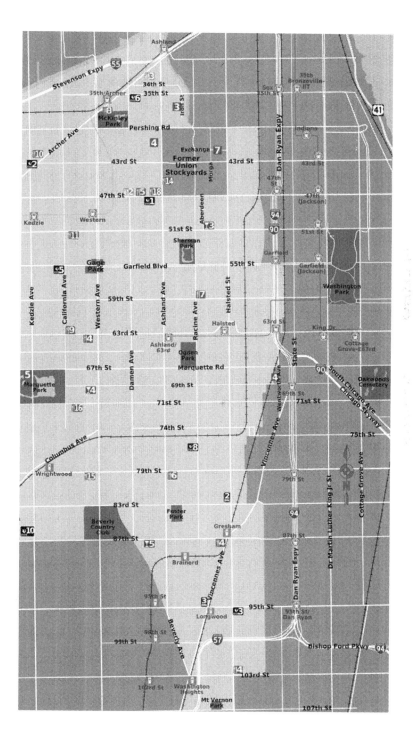

By bus

CTA bus route #62, which travels along Archer Ave from McCormick Center in the Near South *p.95* to Midway, is probably the most convenient route into the Southwest Side from downtown Chicago. Other important routes include the city-spanning north south routes along Halsted, Ashland, Western, Pulaski, and Cicero: #8, #9, #49, #54, and #53. The major east west routes are #47, #55, and #63, which as you might expect run the lengths of 47th, 55th, and 63rd streets.

#62 Archer is the one bus that runs directly from downtown to the Midway Area, but it actually doesn't stop at the airport, so if you're coming from that way, the L is a better option. From the West Side, there are convenient and direct routes along Cicero and Pulaski (#53 and #54). Bus route #55 is by far the best way to travel to Midway from the South Side, and there is a #55 express route that leaves from the Museum of Science and Industry in Hyde Park *p.157*.

By car

The **Dan Ryan Expressway** runs down the eastern edge of the district, and heading west on the 55th/Garfield exit will take you directly to the airport. To get to the Union Stockyard Gate, take the Pershing Road exit from the Dan Ryan. The **Stevenson Expressway** lacks exits on the main roads leading into the eastern parts of the area, but the Damen Ave exit will get you on Archer, from which

you can easily get onto Western, Ashland, or Halsted. For Midway take Cicero; Pulaski is useful for exploring the areas just east of the airport.

Get around

Pretty much the only way to get around the Southwest Side by public transport is by bus, but if this is the route you choose, make a point of it to plan your route ahead of time, as distances are fairly long and the bus routes generally only run along the main streets.

A car is a handy travel companion in the Southwest Side indeed. Attractions, activities, and restaurants are generally spread apart over long distances, and free on-street parking is available just about everywhere. Taxis are also a good option, but do not expect to be able to hail one off the street — you will need to call and arrange rides in advance.

See

The big sights on the Southwest Side are the Union Stockyard Gate. Period. And even that is a pretty small attraction for how out of the way it is. Other sights appeal to narrow sections of society. The Chicago Blues Museum has a magnificent collection for anyone interested in blues history, but it remains to be seen whether it will ever have regular hours. The Balzekas Museum is of obvious interest to Lithuanian-Americans, the Indian Building to *Wayne's World* fanatics and perhaps roadside kitsch-seekers, and the Archives to, well, archivists (and to those who want to trace their roots in the Midwest).

Balzekas Museum of Lithuanian Culture, 6500 S Pulaski Rd, +1 773 582-6500, *www.lithaz.org*, 10AM-4PM daily. The Balzekas museum is a prominent Lithuanian cultural center for the United States, with a fine collection of Lithuanian antiques, folk art, armor, coins, rare historical maps, amber jewelry, and other items exhibited chronologically. The center also includes a state-of-the-art audio-visual center and an impressive research facility for Lithuanian history and genealogy. And the gift shop is a great shopping spot for Lithuanian-related items. Adults: $4, seniors/students: $3, children: $1, free on Tuesday.

Capital Cigar Store Inc (The Indian Building), 6258 S Pulaski Rd. Forget the store, this place is famous for the giant stereotypical-looking Indian statue of Wayne's World fame on the roof. In the movie, his hand is raised in greeting, but he has an arrow through his back. More recently, however, the Midwest Eye Clinic has usurped the cigar sellers, and adopted the Indian as a billboard — the arrow is gone, he now wears large glasses, and bears an odd sign reading "Eye can see now."

Chicago Blues Museum, 3636 S Iron St, +1 773 828-8118, closed temporarily. This museum is *huge* and has an excellent collection of blues paraphernalia and exhibits related to blues in Chicago to-

day and in history. The museum also has exhibits pertaining to Chicago's African-American history in general, especially about the Bronzeville district in the 1920s and 30s. But the collection is on tour, and the museum will therefore be closed at least until the fall.

La Lotería (*4100 S Ashland Ave*). The largest mural in the city (500 ft), painted by Hector Duarte and Mariah de Forest, on the south wall of the Swap-O-Rama building. You can't really see it from the street — you'll need to wander deep into the parking lot for a good look.

National Archives & Records Administration, 7358 S Pulaski Rd, +1 773 948-9050, *www.archives.gov*, M, W-F 8AM-4:15PM, T 8AM-8PM. The enormous Midwest branch of the National Archives is hidden away in the middle of nowhere, but its collection of records is enormous. The public has free and instant access to the census records, for those interested in their family genealogy, while historic federal documents are searchable only by researchers who have applied for a pass in advance.

The Union Stock Yard Gate, 4200 S Peoria St. This limestone structure marks the entrance to the now defunct Union Stockyards that dominated this section of Chicago (and the meatpacking industry of the country) in the late 19th-early 20th centuries. The current stone gate replaced an original wooden gate of the same design.

Do

Marquette Park, 6734 S Kedzie Ave, +1 312 747-6469, 7AM-11PM daily. Marquette Park is huge and is a good place to get away from the urban commotion of the city. Ice skating (on the lagoon) and cross-country skiing are both possibilities during the winter. During the summer, it's likely the South Side's favorite place for a picnic or a pick-up game of soccer (or more accurately in these parts, futbol). The park is also home to the Ashburn Prairie, a fine specimen of the native plant species of the area.

Marquette Park Golf Course, 6734 S Kedzie Ave, +1 312 747-2761, Sunrise-sunset daily. The hidden gem that is Marquette's public golf course is considered one of Chicago's most beautiful. You will feel miles away from the city. Nine holes, 3,187 yards. Weekdays: $8-12, Weekends: $9-13.

Sherman Park, 1301 W 52nd St. Although lesser known than Marquette Park, this 60 acre park is historically and aesthetically its equal. Designed by Daniel Burnham & Co (architects) and the Olmsted Brothers (landscape artists) and located on (a rather unsafe stretch of) historic Garfield Boulevard, this park not only provides open green space and a beautiful lagoon, but also classically designed architecture, and a glimpse into the past (as well as the future) of the Back of the Yards area.

Buy

The Southwest Side is not an enticing shopping destination, unless the endless strip malls on Cicero are your thing. Even Midway Airport lacks a duty free shop, as it only serves a few international flights to Mexico. There really is no reason to *come* to the Southwest Side to go shopping, but if you find yourself here, and need to get something, you can almost certainly find it on Cicero.

Ford City Mall, 73rd St & Cicero Ave, +1 773 767-6400, *ford-city.mallsite.us*, M-F 10AM-9PM, Sa 10AM-7PM, Su 10AM-6PM. This mall, by the way, has a bit of history to its name. In its former life it produced engines for bomber planes during World War II under Ford Company management, and later car engines. If the mall fails to satisfy your needs, rest assured the Cicero Avenue strip malls extending endlessly to the south will.

Izzy Rizzy's House of Tricks, 6034 S Pulaski Rd, +1 773 735-7370, *www.izzyrizzys.com*, M-F 10AM-9PM, Sa 10AM-7PM. You also might want to take a gander at Izzy Rizzy's. The kids will love you if you take them here. Magic kits, fake dog doo, Santa costumes, whoopie cushions galore.

Sanchez Brothers Western Clothes, 1942 W 47th St, +1 773 254-4090, 10AM-8PM daily. Live out your mariachi fantasies here. The Sanchez Brothers carry all sorts of specialty clothing for Mexican bands, from cowboy hats to iguana skin boots! $20-5,000.

Video Strip, 3307 S Archer Ave, +1 773 927-4307, *www.thevideostrip.com*, 11AM-midnight daily. A McKinley Park video rentals shop with an eccentric collection of dvds, including special editions, rare movies, and boxed TV seasons. If you are staying anywhere nearby, they will actually deliver the rentals to you.

Eat

The Southwest Side excels in three culinary areas: Mexican, Polish/Bohemian, and Chicago-style fast food. Avoid the airport hotel restaurants like the plague — there are far better (and more fairly priced) places to eat nearby. If you have a car, drop whatever you are doing and head down Pulaski Ave to Vito & Nick's for the "best pizza, anywhere." If stuck at the airport, Gold Coast Dogs will give you a bonafide Chicago Hot Dog.

Budget

Birrieria Zaragoza, 4852 S Pulaski Ave, +1 773 523-3700, M,W-F 10AM-7PM, Sa-Su 8AM-4PM. This little South Side birrieria has lately found itself featured in just about every major Chicago magazine and newspaper, and while this is surprising, it is not unwarranted. The *birria tatemada* on order is shredded goat, first steamed for hours and then oven roasted, coated with a mild mole, served in tacos, or "en plato" in a tomato consommé. The owner is an artist

first, business owner second, who has studied his narrow trade on a level unique in the city. $2-10.

Bobak's Sausage Company, 5275 S Archer Ave, +1 773 735-5334, *www.bobak.com*, M-Sa 8AM-9PM, Su 8AM-7PM. It's unclear whether the restaurant will ever re-open, but there are tables inside the store for people who like to enjoy sausage at the source, along with other Polish favorites. $4.99/lb. of hot food.

Harold's Chicken Shack. The great South Side fried chicken chain is cheap, usually a little dirty, and always delicious. Crowded at meal times. $2-5.

917 W 87th St, +1 773 224-4621, 11AM-3AM daily.

10259 S Halsted St, +1 773 568-5906, M-Th 10AM-midnight, F-Sa 10AM-1AM, Su 11AM-10PM.

2521 W 63rd St, +1 773 778-9659, Su-Th 11AM-2:30AM, F-Sa 11AM-4AM.

La Cecina, 1934 W 47th St, +1 773 927-9444, 9AM-10PM daily. Come to La Cecina for *la cecina* — a Guerrero-style salt-dried steak that is rehydrated with a marinade and then grilled. But if you are less in the mood for culinary refinement, and more in the mood for eating bull testicles, well, you are in the right place. $2-10.

Lindy's & Gertie's, 3685 S Archer Ave, +1 773 927-7807, M-Th 10:30AM-10PM, F 10:30AM-midnight, Sa 11AM-midnight, Su noon-10PM. Who could go wrong with a South Side institution (since 1924) serving chili, ice cream, and beer? The interior is somewhat of a historic landmark itself, since it's barely been renovated since the roaring twenties. $2-7.

Paletería Flamingo, 2635 W 51st St, +1 773 434-3917, 11AM-10PM daily. Endless (Mexican) flavors of ice cream and Italian ice to choose from — try horchata or maybe cinnamon-apple pie.

Pticek & Son Bakery, 5523 S Narragansett Ave, +1 773 585-5500, *pticeksbakery.tripod.com*, T-F 4:30AM-6PM, Sa 4:30AM-5PM. A small Croatian bakery with a good range of unfamiliar treats (and some rather familiar, gooey chocolate chip cookies).

Racine Bakery, 6216 W Archer Ave, +1 773 581-2258, M-F 6AM-7PM, Sa 6AM-6PM, Su 6AM-5PM. A nice big crowded Polish bakery, with all sorts of pastries, meat/potato pies, jams, mushrooms, juices, and anything else you are missing from Silesia.

Taquería Atotonilco #2, 1659 W 47th St, +1 773 247-5870, M-Th 9AM-1AM, F 9AM-3AM, Sa 8AM-4AM, Su 8AM-1AM. A mostly take-out taquería with a reasonably large seating section that cooks the real deal. $2-4.

Three Sons, 6200 S Archer Ave, +1 773 585-2767, 5AM-11PM daily. An affordable American diner, but since it's in the neighborhood it's in, the best options are in that little Polish section. Full bar. $3-8.

Windy City Hot Dogs, 4205 W 63rd St, +1 773 581-0332, M-Sa 10AM-10PM, Su 11AM-8PM. The place in the area to get your Chicago-style fast food: hot dogs and Italian Beef. $2-4.

Mid-range

Giordano's, 6314 S Cicero Ave, +1 773 585-6100, *www.giordanos.com*, Su-Th 11AM-11PM, F-Sa 11AM-midnight. Located at the southeastern corner of Midway Airport, if you have a layover and want to try real Chicago pizza, take any bus south along Cicero Ave, or you could take a good walk, to the best Chicago chain around for stuffed Chicago pizza. $14-25.

Lagniappe - A Creole Cajun Joynt, 1525 W 79th St, +1 773 994-6375, *cajunjoynt.com*, Tu-Th 11AM-8PM, F-Sa 11AM-10PM. A small little joynt that serves *incredible* gumbo! The cajun seafood entrees are also excellent, and $5 wangs 'n waffles always sounds just about right. $5-15.

Leon's Bar B Que The Original, 1158 W 59th St, +1 773 778-7828, Su-Th 11AM-2AM, F-Sa 11AM-4AM. This is *the* most famous south side barbecue joint, and has fed hungry ribs-lovers since Leon Finney opened it up in 1940. The links are incredible. Leon's also serves good deep dish pizza. Carryout only; no seating. $3-15.

Los Delfines Restaurant, 2750 W 63rd St, +1 773 737-4900, 10AM-8:30PM daily. Tasty Mexican food focusing on the seafood, with a full bar, open late. $9-14.

Los Gallos #2, 4252 S Archer Ave, +1 773 254-2081, M-Th

8AM-1:30AM, F-Sa 8AM-3:30AM, Su 7AM-1:30AM. Deceptively appearing as a small nondescript Brighton Park taquería, this place is actually a culinary find. Breakfast is good, so is the menudo, but the delicious specialty is the Jaliscan-style *carne en su juego* (basically steak soup). The steak is roasted separate from the broth, and then joins a cornucopia of limes, bacon, beans, cilantro, onions, habanero peppers, and radishes. Unless you are planning to feed a family, get the smallest available portion, and make it clear that you want to eat here. $3-12.

Restaurante El Patio, 4527 S Ashland Ave, +1 773 847-2595, 8AM-9:30PM daily. Excellent food and warm, friendly service in this Mexican restaurant. The seafood on offer is especially good. $8-14.

Rhythm & Spice Restaurant, 2501 W 79th St, +1 773 402-9666, *www.rhythmandspicerestaurant.com*, T-W 10AM-4PM, F-Sa 10AM-9PM. A very friendly and authentic Jamaican restaurant with great fish dishes $8-14.

Seklycia, 2711 W 71st St, +1 773 476-1680, M-Sa 7AM-9PM, Su 8AM-8PM. One of the last handful of Lithuanian outposts in the city. A small Lithuanian diner catering to older Lithuanian-Americans in the neighborhood that serves fantastic apple pancakes and other traditional Lithuanian dishes at reasonable prices. $7-12.

Szalas Restaurant, 5214 S Archer Ave, +1 773 582-0300, *szalasrestaurant.com*, noon-11PM daily, bar til 2AM on F-Su. The name means "chalet" in Polish, and that's how the restaurant is designed; not a random quirk, though, because they serve food specific to the Polish highlands. To get in, you'll need to pull the rope over the door and ring the bell. The food's delicious, but plan to hibernate after wading through a hearty meal. $10-30.

Valentina's, 4506 W 63rd St, +1 773 284-5529, Su-Th 9AM-11PM, F-Sa 9AM-midnight. This place, just a few blocks from Midway, serves wonderful taco platters. And the margaritas are just fine too. The decor is light and cheery, on-street parking is plentiful, and service is friendly, all making this a wonderful place to hang out, relax, and have some top-notch Mexican food. $8-15.

Vito & Nick's, 8433 S Pulaski Rd, +1 773 735-2050, *www.vitoandnick.com*, M-Th 11AM-11PM, F-Sa 11AM-1AM, Su noon-11PM. It's a quiet, family-style eatery with a few older patrons chit-chatting at the bar. Widely regarded on the South Side as serving the best thin crust pizza in the city; it bears the slogan "the best pizza... anywhere," and that may well be true — to be clear, this may be the best pizza in the world. The South Side accents are thick, the decor with its carpeted walls and Christmas lights is South Side chic in its purest form — this is an experience to be had. Cash only, sometimes closes early if things are slow. $6-15.

Drink

The Southwest Side does not rank prominently in the minds of Chicagoans when they think of city nightlife, but there are a of worthwhile spots, with good live music.

Groucho's, 8355 S Pulaski Ave, +1 773 767-4838, *www.grouchosbarandgrill.com*, M-F 2PM-4AM, Sa noon-5AM, Su noon-4AM; Kitchen open untill 3AM. A decent South Side rock club featuring better-known local and regional acts. As an added bonus, the kitchen serves bar food all night. Admission: $5, entrées: $5-11.

InnExile, 5758 W 65th St, +1 773 582-3510, *www.innexilechicago.com*, Su-F 8PM-2AM, Sa 8PM-3AM. Gay nightclub that attracts all sorts of people passing through next-door Midway with occasional live performances.

Linda's Lounge (Linda's Place), 1044 W 51st St , +1 773 373-2351. A small, cozy neighborhood dive bar offering live blues and soul.

Natasha's Rome, 2441 W 69th St, +1 773 842-9816, M-F 5PM-2AM, Sa 5PM-3AM, Su 3PM-2AM. This is the nicest club in the Marquette Park neighborhood, with a laid-back bar on each of its two floors. Willie T performs live blues on Fridays, Sundays feature spoken word night, and the rest of the time there is a DJ spinning R&B and other pop music. Locals usually dominate the crowd, except on Fridays and Sundays.

Reese's Lounge (Burnside Lounge), 1827 W 87th St, +1 773 238-1993, 11AM-2AM daily. Live DJs W-Su, Sunday nights are all-jazz. Dress nicely, it's a swanky place. Dinners $5-6.

Tina's, 5440 S Narragansett Ave, +1 773 586-8767, M-Th 4PM-10PM, F-Sa 11AM-11PM, Su 2PM-10PM. A divey neighborhood sports bar that rises above the crowd for its thin-crust and stuffed Chicago style pizzas. Otherwise, cheap drinks and free pool are the draws.

Tony O's Studio 31, 5147 S Archer Ave, +1 773 585-7512, Su-F 8PM-2AM, Sa 8PM-3AM. A bar/nightclub that is plenty friendly, packed on weekends, and miles away from the too-cool-to-sweat clubs downtown. No cover.

Touch of Class, 6058 W 63rd St, +1 773 586-8177, Su-F 9AM-4AM. A neighborhood pub just west of Midway that takes pride in turning off the ear-splitting music that kills conversation in bars across the city. The atmosphere is extremely friendly and laid-back (although Notre Dame games can liven the place up a bit).

Sleep

As it is an airport neighborhood, the Midway Area has a ton of hotels, which mostly fall in to two categories: bland, mid-range, three star business/airport hotels and cheap, but not seedy, motels.

Carlton Inn Midway, 4944 S Archer Avenue, +1 773

582-0900, +1 877 722-7586, *www.carltoninnmidway.com*. Carlton Inn Midway is the **only** Midway hotel located a short walk (1.5 blocks) to the Orange Line L train stop- all other hotels require cabs, shuttles, or long hikes. Free airport shuttle, free parking, free internet, and free breakfast. AAA approved. Clean, comfortable rooms. $92-159.

Crossroads Hotel, 5300 S Pulaski Rd, +1 773 581-1188. Extremely tattered but cheap. Just a couple blocks south of the Pulaski Orange Line station. Rooms from $50.

Four Points Sheraton, 7353 S Cicero Ave, +1 773 735-4694, *www. starwoodhotels.com*. The Sheraton is comfortable enough, recently underwent a big-budget renovation, and the price is a better deal than the Midway Hotel Center offerings. $100-180.

Mainway Midway Motel, 4849 S Cicero Ave, +1 773 735-0550. Another "tattered" budget option located about a half mile north from Midway along Cicero Ave, an easy bus ride. Rooms from $52 Su-Th, $67 F-Sa.

Skylark Motel, 5435 S Archer Ave, +1 773 582-2100. Slightly more expensive than the other budget motels, but the extra cost may be worth it — it really is a good deal nicer. Rooms from $75.

Midway Hotel Center

The Hotel Center is a hotel campus of seven individual options, located two blocks south of the airport (about a half mile from baggage claim) at 65th St and Cicero Ave. Shuttles run between all the hotels and the airport, although (despite claims to the contrary) you cannot always get a shuttle to/from the L station, so expect to have a long trip if you are heading to the city center. If you're here and looking for food, it would be a travesty of taste to go to the center's chain restaurants. Walk a block north to Giordano's for some quality Chicago-style pizza or solid Italian dishes. Better yet, get a taxi to Vito and Nick's.

Chicago Marriott Midway, 6520 S Cicero Ave, +1 708 594-5500, +1 800 228-9292, *www.marriott.com*, Checkin: 3PM, Checkout: noon. A fine business hotel, albeit a small step down from the usual Marriot standards. $140-220.

Courtyard Chicago Midway Airport, 6610 S Cicero Ave, +1 708 563-0200, *www.marriott.com*, Checkin: 3PM, Checkout: noon. Recently renovated, but not quite as nice as the Marriott itself. $110-220.

Fairfield Inn & Suites Chicago Midway Airport, 6630 S Cicero Ave, +1 708 594-0090, *www.marriott.com*, Checkin: 3PM, Checkout: noon. This location is notably nicer than most Fairfield Inns, probably closer to a three-star than a two-star. Free wireless. $110-210.

Hampton Inn Chicago Midway Airport, 6540 S Cicero Ave, +1 708 496-1900, *www.hamptoninn.com*, Checkin: 2PM, Checkout: noon. Recently renovated, bland three

SOUTHWEST SIDE STAY SAFE

star hotel. $130-240.

Hilton Garden Inn Midway Airport, 6530 S Cicero Ave, +1 708 496-2700, *www.hiltongardeninn.com*, Checkin: 3PM, Checkout: noon. Three star hotel with free high speed wireless. $110-200.

Holiday Inn Express, 6500 S Cicero Ave, *www.ichotelsgroup.com*, Checkin: 3PM, Checkout: noon. Probably the best option of the seven (although the differences between them are pretty slight), and has a curious New Orleans theme. $140-210.

Sleep Inn, 6650 S Cicero Ave, +1 708 594-0001, *www.choicehotels.com*, Checkin: 3PM, Checkout: noon. The most price competitive option in the hotel center has a few less frills, and like the others is a bit overpriced, but perfectly sufficient. And the continental breakfast is actually good (waffles!). $85-180.

Contact

Midway Airport offers high speed wireless in several lounges, restaurants, and Air Tran gates, but it is only available to Boingo *www.boingo.com* subscribers. All the following branches of the Chicago Public Library also offer free public internet access.

Back of the Yards Library, 1743 W 47th St, +1 312 747-8367, M,W 9AM-9PM, T,Th 10AM-6PM, F-Sa 9AM-5PM.

Brighton Park Library, 4314 S Archer Ave, +1 312 747-0666, M-

Th 9AM-9PM, F-Sa 9AM-5PM.

Carter G Woodson Library, 9525 S Halsted St, +1 312 747-6900, M-Th 9AM-9PM, F-Sa 9AM-5PM, Su 1PM-5PM.

Clearing Branch Library, 6423 W 63rd St, +1 312 747-5657, M-Th 9AM-9PM F-Sa 9AM-5PM.

Gage Park Library, 2807 W 55th St, +1 312 747-0032, M,W noon-8PM, Tu,Th-Sa 9AM-5PM.

McKinley Park Branch Library, 1915 W 35th St, +1 312 747-6082, M-Th 9AM-9PM, F-Sa 9AM-5PM.

Scottsdale Branch Library, 4101 W 79th St, +1 312 747-0193, M-Th 9AM-9PM F-Sa 9AM-5PM.

Thurgood Marshall Branch Library, 7506 S Racine Ave, +1 312 747-5927, M-Th 9AM-8PM, F-Sa 9AM-5PM.

West Lawn Branch Library, 4020 W 63rd St, +1 312 747-7381, M-Th 9AM-9PM, F-Sa 9AM-5PM.

Wrightwood-Ashburn Branch Library, 8530 S Kedzie Ave, +1 312 747-2696, M-F 9AM-9PM, Sa 9AM-5PM.

Stay safe

As you would expect in such a large district of the city, crime levels *vary* throughout. The northern and western neighborhoods, while sometimes looking gritty, should not worry you in the slightest. Marquette Park is quite safe as well, although it deteriorates a bit southeast of the actual park. Englewood, on the other hand, is a huge neighborhood notorious among Chicagoans for murders, random beatings, and what have you. Auburn-Gresham and Washington Heights rest somewhere in the middle, but they're fairly quiet and peaceful — violent crime is not happening on main streets during the day.

Get out

If your flight is not on the departures display, perhaps you were looking for O'Hare International Airport *p.397*? If so, grab a cab and hope for the best. Most taxis have special rates for the MDW-ORD trip, which should cost about $50-60 at the cheapest and take about an hour. If time is not an issue, you can take the Orange Line to the Loop *p.47* and transfer to the Blue Line to O'Hare for just $2.25, but it will take two hours or more.

If you are staying downtown and just want to get some authentic Mexican food, there are great options closer by in the West Side's Pilsen *p.259* neighborhood.

While you are out this far from the city center, why not head even further south to the Far Southwest Side *p.389* to dig the Irish pubs and brogues.

Hop on the CTA Orange Line and head downtown to the Loop *p.47* to escape the outskirts and see the city you recognize from the postcards.

For more Polish culture, the motherlode is on Chicago's Far Northwest Side *p.363*.

The **Far Northwest Side** of Chicago includes the neighborhoods of **Avondale** and the Polish Village (**Jackowo** and **Wacławowo**), with large Polish communities; **Irving Park** and **Old Irving**, quiet areas with historic homes; and **Forest Glen, Jefferson Park, Norwood Park, Edison Park, Edgebrook, Dunning,** and **Portage Park,** residential areas which have nice parks, old theaters, and some big annual festivals.

These are the neighborhoods closest to O'Hare International Airport *p.397.*

Understand

The Far Northwest Side is, for many travelers, nothing more than a blur of drab buildings seen from the expressway or the Blue Line on their way to O'Hare *p.397.* And only the most fervent of true believers could make an argument that it ought to be anywhere near the top of a first-time visitor's list. None of the city's most famous landmarks are located here; nothing in the best-known history or literature about Chicago happened here. In fact, most Chicagoans would find the Far Northwest Side as unfamiliar as someone right off a plane from the coast.

What *is* here, though, is a group of large, residential communities and a handful of treasures they've grown accustomed to keeping for themselves, unencumbered by style or pace. Sausage shops and old-style Italian restaurants carry on as if health food and celebrity chefs never happened. If you're serious about trying a Chicago-style hot dog at the peak of the form, you'll do well here. Two classic movie palaces awaken for special events, and there are strong contenders for the city's best music venue and original theater venue — the **Abbey Pub** and the **Prop Thtr**, respectively.

Plenty of tourists and locals have tried "going Chinese" for a night in Chinatown *p.175*, but an even more immersive (and less-traveled) experience is "going Polish." English slides to second on the signs, the food makes sweet love to your waist, and the beer flows cheap at your choice of fab discos straight out of Eastern Europe or laid-back dives with you and the regulars. Famously, Chicago has the largest population of Polish people of any city in the world save Warsaw. If you never make it to Poland, at least you can say you've been to Avondale.

So once you're sick of the screaming brats in Lakeview *p.139* and Lincoln Park *p.123*, the scuzz in Uptown *p.273*, the tourist traps on the Mag Mile *p.71*, the crowds in the Loop *p.47*, the hipsters in Wicker Park *p.229*, the confusion in Rogers Park *p.291*, the pretension in Hyde Park *p.157*, the cranks in Bridgeport *p.175* — and you're in the mood to experience Chicago all over again, for the first time — then the Far Northwest Side may have something for you.

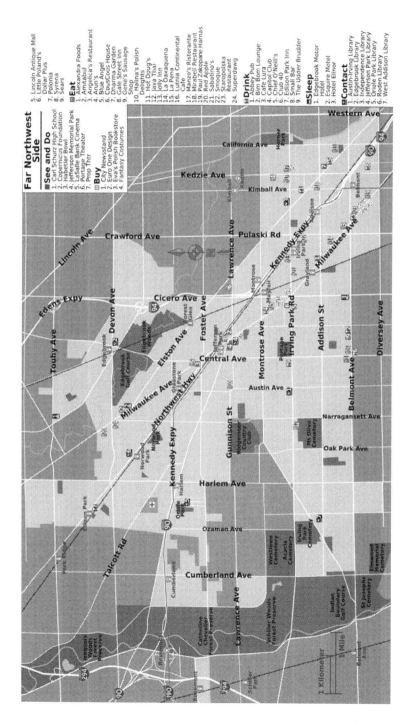

Far Northwest Side

■ See and Do
1. Carl Schurz High School
2. Copernicus Foundation
3. Hanover Bowl
4. Jefferson Memorial Park
5. LaSalle Bank Cinema
6. Portage Theater
7. Prop Thtr

■ Buy
1. City Newsstand
2. Euro One Design
3. Eva's Polish Bookstore
4. Fantasy Costumes

■ Eat
1. Alexandra Foods
2. Amitabul
3. Angelica's Restaurant
4. Arun's
5. Blue Bagel
6. Cucina Roma
7. Dharma Garden
8. Gale Street Inn
9. Gene's Sausage Shop
10. Halina's Polish Delights
11. Hot Doug's
12. Java Thai
13. Jolly Inn
14. La Oaxaquena
15. La Pena
16. Lutnia Continental Cafe
17. Manzo's Ristorante
18. Mirabell Restaurant
19. Paul Zakopane Harnas
20. Red Apple
21. Sabatino's
22. Smoque
23. Staropolska Restaurant
24. Superdawg

■ Drink
1. Abbey Pub
2. Bien Bien Lounge
3. Cafe Lura
4. Capitol Club
5. Chief O'Neill's
6. Club 40
7. Edison Park Inn
8. Small Bar
9. The Uddder Brudder

■ Sleep
1. Edgebrook Motor Hotel
2. Esquire Motel
3. Hotel Elinor

■ Contact
1. Austin-Irving Library
2. Edgebrook Library
3. Independence Library
4. Jefferson Park Library
5. Oriole Park Library
6. Roden Library
7. West Addison Library

Lincoln Antique Mall
5. Lincoln Antique Mall
6. Little Poland's
7. Polonia
8. Syrena
9. Sears

Get in

By train

The CTA **Blue Line** has stops throughout the northwest side of Chicago in Avondale (Belmont, Addison), Irving Park (Irving Park, Montrose), Jefferson Park (Jefferson Park), and Norwood Park (Harlem), before passing into the orbit of O'Hare Airport (Cumberland, Rosemont, O'Hare). You may need to connect with a bus, though, as these stops are pretty far west, and there's a lot of ground between them and the Brown Line to the east.

The end of the CTA **Brown Line** is within reach of Irving Park (Kedzie, Kimball).

The Metra **Union Pacific Northwest Line** has stops in Irving Park, Jefferson Park, Norwood Park, and Edison Park, while the Metra **Milwaukee District North** line stops at Mayfair, Forest Glen and Edgebrook. The former ends at Ogilvie/Northwestern Station and the latter at Union Station, both in the Loop *p.47*.

By bus

This is a fairly large area, covered by a ton of bus routes. Several major ones are listed below. Most connect to the CTA Blue Line or the Metra, and a few spread out into the suburbs.

53 Pulaski runs all night through Irving Park and Avondale connecting with the Irving Park Blue Line & Metra Stations.

54 Cicero runs through the eastern half of the area, although it's not an all-night route.

56 Milwaukee runs from Wicker Park *p.229* and Logan Square *p.247* through the heart of the Polish Village and most the Far Northwest Side ending at Jefferson Park Blue Line/Metra.

68 Northwest Highway runs from the Jefferson Park station to the Park Ridge Metra Station running parallel to the Metra. It also makes connections to the Gladstone, Norwood and Edison Park Metra stations.

77 Belmont connects with the self-named Blue Line station and runs all night. This is handy for trips in Avondale.

78 Montrose connects with the Blue Line at the Montrose station and the Mayfair Metra Station, handy for trips in Portage Park or Irving Park and the Harlem Irving Plaza.

80 Irving Park is, as you might expect, ideal for Irving Park and Old Irving. Connections can be made with the Irving Park Blue Line or Brown Line stops as well as the Irving Park Metra. This route serves the Harlem Irving Plaza.

81 Lawrence runs from Uptown *p.273* to the Jefferson Park and Cumberland Blue Line stations, with a direct connection at the Kimball Brown Line stop providing service all night long.

82 Kimball/Homan connects with the Blue Line at Belmont and the Brown Line at Kimball, and can save you a bit of walking from the Blue Line to places like Abbey Pub.

92 Foster starts at the Jefferson Park station heading east to the lakefront and the Red Line at Berwyn.

Pace buses cover the regions that cross over into the suburbs:

226 Oakton Street starts at the Jefferson Park station heading north along Central Avenue connecting with the Edgebrook Metra station. It then continues up to Skokie heading west on Oakton to Des Plaines.

270 Milwaukee Avenue goes up Milwaukee Avenue from the Jefferson Park Station through Norwood Park and continuing into the suburbs.

290 Touhy Avenue covers Edgebrook and Edison Park and ends at the Cumberland CTA Blue Line.

423 Linden CTA/The Glen/Harlem Avenue starts at the at the Harlem Blue Line covering Norwood and Edison Park and continues up into the suburbs.

By car

I-90/94 (aka "**The Kennedy**") runs through the center of Chicago and then to the western parts of the city, where it joins **I-190**. I-90/190 go to O'Hare Airport, while I-94 splits off to reach the northern and northwest suburbs. The most useful exits are off the Kennedy at Lawrence Avenue and Ill-19/Irving Park Road.

See

Carl Schurz High School, 3601 N Milwaukee Ave (*56 Milwaukee bus*), +1 773 534-3420, *www.schurzhs.org*. A massive 1910 Prairie School masterpiece by Dwight Perkins, possibly the biggest example of the architectural style, and still a working high school. It's an impressive sight.

Copernicus Foundation, 5216 West Lawrence Ave, +1 773 777-8898, *www.copernicusfdn.org*. A Polish Cultural Center in Jefferson Park, housed in the old Gateway Theater movie palace. They host community events and classes throughout the year; highlights include the **Polish Film Festival** *www.pffamerica.com* in November and the **Taste of Polonia** *www.copernicusfdn.org* at the end of August.

Jefferson Memorial Park, 4822 N Long Ave (*Jefferson Park Blue Line*), +1 773 685-3316, *www.chicagoparkdistrict.com*. Beloved local park with seasonal concerts and seven acres of outdoor fun, including fields for baseball, football, soccer, and tennis, as well as a swimming pool and a spray pool. The **Jeff Fest** is held every summer.

Do

Habetler Bowl, 5250 N Northwest Hwy, +1 773 774-0500, *www.habetlerbowl.com*. Longstanding local bowling alley with brand-new facilities. Usually, it's $4 per game for adults ($3 for kids), and shoe-rental is $3.50.

However, it's $2 per game all summer long, and Tuesday nights are always $1 per game.

LaSalle Bank Cinema, 4901 W Irving Park Rd, +1 312 904-9442, Sa 8PM. Movie revival house in Portage Park, with a new old film every weekend. The entrance can be tricky to find if you get there early — go around to the back of the bank. $5 adults, $3 children.

Portage Theater, 4050 N Milwaukee Ave (*Irving Park Blue Line*), +1 773 736-4050, *www.portagetheater. org*. A beautiful old movie palace in Portage Park, built in 1920 with a whopping 1,938 seats. It's only open for special events and festivals like the **Silent Summer Festival** *www.silentfilmchicago.com* and scary movies around Halloween. The Empty Bottle in Ukrainian Village sometimes hosts shows here. Tickets vary by event.

Prop Thtr, 3502 N Elston Ave, +1 773 539-7838, *www.propthtr.org*. Prop is the best place in Chicago to see smart, exciting new dramatic theater, from "Porno Zombies" to Daley biographies. The current production will almost certainly be worth seeing, but the **New Plays Festival** in July offers two shows and a slew of live readings. Most shows $32, $22 students.

Buy

Polish Village

Euro One Design, 3023 N Milwaukee Ave (*56 Milwaukee bus*), +1 773 384-9335, M-Sa 10AM-8PM, Su 10AM-6PM. Search no further: here are the diamond-checkered sweaters you were always meant to have. Euro One Design stocks Polish and Eastern European fashions for women, with a decent selection for men.

Eva's Polish Bookstore, 3034 N Milwaukee Ave (*56 Milwaukee bus*), +1 773 276-0826, M-Sa 10AM-7PM, 10AM-4PM. Almost certainly the largest selection of Polish books in Chicago.

Little Poland's Dollar Plus Store (Polski Sklep), 3067 N Milwaukee Ave (*56 Milwaukee bus*), +1 773 478-0752, 9AM-10PM. Most of the space is given over to standard-issue dollar store junk, but this one stands out not only for the frenetic burst of verbiage on the sign — and the even more effusive exterior walls — but also the small, terrific selection of Polish souvenirs. (While not expensive, most do cost more than a dollar.)

Syrena, 3004 N Milwaukee Ave (*56 Milwaukee bus*), +1 773 489-4435, M-Sa 10AM-8PM, Su 10AM-6PM. The alpha and omega of department stores in Avondale. Frills, lace, fabric roses, and more fill the rows of Polish fashion for women of all ages at Syrena. Even from outside, it's quite a sight.

Others

The Portage Park intersection of Cicero, Milwaukee, and Irving Park is known as the **Six Corners**. In the 1950s, that was the commercial epicenter of the Northwest Side, and one of the busiest in the entire city. These days, it's a mix of a few chains and some intriguing, boarded-up old businesses — check out **Mr. Steer** and the weird Hummel-meets-Star-Trek collection at the old **Crown Gift Shop**, both across from the Portage Theater.

City Newsstand, 4018 N Cicero Ave, +1 773 545-7377, 7AM-11PM. An estimated 60 newspapers and 6,000 magazines from everywhere and south of there, with imports from Prague, Italy, and some kid's basement in Omaha. If it's in print, you stand a very good chance of finding it here.

Fantasy Costumes, 4065 N Milwaukee Ave (*56 Milwaukee bus*), +1 773 777-0222, M-Sa 9:30AM-8PM, Su 10AM-6PM, open later and busy around Halloween, naturally. A *huge*, wonderfully cluttered costume shop in Portage Park, covering almost a full city block. A massive selection of props, costumes, and wigs for kids and adults are available for sale or rental.

Lincoln Antique Mall, 3115 W Irving Park Rd (*80 Irving Park bus*), +1 773 604-4700, 11AM-7AM. An intriguing antique mall in Irving Park with space for dozens of dealers whose eras and offerings vary from Spanish oil paintings to vintage cookbooks. Reportedly, it's a favorite stop for film set designers.

Polonia, 4738 N Milwaukee Ave, +1 773 481-6968, +1 800 210-6451, *www.polonia.com*, M-Sa 10AM-6PM. A very wide selection of Polish books, films, and especially Polish language learning materials. It's a bit of a Polish-American center too, sporting a coffee shop

and even an art gallery.

Sears, 4730 W Irving Park Rd (*80 Irving Park bus*), +1 773 202-2000, *www.searsarchives.com*, M-Sa 9AM-9PM, Su 10AM-7PM. This was a million-dollar store when it was built in the 1930s, and it still thrives despite the economic downturn at the Six Corners. Nothing fancy, but the building has some interest as a retail time capsule of sorts.

Eat

As Hyde Park *p.157* is to academics, as the Near North *p.71* is to department stores, so Avondale is to Polish sausages. Cavernous delis line the streets here, particularly up Milwaukee and Belmont. They're a sight to see even if you're not after some *czarnina* (blood duck soup). A ride on the 56 Milwaukee bus makes for a pretty good off-the-beaten-path culinary tour.

Budget

Alexandra Foods, 3304 1/2 N Central Ave, +1 773 282-3820, M-F 8AM-7PM, Sa 8AM-5PM, Su 9AM-3PM. Wholesale, direct-to-the-public pierogies. Restaurants from around the Midwest buy them in bulk, but you're welcome to enter the grey factory walls and buy as many of the 15-or-so varieties of pierogi as you'd like on the cheap. $3-7.

Angelica's Restaurant, 3244 N Milwaukee Ave (*56 Milwaukee bus*), +1 773 736-1186, 11AM-9PM. Polish diner with big portions and low prices, although vegetarians would be well-advised to stick to the kids menu. $7-10.

Blue Angel, 5310 N Milwaukee Ave (*Jefferson Park Blue Line*), +1 773 631-8700, 24 hours. One of the classic all-night bottomless-coffee diners in Chicago, with respectable diner food. If you have an early morning flight out of O'Hare, you could do worse than camping out in these friendly environs — just tip well. $6-12.

Gene's Sausage Shop & Delicatessen, 5330 W Belmont Ave, +1 773 777-6322, M-Sa 8AM-8PM, Su 8AM-4PM. People come from miles away to get their meat, bread, and beer at this authentic Polish market. Look for the giant cow out front. $7-10.

Hot Doug's, 3324 N California Ave, *www.hotdougs.com*, M-Sa 10:30AM-4PM. In a town known for its sausages (the Chicago-style hot dog), Hot Doug's is unique and nationally renowned. The restaurant only sells sausages but amongst its menu you'll run across bacon sausages, venison sausages, ostrich sausages, and other sausages made from exotic game. These are always done with a gourmet flair, such as Guinness mustard or feta cheese. In addition, on F and S, they offer french fries made with rendered duck fat; it's an interesting treat. However, the line is often out the door. $2-4, cash only.

Java Thai, 4272 W Irving Park Rd (*80 Irving Park bus*), +1 773 545-6200, M-Sa 8AM-10PM, Su 9AM-3PM. All the elements of a

good American coffee house and a good, cheap Thai restaurant form this small, quiet, low-lit hangout, with live jazz during Sunday brunch. $4-7.

Paul Zakopene Harnas, 2943 N Milwaukee Ave, +1 773 342-1464, *www.polishdiner.com*, M-Sa 7AM-10PM, Su 7AM-9PM. Hearty Polish breakfast, lunch, dinner, and booze, with pierogies in-between. $4-$8.

Superdawg, 6363 N Milwaukee Ave (*56 Milwaukee bus*), +1 773 763-0660, *www.superdawg.com*, Su-Th 11AM-1AM, F-Sa until 2AM. For the best hot dogs in town. One "superdawg" comes with pickled tomatoes, mustard, small hot peppers, and a kosher dill. The true Chicago-style hot dog never has ketchup, so save it for your fries! They also sell burgers and sausages, but the superdawg can't be beat. You can also order directly from your car, '50's style with the tray hanging from your car window. $4-6, cash only.

Mid-range

Amitabul, 6207 N Milwaukee Ave (*56 Milwaukee bus*), +1 773 774-0276, *www.amitabul.getwebnet. com*, Tu-Th 1-9PM, F 12-10PM, Sa 10AM-10PM, Su 1AM-8PM. You love Korean food, but you're a vegan. You often find yourself considering how a certain dish would be perfect if the chef had just added a dash of zen cooking energy. You will be very happy at Amitabul. $9-15, according to their website, there's a %10 discount for mentioning you saw them on the web.

CousCous House, 4624 W Lawrence Ave (*81 Lawrence bus* phone='+1 773 777-9801url=http://www.couscoushouse.com/). Friendly and warm staff serve up fluffy couscous, baba ganoush, falafel, and other favorites. Try the mint tea. $9-15.

Dharma Garden, 3109 W Irving Park Rd (*80 Irving Park bus*), +1 773 588-9140, *www.dharmagarden. net*, M-Th 11AM-9:30PM, F-Sa 11AM-10PM, Su 3-9PM. There are several worthwhile Thai restaurants in Irving Park, but Dharma Garden serves vegetarians and seafood lovers especially well, with an emphasis on natural ingredients and healthy preparation. $8-$14.

Halina's Polish Delights, 5914 W Lawrence Ave (*81 Lawrence bus*), Su-M 12-8PM, Tu-Sa 12-9PM. If you are in the mood for breaded fried pork and veal cutlets, there is nowhere else you should be than this corner of Jefferson Park. They serve a fine spread of pierogies, too. The Polish Plate sample platter is available for new diners. English is not part of the staff hiring requirements, so you might want to brush up on your Polish. $7-12.

Jolly Inn, 6501 W Irving Park Rd, +1 773 736-7606, *www.jollyinn. com*, M-Th 10:30AM-9PM, F-Sa 10:30AM-10PM, Su 11AM-9PM. The location — *really* far west — means the buffet at the Jolly Inn is cheap and known only among the Polish locals. The food is unabashedly high-calorie, and yes, that's a bowl of spread-able lard they place on your table. There's a long list of dessert offerings. They get commendably festive at Christmas. $8 weekdays, $10 weekends.

La Oaxaqueña, 3382 N Milwaukee Ave (*56 Milwaukee bus*), +1 773 545-8585, M-Th 9:30AM-11:30PM, F-Sa 9:30AM-12:30AM. A small, casual restaurant serving Mexican food specific to the Oaxacan region. The Oaxaqeño chocolate *mole* sauces are a specialty here, although the excellent seafood dishes can be hard to pass up. $7-15.

La Peña, 4212 N Milwaukee Ave (*56 Milwaukee bus*), +1 773 545-7022, *www.lapenachicago.com*, Tu-W 4PM-10PM, Th-F 4PM-2AM, Sa 4PM-3AM, Su 8AM-2AM. Family-made Ecuadorian food in Portage Park, with a full drinks menu. Friday and Saturday nights have live Andean music, while Sunday nights offer karaoke. Hence, if there's an important conversation to be had over dinner, this may not be the place. $13-18.

Manzo's Ristorante, 3210 W Irving Park Rd (*80 Irving Park bus*), +1 773 478-3070, *www.gcatering. com*, Tu-Th 11AM-midnight, F 11AM-2AM, Sa 4PM-2AM. Most of Manzo's business now comes from catering and delivery, but the cavernous dining room at their location in Irving Park is still open, and looks as well-kept as it did at closing time in 1973, if not as well-attended. Chicago mob aficionados with overactive imaginations will find this fertile ground while being well-fed with good, classic Italian food by the friendly old waitresses, with some of the richest salad dressing you're likely to encounter. Entrees $9-$11; weekdays lunch buffet $7, Su all-day buffet $16.

Red Apple (Czerwone Jabluszko), 6474 N Milwaukee Ave, +1 773 763-3407, *www.redapplebuffet.com*, Su-Th 11AM-9PM, F-Sa 11AM-9:30PM. An enormous, full-service Polski smorgasbord. There is fresh fruit, but vast kingdoms of meat dominate the landscape, with a full complement of quality kielbasa, pierogies, blintzes, and non-diet salads. There's another location further south at 3121 N Milwaukee. The restaurant is quite nice, but the bar is a bit dour. Weekdays $8.49, weekends $9.49.

Smoque, 3800 N Pulaski Rd, +1 773 545-7427, *www.smoquebbq.com*, Su,T-Th 11AM-9PM, F-Sa 11AM-10PM. This new, but very serious barbecue joint serves the best barbecue on the North Side of Chicago. If the brisket and ribs don't satisfy your refined palate, though, you should try the offerings on the Southwest Side before giving up on Chicago barbecue. $4-21.

Staropolska Restaurant, 3028 N Milwaukee Ave (*56 Milwaukee bus*), +1 773 342-0779, 9AM-9PM. The newly renovated Staropolska has been around for ages and is probably the cheapest of the local spreads. Not bad, too, especially the tripe soup. There's a bar right up front. $6.50 buffet weekdays, $10 weekends.

Splurge

Arun's, 4156 N Kedzie Ave (*Kedzie Brown Line*), +1 773 539-1909, *www.arunsthai.com*, Su,Tu-Th 5-10PM, F-Sa 5-10:30PM. One of the finest Thai establishments in the world, including Thailand. One book named it to a list of places to visit throughout the world before you die. prix-fixe meal: $85.

Gale Street Inn, 4914 N Milwaukee Ave (*Jefferson Park Blue Line/Metra*), +1 773 725-1300, *www.galestreet.com*, Mon-Thu 4PM-10PM, F 11:30AM-10:30PM, Sa 4PM-10:30PM, Su 10:30AM-9PM. Chicago's most famous rib joint with a touch of old-time class, right across the street from the Blue Line. It's a good place to eat with parents, and tolerant vegetarians can make do with the portobello mushroom sandwich and some tasty sides. $14-30.

Lutnia Continental Cafe, 5532 W Belmont Ave (*Addison Blue Line*), +1 773 282-5335, Tu-Sa 12-10PM, Su 1-11PM. Not exclusively Polish, as their menu covers a number of culinary styles, but the recent book *Polish Chicago* named Lutnia's tenderloin venison one of the exemplars of Polish cuisine. No buffets here — Lutnia is a strictly fine dining experience, and probably the best fine Polish dining in Chicago. There's sometimes live music on weekends. $14-25.

Mirabell Restaurant & Lounge, 3454 W Addison St, +1 773 463-1962, *www.mirabellrestaurant.com*, M-F 11:30AM-10PM, Sa 11:30AM-11PM. For many years, the foremost outpost of German (and Hungarian) food outside of Lincoln Square. Waitresses in traditional costumes, oompah bands, beer steins, and a noted selection of Hummel figurines set the Bavarian atmosphere for heaping portions of food. $16-25.

Sabatino's Restaurant, 4441 W Irving Park Rd (*Irving Park Blue Line/Metra*), +1 773 283-8331, *www.sabatinoschicago.com*, M-Th,Th 11AM-11:30PM, W 11AM-midnight, F 11AM-12:30AM, Sa 4PM-12:30AM, Su 12-10:30PM. Another fine choice for forgotten-by-time Chicago-Italian ambiance and reasonable prices, with strolling violins Monday through Thursday. It's close to the express-way as well as the train, and offers free valet parking. $14-29.

Drink

If you're looking for swinging Polish nightlife, check the options nearby in Belmont-Cragin, too.

Abbey Pub, 3420 W Grace st (*Belmont Blue Line*), +1 773 478-4408, *www.abbeypub.com*, Box office 11AM-2AM. One of Chicago's essential music venues. The Irish trappings aside, the Abbey Pub does a wider range of great music than almost anywhere else in the city — from surrealist hip hop to English folk rock, with loud stuff, Irish stuff, bluegrass stuff, and foot-stomping stuff thrown in. $8-20.

Bim Bom Lounge, 5226 W Belmont Ave, +1 773 777-2120, Su-F 10AM-2AM, Sa 10AM-3AM. The warped sheet-metal facade outside leads to a friendly Polish punk/rock/metal bar with an especially fierce foosball scene.

Cafe Lura, 3184 N Milwaukee Ave (*Belmont Blue Line*), +1 773 736-3033, Su-F 5PM-2AM, Sa 5PM-3AM. A gloomy (and almost block-long) exterior houses a cheerful bar/cafe with Polish DJs and rock bands, Polish/Czech beer and food, and faux-medieval atmosphere for a Euro-style night at the club. Cover for bands $5-$10, otherwise free.

Capitol Club, 4244 N Milwaukee Ave, +1 773 685-1194, *www.capitolclub.com*. DJs and European sports broadcasts mix up the many pheromones flying around the mirrored walls of this late-night dance club, popular with Polish immigrants. English is spoken, but it's not the first language here.

Chief O'Neill's, 3471 N Elston Ave (*Addison Red Line*), +1 773 583-3066, *www.chiefoneillspub.com*, M-Th 4PM-2AM, F 3PM-2AM, Sa 11AM-3AM, Su 10AM-2AM. Colorful Irish pub in Avondale with a beer garden and *very* popular food, including Sunday brunch (10:30AM-3PM).

Club 40 (Czterdziestka), 3119 N Central Ave, +1 773 777-1231, M-F 4PM-2AM, Sa 4PM-3AM, Su 12PM-2AM. A Polish nightclub for the over-40 set, with the '80s Euro-pop, decor, disco balls and glass walls that the Polish over-40 set like in their nightclubs. In other words, not your average Chicago dive.

Edison Park Inn, 6713 N Olmsted Ave (*Edison Park Metra*), +1 773 775-1404, *www.edisonparkinn.net*, Su-Th 11AM-2AM, Sa 11AM-

3AM. Two-floor pub with food and plenty of games, including pool tables and eight lanes of bowling.

Small Bar, 2956 N Albany Ave, +1 773 509-9888, *www.thesmallbar. com*, Su-F 4PM-2AM, Sa 4PM-3AM. Actually quite small, but with an exemplary beer selection. There's more (and better) food than the usual dive.

The Udder Brudder, 5659 W Irving Park Rd, +1 773 202-1418, M-F,Su 12PM-2AM, Sa 2PM-3AM. A relaxed, friendly Polish beer garden in Portage Park.

Sleep

The vast majority of hotels in the area are clustered around O'Hare International Airport *p.397*, not the neighborhoods. The ones that *are* in residential areas are not in the luxury class, and a couple of owners are notorious for running crime-ridden flophouses. Definitely cast a careful eye over the block and the rooms before you decide to stay there.

Some of the Lincoln Avenue motels are within easy reach, and the Chicagoland suburb of Niles, further down Milwaukee Avenue, has a few places to stay as well.

Edgebrook Motor Hotel, 6401 W Touhy Ave (*290 Touhy bus*), +1 773 774-4200. Unmistakable sign, and unpretentious accommodations — televisions, fridges, and microwaves round out the amenities. It's about fifteen minutes from O'Hare in a quiet, safe area, just east of the Chicagoland sub-

urbs of Niles and Park Ridge. It's also near the Leaning Tower YMCA, a notable roadside oddity on Touhy. You'll want a car to reach the city, though. Rooms from $54.

Esquire Motel, 6145 N Elston Ave, +1 773 774-2700. Friendly accommodations in sleepy Edison Park, five minutes from O'Hare and an easy trip to the city by car down Elston. Rooms have cable and HBO. Rooms from $69.

Hotel Elinor, 3216 N Cicero Ave, +1 773 283-3100. In a classic building near the intersection of Cicero and Belmont. Rooms have full-size beds, bath, and TV, but no other frills. Guests must be 21 and over — no children. Rooms from $45.

Contact

Being heavily residential areas, the neighborhoods of the Far Northwest Side are dotted with small branch libraries that offer free public internet access.

Austin-Irving Branch Library, 6100 W Irving Park Rd (*80 Irving Park bus*), +1 312 744-6222, *www.chipublib.org*, M-Th 9AM-9PM, F-Sa 9AM-5PM. Old Irving.

Edgebrook Branch Library, 5331 W Devon Ave (*84 Peterson bus*), +1 312 744-8313, *www.chipublib. org*, M-Th 9AM-9PM, F-Sa 9AM-5PM. In Forest Glen.

Independence Branch Library, 3548 W Irving Park Rd (*Irving Park Blue Line*), +1 312 744-0900, *www. chipublib.org*, M-Th 9AM-9PM, F-

Sa 9AM-5PM. In Irving Park.

Jefferson Park Branch Library, 5363 W Lawrence Ave (*Jefferson Park Blue Line*), +1 312 744-1998, *www.chipublib.org*, M-Th 9AM-9PM, F-Sa 9AM-5PM. In Jefferson Park.

Oriole Park Branch Library, 7454 W Balmoral Ave (*Harlem Blue Line*), +1 312 744-1965, *www.chipublib.org*, M-Th 9AM-9PM, F-Sa 9AM-5PM. Big, new library near the Oriole Park fieldhouse in Norwood Park.

Roden Branch Library, 6083 N Northwest Hwy (*Norwood Park Metra/68 Northwest Highway bus*), +1 312 744-1478, *www.chipublib. org*, M-Th 9AM-9PM, F-Sa 9AM-5PM. Way out on the fringes of the city in Norwood Park.

West Addison Branch Library, 7536 W Addison St (*152 Addison bus*), +1 312 746-4704, *www. chipublib.org*, M,W,F-Sa 9AM-5PM, Tu,Th 12-8PM. In Dunning.

Get out

The Chicago Polish community flows over these district boundaries, with more to be found on Milwaukee Avenue to the north (in Niles) and to the south (in Logan Square *p.247*, and Wicker Park *p.229*, and Belmont-Cragin *p.331*), and also notably on the Southwest Side *p.347*.

The Chicagoland suburb of Park Ridge, a couple of minutes down Touhy Avenue/Northwest Highway from Edison Park, has the amazing **Pickwick**, a giant classic

movie theater that's still in regular use for second-run movies and occasional holiday revivals.

The **Far Southeast Side** of
Chicago is a huge section
of Chicago with only one
large tourist draw: the Pullman
Historic District. Most travelers
will literally just pass over this district on the Chicago Skyway, but
look closely and something may
catch your eye.

Understand

The Far Southeast side is vast, but
has a much lower population density than the rest of the city and
consequently less to offer a visitor
in terms of amenities and attractions. As it is so big, it is easier to
think of the Far Southeast Side in
terms of its neighborhoods.

Neighborhoods

Greater Pullman (Pullman, Roseland, West Pullman, Riverdale) is

the one dish on the menu for
99% of the Far Southeast Side's
visitors. It is home to the **Historic Pullman District**, important
to American history for its early
planned industrial/railroad community and subsequent strikes
and socialist radicalism, as well as
its attractive and unique architecture.

Southeast Shore (South Chicago,
South Deering, East Side,
Hegewisch) is a once prosperous industrial region around
the mouth of the Calumet River
("The Port of Chicago") that im-
ploded along with Chicago's steel
industry. Today it is one of the
least populous areas of Chicago
and ranges from industrial to
failed-post-industrial in character.
The East Side is the most urban
section of this vast expanse and
has a nice commercial center
along 106th St. Hegewisch is a

particularly odd neighborhood — it is cut off from the rest of the city by Calumet Lake and huge manufacturing districts. As a result, the neighborhood feels almost like an independent, small, Midwestern industrial town (and indeed, a certain mayor not long ago forgot it was part of the city). Though the area has few urban attractions, the Southeast Shore does offer outdoor opportunities around Wolf Lake and Eggers Woods. (But if you are adverse to factory-vistas on the horizon, you may choose to overlook these attractions.)

Pullman history

The history of Pullman — the first modernist planned community in the United States — is a tragic one. George Pullman, the founder, was a liberal railroad tycoon with a reputation as a "welfare capitalist." He founded the Pullman company town with the intention of creating a perfect industrial community which would avoid the vice and extreme poverty found in urban industrial communities and therefore also avoid related worker unrest. To accomplish his goal, he built a very attractive landscaped town in the countryside to the south of Chicago. The company provided wages significantly higher than national averages and state-of-the-art utilities. He met widespread acclaim for his town, including an award for the **"World's Most Perfect Town"**, and visitors came to see Pullman (and the World's Fair Columbian Exposition) from places as far

away as Europe.

A lesson in paternalism and central planning, Pullman controlled nearly every aspect of his resident workers lives. A famous quote sums up this paternalism problem nicely, "We are born in a Pullman house, fed from the Pullman shop, taught in the Pullman school, catechized in the Pullman church, and when we die we shall be buried in the Pullman cemetery and go to the Pullman Hell." The failures of the Pullman company town foreshadowed later 20th century planned communities which had similarly good intentions, but disastrous effects (e.g., the Ida B Wells housing projects of Bronzeville *p.191*).

Following the severe 1893 economic downturn, Pullman company wages decreased while housing and utility costs remained the same, prompting large scale violence and strikes known collectively as The Pullman Strike. The strike shut down the Chicago rail system, effectively cutting off all transportation in the Western half of the U.S. President Grover Cleveland ended the strike by sending in 2,000 US Army troops, the result of which left 13 strikers dead and many more injured.

The Pullman Strike played a significant role in US labor and civil rights history, as A. Phillip Randolph would later rise to prominence in both areas of activism by organizing the largely African-American "Brotherhood of Sleeping Car Porters," a union for the employees of the Pullman Company. Having attained some prominence, Randolph went on to become one of the nation's foremost advocates of civil rights for African-Americans. His achievements and the history of African-Americans in US labor are celebrated today in Pullman's A. Phillip Randolph Museum.

Since the 1970s the Pullman neighborhood, especially the historic district, has gentrified and experienced a racial shift as wealthier, white Chicagoans moved into the neighborhood attracted by the rich architecture and history. Sites and homes of historical interest are currently seeing impressive, painstaking (and slow) restorations. The neighborhood has a very quiet, sleepy feel, so be sure to visit either on a tour or while the museum and visitor center are open, or you might leave disappointed.

Far Southeast Side

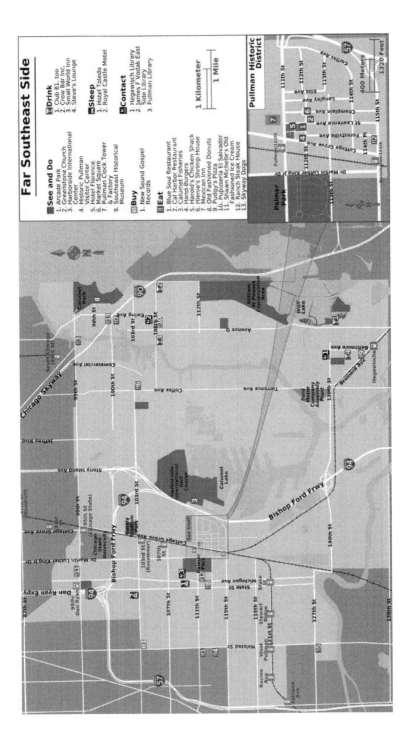

See and Do
1. Arcade Park
2. Greenstone Church
3. Harborside International Center
4. Historic Pullman Visitor Center
5. Hotel Florence
6. Market Square
7. Pullman Clock Tower & Factory
8. Southeast Historical Museum

Buy
1. New Sound Gospel Records

Eat
1. Blu Soul Restaurant
2. Cal Harbor Restaurant
3. Calumet Fisheries
4. Hand-Burgers
5. Harold's Chicken Shack
6. Hense's Shrimp House
7. Maxwell Inn
8. Old Fashioned Donuts
9. Pudgy's Pizza
10. Pupusería El Salvador
11. Shawn Michelle's Old Fashioned Ice Cream
12. Rich's Steak House
13. Skyway Dogs

Drink
1. Club 81, too
2. Cow Bar Inc.
3. Small World Inn
4. Steve's Lounge

Sleep
1. Hotel Toledo
2. Royal Castle Motel

Contact
1. Hegewisch Library
2. James F Vodak East Side Library
3. Pullman Library

1 Kilometer

1 Mile

Pullman Historic District

400 Meters

1320 Feet

Get in

By train

The CTA is not a great way to get to the Far Southeast, as there is only the 95th/Dan Ryan stop in the north of Roseland, far away from everything and anything of interest.

The Metra Electric Line is the best public transportation bet for traveling to the Far Southeast as it has numerous stops in convenient locations. The Pullman/111th St and Kensington/115th St stops are located right next to the Pullman Historic District. Metra also serves Hegewische via the first stop on the South Shore Railroad to South Bend, Indiana.

By bus

To an extent, buses can get you from point to point in the district, but there are no good routes coming here from the city center. If arriving by the CTA Red Line, you can take bus #111 from the 95th/Dan Ryan stop straight to the Pullman Historic District. Bus #30 runs between East Side and Hegwisch along Ewing Ave and Avenue O. East-west transportation is difficult, owing to the industrial wasteland (and Lake Calumet) in the middle.

By car

Since this is the least densely populated section of Chicago, a car is the most convenient method of travel. Free on-street parking is plentiful.

The most important highway for getting around is route I-94 along the **Dan Ryan Expy** and further south along the **Bishop Ford Fwy**. Exit at 111th for Historic Pullman or to get to Michigan Ave in Roseland, otherwise 95th and 103rd (to 106th) are useful to cross over to the East Side, and 130th is the exit of choice for Hegwisch.

The **Chicago Skyway** is the other main highway, which cuts across the East Side on its way to Indiana. Exits 108 (Anthony Ave/92nd St) and 110 (Indianapolis Blvd/US-20/US-41) will both let you off on the East Side, from which Historic Pullman and Hegwisch are both relatively easy drives. **US-41**, which cuts through the northeastern section of the East Side, is the old pre-Skyway route along the lake, and is way slower, but a good deal more interesting (and toll-free). It connects up with **Lake Shore Drive** farther north.

103rd/106th, and 130th Streets are the main roads for traversing the industrial wastelands lying between the western and eastern neighborhoods in the south of the district.

See

A Philip Randolph/Pullman Porter Museum, 10406 S Maryland Ave, +1 773 928-3935, *www.aphiliprandolphmuseum.com*, Open April-Dec 1 and in Feb for scheduled Black History events; Th-Sa 11AM-4PM. A museum in tribute to A. Phillip Randolph, which focuses on African-American culture and history, the Pullman Historic

Pullman Market Square

District, and US labor history. The interior has a big and rare manual tracker Organ. Admission $5.

Greenstone Church, 11211 S Saint Lawrence Ave, +1 773 785-1492. A landmark church in the heart of the historic Pullman community. It was initially intended to be a Unitarian church, where all the workers would go to service. That did not catch on and the church sat empty for years before becoming a Presbyterian and then Methodist church.

Historic Pullman Foundation Visitor Center, 11141 S Cottage Grove Ave, +1 773 785-8901, *www.pullmanil.org*, T-Su 11AM-3PM. The first stop to any Pullman visit houses a 20 minute video about the town's history, several

exhibits, and a gift shop. Offers guided walking tours every first Sunday of the month, as well as events and self-guided tour brochures. Be sure to head around to the back of the building (North side) to check out the impressive mural, "Visual Interpretations of Pullman," which depicts the former Pullman Arcade building coupled with an interpretation of the Pullman town and its laborers. 2 hour guided walking tours: 5$, 4$ (seniors), 3$ (students).

Hotel Florence, 11111 S Forrestville Ave, +1 773 660-2341, By appointment M-F 10AM-4PM. The Hotel Florence, named after Pullman's favorite daughter, is the most splendid building in the district. It was built in 1881 to accommodate visitors from all over the United States and Europe who came to see Pullman's "perfect town." The hotel is currently closed as it is going through a $1.2 million restoration and renovation program, but interior tours, focused on the restoration itself, can be arranged through the Historic Pullman Foundation.

Market Square (*2 blocks east of the Visitor Center at the intersection of E 112th St and S Champlain Ave*). Market square is just lovely. The Market Hall, which served as a grocery store, is currently being restored as it has suffered from several fires over the years.

Pullman Clock Tower and Factory, 111th St and Cottage Grove Ave (*just north of the Hotel Florence*), +1 773 660-2341. One of the world's most beautiful factories is undergoing a $3.4 million restoration, after it was badly damaged in 1998 by an arsonist. 90 minute guided tours, which focus on the restoration itself, are available by advance appointment.

Southeast Historical Museum, 9801 S Avenue G (*in the Calumet Park Fieldhouse*), +1 312 747-6039, *www.neiu.edu*, Th 1PM-4PM. A small history museum with exhibits celebrating the area's once mighty steel industry and labor history.

Do

Annual Historic Pullman House Tour, +1 773 785-8901, October 13-14 11AM-5PM. Includes a tour of about eight historic Pullman district homes as well as the visitor center and Greenstone Church. Reservations strongly recommended. $20, $17 (seniors or advance purchase).

Avalon Park Ice Skating, 1215 E 83rd St, +1 312 747-6015, *www.chicagoparkdistrict.com*, Outdoors 7AM-11PM daily, Indoor rink M-F 9AM-10PM, Sa-Su 9AM-5PM. Free skating; 3$ skate rentals.

Harborside International Golf Center, 11001 S Doty Ave, +1 312 782-7837, *www.harborsidegolf.com*, Open 1 April–30 November, sunrise-sunset. 36 holes of golf on the shores of Lake Calumet with some classic Far South views of the distant skyline and nearby decaying steel mills. Lighted driving range. 18 holes $65 weekdays, $75 weekends, $40 twilight.

William W Powers Conservation Area (Wolf Lake), 12949 S Avenue O (*entrance at 126th St and Avenue O*), +1 773 646-3270, *dnr.state.il.us*, sunrise-sunset, office: M-F 8AM-4PM. A conservation area around large Wolf Lake that is a study in contrasts between the industrial surroundings and the local cattails. It's a surprisingly good spot for fishing and even some hunting. In the winter, come here for ice skating and ice fishing.

Buy

New Sound Gospel Records and Tapes, 10723 S Halsted St, +1 773 445-1899, M-T 10AM-7PM, Th-Sa 10AM-6PM. A huge collection of new and used gospel records, tapes, CDs, and sheet music. Also sells gospel-related clothing and instruments.

Eat

Budget

Hand-Burgers, 11322 S Halsted St, +1 773 468-4444, M-Sa 11AM-7PM. A South Side fast food institution that does a robust trade in cooked-to-order burgers and fresh-cut fries. The basic burger will do you right, but there are a bunch of other interesting options, like fiery burgers made with hot peppers ground into the beef. The decor, as with many established South Side eateries, celebrates Chicago's black history, with old photographs of Mayor Harold Washington and a not-so-old Barack Obama signature. As you leave, cast a derisive glance at that McDonalds across the street. $4-6.

Harold's Chicken Shack, 12700 S Halsted St (*Multiple locations*), +1 773 785-4153, 11AM-2AM daily. The great South Side fried chicken chain is cheap, usually a little dirty, and always delicious. $2-5.

Old Fashioned Donuts, 11248 S Michigan Ave, +1 773 995-7420, M-Sa 6AM-6PM. Michigan Ave in Roseland is far out o the way, and not a pleasant place for a stroll, but this nearly 40 year old establishment is worth the trek for some of the freshest, most mouth-watering donuts you'll ever have. Old Fashioned Donuts is written up in the main Chicago papers every year as having the best donuts in the city (Dat Donuts is a mere tribute band). $0.20-2.

Pupuseria El Salvador, 3557 E 106th St, +1 773 374-0490, M 10AM-8PM, W-Th 10AM-9PM, F 10AM-9:30PM, Sa 10AM-9:30PM, Su 2:30PM-6:30PM. You have to travel far and long in Chicago to reach the city's Salvadoran community, but if you haven't tried pupusas before, it might be worth it. $2-6.

Shawn Michelle's Old Fashioned Ice Cream, 332 E 95th St, +1 773 785-1232, M-Sa noon-8PM, Su 1PM-6PM. Homemade ice cream in some surprising flavors.

Skyway Dogs, 9480 S Ewing Ave, +1 773 731-2000, M-Sa 10:30AM-10PM, Su 11AM-8PM. This is about as far from the city center as you can get, but this ramshackle little hot dog stand serves up some of Chicago's best hot dogs. They've got a drive thru, and there are usually a couple hungry squad cars "refueling" in the line. The picnic tables outside are a great place to soak up the local atmosphere, watching riced-out cars and other hungry patrons roll by. $1.50-4.

Mid-range

Blue Soul Restaurant, 11142 S Halsted St, +1 773 264-5433, 8AM-8PM daily. If it wasn't clear, this place serves soul food. The eatery is modest, and does more take-out business than dine-in, but it's nonetheless a fine place to enjoy a meal. The specialty is the chicken and waffles, and you should take that recommendation to heart. $7-12.

Calumet Fisheries, 3249 E 95th St, +1 773 933-9855, 10AM-9:45PM daily. One of the last great waterside shrimp and fish shacks from the glory days of the Port of Chicago. Calumet Fisheries offers all sorts of breaded and fried seafood, but the slow-smoked offerings might be the top draw. They recognize this too — they advertise their smoked chubs as **"fish crack."** The atmosphere here is just right too, it's right by the 95th St bridge (which the Blues Brothers jumped in their car), and boasts some serious industrial vistas. $7-18.

The Cal Harbor Restaurant, 546 E 115th St, +1 773 264-5435, M-Sa 5:30AM-5:45PM, Su 6AM-5:45PM. Serving the historic Pullman neighborhood, a classic South Side diner with all that entails. 3-9$.

Hienie's Shrimp House, 10359 S Torrence Ave, +1 773 734-8400, 11AM-midnight, F-Sa 11AM-1AM. Hienie's has been around for decades (albeit not in the same spot) and proudly upholds grand tradition of roadside shacks full of fried seafood and chicken catering to industrial workers. Their shrimp and gizzards are simply outstanding, and their hot sauce is beloved enough by the East Siders that it's made its way into local grocery stores. Any way you slice it, the piping hot, cholesterol laden, made to order food here will be great, but it's best enjoyed on the hood of your car while gazing off into the nearby smokestacks. $4-17.

Mexican Inn, 9510 S Ewing Ave, +1 773 734-8957 , Tu-Su 11AM-10PM. Fine authentic Mexican food served up in the East Side's most pleasant and most narrow restaurant. The Mexican Inn is a true South Side establishment, and has been around for nearly 50 years, making it one of the cities oldest taquerías. Unique among Chicago's taquerías, the Mexican Inn is actually renowned for its *hard-shell* tacos. $5-10.

Ranch Steak House, 11147 S Michigan Ave, +1 773 264-0320, Su-Th 7AM-10PM, F-Sa 7AM-11PM. This steak house, despite the inauspicious location, is actually quite good and strikingly cheaper than what you would pay for comparable food downtown. $10-15.

Pudgy's Pizzeria, 13460 S Baltimore Ave, +1 773 646-4199, Su-Th 4PM-11PM, F-Sa 4PM-midnight. There are a lot of good pizzerias in Hegwisch, most of them bearing a name oddly similar to Pudgy's, but this is the great one. The Chicago-style thin crust pizzas here hold up well against the best in the city, with the famous entree being the garlic-drenched "Bob's Mistake." Downsides include high prices (for thin crust) and very limited seating — just two small tables, usually taken up by people waiting for their order. $5-30.

Drink

If you're in Pullman and in the mood for a beer, you're in for more trouble than you would think. The famous Pullman Pub closed just recently under mysterious circumstances (asking a local about this is a *very* good way to start a conversation). If you like an early afternoon tipple, try the Frank Loyd Wright-style golf course club house off of 111th street just before Route 57 (open April through October, *www.stefanirestaurants.com*); the Cal Harbor also has a bar, which is sometimes open, sometimes not. Otherwise head over to the better options on the East Side on 106th or in Hegewisch.

Club 81, Too, 13157 S Avenue M, +1 773 646-4292, 11AM-2AM daily. The bar at the end of Chicago. Seriously, if you stumble out the wrong way, you'll fall into Wolf Lake. Old-timey moose-head decor might make you long for those bygone days of a fine cigar with your evening's whiskey, but even without the smoke, this is a great place for a beer with the establishment's legendary fish fry or Polish food.

Crow Bar Inc., 4001 E 106th St, +1 773 768-6985, 10AM-2AM daily. Probably the nicest neighborhood bar on the East Side, with strong drinks, friendly clientele, and sports on the television. It's also not a bad place to grab a corned beef sandwich.

Small World Inn, 3325 E 106th St, +1 773 721-2727, 11AM-11PM daily. This would seem to be yet another run of the Mill workingman's watering hole, except for the fact that it has served as a Yugoslav-American cultural center for decades. A drink here is a pleasant occasion, but focus on the menu — the Serbian cevapcicci (cheh-VAHP-chee-chee) will open your eyes to sausage possibilities you never knew existed. Entrees: $3-8.

Steve's Lounge, 13200 S Baltimore Ave, +1 773 646-1071, Tu-F 2PM-close, Sa-Su 3PM-close. One of the favorite (and most prominently-located) bars in Hegewisch, renowned not simply for being a nice laid-back bar, but rather for their legendary fried chicken. Their dining area is only open on Fridays 4PM-8PM, but you can get the fried chicken to go whenever you like if you call ahead of time.

Sleep

None of the Far Southeast Side's hotels are very nice and they are *far* from most of what you want to see in the city, so think carefully about whether it might make sense to stay elsewhere before you book a room.

Hotel Toledo, 10928 S Michigan Ave, +1 773 568-2643. Transient hotel, often at full capacity. Rooms include a shower and television. $40 for eight hours, $50 overnight on weekdays, $60 on weekends.

New Riviera Motel, 9132 S Stony Island Ave, +1 773 221-6600. Offers king-size beds, televisions, clock radios, and some furniture. $50 for ten hours, $66 overnight.

Royal Castle Motel, 45 W 103rd St, +1 773 468-8100. Just off State Street in Roseland. $50 for ten hours, $60 overnight.

Contact

There are **three public libraries** in the Far Southeast Side, all offering free public internet access:

Hegewisch Branch Library, 3048 E 130th St, +1 773 747-0046, M-F 10AM-9PM, Sa-Su 9AM-5PM.

James F Vodak East Side Branch Library, 10542 S Ewing Ave, +1 312 747-5500.

Pullman Branch Library, 11001 S Indiana Ave, +1 312 747-2033, M-Th 9AM-8PM, F-Sa 9AM-5PM.

Stay safe

Avoiding high crime areas in the Far Southeast Side is very simple: basically anything west of the Bishop Ford Fwy aside from Historic Pullman is gangland territory (although, obviously, that varies widely from block to block). It is unlikely that any visitors would find themselves in the far-flung and benighted communities of Riverdale, West Pullman, and Roseland, aside from the steady stream of foodie pilgrims to Old Fashioned Donuts. But if you are there for reasons other than sightseeing (there are no sights), stick to main streets and avoid walking around at night and you should be fine. All areas east of the Bishop Ford, on the other hand, often look gritty, but this is because they are poor — not crime ridden. Hegewisch and East Side are some of the safest communities in the city.

Get out

Travelers interested in the **labor history** of Chicago should also mosey on over to the **Back of the Yards** neighborhood on the Southwest Side *p.347*, former home to

the sprawling Union Stockyards made infamous by Upton Sinclair's *The Jungle*.

Pullman was not the only utopian planned industrial community in these parts. Just across the Indiana border is Marktown, a community modeled on an English village, but surrounded on all sides by three steel plants and the world's largest oil refinery.

The **Far Southwest Side** of Chicago is home to a large Irish-American community, a ton of Irish pubs, and even a replica Irish castle.

Understand

Chicago's Far Southwest Side is absolutely not one of the city's main tourist attractions, but it does offer an interesting mix of South Side and Irish culture (i.e., the authentic **Irish pubs** are here). Until 2009, the area was a major international tourist destination on Saint Patrick's Day for its magnificent parade, the largest **Saint Patrick's Day** neighborhood parade in the world outside of Dublin. Today however, perhaps owing to a desire to avoid greatness and to become yet another boring, middling, mildly suburban area of little distinction, the

neighborhood has decided to end the parade because it "had become something too big."

Beverly is the most distinctive of the Far Southwest neighborhoods and probably has the most to offer travelers. Here you will find Givens Castle, the Ridge Historical Society of Beverly and Morgan Park, and *plenty* of Irish pubs. You might want to visit just for a change in topography — Beverly is the only neighborhood in Chicago with hills, lending it the odd-sounding nickname Beverly Hills. Along with **Morgan Park** to the south, Beverly is one of Chicago's few racially integrated neighborhoods, with a sizable African-American minority living side-by-side with the neighborhood's large Irish-American community.

Mount Greenwood is a large middle class area of Chicago, home to many of the city's Irish-American firefighters and police officers and to St Xavier University. For those in search of an authentic Irish-American neighborhood, look no further. *No* tourists make it out here and the pubs will transport you straight back to the Emerald Isle.

Get in

By car

If you have a car at your disposal, use it. Chicago's Far Southwest Side is not well served by mass transit and parking is plentiful throughout the district. If coming from the north, take Pulaski Rd or Western Ave; both are major roads and will get you there quickly. From I-57, take either the US-1/Halsted Avenue exit south to 103rd St, or the 111th St exit. From I-294, the simplest route is to head north from the Cicero Avenue exit and then to turn right on 115th or 111th St.

By train

The Metra Rock Island line to Joliet passes through Beverly and Morgan Park. A one-way trip from downtown LaSalle Station to 103rd St will cost $3.05.

By bus

If taking the bus is an absolute necessity, then the best way to reach this area from the north is via CTA Route 49 (Western), with a transfer to Pace Route 349 (South Western) at 79th St. Route 349

will take you within walking distance of most attractions in the district. Do not take any routes running any east of Western, as they both end short of the district as well as run through some rough neighborhoods. All transit service in this area ends after midnight, so make sure you have enough money to get back via taxi (you will need to call for one) if you plan to spend the night at one of the neighborhood pubs.

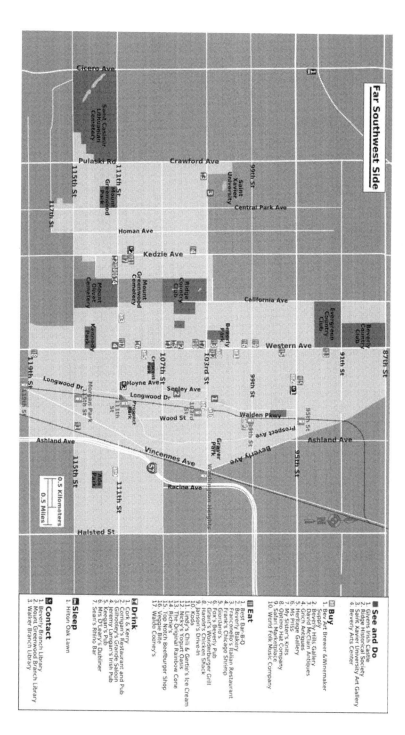

Far Southwest Side

See and Do
1. Givens Irish Castle
2. Ridge Historical Society
3. Saint Xavier University Art Gallery
4. Beverly Arts Center

Buy
1. Bev Art Brewer & Winemaker Supply
2. Beverly Hills Gallery
3. David Clark Antiques
4. Grich Antiques
5. Heritage Gallery
6. Ms Priss
7. My Sister's Knits
8. Optimo Hat Company
9. Safari Marketplace
10. World Folk Music Company

Eat
1. Best Bar-B-Q
2. Beverly Bakery
3. Franconello's Italian Restaurant
4. Frank's Chicago Shrimp House
5. Giordano's
6. Fox's Beverly Pub
7. Grant's Wonderburger Grill
8. Harold's Chicken Shack
9. Janson's Drive-In
10. Koda
11. Lindy's Chili & Gertie's Ice Cream
12. Nick's Yogurt Oasis
13. The Original Rainbow Cone
14. Richie's
15. Top Notch Beefburger Shop
16. Veggie Bite
17. Waldo Cooney's

Drink
1. Cork & Kerry
2. Corrigan's Restaurant and Pub
3. Gilhooley's Grande Saloon
4. Jeremy Langan's Irish Pub
5. Keegan's Pub
6. Mrs. O'Leary's Dubliner
7. Sean's Rhino Bar

Sleep
1. Hilton Oak Lawn

Contact
1. Beverly Branch Library
2. Mount Greenwood Branch Library
3. Walker Branch Library

FAR SOUTHWEST SIDE BUY

See

Givens Irish Castle (Beverly Unitarian Church), 10244 S Longwood Dr, +1 773 233-7080, *www.beverlyunitarian.org*, Call in advance for hours. Certainly the oddest sight in Chicago's Far Southwest Side, this building is a replica of castle on Ireland's River Dee, built by a nostalgic and wealthy Irish-American for his fiancee in 1885. Today, the castle houses Beverly's Unitarian congregation and offers a yearly Halloween "Haunted Castle." Beyond the deliberate scares, the castle is purportedly haunted by an actual ghost: a young girl who used to live here. She tends to show up, wearing a long dress, during weddings or parties where alcohol is being served.

Ridge Historical Society, 10621 S Seeley Ave, +1 773 881-1675, *www.ridgehistoricalsociety.org*, Su-Th 2PM-5PM. This historical society focuses on the Beverly and Morgan Park neighborhoods and offers tours, assistance with area research, and small, thoughtful exhibits such as a costume room and a doll house collection.

Saint Xavier University Art Gallery, 3700 W 103rd St, +1 773 298-3081, *www.sxu.edu*, M-F 10AM-5PM, Sa 10AM-3PM. A rotating gallery of works by professional artists.

Do

Beverly Arts Center of Chicago, 2407 W 111th St, +1 773 445-3838, *www.beverlyartcenter.org*, M-F 10AM-9PM, Sa 10AM-6PM, Su noon-5PM. The Beverly Arts Center is a community arts center offering film screenings, dance and dramatic performances, and monthly art gallery exhibits.

Buy

Irish

Heritage Gallery, 1915 W 103rd St, +1 773 233-0084, *www.simmerling.com*, M-F 10AM-5PM, Sa 10AM-3PM. This art gallery features the original works of its owner, Jack Simmerling, who specializes in pen-and-inks of Chicago landmarks and watercolors of Ireland.

Beverly Hills Gallery, 2133-35 W 95th St, +1 773 239-7460, M, Sa 10AM-7PM, T-F 10AM-7PM. This gallery sells fine art from all over the world and specializes in Celtic art by Courtney Davis.

World Folk Music Company, 1808 W 103rd St, +1 773 779-7059, *www.worldfolkmusiccompany.com*, M-Th 10AM-9PM, F 10AM-6PM, Sa 9AM-5PM. A music shop selling instruments, sheet music, and CDs, which also hosts concerts by local folk musicians.

Other

Bev Art Brewer and Winemaker Supply, 10033 S Western Ave, +1 773 233-7579, *www.bev-art.com*, Tu-Sa 6AM-7PM. Come here to make your own wine and beer, under the store's guidance. It also sells all the equipment you'd need to brew at home (or your hotel), if you prefer to get even deeper into Chicago history with a Prohibition-style experience.

David McClain Antiques, 2716 W 111th St, +1 773 239-4683, noon-6PM daily. David McClain runs his antique business out of his house and offers a quite large collection of furniture and some paintings and sculptures.

Grich Antiques, 10857 S Western Ave, +1 773 233-8734, M-Sa 11AM-3PM. Grich has *a lot* of antiques and a wide selection on offer. Come prepared to bargain.

Ms Priss, 9915 S Walden Pkwy, +1 773 233-7747, *mspriss.homestead. com*, T-F 11AM-6PM, Sa 11AM-4PM. Women's boutique shopping is not Beverly's forte, but Ms Priss will definitely beat your expectations.

My Sister's Knits, 9907 S Walden Pkwy, +1 773 238-4555, *www.mysistersknits.com*, T-Th 11AM-6:30PM, F noon-9PM, Sa 10AM-4PM, Su noon-4PM. A small, friendly, and rather bohemian, knitting and yarn shop.

Optimo Hat Company, 10215 S Western Ave, +1 773 238-2999, *www.optimohats.com*, M-Sa 10AM-6PM. A very snazzy specialty custom hat shop. $200-300.

Safari Marketplace, 1403 W 111th St, +1 773 233-8307, 8AM-6PM daily. An eclectic store offering African-American related items from audio tapes of Louis Farrakhan to African clothing and board games. The store also has a section devoted to world musical instruments.

Eat

Budget

Best Bar-B-Q, 1648 W 115th St, +1 773 239-1522, Tu-Su 11AM-2AM, M 11AM-10PM. Southside carry-out ribs and chicken joint. $3-6.

Beverly Bakery & Cafe, 10528 S Western Ave, +1 773 238-5580, Tu-F 5:30AM-4PM, Sa 7AM-5PM, Su 8AM-1PM; breakfast & lunch served until 3PM daily. This family-owned bakery is always a tasty place to stop by, but is an especially good stop around St Patrick's Day, when it offers various Irish treats.

Frank's Chicago Shrimp, 10410 S Kedzie Ave, +1 773 445-3100, Su-Th 11AM-9PM, W-Sa 11AM-10PM. A small hole-in-the wall with that has been serving Chicago-style shrimp, mostly for take-out, for decades. $3-5.

Grant's Wonderburger Grill, 11045 S Kedzie Ave, +1 773 238-7200, M-Sa 10:30AM-8PM. A family-owned local landmark serving burgers and curly fries since 1959. $2-5.

Harold's Chicken Shack, 11857 S Western Ave, +1 773 779-9911, 11AM-2AM daily. The great South Side fried chicken chain is cheap, usually a little dirty, and always delicious. $2-5.

Janson's Drive-In, 9900 S Western Ave, +1 773 238-3612, M-F 10AM-10PM, Sa 11AM-10PM, Su 11AM-6PM. A classic, neon-adorned, drive-in fast food joint with great Chicago hot dogs. $2-5.

Lindy's Chili & Gertie's Ice

FAR SOUTHWEST SIDE EAT

Cream, 11009 S Kedzie Ave, +1 773 779-7236, *www.lindyschili.com*, M-Th 10:30AM-10PM. A chili and burgers joint sharing the space with a traditional ice cream parlor. $2-6.

The Original Rainbow Cone, 9233 S Western Ave, +1 773 238-7075, 11AM-10:30PM daily, March-December. For over *80 years* South Side families have enjoyed the rainbow cone, a five-flavored ice cream treat of chocolate, pistachio, strawberry, Palmer House, and orange sherbet.

Richie's, 3123 W 111th St, +1 773 298-1548, *richiesrestaurants.com*, T-Th 11AM-10PM, F-Sa 11AM-11PM, Su 4PM-9PM. A good value Italian restaurant. Don't pass up the seafood. $9-14.

Top Notch Beefburger Shop, 2116 W 95th St, +1 773 445-7218, *www.topnotchbeverly.com*, M-Sa 7AM-8PM. A south side burger institution since the 1950s with seriously juicy burgers made from quality beef. $2-8.

Nicky's Yogurt Oasis (Yogurt and Hot Dogs), 10255 S Western Ave, +1 773 233-3072, 10AM-10PM daily. Beverly's top Chicago style grilled fast food option, with an extra dose of frozen yogurt and ice cream. It's a beloved shop, and it's almost always crowded. $2-5.

Mid-range

Fox's Beverly Pub, 9956 S Western Ave, +1 773 239-3212, M-Th 11AM-11PM. A neighborhood Irish pub that is more of a restaurant than a bar, offering Irish and Italian food, as well as *superb* Chicago thin-crust pizza. $8-13.

Franconello's Italian Restaurant, 10222 S Western Ave, +1 773 881-4100, M-Th 11AM-10PM, F 11AM-10:30PM, Sa 3PM-10:30PM. An Italian restaurant serving hearty portions of solid (if a bit over-priced) food. $9-14.

Giordano's, 9613 S Western Ave, +1 773 445-6255, *www.giordanos.com*, Su-Th 11AM-11PM, F-Sa 11AM-midnight. One of the best locations for Giordano's pizza. The restaurant's specialty is its heart-devastating stuffed Chicago pizza, although it also serves plenty of other Italian entrees. It also makes a fine thin-crust pizza, but if you are in the Far Southwest, you should probably get your thin crust from the masters at Vito & Nick's or Fox's. $10-23.

Veggie Bite, 3031 W 111th St, +1 773 239-4367, *veggiebite.net*, noon-10PM daily. A Chicago junk-food establishment with a surprising *all vegan twist*. Try the Italian "beef" melt (made with organic flour and soy cheese?!) and wash it down with a glass of carrot juice. $8-12.

Waldo Cooney's, 2410 W 111th St, +1 773 233-9781, *www.waldocooneyspizza.com*, M-Th 11AM-11PM, F-Sa 11AM-12:30AM, Su noon-11:30PM. A quality pizzeria serving thin crust and stuffed Chicago pies. $7-18.

Splurge

Koda, 10352 S Western Ave, +1 773

445-5632, *kodabistro.com*, Lunch M-F 11AM-2PM; Dinner: T-Sa 5PM-10:30PM, Su 4-9PM. An upscale French bistro and bar with a contemporary and interesting menu. Don't be fooled into thinking this will be good "for the South Side" — the food here is really top-notch. $20-30.

Drink

A pint may be the number one reason to make the trek out to the Far Southwest Side. Chicago is a city full of fake Irish pubs, but the only ones where the clientèle and servers speak with a brogue are down here, mostly along Western Avenue.

Irish pubs

Cork & Kerry, 10614 S Western Ave, +1 773 445-2675, *www.corkandkerrychicago.com*, M-F 2PM-2AM, Sa noon-3AM, Su noon-2AM. An unpretentious neighborhood Irish pub that doesn't serve food and has a great beer garden for the summer months.

Corrigan's Restaurant and Pub, 3047 W 111th St, +1 773 298-1315, Bar: M-F 3PM-2AM, Sa 11AM-3AM, Su 10AM-midnight, Restaurant: Su-Th 3PM-10PM, F 3PM-midnight, Sa noon-midnight. A community-oriented Irish pub that serves corned beef and cabbage if you are feeling in an Irish mood.

Gilhooley's Grande Saloon, 3901 W 103rd St, +1 773 233-2200, *gilhooleyssxu.com*, M-Th 11AM-1AM, F-Sa 11AM-2AM,

Su 11AM-9PM. A rather upscale, stylish, and attractive pub across the street from St Xavier's, offering a small selection of sandwiches and burgers to accompany a very large selection of drinks. Live bands perform F-Sa, while the neighborhood performs on open-mic Wednesdays. $5-8.

Jeremy Lanigan's Irish Pub, 3119 W 111th St, +1 773 233-4004, Su-F noon-2AM, Sa noon-3AM. Come here to drink and reminisce about the old country. This pub is frequented by Irish nationals and puts on amateur live Irish music F-Su.

Keegan's Pub, 10618 S Western Ave, +1 773 233-6829, M-F 2PM-2AM, Sa noon-3AM, Su noon-2AM. A friendly neighborhood pub that may well serve the best pint of Guinness in Chicago. It's also right next door to Cork & Kerry, so you can switch between the two if you're unsatisfied with the one.

Dubliner, 10910 S Western Ave, +1 773 238-0784, Su-F noon-2AM, Sa noon-3AM. Well, the name probably gives away that this is an Irish pub. It is very low-key and very popular with Irish immigrants. It's *arguably* the most authentic pub in the area.

Sean's Rhino Bar & Grill, 10330 S Western Ave, +1 773 238-2060, M-F 1PM-2AM, Sa noon-3AM, Su noon-2AM. More of a sports bar than the rest, but in this neighborhood everything pretty much winds up being an Irish pub. Live bands perform on Saturday nights.

Sleep

Chicago's Far Southwest Side is a black hole as far as travel accommodations are concerned; if you are planning to stay in the area, you should try the Hilton just across the city boundaries in Oak Lawn, one of the Midway Airport-serving hotels in Bedford Park, or one of the many hotels by the Tri-State Tollway in Alsip.

Hilton Oak Lawn, 9333 South Cicero Avenue, +1 708 425-7800, *www1.hilton.com*, Checkin: 3PM, Checkout: noon. A fairly standard Hilton, which offers a free shuttle to Midway Airport. $141.

Contact

Beverly Branch Library, 2121 W 95th St, +1 312 747-9673, M-F 9AM-9PM, Sa 9AM-5PM. A *big*, modern facility with free public internet access as well as a very large selection of books. Its 3,500-item "Irish Collection" is especially noteworthy.

Mount Greenwood Branch Library, 11010 S Kedzie Ave, +1 312 747-2805, M-Th 9AM-9PM, F-Sa 9AM-5PM. Free public internet access.

Walker Branch Library, 11071 S Hoyne Ave, +1 312 747-1920, M-Th 9AM-9PM, F-Sa 9AM-5PM. Free public internet access.

Get out

The Far Southwest Side has the city's largest Irish-American population, but the more famous (and politically-connected) one is in Bridgeport *p.175*, home of the Daleys.

O'HARE AIRPORTUNDERSTAND

O'Hare International Airport *www.ohare.com* (IATA: **ORD**) is one of the biggest and busiest airports in the world. It serves the city of Chicago and the rest of the Chicagoland area, with connecting flights to smaller cities throughout the Midwest.

Understand

This is no Changi, no Kansai; in other words, it's nobody's favorite airport. O'Hare is huge, but it's from an era before airports had much in the way of amenities, and it's been stretched beyond capacity for a while now. Although safety has never been a concern, O'Hare has one of the worst on-time records of any major airport. However, most of the world's airlines fly though O'Hare, so international travelers aren't likely to

have much of a choice, other than possibly Chicago's Midway or Milwaukee's General Mitchell International (connected to the Loop *p.47* via the Amtrak Hiawatha *www.amtrakhiawatha.com* train service).

O'Hare has four passenger terminals. **Terminals 1-3** handle domestic traffic (and some international departures); **Terminal 5** handles all international arrivals and international departures that are not covered by Terminals 1-3. (Terminal 4 is something of a fnord, its temporary space since re-appropriated as the shuttle bus depot; the name has been set aside for potential future expansion).

United Airlines has a significant presence at O'Hare, since its corporate offices are located in downtown Chicago. O'Hare is also a major hub for **American Air-**

lines. As such, a rule of thumb is that Terminal 1 is dominated by United and its alliance partners; Terminal 3 is given over to American and its partners, and Terminal 2 is everybody else, plus some United Express gates that wouldn't fit in Terminal 1. More precisely:

Terminal 1 All Nippon, Lufthansa (departures only), Ted, United Airlines (domestic arrivals and departures) (international departures only), United Express

Terminal 2 Air Canada, Continental Airlines, Jet Blue, Northwest Airlines, US Airways, United Express

Terminal 3 Alaska Airlines, American Airlines (domestic and international departures), American Eagle, Delta Air Lines, Iberia Airlines (departures only), Spirit Airlines

Terminal 5 Aer Lingus, Air France, Air India, Air Jamaica, Alitalia, All Nippon, American Airlines (International arrivals only), Asiana Airlines, Austrian Airlines, British Airways, Cayman Airways, Iberia Airlines (arrivals only), Japan Airlines (JAL), KLM, Korean Air, LOT Polish Airlines, Lufthansa (arrivals only), Mexicana, Royal Jordanian, Scandinavian Airlines, SWISS, TACA Airlines, Turkish Airlines, USA 3000, United Airlines (international arrivals only), Virgin Atlantic

O'Hare International Airport

Parking Lot

Lounge

ATS Stop

CTA Blue Line Station

Hotel Courtesy Shuttle

0.25 Kilometers

0.25 Miles

Get in

Chicago's Far Northwest Side *p.363* is the closest part of the city to O'Hare. While it does have some charms, the most popular attractions for tourists are much further on, in the Loop *p.47*, Near North *p.71*, and Near South *p.95*.

By train

The CTA **Blue Line** *www.transitchicago.com* terminates at the space-age station for O'Hare, designed by the firm of architect Helmut Jahn. Trains run 24 hours a day, as frequently as every six minutes during peak periods and as infrequently as every half-hour overnight. The trip to the Loop *p.47* should take about 48 minutes, but never cut things close with the CTA. The station is located beneath the Bus/Shuttle Center, closest to Terminal 2 but easily accessible by underground passages, with moving walkways, from Terminals 1 and 3. Those arriving at or departing from Terminal 5 (international) must take the automated Airport Transit System between Terminals 2 and 5.

Metra *www.metrarail.com* North Central Service trains stop at the "O'Hare transfer" station, located adjacent to parking lot F (with shuttle bus service connecting to the ATS). The train reaches Chicago's Union Station in approximately 30 minutes, but service is infrequent, operates only on weekdays and is concentrated in the peak commute direction.

By bus

Pace *www.pacebus.com* routes **250** (Dempster Street for Evanston and Skokie) and **330** (Mannheim/La Grange) stop at the terminus of the Airport Transit System in parking lot E.

Several bus companies run scheduled and charter services to other communities; these usually drop passengers off at the departure-level curb and pick passengers up at the Bus/Shuttle Center.

By taxi

Most taxis offer a fixed rate for the O'Hare trip from the Near North *p.71* or the Loop *p.47*. The price will vary from other locations, but shouldn't exceed $30 from the city center or anywhere on the North or West Side; parts of the South Side may be more expensive.

Of the many shuttle/limo services, **Airport Express** *www.airportexpress.com* vans are the most commonly seen doing the rounds of downtown hotel pick-ups. Fares are $27/19/14 (per person) for one/two/three or more, with a discount for a return ticket if bought in advance and lower fares for children under 14.

By plane

The **Omega Airport Shuttle** provides transfer service to Midway Airport for $16, with hourly departures from the Bus/Shuttle Center. Service is offered 6:45AM-11:45PM, daily. Most taxis offer fixed rates for the Midway/O'Hare trip in the vicinity of $35-40.

By car

Access to O'Hare's terminals is via **I-190**, which originates near the interchange between **I-294** (the **Tri-State Tollway**) and **I-90** (the **Northwest Tollway** to the northwest and the **Kennedy Expressway** to the east). From downtown Chicago, follow **I-90/94** northwest, continue on I-90 when I-94 splits off, then follow I-190 into the airport, which splits eventually into arrival (lower-level) and departure (upper-level) roadways serving Terminals 1, 2, and 3 in turn. For Terminal 5, exit on Bessie Coleman Drive. This exit also serves numerous rental car companies and the economy parking lots. To drop off a passenger without the harrowing experience of navigating the departures roadway, try **Kiss n'Fly**: follow signs for remote **lot E** where you can leave your friend at the terminus of the **Airport Transit System,** just a short ride away from the terminals.

Most major car rental companies have gigantic lots at O'Hare and offer complimentary shuttle buses to and from the passenger terminals.

Parking

O'Hare runs a parking hotline (+1 773 686-7530) and broadcasts parking information on 800 AM within two and a half miles of the airport. Needless to say, then, parking at O'Hare is no simple af-

fair. If you're the sort of person who likes to meet friends at baggage claim with a cordial "Come on, run with those bags!" you'll be glad to know that parking in the main garage is **free** for stays of under 10 minutes. For the rest of us...

Short-term Level one of the main garage (**lot A**) is designated for short-term parking, charging $2 for the first hour, and $4 for stays of up to three hours. But keep an eye on the clock, as a fourth hour sees the rate jump to $21, and it doesn't take long to reach the $50/day maximum. Other lots (under long-term, below) also charge $2 for the first hour, but rates increase faster, and as they are further away from the terminals, this option really only benefits you if the hourly parking area is full.

Lot D, adjacent to Terminal 5, also offers short-term parking: $2 for an hour, $6 for two hours.

A portion of remote **lot F** is now the **cell phone lot** where you can park for free and *wait in your car* for an arriving passenger to call your cell phone, at which point you can pick up your friend curbside without circling endlessly.

Long-term If leaving a vehicle at the airport during a trip, numerous options are available. The upper levels of the main garage (**lot A**) and the adjacent surface lots (**lots B and C**) charge $30/day.

Lot D charges $50/day.

Remote **economy lot E** charges $16/day, **lot G** charges $13/day, and the more remote **lot F** charges $9/day. A shuttle takes you between lots F, G, and the ATS terminus in lot E.

And if money is no object, **valet parking** is available at $10/$16 for one/two hours and $45 for the day.

Visitors are advised to notify the above parking hotline if they plan to park for longer than thirty days.

Get around

On foot

Passengers may walk between Terminals 1, 2, and 3 both landside (prior to clearing security) and air-side. The distance can be considerable; make sure to allow adequate time for layovers between different terminals. United Airlines also runs an air-side shuttle bus between its gates in Terminal 2 and Terminal 1.

Airport Transit System

O'Hare has an automated, landside, transit system cleverly called **Airport Transit System** or **ATS.** Stops are made at all four terminals as well as remote parking **lot E.** This is the only way to reach the three domestic terminals and the Blue Line station from the international terminal, which means that passengers connecting to or from a Terminal 5 flight should allow abundant time for border formalities, inter-terminal transit, and a second security screening.

See & Do

O'Hare doesn't have much in the way of amenities, but there are a few:

Brachiosaurus skeleton (*Terminal 1, Concourse B*). Airports are big affairs with large budgets, but only O'Hare can boast a complete dinosaur skeleton. And not just any skeleton, but that of the largest animal ever to walk the earth. The Brachiosaurus skeleton is in Terminal 1's Concourse B indefinitely as part of a promotional agreement between the airport and the Field Museum in the Near South. It's certainly worth a look if you are in the terminal, and don't worry — you can't miss it.

Butch O'Hare's fighter plane. A replica of the F3F-4 fighter plane flown by the airport's namesake hangs in the main hall of Terminal 2.

There are three **family/companion restrooms** in Terminal 2, and one in Terminal 3.

Interfaith Chapel, Terminal 2, +1 773 686-2636, *www.airportchapels. org*, The chapel is open 24 hours. If flight delays are making you question your faith, then head right over. There are chaplains for Catholics, Protestants, and Muslims during office hours, M-F 8AM-2:30PM.

Kids Play interactive exhibits are located in Terminal 2 ("Kids on the Fly") and Terminal 5 ("Play It Safe"), operated by the Chicago Children's Museum from Navy Pier. They're open during airport hours.

O'HARE AIRPORT EAT

Travelers and Immigrants Aid, Terminal 2, upper level, +1 773 894-2427, M-F 8:30-9PM, Sa-Su 10AM-9PM. Provides information, directions, and assistance for travelers. There are also information booths in all three terminals staffed from 2-7PM M-F 2PM-7PM, Su 3-7PM.

UIC Medical Center, Terminal 2, +1 773 894-5100, M-F 7AM-7PM, Sa-Su 9AM-5PM. Operated by the University of Illinois at Chicago. They can provide emergency treatment/urgent care, X-rays, immunizations, and other services.

If you just can't wait, there are HeartSave defibrillators (+1 773 462-7283) in all four terminals, intended to be within a minute's reach from any point in the airport.

The U.S.O. has a center for military personnel in Terminal 2 (24 hours).

O'Hare in the movies

Scenic beauty it ain't, but O'Hare does have a cinematic legacy. For example, in the first two "Home Alone" movies, the McAllister family departed for Paris and Miami in American Airlines' Terminal 3. If you feel like playing with a Talk-Boy, chasing a man in a Burberry coat, or running on to the jetway of your flight moments before you leave, here's the place.

Buy

There are, of course, duty free shops in Terminals 1, 2, 3, and 5.

Chicago Historical Society Gift Shop, 8AM-9PM daily, has a better class of Chicago Souvenir than most. They're in Terminal 3.

Field Museum Store, 8AM-8PM daily, takes the gift shop from the great museum to Terminal 1.

Hudson's Booksellers, 7AM-9:30PM daily, has a reasonable selection of books in Terminals 1, 2, and 3.

Eat

There isn't much good to say about food at O'Hare. You'll pay more than you should for meals you won't remember anything about, save for the grease. Nevertheless, there are plenty of places to eat. A full list can be found on the O'Hare website *www.flychicago.com*.

Budget

McDonald's, 5AM-11PM daily, has its greasy claws in all four terminals and is notable mainly for being open later than anyone else.

Gold Coast Dogs, 6AM-8PM daily, serves airport versions of Chicago-style hot dogs in Terminals 3 and 5. It would be a crime against taste if this was your only encounter with a Chicago-style hot dog, with Superdawg only a short distance away on the Far Northwest Side *p.363!*

Nuts on Clark *www.nutsonclark.com*, 6AM-10PM daily in Terminals 1, 2, and 3, has tasty popcorn & nuts for a takeaway salty fix.

Sky Bridge, 5AM-9PM daily, is run by Greeks and serves gy-

403

ros, kebabs, and some other Greek fare along with the basic burger and dog. A step up for the usual fast food joint, most meats here aren't cooked until you order. The omelets are good, the hash browns greasy. Terminal 2, near F9.

Mid-range

Billy Goat Tavern & Grill, 6AM-9:30PM daily, serves beer, steaks, and cheeseburgers in Terminal 1. For the sake of any locals who might be around, travelers should take it as a given that everyone has already heard their John Belushi impression, thanks.

Chili's, 5:30AM-9PM daily, serves a limited version of their burgers-and-pasta menu in Terminals 1, 2, and 3.

Pizzeria UNO, 5:15AM-9:30PM daily, slums it in Terminals 2, 3, and 5, pushing watery versions of Chicago's hallmark deep dish pizza, while **Connie's Pizza** does the same in Terminal 1 and **Gino's East** in Terminal 3.

Splurge

The Berghoff, 5:15AM-10:30PM daily, lives on in Terminal 1, outlasting the original location in the Loop. Bratwurst loyalists will have to take the classic German food wherever they can get it.

Wolfgang Puck, 5AM-10PM daily, in Terminals 1 and 3 has an extremely limited menu to compensate for demand and limited preparation space. It's overpriced and not tasty enough to justify the price, but if you're on an expense account, go for it.

Drink

There are a few options for booze in O'Hare. Some restaurants, including **Billy Goat** and **The Berghoff**, also have liquor licenses. As with food, options are more limited in the international terminal.

Goose Island Brewing Company, 8AM-8PM daily, in Terminal 2.

Prairie Tap, 6AM-10PM daily, in Terminal 3.

Sleep

Many hotels serving O'Hare are actually located in the nearby suburbs of Rosemont and Schiller Park, among others. They tend to be nice, clean, bland, and expensive. Amenities are fairly standard, with an eye toward business travelers. Virtually all hotels run shuttles to and from the airport. Some run on a schedule and do regular pick-ups, while others have to be called from the airport concierge. Shuttle stops are clearly sign-posted. Make sure the shuttle is going to your specific hotel — Marriott, for example, runs separate shuttles for each of its brands. A taxi should cost $10-15 at the most.

If you're driving to a hotel, get on **I-190**, the small expressway that operates to/from the airport. Most hotels are clustered on Mannheim Road or River Road, which have exits from the expressway, or off roads that connect with

Mannheim going north (Higgins, Touhy) or south (Irving Park). I-190 merges with I-90/94, which heads to the center of Chicago.

Budget

Cheap hotels near O'Hare tend to be cheap for a reason — don't be shy about asking to see the room first.

Comfort Inn O'Hare (Des Plaines), 2175 E Touhy Ave, Des Plaines, +1 847 635-1300, *www.comfortinn.com*. About two miles from the airport. Rooms from $90.

Comfort Inn O'Hare (Elk Grove Village), 2550 Landmeier Rd, Elk Grove Village, +1 847 364-6200, *www.comfortinn.com*. About five miles from the airport. Rooms from $80.

Econo Lodge O'Hare Airport, 2080 N Mannheim Rd, Northlake, +1 708 681-0220, *www.econolodge.com*. Rooms from $60.

Quality Inn O'Hare Airport, 3801 N Mannheim Rd, Schiller Park, +1 847 678-0670, *www.qualityinn.com*. About two miles from the airport. Rooms from $60.

Quality Inn & Suites, 100 Busse Rd, Elk Grove Village, +1 847 593-8600, *www.qualityinnelkgrove.com*. About five miles from the airport. Rooms from $85.

Mid-range

Best Western At O'Hare, 10300 W Higgins Rd, Rosemont, +1 847 296-4471, *book.bestwestern.com*. The rooms are a little dingy and the in-

ternet was spotty at last check, but it's not bad. Has a sports bar and a diner on-site. Rooms from $130.

Comfort Inn O'Hare (Franklin Park), 3001 N Mannheim Rd, Franklin Park, +1 847 233-9292, *www.comfortinn.com*. About five minutes from the airport. Rooms from $130.

Comfort Suites O'Hare (Schiller Park), 4200 N River Rd, Schiller Park, +1 847 233-9000, *www.comfortsuites.com*. Big hotel with a sports bar and grill on-site. Rooms from $120.

Doubletree Hotel Chicago Arlington Heights, 75 West Algonquin Road, +1 847 364-7600, *www.doubletreeah.com*. Free Shuttle (based upon avilability) near Woodfield Mall. Rooms as low as $89 on weekends, higher during the week.

Embassy Suites Chicago O'Hare/Rosemont, 5500 N River Rd, Rosemont, +1 847 678-4000, *www.embassysuites.com*. About one mile from the airport. Rooms as low as $119, but reservations can be difficult to get.

Four Points by Sheraton, 10249 W Irving Park Rd, Schiller Park, +1 800 323-1239, *www.kinseth.com/ohare.asp*. Lounge, restaurant, pool, and the rest. For travelers who like to cut it close, shuttles run to O'Hare every 20 minutes, 24 hours per day. Rooms from $155.

Hampton Inn Chicago O'Hare Airport Hotel, 3939 N Mannheim Rd, Schiller Park, +1 847 671-1700, *www.hamptoninnohare.com*. About

1.5 miles from the airport. Rooms from $146.

Holiday Inn Express Hotel & Suites, 6600 N Mannheim Rd, Rosemont, +1 847 544-7500, *www. ichotelsgroup.com*. About five miles from the airport. Rooms from $163.

Hyatt Regency O'Hare, 9300 W Bryn Mawr Ave, +1 847 696 1234, *ohare.hyatt.com*. Contemporary facility with newly renovated guest rooms and meeting space. Rooms from $159.

Radisson Hotel Chicago O'Hare, 1450 E Touhy Ave, Des Plaines, +1 847 296-8866, *www.radisson.com*. About 1.5 miles from the airport. Rooms from $169.

Residence Inn Chicago O'Hare, 7101 Chestnut St, Rosemont, +1 847 375-9000, *marriott.com*. Home-y hotel with separate kitchens. Rooms from $149.

Renaissance Chicago O'Hare Suites Hotel, 8500 W Bryn Mawr Ave, +1 773 380-9600, *renaissanceohare.com*. Indoor swimming pool. Rooms from $179.

Sheraton Suites Elk Grove Village, 121 Northwest Point Blvd, Elk Grove Village, +1 847 290-1600, *www.starwoodhotels.com*. 253 suites with separate living rooms and bedrooms. Rooms from $159.

Wyndham O'Hare alt, 6810 N Mannheim Rd, Rosemont, +1 847 297-1234, *www.wyndham.com*. Just five minutes from the O'Hare International Airport. Among the standard amenities is one you

don't find everywhere: a kosher kitchen. Rooms from $159.

Splurge

If you're going to spend a lot of money on a hotel and you plan to be in town for more than one night, you'll have a much better time in downtown Chicago. That said, these hotels are *big* and do a lot of business.

Chicago Hilton O'Hare, O'Hare Intl Airport, PO Box 66414, Chicago, +1 773 686-8000, *www.hiltonchicagoohare.com*. The only hotel located on-site at the airport, in Terminal 2 (close to the CTA Blue Line), with more than 850 rooms and sound-resistant windows. Rooms from $299.

Chicago Marriott Suites O'Hare, 6155 N River Rd, Rosemont, +1 866 614-8410, +1 847 696-4400, *marriott.com*. Just five minutes from the airport. Rooms from $269.

Crowne Plaza Hotel, 5440 N River Rd, Rosemont, +1 847 671-6350, *www.ichotelsgroup.com*. Giant hotel about 1.5 miles from the airport, with copious meeting space. Rooms from $188.

Doubletree Hotel Chicago O'Hare, 5460 N River Rd, Rosemont, +1 847 292-9100, *www.doubletree.com*. About five minutes from the airport. Rooms from $239.

Holiday Inn Select, 10233 West Higgins Rd, Rosemont, +1 847 954-8600, *www.ichotelsgroup.com*. Newly renovated in 2007, about one mile from the airport. Rooms from $199.

Sheraton Gateway Suites Chicago O'Hare, 6501 N Mannheim Rd, Rosemont, +1 847 699-6300, *www.starwoodhotels.com*. Close to O'Hare and the Donald E. Stephens Convention Center in Rosemont. Rooms from $239.

Sofitel Chicago O'Hare, 5550 N River Rd, Rosemont, +1 847 678-4488, *www.sofitel.com*. Offers "a touch of France" amid the anonymous sprawl around O'Hare. It's connected by walkway to the Donald E. Stephens Convention Center in Rosemont. Rooms from $229, but much cheaper with advance booking.

The Westin O'Hare, 6100 N River Rd, Rosemont, +1 847 698-6000, *www.westinohare.com*. More than 500 pretty rooms with a long list of amenities. Rooms from $329.

Contact

Wi-fi is available throughout O'Hare Airport from **Boingo** *www.boingo.aero*. Day passes cost $6.95, while monthly rates are $9.95 for the first three months and $21.95 thereafter.

Laptop Lane, M-F 6:30AM-11PM, Sa-Su 8AM-4PM, *offices.regus.com*. *ph* provides secure internet connections and office services for business travelers in Terminal 1. $5 gets you five minutes.

ACKNOWLEDGEMENTS

This guidebook is licensed under **Creative Commons Attribution-ShareAlike 1.0**. You may freely redistribute and modify this guidebook and any part thereof as long as the conditions of the license are followed; in particular, you must give *attribution* to all authors, you must make all derivative works available under the same license, and you must notify readers of this license. The full legal text of the license is available at *creativecommons.org/licenses/by-sa/1.0*.

Content in this guidebook is based on work by Wikitravel users 2old, ALT wikignome, AVLann, Agenbite, Alexa52, Allioop, Aphcoinc, Asterix, Aude, Bill-on-the-Hill, Cacahuate, Cargirl, Celticevergreen, ChicagoChica, Cjensen, Clarkanddivision, Danielk2, DavidG, Dforest, Dgkwong, Dguillaime, Donjuansw, Eco84, Edmontonenthusiast, Fastestdogever, George Furimidad, Gilliam, Gorilla Jones, H3O, Hiwhispees, Inas, Iseguban, JYolkowski, Jamesbrownontheroad, Jonathan 784, Jonboy, Jpatokal, Jtesla16, Kevin Forsyth, Lame, Lauren stevens, Leprofenhistoire, Locano, MarinaK, Mark, Morph, Msainz, N. Paul Inast, NEMN, NJR ZA, Nklimovi, Orestek, Padraic, Pastor Bentonit, PerryPlanet, PeterfitzgeraId, Peterfitzgerald, Rickvaughn, Rouge, Rpmprguy, Sapphire, Sertmann, Shan64, Shaund, Showercurtain, Tailwinds, Tatata7, Texugo, Vidimian, Wandering, Wikitravel's anus is raped by Grawp's massive cock., Wrh2, Ypsilon, Zol87, and anonymous users of Wikitravel.

Editor **Peter Fitzgerald** is an alumnus of the University of Chicago. He grew up in Washington, D.C. and loves to travel through Russia, the Caucasus, and Baltimore. Some articles he had an especially heavy hand in drafting include all of those on the South Side, the Far West Side, the Loop, and the Loop Art Tour. He is also the sole author of every map in the book, save the CTA L lines chart.

Marc Heiden is a native of Rogers Park, and has also lived in Hyde Park, Ukrainian Village, Lakeview, Streeterville, and Albany Park in Chicago, as well as three splendid years in Kyoto and Hiroshima, Japan. For the research phase, he owes great thanks to Eric Rampson and Mike Renaud (West Side), Joe Camp, Noel Carroll, Andrew Edeker, Rory Leahy, and Mike Saul (North Side), Sashank Varma (Along the Magnificent Mile), and Kelli Weber (around town). Publishers who are interested in a nearly-complete epic novel about a monkey may start bidding now.

A special thank you in no particular order to Josh Evnin and Joe Goldberg for images used in this guide under the CC Attribution-ShareAlike 2.0 license; to Richie Diesterheft, L.W. Yang, John Picken, Michael Hicks, Jordan Fischer, Tammy Green, Keng-Yu Lin, Esparta Palma, and David Kinney for images used in this guide under the CC Attribution 2.0 license; and to Wikipedia User:Xyboi for images used in this guide under the CC Attribution 2.5 license. For image-specific licensing information, please log

ACKNOWLEDGEMENTS

on to *wikitravel.org.* "Wikitravel" and the Wikitravel "Compass Rose" logo are trademarks of Internet Brands, Inc and are used here under license. All other trademarks are the property of their respective owners.

This guide has been produced and typeset using the *Yucca* engine under license from Contentshare *(www.contentshare.sg).* Book design by Ideaprism *(www.ideaprism.com).*

Every effort has been made to ensure that the facts in the guidebook are accurate, but travellers should still obtain advice from their embassies about current travel and visa requirements before travelling. *The authors and publishers cannot accept responsibility for any loss, injury or inconvenience however caused.*

INDEX

INDEX

413

INDEX

415

INDEX

INDEX

INDEX

INDEX

INDEX

INDEX

INDEX

Wikitravel Press
Free, complete, up-to-date, and reliable

4690 rue Pontiac
Montreal Quebec H2J 2T5
Canada
info@wikitravelpress.com

Why choose Wikitravel Press?
Wikitravel Press guidebooks are updated every month, so the information in them is always up to date. And you don't have to wait for them to show up in your neighborhood bookstore: when you order online, you will always get the newest version!

Share your world
Our guides are written by travellers, for travellers, and *you* can help make a difference. Did you find a great restaurant that the world needs to know about, or a horrible tourist trap to stay away from? Tell us, and it will be *in this very guide* next month. Better yet, log onto *wikitravel.org* and add it in yourself!

Join our team
Ever wanted to be a travel writer? We're hiring! Editors should have exceptional writing and researching skills; first-hand knowledge of the region or city they're covering; and experience with wiki collaboration, especially on Wikitravel. Send your CV and book proposal to *proposals@wikitravelpress.com.*

Find your next destination

Out now   **Coming soon**

Cairo   Paris   Copenhagen Washington DC
Chicago   San Francisco Hiroshima   *and more...*
Helsinki Singapore   Kuala Lumpur

http://wikitravelpress.com

The Wikitravel Story

In 2003, Evan Prodromou and Michele Ann Jenkins arrived at a remote Thai island late in the evening and checked their guidebook to find a place to stay for the night. The book told them to walk around the pier and follow the beach to reach a bungalow-style hotel with an ocean view, but when they came around the corner with their backpacks on, exhausted, there was only a mouldering pile of planks left. How many others would make the same mistake, and how could they warn them? Their answer: creating a travel guide where travelers can change and update the entries themselves!

Today, Wikitravel offers over 30,000 travel guides in 17 languages, with over 10,000 editorial contributions per week. The site won the Best Travel Website category in the 2007 Webby Awards.

How Wikitravel Works

Built on the principle that travelers often get their best information from other travelers, Wikitravel uses wiki-based collaborative editing technology that lets *everybody* contribute. At Wikitravel, "feedback" isn't just an afterthought, it's the whole reason the site exists. Join our lively community, read up on the latest information from around the world, and chip in to share your new finds and travel experiences!

Plunge forward!
http://wikitravel.org

Made in the USA
Lexington, KY
18 June 2010